ᴵA Insᴛ ᴵᴵ ᴬ Rᵀ

The world of public services and administration – including local authorities,
quasi-governmental bodies and the agencies of public-private partnerships – has seen
massive changes in the United Kingdom and other western democracies. The original
aim of the **Government Beyond the Centre** series was to bring the study of this often-
neglected world into the mainstream of social science research, applying the spotlight
of critical analysis to what had traditionally been the preserve of institutional public
administration approaches.

The replacement of traditional models of government by new models of governance
has affected central government, too, with the contracting out of many traditional
functions, the increasing importance of relationships with devolved and supranational
authorities, and the emergence of new holistic models based on partnership and
collaboration.

This series focuses on the agenda of change in governance both at sub-central level
and in the new patterns of relationships surrounding the core executive. Its objective
is to provide up-to-date and informative accounts of the new forms of management
and administration and the structures of power and influence that are emerging, and
of the economic, political and ideological forces that underlie them.

The series will be of interest to students and practitioners in central and local
government, public management and social policy, and all those interested in the
reshaping of the governmental institutions which have a daily and major impact on
our lives.

Government Beyond the Centre
Series Standing Order
ISBN 0–333–71696–5 hardcover
ISBN 0–333–69337–X paperback
(outside North America only)

You can receive future titles in this series as they are published by placing a standing
order. Please contact your bookseller or, in the case of difficulty, write to us at the address
below with your name and address, the title of the series and the ISBN quoted above.

Customer Services Department, Macmillan Distribution Ltd
Houndmills, Basingstoke, Hampshire RG21 6XS, England

GOVERNMENT BEYOND THE CENTRE

SERIES EDITORS: GERRY STOKER AND DAVID WILSON

Local Government in the United Kingdom

Third Edition

David Wilson

and

Chris Game

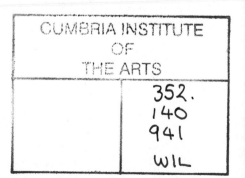

First edition 1994
Second edition 1998
Third edition 2002

Published by
PALGRAVE MACMILLAN
Houndmills, Basingstoke, Hampshire RG21 6XS and
175 Fifth Avenue, New York, N.Y. 10010
Companies and representatives throughout the world

PALGRAVE MACMILLAN is the global academic imprint of the Palgrave Macmillan division of St. Martin's Press, LLC and of Palgrave Macmillan Ltd. Macmillan® is a registered trademark in the United States, United Kingdom and other countries. Palgrave is a registered trademark in the European Union and other countries.

ISBN 0–333–94860–2 hardback
ISBN 0–333–94859–9 paperback

This book is printed on paper suitable for recycling and made from fully managed and sustained forest sources.

Catalogue records for this book are available from the British Library and the US Library of Congress.

Copy-edited and typeset by Povey–Edmondson
Tavistock and Rochdale, England

Printed and bound in Great Britain by
Antony Rowe Ltd, Chippenham and Eastbourne

Contents

Part 2   The Politics and People of Local Government

List of Figures and Boxes

Figures

Boxes

List of Exhibits

Preface to the Third Edition

Margaret Thatcher, in the eleven years of her premiership, appointed no fewer than nine Ministers for Local Government: quite a record for someone who claimed not particularly to like ministerial reshuffles. They could make up a rather abstruse series of 'Where are they now?' on their own. The speed with which they came and went is no doubt a reflection of what she thought of them, as well as, very obviously, what she thought about local government.

By that standard alone, the period between this book's second and third editions has been one of what scientists might term homeostasis – stable equilibrium – with a single local government minister, Hilary Armstrong, throughout the whole of the 1997 Labour Government. By almost any other standard, though, the scale of change has been every bit as great as that recorded in our previous two editions.

It was always clear to us, therefore, that this edition would require at least as much revision as the previous one. We had had four years of a new and self-styled modernising government, elected on a manifesto of unprecedentedly radical devolutionary reform, which might or might not filter through to a local level. We had seen that government's overwhelming re-election in June 2001 and its second term agenda. If this edition was to be as up-to-date as its predecessors, it seemed unlikely that any chapter would survive entirely intact. None did, and neither did the previous twenty-chapter format.

To incorporate sections on the institutional reforms in Scotland, Wales, Northern Ireland and London, plus the advent of executive local government, the previous single chapter on current structures has been split into two. The reverse, as some of our students will be delighted to learn, has happened to local finance. There is an almost completely new chapter on partnerships and the ever increasing complexities of local governance. Probably the biggest change, though, has been to Part 3. We have endeavoured to divide the whole of New Labour's 'modernisation agenda' and the previous reforms on which it built into those that are primarily 'managerial' and those that are primarily 'governmental'. It is a rough-and-ready distinction, but one whose relevance seemed confirmed by the Government's December 2001 White Paper and one that we obviously hope will help our readers to make sense of a potentially bewildering catalogue of initiatives and changes.

The rest of the world moves on too, and a small measure of just how quickly it does so is that a key discussion point when we were first contemplating this third edition was how we should deal with web site references. It had barely been an issue on the horizon for the first edition, written in 1992–3. Even when we wrote the second edition in 1996–7, only the most entrepreneurial of local authorities or other public bodies had sites likely to be of any real value to our readers. For this edition, though, a host of web site citations seemed unavoidable – until the arrival of Google.

Were we into dedications, strong candidates indeed would be Larry and Sergey, as they are known to their friends, or Lawrence Page and Sergey Brin, as they should be even better known to the world than they already are. Their matchless claim to fame is that they were the developers of the core technologies that have given us Google, that most admirable leader among Internet search engines. Their claim on our gratitude is that they have saved us the trouble of having to list, then recheck, the dozens of web sites of authorities, organisations and subjects referred to in our text. It really is now hardly worth adding, say, the Department of Transport, Local Government and the Regions or the Local Government Association to your 'favourites', as Google can get you straight not just to their home pages, but probably to the specific subject or document you require. Nor do you need to remember precisely how any individual, and individualistic, local authority needs to be cited before the standard 'gov.uk'; Google will know.

There are, of course, other good search engines, and Google pays us no agents' fees. The acknowledgement is mainly a device for explaining – and without apology – why you should *not* expect to find the strings of web sites included in some other recent texts on the operation of government. It is not that we consider them unimportant, or even optional; quite the reverse. They are *the* best means of keeping up with what is going on in the 'real' world of local government practice, which, just as in previous editions, is the one to which we are trying to introduce our readers. In updating this edition, we ourselves have plundered the Internet constantly, and we hope you will be encouraged to do the same.

Some things, however, in this inconstant world, do not change – one being the debts of gratitude incurred in producing a volume of this attempted type and range. First must come our academic colleagues, headed, as from the outset, by Professors John Stewart and George Jones. Without the latter, the first edition and therefore its successors would have taken a very different, and undoubtedly inferior, form. Without the former, the book quite simply could never have existed. Others too have contributed even more than an enumeration of their footnote references might suggest, most notably Professors Gerry Stoker and Steve Leach.

Particular thanks too must go to Ranjna Mistry from the Department of Public Policy at De Montfort University – for the excellence of her administrative and secretarial skills, her diligence and unfailing good humour. Aileen Kowal and Caroline Laird also provided secretarial support of the highest standard. Then comes our publisher, Steven Kennedy. Rather as Colin Dexter revealed Inspector Morse's first name to be Endeavour, we can exclusively confirm that Steven's middle name is Forbearance. For the cartoons we and the publishers are pleased to thank Patrick Blower and the *Local Government Chronicle* for permission to reproduce those in Figures 5.1 and 9.2, John Clark and the Local Government Information Unit for that in Figure 10.1, and Harry Venning and *The Guardian* for that in Figure 13.1.

We trust that these and the other illustrations contribute to the book's interest and merit. For whatever defects and errors you detect and for the views expressed, we, of course, accept responsibility.

DAVID WILSON
CHRIS GAME

Part 1

Local Government –
The Basics

Chapter 1

Introduction – Our Aims and Approach

The licence plate view of local government

For most Americans vehicle licence plates tell them all they feel they need to know about British local government:

> [British] licence plates are unimaginative and uninformative. There is no 'Kent: The Garden County' or 'Cumbria: Land o' Lakes'. I wonder what games British children play on long trips. (Seitz, 1998, p. 270)

The author of this observation was Raymond Seitz, one of the outstanding and most anglophile of recent American ambassadors to Britain. The reference to children's games came from his recollections of being driven across the United States as a young boy and playing an I-spy game of spotting licence plates, each of which displayed some slogan or nickname related to its state of origin: 'New York: the Empire State', 'Tennessee: The Volunteer State', and, more disconcertingly, 'New Hampshire: Live Free or Die'. The early lesson in government that Seitz learned from this experience was that every state had its own special character and identity. State and even local governments had real authority and their residents had a fierce pride in being different from their neighbours across a shared boundary. American states had their own constitutions and legislatures. They could raise capital and tax their citizens, with taxes that varied from state to state. America was a federal and genuinely pluralist country.

By comparison, Seitz found the United Kingdom a unitary and uniform country. Local government seemed constantly to be undergoing some reorganisation, with boundaries changing and councils coming and going without anyone apparently caring very much. Services, benefits, taxes and even licence plates are more or less the same everywhere:

> Central government divvies up the public purse and distributes the funds evenly across a homogeneous society. Who gets what is a national responsibility and a national preoccupation. (p. 270)

The egalitarianism may be admirable, but the cost, concludes Seitz, is a 'feebleness' of local government and a 'super-centralism' of policy-making in which 'local government is directed from London in a semi-colonial fashion.' (p. 274)

The excited Professor

We shall examine such views in more detail later on in this book. For the moment we will simply set them against the rather differing assertions of an even more experienced British observer, Professor John Stewart, to whom we pay tribute in our Preface. Invited to give evidence to an important all-party House of Lords Select Committee investigating UK local government, Professor Stewart introduced himself with the following remarks:

> Reading some reports of your evidence, I get the impression that some people have been saying that local government is a dull world. I can quite understand that, if you are looking at the *national* world of local government – because, once you reduce local government to a uniform view, it is rather a dull world.
>
> I have had the good fortune to visit 300 local authorities over the last few years, interviewing leaders and chief executives, and what impresses me is *the excitement of local government*. It is the excitement of how one authority differs from another, because of the nature of the area, and because of the quality of the leadership. I am impressed too by the extent of innovation that has been taking place, sometimes in response to government legislation, but sometimes by the local authorities themselves. It is very exciting ... to see city or town leaders wrestling with tremendous urban problems. I do not want you to get the impression that the world of local authorities is dull. (House of Lords, 1996, Vol. II, pp. 461–2, emphasis ours)

Professor Stewart has since expanded upon these themes of the parallelism of diversity and uniformity and the excitement of local innovation in a book appropriately entitled *The Nature of British Local Government* (Stewart, 2000). Get out of London more, and get real, might be his message to the former US ambassador. Of course there are not the same extremes of government in the United Kingdom as in the United States, nearly 40 times its size. It is true too that British local councils are subject to significantly greater central government control and direction than are their American or most of their European counterparts. But look a bit more carefully and you will see forces of diversity as well as forces of uniformity: differing locations, histories, cultures, economies, social class structures, politics – all of which militate against even neighbouring councils being the undistinguishable 'administrative units' that Seitz thought he saw (p. 271).

And if that was true in the past, it ought to be even more so in the future. For, following the Local Government Act 2000, local authorities have for the very first time a statutory power of community leadership: the power 'to promote the economic, social and environmental well-being of their area'. It may not sound very remarkable, and in most European countries it would not be. But for at least the more pro-active and forward-looking British councils it offers an unprecedented opportunity to identify and respond to the particular needs and circumstances of their unique localities.

A dull world? Not any more!

One of our chief aims in this book is precisely the same as the task Professor Stewart set himself in talking to the House of Lords Committee – to dispel any idea you, our readers, may have that the world of local government is narrow, uniform or dull. It is, in fact, quite the reverse.

Narrow is something local government has never been. That local authorities 'look after you from the cradle to the grave' – or from sperm to worm – is both a cliché and an unfashionably paternalistic view of councils' wide-ranging responsibilities. But it is also literally true, in that they will register your birth, death and, if necessary, any intervening marriage, and then finally dispose of you, in cemetery or crematorium according to taste. Much more to the point, our local councils and the services that they provide have a far more immediate, continuous and comprehensive impact on all our daily lives than many of the so-called 'bigger' issues that make the parliamentary headlines.

Nor have these local councils ever been uniform – except in the sense that the whole land mass of our planet would look uniform if viewed from far enough away. Local government is the government of localities, and an institutionalised recognition of their widely varying characteristics – geographic, demographic, social, economic and, by no means least, political. We cannot take you physically on Professor Stewart's tour of local authorities, but we try to do the next best thing – by illustrating, wherever possible, the differences that exist even between councils of the same type and a similar size, and also by encouraging you to discover for yourselves the uniquenesses of your own local councils, or what you might call the microcosmos of local government.

As for being dull, the very suggestion would be likely to raise a pitying, and self-pitying, smile from most of those working in or with local government over the past few years. What area of the private sector, they would ask, has had to come to terms with more change and upheaval on every front: privatisation and the contracting out of services; compulsory competitive tendering (CCT) and now Best Value; opt-out ballots of tenants and school parents; the introduction and almost instant abandonment of a 'poll tax', followed by a council tax, and tax capping; neighbourhood offices, customer contracts, complaints hot-lines, one-stop shops, service guarantees, environmental audits, enabling councils, private finance initiatives, performance indicators and league tables ... all against a backdrop of continuous financial constraint and the actual or threatened rearrangement of the country's whole local government structure.

Few of these ideas and developments would or could have found their way into a book on local government published even a dozen or so years ago. Their origins are mixed. Some came from within the world of local government itself. But many, as both Seitz and Stewart noted, stem from central government and from the unprecedented quantity of legislation directed at local councils in recent years. It has been this interventionist and legislative attention of central government that has raised the profile of local government, made it regular front-page news, and thereby:

> succeeded in doing the unthinkable [and] rescued students from the terminal boredom of lectures on local government by making the subject interesting, even humorous for those with a taste for black comedy. (Rhodes, 1991, p. 86)

But whose responsibility was it that there was an image of 'terminal boredom' to dispel? Partly, presumably, local councils themselves, who have all too often failed to project themselves in such a way as to stimulate the interest – let alone the sympathy and support – of those they claim to represent and serve. To be fair, this criticism is one that many of them would now acknowledge and claim to be doing their best to rectify. We shall be drawing attention to some of their more noteworthy efforts throughout this book.

Authors too, however, have their responsibilities. Part of our job must be to stimulate the interest of *our* public in the activities of local government: to convey, as directly as possible, a sense of its 'feel' and atmosphere. So who are our public?

You and us

We assume that most of our readers will not themselves have worked in local government, or at least not for any great length of time. We assume that, for most of you, your principal experience of local government will have been as customers, consumers, clients and citizens; perhaps also, to add a fifth 'C', as complainants. You will probably have had various more or less memorable contacts over the years with council officials and employees, and perhaps also with your locally elected councillors. You will certainly be at least one and probably several of the following: council tax payers, education grant recipients, state school or college students, council house tenants, social services clients, library borrowers, sports and leisure centre users, pedestrians, bus travellers, car drivers, taxi riders, planning applicants or protesters, domestic refuse producers, and so on. You will probably be registered local electors, and possibly actual voters. Yet perhaps oddly, given this degree of personal involvement, you are likely to consider yourselves to be 'outsiders' in relation to the world of local government.

If so, then in this sense we too are outsiders. We are not employed in local government either; but we do work very closely with local government. In various ways – through teaching and lecturing, research and consultancy – we are in virtually daily contact with local councils, their members and staff. A key part of our jobs involves trying to link together, or at least narrow the gap between, the 'academic' and 'practitioner' worlds of local government, and that is the task we have set ourselves in this book.

Our aim is to present a picture of local government comprising both facts and 'feel'. The balance, we believe, is vital. Certainly, we would reject what might be labelled the 'Gradgrind' approach, after Charles Dickens' schoolmaster in *Hard Times*: 'Now, what I want is Facts. Teach these boys and girls nothing but Facts. Facts alone are wanted in life.' But if facts alone are insufficient, *some* facts are indispensable – and not just for those of you required to sit exams. We are concerned, therefore, that our readers acquire a factually accurate knowledge of what local government is about and how it works. We are even more concerned, though, that you acquire something of what we describe as the 'feel' of local government: an appreciation of the interests, viewpoints, motivations, satisfactions and frustrations of those involved, and an awareness of the range, the nature and the complexities of the issues they face.

Welcome to gov.uk

With this latter objective in mind, we now put forward a few important suggestions or recommendations. First, you should try to make whatever use you can of the fact that you yourselves will, depending on exactly where you live, be residents of at least one local council, and possibly two or three. These councils produce a mass of information in different forms about the services they provide and the activities with which they are involved. They may produce and circulate their own council newspaper, or insert a couple of pages regularly into one of the local daily or weekly papers. They will certainly deliver to you personally a statement of their annual budget to accompany your local council tax demand.

Exhibit 1.1 Test out your own council's web site

Four (of the many) ways of finding your council's site

1. *Most comprehensive*: the Government's official web site –
   www.open.gov.uk
   Organisational index lists all public sector web sites – clunky, often out of
   date, but ultimately indispensable; you might as well get used to it.

2. *Easier and still comprehensive*: the Tagish Directory –
   www.tagish.co.uk/links/localgov.htm
   Lists all local authority sites alphabetically, including town and parish
   councils, plus other useful local government-related sites.

3. *More fun*: the Keith Edkins Family Index – www.gwyrdir.demon.co.uk
   Sites retrievable through clickable maps; also lots of election stuff, table of
   council political compositions, etc.

4. *Most fun*: the Oultwood Local Government Web Index –
   www.oultwood.com
   Sites retrievable by both maps and initial letter, and can be compared with
   council sites in Australia, New Zealand, Canada, South Africa and Eire.
   Look especially for 'good example' sites, bus traffic signs – 'heavyweight
   sites, with busloads of good content', webcam and disabled icons. Avoid
   'no through road' signs – home page only. Also lists councils without
   sites. Check out too the (still sadly few) pages of individual councillors,
   like Blandford Forum Town Councillor, Ieke van Stokkum: sign her guest
   book, add to her cookie league table.

They will also produce all sorts of other leaflets, brochures, cards and
pamphlets about particular services that should be available from your
local town or county hall. So go along and ask! That was our advice in the
two previous editions of this book and it still holds good. But, as ever with
local government, the world has moved on. Virtually all principal councils
now have their own web sites, and indeed are a key part of Tony Blair's
rash, if vaguely defined, pledge that 25 per cent of public services should be
available electronically by 2002 and 100 per cent by 2005 – regardless
apparently of whether they might be more appropriately delivered in
person or telephonically. It means, though, that there really is no better
– not to say lazier and more enjoyable – way of finding out both about
your own council and local government in general than by surfing and
comparing these hugely assorted council sites (see Exhibit 1.1).

University web sites – what we might call dot.ac sites, ending as they do
in ac.uk – vary greatly, from those offering little more than long lists of
courses and departments to those with virtual tours of campuses,
webcams, and much else besides. Council sites – almost all ending in

---

Exhibit 1.1 continued

Some test questions for any council site

1. Would you say the site was aimed more at prospective business investors or residents with problems?
2. How recently was the site last updated? Is there stuff clearly past its sell-by date?
3. Could it give you satisfactory information if you were looking for long-term care for an elderly parent?
4. Is there a clear statement of which political party or parties control the council?
5. Could you find your own councillor(s) using only your address or postcode – i.e. if you don't happen to know the name of the ward you live in?
6. Does the A–Z of services include those provided by other councils or organisations in the area?
7. Is there a listing for 'wheelie bins' or only 'refuse collection' or even 'wheeled bin'? Could you find out which day your wheelie bin would be emptied simply by typing in your street name?
8. What information, if any, is available in languages other than English?
9. Could you download useful maps of the council area?
10. Are committee papers – agendas, reports, minutes – available online?
11. Could you search planning applications?
12. Could you find details of how to complain to, or compliment, the council?
13. Could you find out who is the largest employer in the area, and what the current unemployment rate in your own ward is?
14. Does the council appear to have any policy on sustainable development?

---

gov.uk – vary much, much more and are correspondingly more informative, both directly and indirectly. If your council proves to be one with a web site that proclaims, directly or indirectly, that it was last updated several months ago, it is in its own way making as eloquent a statement about itself as those councils with some of the more ambitious and interesting sites listed in Exhibit 1.2. Judge for yourself, by comparing it with these and other sites or by using our short list of questions in Exhibit 1.1, how useful, practical and enterprising your council's site is.

An early definition

Even an average council web site is likely to offer an A–Z listing of services, something about the way in which the council organises itself, and a news page of recent initiatives and forthcoming activities. Our guess is that, after no more than half an hour's surfing and browsing in the way we have suggested, even if you were to have started with no previous

Exhibit 1.2 Tameside and other good council web sites

Tameside Borough Council (east of Manchester) and its Customer First programme won the Microsoft Digital Britain award in 2000 for the best use of IT by a public sector organisation. The Customer First programme embraces far more than IT, but its core aim is to provide the borough's 221,000 residents with fast, efficient access to information and services by means of web-based technology, as well as by telephone, post, and face-to-face contact with council staff.

What's good about www.tameside.gov.uk?

It provides what the council's customers, when questioned, said they wanted:

1. easy access to basic general and personal information – council tax balances, library opening times, refuse collection dates, progress of a planning application, etc.;
2. to be able to report information to the council and other relevant organisations – e.g. a change of address, a death – easily and quickly;
3. to be able to request services – e.g. an appointment with a planning or welfare officer, the removal of bulky waste or an abandoned vehicle – without inconvenience;
4. to be able to make payments – council tax, housing rent, business rates, car parking fines – swiftly and securely (the first UK council to provide this facility).

knowledge at all about local government, you would be able to piece together a reasonable preliminary impression of the kind of institution a local council is (Box 1.1). This is by no means a fully comprehensive definition of what a local council is and how it operates, but it is a useful starting point.

Box 1.1 Your local council

- A large, geographically-defined, multi-functional organisation,
- pursuing a variety of social, political and economic objectives,
- either through the direct provision,
- or through the sponsorship, indirect funding, regulation, or monitoring of
- a very extensive range of services to its local community.

Exhibit 1.2 continued

How is it accessed?

1. from one of the council's five specially designed Customer Service Centres;
2. from one of several satellite centres across the borough, like libraries, housing cybercafés;
3. from home.

Other sites that were worth visiting in 2000/01 — authors' own list, alphabetical order only:

Brent LBC – good on local democracy issues, public consultation, and links to other sites

Camden LBC – first offering online payment for parking tickets and council tax

Devon CC – webcam at Junction 30 of M5: seriously weird

Dundee CC – Scotland's 4th city, but one of the first with online 'life events' pages

Gwynedd CC – live bilingual webcasts in RealVideo of council and committee meetings

Hampshire CC – consistently good and comprehensive site, covering the whole county

Kirklees MBC – exceptionally user-friendly

Newtownabbey BC – one of Northern Ireland's best

Oldham MBC – especially Best Value and BV consultation

Rutland CC – Local Government Association Web site of the Year, 2000

Waveney DC – check out its cemetery index!

Western Isles – wonderful area, fun site – bilingual too

Wrexham CBC – Croeso i wefan Cyngor Bwrdeistref Sirol Wrecsam!

Your council's *Annual Report*

One way or another, by personal or electronic visit, you should also be able to obtain at least a summary version of your council's *Annual Report*. This document is something that, together with a set of audited *Annual Accounts*, all councils are required by law to produce. As with council web sites – and a great deal else that ultimately depends on the inclinations and priorities of local authorities themselves – you will find that the formats of these *Annual Reports* vary enormously: from the glossily illustrated and expensive-looking brochure-cum-book to the more downbeat, down-market tabloid newspaper format, designed for comprehensive circulation among the council's residents. But, whatever its style, a council's *Annual Report*, like its web site, can tell you a great deal about itself: both about the kind of organisation it is, and also about the kind it wishes to be seen as being. Like a university's prospectus, it is one of the council's best opportunities to make a public statement and presentation of its activities and achievements, its internal management and external relations, its future plans and its past performance.

In particular, a good *Annual Report* is likely to contain two useful features that we shall refer to explicitly in later chapters. First, there will be a presentation of the council's *budget* and overall *financial profile*: how much was spent, on what services, and where the money came from. Since you yourselves will have provided at least some of that money – in the form of local and national taxation, local fees, charges and rents – and since you will also be users of some of the council's services, we feel that one of the best ways of introducing the sometimes rather threatening topic of local government finance is through your own council's budget and accounts. Understand how your own money is spent, and the services it helps to provide, and you are well on the way to understanding the system.

A second feature of many *Annual Reports* is the *comparative* one. All councils are required to compare the scale, costs and efficiency of their services – their so-called Performance Indicators – with those of other authorities of the same general type. Some councils will provide this comparative information in their *Annual Reports*, but all are required to make it available somehow through the local press. So try to get hold of your council's most recent publication of its performance indicators and check for yourself how, say, its pupil–teacher ratios, provision of nursery school places, *per capita* library loans, housing rent arrears, household waste recycling record, or council tax collection rates compare with those of other authorities – and, more importantly, see what explanations may be offered for any apparently unfavourable figures.

Organisation of the book

The book is divided into three parts. Part 1 is concerned with the *basics* of local government. The aim is to provide you with a good basic knowledge of the purposes and origins of local government, its structures, functions and finances, and the context in which it operates. At the end of Part 1 you should, we hope, feel reasonably confident about the fundamentals of local government.

Part 2 looks at the *dynamics* that drive the system. What makes local government 'tick'? The focus moves on to the people and institutions that make decisions, provide services and seek to influence the activities of their locality. We become more directly concerned with politics, since our aim is to understand how various 'stakeholders' involved in local government perceive their situation and try to realise their objectives.

Part 3 turns to the agenda of *change*: changes that in 2001 were already being implemented and, slightly more speculatively, possible changes in the less foreseeable future. The absence of any major Local Government Act in the re-elected Labour Government's first Queen's Speech misleads no one who has followed the subject in recent years. Within the lifetime of this Parliament, let alone the decade, local government will have evolved and changed at least as much as during the 1980s or 1990s.

Guide to further reading

First, to complement Ambassador Seitz, a couple of highly readable journalistic views of local democratic government and why it matters. Former *Times* editor, Simon Jenkins (1995), ranges over the whole of British government during the Thatcher years, while *Guardian* columnist, Jonathan Freedland (1998), compares Britain, ruefully, with the United States, but they both care, entertainingly. An additional way of developing your 'feel' for local government and politics is through the so-called 'trade press' of local government: the weekly or fortnightly publications that are read mainly by local government personnel themselves, not least for the job advertisements. Most useful are probably the *Local Government Chronicle*, the *Municipal Journal*, and *Public Finance*. If you have the opportunity to read these 'practitioner' publications, particularly their 'front-end' news sections, we would strongly recommend it; and don't ignore completely those job adverts – they (and their salaries) can be quite revealing. *Local Government Chronicle* has its own web site (www.lgcnet. com), as do *Public Finance* (www.cipfa.org.uk/publicfinance) and the Local Government Association (LGA) (www.lga.gov.uk), another invaluable source of current news, briefing papers and suchlike. Both the *Chronicle* and the LGA have their own additional password-controlled pages, but don't be put off: they produce plenty of freely available material. It is even more important that you scan as frequently as possible the local government news items in both the national and your local press. Hardly a day passes without there appearing at least one or two news articles about the activities of local councils, which will illustrate, expand upon, or update the contents of this book.

Chapter 2

Themes and Issues in Local Government

Introduction – follow those headlines!

This chapter introduces some of the main current themes and issues in UK local government and the key defining characteristics of the local government system. We start by trying to demonstrate the value of our own advice about the benefits of following local government in the national and local media. If, for example, you had been scanning the press during 2001, the headlines that might have caught your eye would almost certainly have included some of those in Exhibit 2.1.

Change and uncertainty

Our news headlines collectively illustrate several of the most prominent themes of local government around the turn of the century,[1] starting with its state of apparently perpetual motion. In almost every aspect it continued – as throughout the 1980s and 1990s – to be subject to change, much of it of the most fundamental kind (Items 1–3, 5–7 in Exhibit 2.1).

Throughout the mid-1990s even the total number of councils was changing – or, to be specific, falling – from year to year. When the first edition of this book was published in 1994, there were 540 local councils in the UK – already, by comparative international standards, a very small number. By 1998, when the second edition appeared, 77, or one in every seven, had disappeared, the victims of national governmental reorganisation (Wilson and Game, 1998, p. 14). In Wales the number had been cut by more than half, from 45 counties and districts to just 22 new 'unitary' or

---

[1] Although, as more thoughtful readers may have guessed, in the case of Item 12, it was the turn of the nineteenth century, in the summer of 1900!

Exhibit 2.1 Selected news headlines, 2001

1. **MAYOR KEN CALLS FOR FEWER BOROUGHS**
   London Mayor, Ken Livingstone, calls for the 33 London boroughs to be cut by half to make them more effective, and predicts the new Greater London Authority will become the capital's health authority and lead to elected regional government elsewhere in England.

2. **PRESCOTT CONCEDES 4th OPTION FOR SMALLER DISTRICTS**
   The then Environment Secretary, John Prescott, reluctantly allows 86 district councils with populations under 85,000 to retain modified committee systems, rather than having to adopt one of the Government's three preferred executive styles of political management.

3. **TORIES WOULD SCRAP LEAs**
   Conservatives announce a 'Free Schools' plan, which would pass budgets direct to school heads, bypassing Local Education Authorities and effectively ending local government's education role.

4. **NEW LICENSING POWERS FOR COUNCILS**
   Government White Paper on modernising licensing laws proposes that councils, rather than magistrates, should have new powers to issue alcohol licences, including 24/7 opening hours.

5. **SCOTTISH MINISTERS RESTRICT TENANTS' RIGHT TO BUY**
   To stop councils losing all their low-cost rented accommodation, Scottish communities minister, Wendy Alexander, says that new tenants must wait 5 years instead of two before applying to buy their homes, and accept reduced percentage discounts.

6. **WELSH TO SCRAP SCHOOL LEAGUE TABLES**
   Welsh Education and Lifelong Learning Minister, Jane Davidson, announces that, following consultations, the Assembly will no longer follow the English practice of publishing each school's exam results.

7. **TWO-THIRDS OF NI COUNCILLORS TO GO?**
   A restructuring of local government could cut Northern Ireland's 26 district councils to 10 and the number of councillors by two-thirds.

8. **NHS EXECUTIVES GET DEMOCRATIC SCRUTINY**
   Government's *NHS Plan* proposes that unelected community health councils be abolished, and that council overview and scrutiny committees will also monitor local health services and hospital provision.

9. **OUTSOURCING WORSENS TAX COLLECTION RATES?**
   Government figures show council tax collection rates in 1999/2000 ranged from 99.9 per cent to 67.9 per cent, with the two worst-performing councils, Hackney and Southwark, having contracted out (outsourced) tax collection to private companies.

10. **MINISTER PRAISES BRUM'S NOISE MAP**
    Birmingham City Council's 'sound emission contour map', providing a coloured illustration of the combined road, rail and aircraft noise across the city, is commended by Environment minister, Michael Meacher, to other urban areas.

11. **SHOWING RACISM THE RED CARD**
    Oxfordshire County Council, the Oxfordshire Racial Equality Council and Oxford United Football Club launch a joint campaign to distribute 10,000 'Show Racism the Red Card' posters to youth and community organisations across the county.

12. **ST HELENS FIRST WITH MUNICIPAL MILK DEPOT**
    St Helens Council, the first UK local authority to set up its own milk depot, also uses its birth register to send a council employee to visit all new parents with advice on feeding.

single-tier councils. In Scotland the 65 former regions and districts had been reduced to 32 unitaries. In England 46 new unitary councils had replaced five counties and 58 districts. Only Northern Ireland's local government structure remained intact, and even that was looking likely to change with the ending of direct rule from London and an anticipated transfer of more responsibilities to a smaller number of more powerful councils (Item 7).

If, as a reader, you think all this structural tinkering might make for confusion and uncertainty, just try imagining yourself as a council worker, not knowing whether your employing authority will still be in existence in a couple of years' time, let alone what powers and service responsibilities it might have (Items 3, 4), or how it might be managed and organised (Item 2).

Structural change did not, of course, stop in 1998. Quite the contrary, for the new Labour Government came into office in 1997 with the century's most far-reaching agenda for constitutional reform, including a radical programme of devolution. Within two years the Scots had, for the first time in nearly 300 years, their own legislative Parliament and their own Executive (the equivalent of the Cabinet), with Ministers very ready to distance themselves from Westminster policy if they consider it to be in Scotland's interests (Item 5). Wales too had its own Assembly, though without the powers to vary tax or pass primary legislation. It has, however, a say in the implementation of legislation (Item 6), and it is possible that, had it been in existence 10 years earlier, it might even have been able to opt out of the poll tax.

Northern Ireland's new Assembly, its first since Edward Heath's Government assumed direct rule over the province in 1972, had the most stuttering infancy, having been elected in June 1998, convened and adjourned in July 1999, reconvened in November 1999, suspended in February 2000, and reinstated in May 2000. Like the Scottish Parliament, though, it has legislative powers, including over what may eventually prove to be a greatly transformed and strengthened system of local government.

There has been further structural reform in England as well, with almost certainly more to come. London, without a capital-wide elected Authority since the Thatcher Government's abolition of the Greater London Council (GLC) in 1985/86, now has one again. In May 2000 Londoners elected both a 25-member Assembly and the country's very first directly elected executive mayor: the same Ken Livingstone who had been the last (Labour) leader of the GLC, but who now stood and won as an Independent.

Predictably enough, the new mayor was quick to reveal his own ideas about the future of London government and that of the English regions (Item 1). The latter had acquired under the Labour Government business-led Regional Development Agencies (RDAs), but with linked 'chambers' or assemblies of councillors, business people, trade unionists and religious leaders that were entirely nominated, rather than directly elected. If, as the Government's policy envisaged, some or all of these regional assemblies were eventually to become directly elected, the move would almost certainly be accompanied, as in Scotland and Wales, by the spread of unitary local government across the country: in short, yet further reorganisation.

It was the *internal* structure of councils, though, that in 2001 was set to change more immediately. Through its Local Government Act 2000, in addition to introducing a 'promotion of well-being' role (see Chapter 1), the Blair Government was attempting to 'modernise' the whole way in which, throughout their history, councils had organised themselves and conducted their business. Previously, all elected councillors were involved, through their membership of committees, in the policy-making of their councils. In future, the Government wanted policy determination to be the responsibility of either a single directly elected executive mayor – as in the Greater London Authority – or at least of a small cabinet of leading councillors. The remaining non-executive councillors would critically examine and scrutinise council policy (and health service policy too – Item 8) and, of course, represent their communities and constituents. Initially at least, these highly prescriptive proposals were not enthusiastically received in the local government world, and, despite its large House of Commons majority, the Government was forced to make certain concessions to meet the demands of particularly many relatively smaller councils (Item 2).

In addition to all this organisational change, other government legislation was, as ever, adding to or subtracting from local authorities' powers and responsibilities. 2000, for example, saw the formal end of Compulsory Competitive Tendering (CCT) – the requirement, introduced under the Thatcher Governments, that councils put out to private competition various specified services – though councils could continue on their own initiative to contract out (outsource) services, and accept the not invariably beneficial consequences (Item 9). CCT was replaced by Labour's Best Value (BV) regime, a more comprehensive and less finance-driven means of attaining essentially similar objectives. There was the suggestion of councils being allocated modest new licensing powers (Item 4), and the, in every respect, far more serious possibility of a future Conservative government ending altogether local government's involvement in education (Item 3). For a country once used to long-term stability in its governmental institutions, this breadth, scale and speed of change are at least remarkable and, to many, constitutionally and democratically threatening. Inevitably, it is one of this book's key themes.

Non-elected local government and 'local governance'

There is a trend detectable in much of this recent change to which we have already alluded in relation to both the health service and the English regions (Items 1, 8): the spread of non-elected or indirectly elected local government. It is not in itself a new phenomenon. The original National Health Service (NHS) structure and the newer self-governing hospital and primary care trusts have been completely non-elected since 1974; so too were the New Town Development Corporations (NTDCs), and the Scottish and Welsh development agencies, on which the English regional development agencies are modelled.

The scale of non-elected government, however, increased enormously during the 1980s and 1990s, frequently at the *direct expense* of elected local councils. Under national governments of both major parties, service responsibilities were removed from local authorities and given to mainly single-purpose Government-appointed agencies: Urban Development Corporations (UDCs) for inner city development, Training and Enterprise Councils (TECs), Housing Action Trusts (HATs) and governing bodies of grant-maintained schools and further education colleges, for example. Collectively, these bodies are conventionally known as local 'quangos' – quasi-autonomous non-governmental organisations – and it is no exaggeration to talk of there having been a 'quango explosion', involving the creation of some 6,000 of these special-purpose bodies and the appointment of a 'quangocracy' of over 70,000 board members – in both cases, several times the numbers of elected councils and councillors. It has amounted, in the judgement of Jones and Stewart (1992, p. 15), to a 'fundamental change' in our system of local government:

> Government is being handed back to the 'new magistracy' from whom it was removed in the counties more than 100 years ago. Elected representatives are being replaced by a burgeoning army of the selected ... the unknown governors of our society.

So fundamental have been these changes, and so fragmented has local service provision become as a consequence, that some political scientists claim that local government has evolved into something better termed local 'governance'. This latter concept, it is claimed, more effectively describes the extensive network of public, voluntary and private sector bodies that are nowadays involved in policy-making and service delivery at the sub-central level (see, e.g., Rhodes, 1997; Stoker, 1998, 1999a, 2000; Leach and Percy-Smith, 2001). We would not disagree with the analysis, but neither have we been seriously tempted to retitle or fundamentally refocus our book. While giving plenty of attention to relevant non-governmental organisations, this particular book's focus remains *elected local government*, which remains, as democratically accountable service provider and major resource holder, at the very heart of any network or process of local governance.

The new non-elected bodies were a deliberate challenge to elected local government – all too often itself 'unknown' to its citizens – and the challenge has been positively taken up, in the form of more collaborative and partnership working. While continuing to argue the case for quangos operating more openly, democratically and accountably, councils nowadays are increasingly working *with* and *through* these external organisations – to deliver services, monitor other organisations' service provision, and apply for government grant funding.

Diminished discretion

As some powers have been taken away from local government, those retained have been increasingly constrained – subject to greater national direction and control. Switchback changes in local government finance, particularly during the 1980s and early 1990s, were accompanied by the imposition of steadily tighter conditions – Government ministers and civil servants becoming more directly involved in declaring what *they* calculate each local council ought to be spending on different services. The outcome, as suggested in Figure 2.1, has been a perceptible reduction in local discretion, in the ability of local councils either to decide for themselves or to finance effectively services that they would wish to provide for their local communities.

We shall be encountering later many of the specific governmental initiatives itemised in Figure 2.1. We shall note too the contrast between this centralising trend in the United Kingdom and the generally decentralising policies that were being pursued by most other European central governments, but which here have been more the exception than the rule. For the present we merely draw attention to the general shape of what we label the 'funnel of local authority discretion'.

Like a funnel, there is a definite tapering from one end to the other. But there is no suggestion that all local discretion has been eliminated. Councils still have some opportunity, Figure 2.1 implies, to determine their own political priorities and to embark on their own policy initiatives in response to the needs and wishes of the residents in their particular local communities. They may feel increasingly hemmed in by central government dictates and directives, they may protest their unfairness, but they have by no means been robbed of all initiative and individuality.

Figure 2.1   *The funnel of local authority discretion*

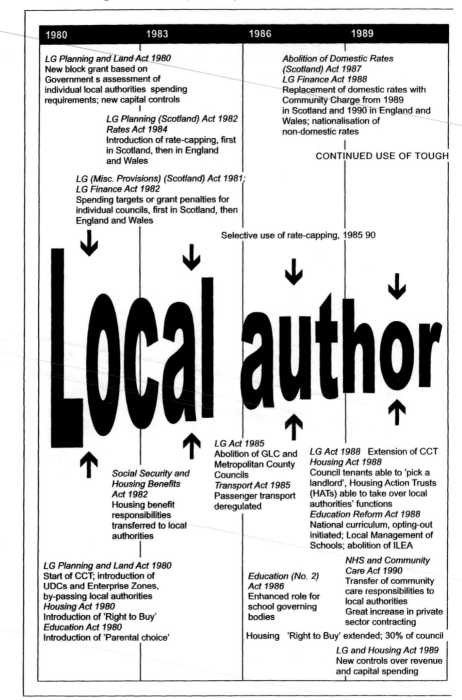

1980	1983	1986	1989

LG Planning and Land Act 1980
New block grant based on
Government s assessment of
individual local authorities spending
requirements; new capital controls

LG Planning (Scotland) Act 1982
Rates Act 1984
Introduction of rate-capping, first
in Scotland, then in England
and Wales

LG (Misc. Provisions) (Scotland) Act 1981;
LG Finance Act 1982
Spending targets or grant penalties for
individual councils, first in Scotland, then
England and Wales

Abolition of Domestic Rates
(Scotland) Act 1987
LG Finance Act 1988
Replacement of domestic rates with
Community Charge from 1989
in Scotland and 1990 in England and
Wales; nationalisation of
non-domestic rates

CONTINUED USE OF TOUGH

Selective use of rate-capping, 1985 90

Social Security and
Housing Benefits
Act 1982
Housing benefit
responsibilities
transferred to local
authorities

LG Act 1985
Abolition of GLC and
Metropolitan County
Councils
Transport Act 1985
Passenger transport
deregulated

LG Act 1988   Extension of CCT
Housing Act 1988
Council tenants able to 'pick a
landlord', Housing Action Trusts
(HATs) able to take over local
authorities' functions
Education Reform Act 1988
National curriculum, opting-out
initiated; Local Management of
Schools; abolition of ILEA

LG Planning and Land Act 1980
Start of CCT; introduction of
UDCs and Enterprise Zones,
by-passing local authorities
Housing Act 1980
Introduction of 'Right to Buy'
Education Act 1980
Introduction of 'Parental choice'

Education (No. 2)
Act 1986
Enhanced role for
school governing
bodies

NHS and Community
Care Act 1990
Transfer of community
care responsibilities to
local authorities
Great increase in private
sector contracting

Housing   'Right to Buy' extended; 30% of council

LG and Housing Act 1989
New controls over revenue
and capital spending

Source: Adapted from Hollis *et al.* (1990), p. 22.

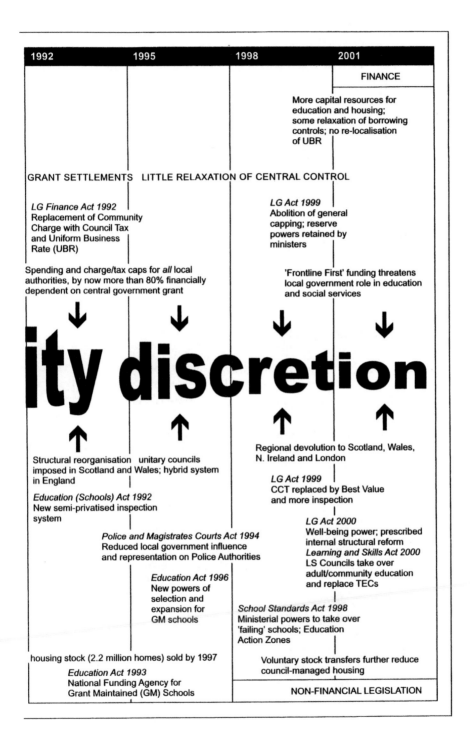

1992	1995	1998	2001

FINANCE

More capital resources for education and housing; some relaxation of borrowing controls; no re-localisation of UBR

GRANT SETTLEMENTS   LITTLE RELAXATION OF CENTRAL CONTROL

LG Finance Act 1992
Replacement of Community Charge with Council Tax and Uniform Business Rate (UBR)

LG Act 1999
Abolition of general capping; reserve powers retained by ministers

Spending and charge/tax caps for *all* local authorities, by now more than 80% financially dependent on central government grant

'Frontline First' funding threatens local government role in education and social services

ity discretion

Regional devolution to Scotland, Wales, N. Ireland and London

Structural reorganisation   unitary councils imposed in Scotland and Wales; hybrid system in England

Education (Schools) Act 1992
New semi-privatised inspection system

LG Act 1999
CCT replaced by Best Value and more inspection

Police and Magistrates Courts Act 1994
Reduced local government influence and representation on Police Authorities

LG Act 2000
Well-being power; prescribed internal structural reform
Learning and Skills Act 2000
LS Councils take over adult/community education and replace TECs

Education Act 1996
New powers of selection and expansion for GM schools

School Standards Act 1998
Ministerial powers to take over 'failing' schools; Education Action Zones

housing stock (2.2 million homes) sold by 1997

Voluntary stock transfers further reduce council-managed housing

Education Act 1993
National Funding Agency for Grant Maintained (GM) Schools

NON-FINANCIAL LEGISLATION

Diversity and innovation

Proof of that last assertion may be found among our own news items in Exhibit 2.1, and will surely be in any similar selection you may assemble for yourselves. Examples will range from the momentous and contentious to the barely newsworthy. But Birmingham's noise map (Item 10), its voluntary testing of 5-year old school pupils that featured as a news item in our previous listing (Wilson and Game, 1998, p. 12) and Oxfordshire's campaign against racism in football (Item 11) all share one thing in common. They are all examples of local councils freely deciding to do something differently from how it was being done before, differently from what other councils were doing, and *not* merely in response to any central government demand or requirement. As Item 12 demonstrates, councils have always taken such initiatives, and – except that the twenty-first-century council official would be a social worker rather than a sanitary inspector – they are just as ready and willing, if not always quite as able, to do so today.

Contracting, competing, enabling

The picture of contemporary local government that is emerging is one of inevitable subordination to central government, but hardly craven subservience; councils with perhaps less freedom of action than previously, but far from emasculated.

As for the future, the goal that the Conservative Governments of the 1980s appeared to have in mind at one time was expressible as a pun. The combination of the Government's removal of some functions from the control of local authorities and its encouragement of the contracting out of others to the private sector led to the coining of the term: 'the *Contracting Authority*'. Both in size and in the nature of its work, the local authority of the future, it was suggested, would be a contracting one!

The end of the 1980s brought a slight change in terminology. Contraction was still the objective, and contracting out still one of the key means to that end. But there were other means too, spelled out in the Government's 1987/88 legislative programme, in which a whole clutch of measures signalled a fundamental change in the role and operation of local authorities.

There was the extension of the controversial community charge or poll tax from Scotland to England and Wales and the introduction of the uniform business rate – of which more in Chapter 10. Of even greater long-term significance, though, were the plans for housing, education and many of the technical services provided by local councils. Council tenants would be able to choose their own landlords and vote themselves out of local authority control. Similarly, the parents of children in state schools could vote to 'opt-out' of their Local Education Authority and become grant maintained directly by the then Department for Education. Services such as refuse collection, street cleaning and school catering, which most councils had been used to providing themselves with their own workforces, would now have to be open to competitive tenders or bids from the private sector: the Compulsory Competitive Tendering (CCT) we referred to above.

One depiction of the future, therefore, was that of 'the *Competitive Council*' (Audit Commission, 1988): required to compete with private companies, with the voluntary sector, and even with central government itself, if it wished to continue to provide some of its most long-standing services. It was given an additional twist during the 1990s with urban regeneration initiatives like City Pride and City Challenge, in which councils were required to compete against each other for the limited funds that ministers were prepared to make available.

The phrase, though, that achieved wider currency than either the Contracting or the Competitive Council was that of the *Enabling Council* (Clarke and Stewart, 1988; Brooke, 1989; Ennals and O'Brien, 1990; Wistow *et al.*, 1992; Leach, Davis *et al.*, 1996). Local authorities' traditional role as large-scale and mainly self-sufficient service *providers* would – in almost any conceivable political future, it was argued – be reduced, and they would instead become 'enablers'. They might in many instances retain the ultimate responsibility for service provision. But, rather than do everything themselves, with their own directly employed workforces, they would stimulate, facilitate, support, regulate, influence and thereby *enable* other agencies and organisations to act on their behalf. The Enabling Authority thus became the new vogue term – and sometimes, it seemed, the new vague term, given the widely varying interpretations put upon it. It paved the way for the increasingly explicit emphasis in local government today on *partnerships* and partnership working. It is hardly a novel idea, but it will undoubtedly receive more references in this edition than in the previous one, whereas in the first edition we were intrigued to find that it was not indexed at all!

The quest for quality

By no means all recent change in local government has been externally prompted. Increasingly over the past two decades local councils have begun of their own volition to examine more self-critically their performance record and to look for ways of improving it and thereby enhancing their public image. They have sought to develop – to quote two now rather dated buzz phrases – a public service orientation or customer service culture.

Too often in the past, councils will now concede, they were inclined to act as what in many ways they were: unchallenged monopolistic service providers *to* – rather than *for* or *with* – a largely captive public. The last distinction is a crucial one. Rarely, until fairly recently, were service recipients actually asked about the type or quantity or quality of service they required or were prepared, through their own local taxes, to finance. Rarely, in short, were they treated as customers: people able to make choices, with the right to the information on which to base those choices, the right of redress if dissatisfied with the service received, and the right to go to other providers.

Local council services were, for the most part, professionally managed, competently delivered, and tolerably efficient. But the emphasis tended to be on quantity rather than quality, with relatively little consideration paid to issues of flexibility, variety and consumer relevance. This emphasis was already changing – in advance of, as well as in response to, John Major's Citizen's Charter initiatives under the 1992–7 Conservative Government.

Local authorities have been developing a wide range of their own initiatives to improve the quality of their services and get 'closer to their customers': neighbourhood offices, 'one-stop shops', community meetings, public attitude surveys, 'focus group' discussions on specific issues with selected groups of residents, council newspapers, complaints hot-lines, public question times at council meetings and, most recently, customer service centres, as already noted in Tameside. Once again, keep a look out for anything noteworthy your own council may be doing.

The present system – defining characteristics

Having identified some of the principal themes and concerns of modern-day local government, we now pause for some stocktaking. If the world of local government is changing as fundamentally as we suggest, what is it changing from? What, in broad introductory terms, does the present system look like? What are its main features and its overall rationale? In the remainder of this chapter we introduce some of the key defining characteristics of our local government system.

Local government, not local administration

We should start with a vital distinction, and explain why we have so far been using, unquestioningly, the term 'local government', rather than 'local administration'. It will serve too as a further introduction: to why the university department for which one of us works is called the Institute of Local *Government* Studies (INLOGOV), and not Local *Administrative* Studies.

All countries of any significant size find it necessary to decentralise or disperse some of the basic tasks of governance. Some do so much more extensively and more enthusiastically than others. Switzerland, for example – albeit a somewhat exceptional one – has never had a national Ministry of Education or a Ministry of Health (Allen, 1990, p. 1). The Swiss decentralise these services entirely to the control of local authorities, and mostly very much smaller authorities than those in Britain.

When central governments decentralise, they may choose to do so in different ways and to different degrees:

- *Administrative decentralisation, or delegation*
  They may choose to delegate purely administrative decision-making to dependent field offices of a central ministry. All major policy decisions will continue to be taken centrally, but the service will be delivered and routine administrative decisions taken by locally based but centrally employed civil servants. The most obvious example in Britain is the Department for Work and Pensions' Jobcentre Plus, whose *cash payments* to the sick, disabled and unemployed are made from local offices of the DWP or in Northern Ireland the Social Security Agency. They are thus largely separated – unlike the practice in many countries – from the local authority social *services* provided to many of the same people.
- *Functional decentralisation*
  Secondly, central government can create semi-independent agencies to run specific services. Here the most obvious example is the NHS, with its structure of strategic health authorities and trusts, overseen by boards of appointed and nominated members. It may look a little like the structure of local councils, and in many countries the health service is a fully integrated part of the local government system. But, though they work closely with and may in future be scrutinised by local authorities, Britain's health authorities and trusts are quite separate: funded by and ultimately accountable to central government, and thus part of the growing 'quangocracy' referred to above.
- *Political decentralisation, or devolution*
  Thirdly, central government can devolve policy-making responsibilities in a wide range of service areas to relatively autonomous and directly elected regional, provincial or local governments. This political decentralisation – the process that produced the Scottish Parliament, the Welsh and Northern Ireland Assemblies, and the GLA – in which a constitutionally superior body chooses to hand over certain powers to constitutionally dependent ones, is clearly distinguishable from *federalism,* in which *both* the national (or federal) and the local bodies are assigned their powers equally and separately by the constitution. But it is just as clearly distinguishable from local administration.

Local authorities are far more than simply outposts or agents of central government, delivering services in ways and to standards laid down in detail at national ministerial level. Their role, as representative bodies elected by their fellow citizens, is to take such decisions themselves, in accordance with their own policy priorities: to govern their locality. If this were not so, there would not be the often dramatic variations in the service costs and performance measures revealed in councils' *Annual Reports*, and in the increasingly popular league tables of local council statistics. Nor would we have seen in several of our Items in Exhibit 2.1 examples of ways in which councils can, to a certain extent at least, determine and pursue their own initiatives.

Local self-government?

So, does the system of local government – councils of elected politicians making policy decisions on behalf of their local communities – amount to local *self-government*? Do localities and communities have the rights and resources genuinely to manage their own public affairs in what they see as their own best interests? Some writers appear to think so, and use the terms 'local government' and 'local self-government' almost interchangeably.

Others, however, are more hesitant. Local government *ought* to mean local or community self-government, they seem to suggest; it ought to be about democratically elected representatives collectively deciding how best to respond to all the differing needs and wishes of the residents of their area. In practice, though, that is not how it has worked in the United Kingdom. Let us look at a particularly forceful quote from the Bains Committee, responsible in the early 1970s for one of the most influential reports on post-war local government:

> Local government, in our view, is not limited to the narrow provision of a series of services to the community ... *It has within its purview the overall economic, cultural and physical well-being of the community.*'
> (Bains, 1972, para. 2.10, emphasis ours)

It sounds like the first half of an exam question, followed perhaps by: 'Discuss, with reference to UK local government over the past twenty years.' If it were an essay question, you would certainly want to focus on that slightly quaint word 'purview'. For it has at least two shades of meaning. One is that which the Bains Committee apparently had in mind: scope of outlook or concern. Local councils, they were saying, *should* properly be concerned with and involved in *all* aspects of community life, not just those areas of responsibility allocated to them by Parliament.

That is the situation in many countries, especially those formed historically by the coming together of several small communities for mutual help and support – e.g. Switzerland, the Netherlands, Italy, the Scandinavian countries. Local councils or municipalities in such countries have, on average, much smaller populations than UK local authorities. Yet they have something that British councils historically have not had: a *power of general competence*. They have a general right to undertake any activities that they feel to be in the interests of their citizens, unless such activities are actually forbidden or assigned to other bodies. Like private citizens, they can do anything they are not expressly forbidden from doing. In these countries, as Allen puts it (1990, p. 23):

> Local government is not looked upon as just a mechanism. Rather, it is seen as the organic self-expression of the people themselves, whose powers are not yielded to the centre, but retained by the citizens of each community in the country to provide necessary local services for themselves.

In the United Kingdom, with its long monarchical history, the formal constitutional position is almost precisely the reverse: local councils have been able to do *only* what they are statutorily permitted to do. Their rights and competencies are not general, but specific. To quote Allen again (1990, p. 22), almost echoing Ambassador Seitz from our opening paragraphs:

> Local government is looked upon essentially as a subordinate mechanism created by the state for its own convenience. It is no more than one of several alternative agencies through which the paternalist central government can arrange the provision of services for the state's citizen-subjects.

Underlying their subordinate status, the common law doctrine under which councils operate is known as *ultra vires*, a Latin term which translates as 'beyond the powers'. If a local council does something or spends money that it is not statutorily authorised to, it will be deemed to have acted *ultra vires*: beyond its powers, and therefore illegally. Moreover, until the practice was finally abolished in the Local Government Act 2000, the elected councillors who collectively agreed to the action became individually punishable and personally liable to refund any money illegally spent.

This reference to the legal framework of UK local government brings us back to the Bains Committee. For 'purview' has an alternative narrower and particularly legal meaning: the body of a statute, containing the enacting clauses. This meaning was probably not that intended by the Bains Committee, but it has served as a cautionary reminder that, legally and constitutionally, local government in the United Kingdom could concern itself with the 'overall economic, cultural and physical well-being of the community' *only* in as far as the national Parliament gave it the statutory authority to do so. Observant readers, however, will have noted that this is not the first reference made to community 'well-being'. As we noted in Chapter 1, following that same Local Government Act that abolished the councillor surcharge, councils now have the power 'to promote the economic, social and environmental well-being of their area' – in other words, something close to a power of general competence. They do not have any additional resources to accompany this power, and we see no reason yet to contemplate widening the neck of our funnel of discretion. But the 'well-being power' does offer a potentially far-reaching opportunity to councils prepared to use it.

Creatures of statute

Like all of local councils' more specific powers and competencies, though, this well-being power derived from legislation, and it thus reinforces, rather than undermines, local government's necessarily subordinate position in our constitution. The doctrine of parliamentary supremacy derives from the fact that the United Kingdom, like over 80 per cent of the world's nations, is a *unitary* state, not a federal one. There is a single source of constitutional power and authority: the Westminster Parliament, in which usually nowadays one party has an overall majority of members and thus forms the Government of the day. Parliament, processing legislation introduced by the Government, can make or unmake law on any subject whatever – including local government.

In federal systems – the United States, Canada, Australia, India, Germany and Switzerland, for example – legislative power is divided, between the federal government at the centre and the governments of decentralised states or regions. No such division exists in Britain. Constitutionally, local authorities are in the same subordinate position as are the Scottish Parliament and the Welsh and Northern Ireland Assemblies. They are literally the creatures, the creations, of parliamentary statute. Their boundaries, duties, powers, memberships and modes of operation are laid down by Acts of Parliament. Naturally, therefore, they can be abolished by Parliament and, as we have seen, restructured and reincarnated at Parliament's will.

Partial autonomy

To summarise: the United Kingdom has a constitutionally subordinate system of local government, without historically the wide-ranging competence of many European continental systems, yet which is far more than a network of field agencies of central government. It could be described as semi-autonomous.

There are semantic purists who will insist that there can be no such phenomenon as partial autonomy, but we find it useful to be able to describe one governmental institution as having relatively less autonomy than another, or less than it possessed itself at some time in the past. Indeed, such imprecise terminology fits appropriately our uncodified and convention-based constitution. Most European countries have formal, written constitutions, which usually include some provision for, and protection of, the principle of local self-government.

In the United Kingdom, with no comparable single constitutional document, there is in theory no limit to the sovereignty of Parliament. There is correspondingly no constitutional protection for local government: neither for the rights of individual councils nor for the system as a whole.

In practice, however, as we shall see in Chapter 4, much of the history of UK local government, particularly during the early decades of the twentieth century, has been about governments determining and Parliaments legislating to devolve powers and responsibilities to local authorities. Local councils have been seen, in Allen's phrase, as a usefully democratic and effective 'subordinate mechanism' for the delivery of all kinds of services which central government has decided should be publicly provided.

Statutory powers can assume various forms. At one extreme they may be *detailed* and *compulsory*, requiring local councils to undertake certain activities to tightly defined and rigorously enforced standards. Alternatively, they may be *permissive* or *discretionary*, leaving councils to decide for themselves whether or not to provide a particular service, and to what standard. Traditionally, much of the legislation affecting local government has had what might be termed a high 'discretion factor'. Local councils have had considerable say in how they deliver their services and, in some cases, whether or not they do so. But discretion has no guarantee. It can be curtailed and ultimately withdrawn: hence the aptness of the label 'partial autonomy'.

Directly elected

The characteristic responsible above all others for whatever degree of autonomy local authorities do possess is that of their direct election. They are not composed of locally based civil servants or central government appointees. They consist of local people, chosen at regular and regulated elections to represent the interests of the communities in which they themselves also live and work.

These representatives – known as *councillors* or *elected members* – collectively constitute the local council and are the embodiment of its legal authority. On the basis of that authority, they recruit and employ a wide range of staff – professionally qualified 'officers', other administrative, technical and clerical 'white-collar' staff, and various categories of manual or 'blue-collar' workers – to carry out the policies and deliver the services that they, as democratically elected representatives, determine.

Direct election does not, in the United Kingdom's unitary system of government, make councillors the constitutional equals or rivals of Members of Parliament. Councillors may have to face their electorates more frequently than MPs, and there are far more of them: nearly 40 times as many. But elections can always be suspended, just as councils can be abolished, at any time that the Government, through Parliament, decrees. Until that happens, though, councillors' elected status accords them a legitimacy quite different from that of, say, the appointed members of health authorities or urban development corporations (UDCs).

Councillors have had to present themselves and their policy proposals for consideration and approval by the electorate. That local democratic approval represents a uniquely potent bargaining counter in any subsequent negotiations, whether with ministers, Whitehall civil servants, or their own local officers. Their critics may, perhaps with some cause, question voters' genuine understanding of the complex issues involved and their relatively low turnout rates in local elections. But the very fact of electoral backing in any even aspiring democratic society has a force of its own.

Multi-service organisations

If electoral accountability is the primary distinguishing feature of local authorities, the second is their range of responsibilities. They are involved in some way or other, it can sometimes seem, with an almost infinite variety of different services.

We referred earlier to councils looking after people from womb to tomb. Another way of illustrating the same point is through the A–Z service directories that most councils now produce. The directories are designed for the councils' own sometimes understandably confused residents: to publicise the services that may be available to them and, even more importantly, where to go for them and who to contact. It has been estimated that a typical unitary authority has at least 700 'lines of business', which is far more than even most multinational companies, and, it could be argued, make it correspondingly far more demanding to manage. If you doubt it, take a look at Exhibit 2.2 which lists a selection of just the A-initialled services that such a council might in some way be involved with – all we had room for.

Multi-functional organisations

All the services listed in Exhibit 2.2 have some degree of council involvement. But by no means are they all directly provided by the council itself. Historically it is true that councils' principal function has been that of *direct service provider*. They themselves have purchased the land, provided the buildings and equipment, and employed all the staff necessary to deliver their services.

Councils have always, though, had other functions and roles as well, and it is these roles that are becoming relatively more important nowadays. In many cases the local authority is the *regulator* or *monitor* of the activities of other agencies and organisations. They issue licences for public entertainments, theatres, cinemas, sex establishments, street trading, taxi drivers, animal boarding establishments, hairdressers, late night cafés, performing animals, pet shops, caravan sites acupuncturists. Similar responsibilities include the *registration* of private residential homes, and the *certification* of sports ground safety, as the public became acutely aware following the Bradford and Hillsborough football disasters.

A further role is as *facilitator*, providing advice, assistance and possibly finance to individuals or organisations undertaking activities consistent with the policy of the council. Thus a Local Action Team of council officers will provide help in setting up credit unions as part of the council's work in alleviating poverty and debt. Start-up grants and loans are available for the establishment of new businesses and workers' co-operatives, and grants are given also to an extensive range of arts, recreation, social and community groups. Finally, moving a further step away from direct service provision, there is that most rapidly developing of council roles to which we have already alluded: that of *service contractor*.

Power of taxation

Vital though we argued that it is, electoral authority is essentially a moral force. To be effective, it needs something more tangible: the right to tax. A further crucial characteristic of local authorities, therefore, is that they have the power to tax local residents. Other local agencies are funded by government grants and from their own trading income. Local authorities too receive much – indeed most – of their income from these sources. But for almost 400 years they were also able set the levels of, as well as collect, their own taxes.

Since 1980, however, the local tax system has undergone an unprecedented series of reforms. Part of the outcome has been that local authorities' taxation power is no longer, as lawyers might say, an unfettered one. As recorded on our funnel of local authority discretion, Conservative ministers in the 1980s took statutory powers to cap or limit

Exhibit 2.2 An A–A of council services

Service department/office	Possible contact
Abandoned vehicles, removal of	Environmental & Consumer Services
Abnormal loads	Highways
Abuse of children	Social Services
Access, for disabled	Planning & Architecture
Accessible transport	Travel Information Centre
Accident prevention	Environmental & Consumer Services
Accidents, road clearance	Highways
Accommodation, hotels and guesthouses	Tourism
Accommodation, for homeless	Housing
Accounts, of the Council	Finance/Treasurer's
Acupuncture, registration of	Environmental & Consumer Services
Admissions and transfers to schools	Education
Adoption, of children	Social Services
Adoption, of roads	Highways
Adult education	Education/Leisure & Culture
Adult protection (vulnerable older people)	Social Services
Adventure playgrounds	Leisure & Community Services
Advertisements and signs, control of	Planning/Development Control
Advice, neighbourhood offices	Neighbourhood Advice & Benefits
Advice bureaux (of ward councillors)	Members' Services
After-school activities	Leisure & Community Services
AIDS/HIV, advice on	Social Services
Air quality, measurement of	Environmental & Consumer Services
Alcohol abuse, advice on	Social Services
Allotments, hire of	Leisure & Community Services
Alteration of buildings	Planning/Development control
Aluminium recycling	Environmental & Consumer Services
Amusement machines, licensing of	Environmental & Consumer Services
Animal welfare, enforcement of regulations	Environmental & Consumer Services
Antique markets, information on	Environmental & Consumer Services
Ants, control of	Environmental & Consumer Services
Approved lists, of contractors and service suppliers	Finance/Treasurer's
Architecture, listed buildings	Planning
Arts and entertainment, information on	Leisure Services
Asbestos, removal of	Environmental & Consumer Services
Assistance to industry	Economic Development
Awards, student	Education

councils' levels of spending and their right to tax their own residents, thereby effectively controlling their budgets. The 1997 Labour Government abolished what it called the 'crude and universal capping' system it inherited, but ministers retain a seemingly arbitrary reserve power to intervene and cap selectively the budget and council tax levels of any council proposing to spend in a way that they decide is 'excessive'. So, while the power to tax still distinguishes local councils from other agencies of public administration, it is a power exercised nowadays with central government constantly looking over their shoulders.

Conclusion

We have identified in this chapter a set of characteristics that, individually and collectively, serve as a definition of UK local government (Box 2.1). This is a slightly more elaborate definition than that we worked out in Chapter 1, and it will serve as a reference point for several of the remaining chapters in Part 1 of the book.

Box 2.1 UK local government defined

- A form of geographical and political decentralisation,
- in which directly elected councils,
- created by and subordinate to Parliament,
- have partial autonomy
- to provide a wide variety of services
- through various direct and indirect means,
- funded in part by local taxation.

Guide to further reading

Our first recommendations for further study are those we made in Chapter 1. Find out about the practical workings of local government from your own local councils – either by going along and testing their customer responsiveness in person or by checking out their web sites. Couple this with a regular – if possible daily – scanning of the Home News pages of a 'quality' or 'broadsheet' national newspaper: *Guardian, Independent, Telegraph* or *The Times* – also available on the internet (www.guardian. co.uk etc.). And don't forget your local press – including your council's own newspaper, if it has one – especially around the January/February budgeting and April/May election times. For a more cynical view there is

Private Eye's regular 'Rotten Boroughs' column. The most comprehensive textbook introduction to 'how it all works' (to quote its subtitle) is Byrne (2000), but, as you will have gathered, the world of local government changes fast and, if you have access to it, there is no better way of staying in touch (or revising!) than through the internet. Try initially the Local Government Association – www.lga.gov.uk and the Department for Transport, Local Government and the Regions – www.dtlr.gov.uk. And if you're really keen, you can register (free) for a daily email bulletin from www.info4local.gov.uk – a one-stop gateway for local government information published by relevant government departments.

Chapter 3

Why Elected Local Government?

Introduction

In identifying in Chapter 2 the defining characteristics of the UK local government system, we emphasised why this book's primary focus is very definitely on *elected local government*, rather than the boundary-blurring networks of local *governance*. We look now, therefore, at the principles underpinning that governmental system, at its rationale and *raison d'être*, its value and values. Inevitably, we will be discussing, though not uncritically, the benefits and positive attributes of elected local government, reflecting one bias to which we do readily admit: a predisposition in favour of decentralisation of power and against its undue concentration.

The problems of local government

To central government, it often seems, the commonest 'problem' of local government is when it refuses to do what central government wishes: when local councils pursue demonstrably different goals from those of the party in power nationally. An alternative interpretation of such a battle of wills is that it demonstrates the health and robustness of a governmental system. Far from constituting a problem, it ought to be seen as an affirmation of precisely what local government should be about: locally elected and accountable representatives developing policies embodying *their* judgement of the best interests of *their* local community, not the judgement of the centre.

Our own reference to 'the problems of local government' is intended to suggest something rather more subtle and complex. We mean the potential costs and considerations involved in any decision to devolve administrative responsibility, let alone political power. In several cases these potential costs are merely the obverse of possible benefits. But it is still useful to enumerate some of what Allen (1990, Ch. 1) terms the disadvantages of decentralisation.

The first argument deployed against decentralisation is that of *financial cost*. Decentralisation duplicates scarce financial resources and staff. Things could be run more cheaply from the centre, critics suggest, whether the centre in question is London or, when considering the case for area or neighbourhood offices, from a council's own headquarters.

Closely linked to finance is *efficiency*. It may be difficult to attract experienced staff and enterprising management, especially if the decentralised units are relatively small and poorly resourced. The argument loses some of its force, however, if you have a national government responsible (or irresponsible) for, among other managerial embarrassments: the Millennium Dome; a Millennium-celebrating 'wall of fire', visible only by helicopter; a Jubilee Line extension costing nearly twice its promised £2.1 billion; army SA80 rifles (in Kosovo) that jam during rapid firing and Clansmen radios unable to either transmit or receive messages; railway signals positioned so badly that there is a jargonised abbreviation ('spads') for the frequency with which they are passed at danger – and a poll tax. In Britain at least, policy inefficiency is not confined to any single level of government.

A different kind of argument is that of *inequality*. The more genuinely decentralised a service, the greater, inevitably, will be the resulting disparities among geographical areas and social groups. These disparities generate public and electoral demands for greater 'fairness' and minimum national standards, followed by central government's intervention with resource distribution formulae, bringing greater territorial equity but at the cost of local political and financial discretion. This apparent national intolerance of locally varying service provision is a particularly British phenomenon, and perhaps the biggest dilemma facing genuine local government reformers, as opposed to instinctive centralisers or abolitionists.

Finally, there is the charge of potential *corruption*, levelled probably more frequently at local than at national government, and at least as much in the news today as it was in the 1970s, at the time of the notorious 'Poulson Affair'. In 1974 several leading politicians and senior public sector employees were found guilty of having improperly and corruptly secured contracts for the Yorkshire private architect, John Poulson. The case led to the important formulation of a National Code of Conduct for the guidance of both councillors and officers. Perhaps for this reason, it is remembered primarily as a case of *local* government corruption, despite the fact that 'Poulson's cadre' (Doig, 1984, p. 142) embraced a cabinet minister, MPs of both parties, civil servants, health service and nationalised industry employees, as well as councillors and officers.

The equally high-profile case of the 1980s and 1990s – much more to do with political power than personal financial gain – was the 'homes for votes' affair involving Dame Shirley Porter, then Leader of Westminster City Council. Dame Shirley and five councillor and officer associates were found by a local government district auditor to have operated a housing sales policy specifically for the electoral benefit of the Conservative Party, thereby costing their council many millions of pounds. This verdict was overturned by the Court of Appeal in 1999, before which time aspects of the case were considered in 1996/97 by the Government's Committee on Standards in Public Life, chaired by Lord Nolan. But it should also be remembered that that Committee was set up in the first place to investigate allegations of misconduct and 'sleaze' in the *Palace*, not the City, of Westminster, and on the part of MPs and ministers, who significantly had no equivalent of councillors' Code of Conduct to guide their behaviour.

Our point is not that any set of politicians – local or national, male or female, Party *A* or Party *B* – is intrinsically more virtuous or more corruptible than any other. It is merely that we should retain a sense of perspective and keep in mind Allen's warning (1990, p. 12) that, despite all the national and international evidence that

> central agencies are often at least as incompetent, inefficient or corrupt as local bodies, local authorities are perennially in the news for alleged corruption and graft ... one or two notorious cases can suffice to keep the whole concept of local government in disrepute.

The values of local government

These alleged 'problems' of decentralisation are not to be dismissed lightly. But they can be more than balanced by its positive features or, as various authors have phrased it, the justifications of local government (Smith, 1985, Ch. 2; Young, 1986b; Clarke and Stewart, 1991, Ch. 3). In the remainder of this chapter we group our justifications under the seven headings itemised in Exhibit 3.1. It is a grouping derived from an important and enduring literature – dating back at least 150 years to the still relevant writings of Joshua Toulmin Smith and John Stuart Mill.

Exhibit 3.1 The values or justifications of elected local government

Elected local government is likely to be better than a combination of central government and local administration at:

1. Building and articulating community identity
2. Emphasising diversity
3. Fostering innovation and learning
4. Responding swiftly, appropriately, corporately
5. Promoting citizenship and participation
6. Providing political education and training
7. Dispersing power.

Building and articulating community identity

In Chapter 2 we concentrated particularly on local *government* and its contrast with local administration. We now focus on *local* government: the government of a particular geographical area and, if the relevant boundaries have been appropriately drawn, the government of a community. The institutions of local government ought both to reflect and reinforce people's sense of place and of community:

> A local authority has the capacity to shape an area, to preserve it, to develop it, to change it, and in doing so to give it a new identity. (Clarke and Stewart 1991, p. 29)

But necessarily these things take time and need encouragement, both of which have been at a premium in recent years. We contrasted in Chapter 2 the kind of 'bottom-up' local self-government found in some European countries, which grew out of local communities coming together for mutual help and support, and the United Kingdom's more 'top-down' version, deriving from parliamentary statute and the drawing of boundary lines on maps. The inevitable danger of over-frequent 'top-down' restructuring is the severing of any link between a local authority and community identity, the most visible sign of which must be the imposition of alien council names that at best bewilder and at worst infuriate.

The reorganisation of the early 1970s produced countless examples of these 'artificial' names, initially as unfamiliar to their own residents as they still are to many outsiders. Some have already disappeared in the 1990s reorganisation: the non-metropolitan counties of Avon, Cleveland and Humberside, together with the equally short-lived and much-mispronounced Welsh counties of Clwyd and Dyfed. But plenty of others remain: the metropolitan districts of Calderdale and Kirklees (respectively the areas around Halifax and Huddersfield), Knowsley (east of Liverpool) and Sandwell (West Midlands); and, among the many non-metropolitan district candidates, Adur (West Sussex), Craven (North Yorkshire), Gravesham (Kent), Three Rivers (Herts), and the doubly confusing Wyre (coastal Lancashire) and Wyre Forest (Worcestershire).

Then there are all the 'compass point councils' – real towns and neighbourhoods considered too small to govern themselves that have been grouped and anonymised by boundary commission bureaucrats into meaningless geographical mongrels – North Hertfordshire, South Somerset, East Northamptonshire, West Lancashire, and dozens like them. As it happens, each of these four contains a town of at least 30,000 – respectively, Letchworth, Yeovil, Rushden, and Skelmersdale – that would qualify for self-governing status in almost any other country in Western Europe. In Britain, however, they and their like can be seen as testaments to a national political culture that is inclined to build and restructure its local government system 'more on bureaucratic and professional principles than upon local needs and community identities' (Lowndes, 1996, p. 71).

Emphasising diversity

A sense of place and past implies *distinctiveness*: of an area's distinctive geography, history, economy, social and political culture, and of its consequently distinctive preferences and priorities. It is the recognition that even local authorities of the same type, with the same statutory powers and responsibilities, can be utterly different from each other and have completely different governmental needs.

In a federal system like the United States, where the states can pass as well as promote their own legislation, the diversity of local demands and circumstances can appear extreme and even bizarre. In Indiana it is illegal to ride on a bus within four hours of eating garlic, in South Carolina to drink water in a bar, and in Kentucky to carry an ice cream cone in one's pocket. But UK local authorities too can differ so greatly in character that it is possible to imagine their enacting almost equally singular legislation, given the chance.

Basildon, Berwick-upon-Tweed and Bolsover are all English non-metropolitan districts. Yet, apart from their initials, they share little in common. Basildon, heartland of 'Essex girl' jokes, was the first of the country's post-war New Towns. After 50 years it has grown to well over 100,000, yet has to share its council with the two inevitably overshadowed townships of Billericay and Wickford, the total 165,000 population making it the third largest of England's 238 non-metropolitan districts. It is London commuter territory, but the local economy is also thriving, with government recognition as an area of potential industrial development, and large-scale recent investment in a regional shopping centre, Festival Leisure Park, and – not to be overlooked – the National Motorboat Museum. It is vulnerable, though, to disinvestment decisions by foreign-owned companies, and there are pockets of deprivation amid the growing prosperity. In 2001 the 41-member Council remained Labour-dominated, as for almost all of its history, though not perhaps indefinitely.

Berwick-upon-Tweed Borough Council covers nearly nine times the area of Basildon but has about one-sixth of its population. By this latter criterion it is almost the smallest council in England. Notwithstanding its team's membership of the Scottish Football League, the medieval walled town itself lies two miles south of the Scottish border. But most of the borough is rural, its economy based on agriculture, fishing and light industry, plus summer tourism attracted by its picturesque coastline and the Northumberland National Park. The politics of the 29-member council are predominantly Liberal Democrat, with Independents in second place.

Bolsover's voters in North-East Derbyshire, by contrast, have never elected a Liberal Democrat councillor and only very occasionally a Conservative. Probably better known nowadays for its MP – 'Beast of Bolsover', Dennis Skinner – than for its council, the area was for more than 100 years a centre of the country's mining industry, although its castle and market charter date back to the thirteenth century. Today there are no mines, nor railways. An enterprise park has replaced the colliery, small businesses are being developed, mining landscapes reclaimed, and heritage sites restored. The council itself, as by far the town's largest employer, is leading the search for a new identity in a coal-less age.

Any other random selection of B-initialled districts would produce just as great a diversity. Yet central government's instinct tends to be to focus on the relatively few similarities of such authorities and to play down their obvious contrasts. Ministers and civil servants struggle to devise formulae that will enable all such councils to be dealt with as a single group. A thriving local government does the reverse. It emphasises and gives voice and expression to the distinctiveness of local communities. It is the *government of difference* or of diversity – or, more accurately still, of multiversity.

Fostering innovation and learning

By responding to diverse local circumstances and acting as the government of difference, local authorities are almost bound to enhance the learning capacity of government. They will develop their own solutions and initiatives, some of which may prove unsuccessful or applicable only to their specific locality, but some of which may be adaptable – either by other local authorities or even by central government.

Local authorities are constantly learning from each other – through official bodies like the Audit Commission and the Improvement and Development Agency (IDeA), publicising examples of 'best practice'; through the dozens of local government professional magazines and journals, conferences and seminars; and by simple word of mouth. Refer back to our own selection of News Items in Exhibit 2.1. You can be sure that, with or without ministerial encouragement, other councils will soon be producing their own sound emission contour maps – just as, in another environmental initiative, the London Borough of Hammersmith and Fulham readily acknowledged the lead given by their neighbours, Camden and Westminster, in collecting waste glass left at the roadside and crushing it into reusable sand.

Almost every local authority in the country has developed or piloted some new service that has subsequently been adopted or adapted for use elsewhere. Bradford reduced its burglary rate by fitting laminated windows and steel-framed doors in its council houses. Bracknell Forest pioneered, with BT, a multi-function smart card to purchase local services, borrow library books, and participate in local retail loyalty schemes. Broadlands District in Norfolk recycles Yellow Pages telephone directories and shreds them into animal bedding. Lambeth has a team of street care agents to patrol the borough and respond to the public's concerns with graffiti, illegal dumping, abandoned vehicles and other street issues. Liverpool, self-styled 'most library-friendly city in the UK', opens several of its libraries on Sundays. Neighbouring Knowsley runs a 'Snack, Classics and Pop' breakfast service, accompanied by classical or pop music, for schoolchildren not getting breakfast at home; also a 'Plus One Challenge' incentive scheme to reward pupils improving their GCSE results via the council's revision web site and text messaging service.

The list is endless, and we defy you to find a council that can *not* produce some service innovation to boast or bore about. Most, indeed, are likely to be involved in one or more of the government pilot schemes that have proliferated under Labour Ministers who have recognised much more than their predecessors the testing and learning opportunities provided by local government. 'We have more pilots than British Airways', boast overburdened chief executives, confronted with ministerial calls to pilot best value and postal balloting, initiatives to deal with runaway children, and to produce 'Better Government for Older People', measures to improve the quality and 'greenness' of local bus services and cut levels of greenhouse gas emissions.

Responding swiftly, appropriately, corporately

Distance delays. It can also distort perception. Being the multi-service multi-functional organisations that they are, local councils on the spot ought to be able to identify better and faster than can central government the most appropriate response to any local situation. They should also be able to organise that response themselves, quickly, co-ordinatedly and, possibly, more economically. Sharpe (1970, pp. 155, 165) terms this ability the 'knowledge value' of local government:

> central government is not equipped to grasp the inimitable conditions of each locality. Local government is preferable precisely because locally elected institutions employing their own specialist staff are better placed to understand and interpret both the conditions and the needs of local communities ... out-stationed field agencies could not ... co-ordinate their activities with each other.

An exceptional but vital example of such co-ordination was provided by Kent County Council's emergency support operation following the bomb explosion at the Royal Marines' barracks at Deal in September 1989 which killed 11 bandsmen. The operation involved almost the whole range of council departments:

- the Fire Service
- the Police, who initially notified ...
- the Emergency Planning Unit, who co-ordinated the ensuing support work, calling in, where necessary, organisations like the British Red Cross, the ambulance service, and Dover District Council
- Social Services, providing temporary shelter for those evacuated from their homes, meals-on-wheels, care and counselling support
- Education, as schools were requisitioned as rest centres
- the Schools Meals Service, providing food and hot drinks for both the rescued and rescuers
- Building Design and Highways, whose structural engineers were needed to advise on partially collapsed buildings
- Supplies, called upon to provide waterproofs and other protective equipment.

The traditional management jargon here is 'horizontal integration', as explained in the Widdicombe Committee Report:

> Local authorities can respond corporately to multi-dimensional local issues, such as inner city problems, in a way which national services are less able to do. This is an advantage of multi-purpose units of government which is not easily replicated in a system of local administration. Thus, while the health service might maximise efficiency in its vertical integration of a single service between district health authority and Whitehall, local government will tend to have the advantage in horizontal integration of a range of services at local level. (Widdicombe, 1986a, p. 52)

'Holistic' or 'joined-up' government (see Perri 6, 2002) are the more contemporary terms for the same phenomenon, the contrast being the 'silo' organisation: long, vertical towers making policy pronouncements and attempting to deliver services independently of one another. Those in multi-functional local authorities can find it disconcerting to be lectured about the virtues of joined-up government by ministers in their apparently less effectively integrated Whitehall departmental silos. Many of our most intractable policy problems – crime, community safety, social exclusion, job creation, drugs (see Exhibit 3.2) – require the kind of cross-cutting, multi-service intervention that local authorities, with their wide range of duties, powers and services, are ideally placed to both provide and co-ordinate.

Exhibit 3.2 Local government's contribution to a joined-up drugs policy

Social Services departments – plan and provide for social care needs of problem drug users

Housing departments – provide housing for recovering drug users; manage and control drug use in areas of social housing

Education and Youth Services – provide drug awareness education, in and outside school; can develop a community drug prevention strategy, using youth and outreach workers and community development officers

Environmental Services – are responsible for collection and safe disposal of used syringes; license premises for public entertainment, register door supervisors, etc.

Leisure and Recreation – can provide young people with appropriate and accessible leisure facilities

Training and Personnel – can contribute to drug prevention strategies; provide help for employees who themselves have drug problems

Economic Development – provide employment opportunities to deter drug dealing and usage

Youth Offending Teams – direct young drug-using offenders towards drug treatment.

PLUS, CORPORATELY, local authorities are almost certainly the best equipped organisations to liaise with representatives from the police, customs and excise, the probation and prison services, health authorities, and the voluntary sector.

Promoting citizenship and participation

Local *administration* is about acceptance: local officials' acceptance of nationally determined policy, and service recipients' acceptance of those officials' implementation of that policy. Local *government* is about choice and challenge. It actively encourages, particularly nowadays, citizen involvement and participation. It has what Sharpe (1970, p. 160) calls 'democratic primacy' over central government, 'because it does enable more people to participate in their own government'.

Most obviously, elected local government involves citizens as voters and elected representatives. The regularity of local elections means that we have the chance to vote for our councillors far more frequently than for our MPs, even if only a minority of us actually do so. It is interesting, bearing in mind recent low local election turnouts, that, compared to many countries, the United Kingdom has an exceptionally small number of councils and councillors – who are unknown personally, therefore, to most electors – and an exceptionally large number of MPs. Even so, for every MP or parliamentary candidate there are roughly 40 councillors or candidates in our so-called 'principal' councils – that is, counties, districts, boroughs and unitaries.

These figures, moreover, completely exclude the 90,000 or so elected members of the country's 'local' – that is, parish, town and community – councils. There are 8,000 parish and town councils in England, and some 2,000 community councils in Wales and Scotland, with an average of nine elected members each, albeit some of them doubling as councillors on principal authorities as well. Some of these councils are larger than our smaller district councils, representing communities of over 30,000 people, and in many countries they would be powerful and important institutions. In the United Kingdom, by contrast, as we shall see in Chapter 5, their powers are limited mainly to the discretionary provision of relatively minor and very localised services, and to representing the views of their residents to principal councils and other agencies. Not surprisingly in the circumstances, many elections go uncontested, but these councils remain democratically constituted and accountable bodies and offer to a great many citizens the means of participating directly in the government of their communities.

There is, in any case, immensely more to participation in local government than standing and voting in local elections. Elections are only the tip of the participation iceberg, as has been emphatically shown by researchers at De Montfort University who have recorded and categorised the many and varied methods modern councils use to try to get us involved in their decision making (see Exhibit 3.3). Their efforts may not always be successful. Many, even most, people may decide that they do not wish to participate: that their interests are already adequately represented and they have better things to do with their lives. But elected local government offers them the right and opportunity to participate – and was doing so, often in some genuinely innovative ways, long before 'getting closer to the community' became part of the Blair Government's modernisation agenda for local government.

Providing political education and training

Participation is itself a form of political education. In the United Kingdom political education has traditionally been a largely neglected field of study in our schools and colleges. Not before time, that situation is being remedied, with Citizenship Education becoming a compulsory subject on the secondary school curriculum and part of the Personal, Social and Health Education and Citizenship framework in primary schools. In time, these developments will hopefully raise levels of political literacy and

Exhibit 3.3 How local authorities try to get us participating

	% of councils saying used in 1997
1. TRADITIONAL METHODS	
• Public meetings/consultation documents	85+
• Co-option to council committees	60
• Public question and answer sessions at council or committee meetings	45
2. CONSUMERIST METHODS – concerned mainly with aspects of service delivery	
• Complaints/suggestion schemes	90+
• Service satisfaction surveys, service-specific or authority-wide	85+
3. CONSULTATIVE METHODS	
• Interactive web sites	25
• Citizens' panels – statistically representative samples of 1000+ residents	20
• Local referendums	2
4. FORUMS – gatherings of residents with a shared background or experience	
• Service user forums	60+
• Area or neighbourhood forums	60
• Issue forums	50
• Shared interest forums	40
5. DELIBERATIVE METHODS – to encourage in-depth consideration of issues	
• Focus groups – small discussion groups of 10–12 selected residents	50
• Community plans/ needs analysis – setting priorities for local service provision	45
• Visioning exercises – getting participants to 'vision' some aspect of the future	25
• Citizens' juries – extended and evidence-based consideration of policy area	5
6. USER MANAGEMENT – direct citizen control over local services	
• e.g. tenant management co-operatives, community-run nurseries and youth clubs	20+

Main source: Lowndes *et al.* (2001).

community involvement. Even then, though, governmental institutions themselves – particularly at the local level – will continue to have a vital role to play as stimuli of political learning.

Local elections are especially important. Even non-voters are likely to have their political awareness and governmental knowledge increased through the heightened media attention given to local issues and candidates during the campaign period. All UK local elections take place in April or May, shortly after councils have made their budgets for the new financial year and sent out their local tax demands. Councillors and candidates, through their election addresses and manifestos, have to defend their actions or propose alternative policies. Statistics are produced, challenged and debated. Surveys may show that many people still remain unaware of who our councillors are and what our councils do, but without elections that ignorance would be almost total.

For its most active and involved participants local government provides not just education, but a training and apprenticeship for a professional political career. In recent General Elections there has been no single more important recruiting ground than local government – for all political parties. Of the record 1997 intake of 259 new MPs, 161 (62 per cent) had served as councillors, bringing the Commons total as a whole to 368 (56 per cent). This latter figure included two-thirds of Labour MPs, over 60 per cent of Liberal Democrats, and 30 per cent of Conservatives.

Striking though these figures are, the key term in those last two sentences is 'had served', for almost all of that 62 per cent will have resigned from their councils at the earliest political opportunity, even if their parliamentary seats happen to be within the council area. In this respect there is generally in Britain much less career overlap between national and local politics – and local government has a correspondingly less powerful voice nationally – than in many countries.

Dispersing power

Last, though anything but least, we come to arguably the most fundamental value or justification of local government: that of pluralism. To quote the Widdicombe Report on the Conduct of Local Authority Business:

> the case for pluralism is that power should not be concentrated in one organisation of state, but should be dispersed, thereby providing political checks and balances, and a restraint on arbitrary government and absolutism. (Widdicombe, 1986a, p. 48)

Ten years earlier another Government report, this time by the Layfield Committee of Inquiry into Local Government Finance, had seen local government's role in almost identical terms:

By providing a large number of points where decisions are taken by people of different political persuasion ... it acts as a counterweight to the uniformity inherent in government decisions. It spreads political power. (Layfield, 1976, p. 53)

It is the same idea that is to be found on the opening page of any dictionary of quotations: Lord Acton's famous aphorism that 'power tends to corrupt, and absolute power corrupts absolutely'. Like many supposedly well-known sayings, it is frequently misquoted, but for our purposes the placement of the emphasis is insightful. The dispersal of power *may* lead to corruption, but Acton's certainty is reserved for its concentration.

Conclusion

Let us be clear. We are not in this chapter putting forward an idealised and uncritical case for decentralised government, certainly not as it currently exists in the United Kingdom. Our local authorities can easily be shown to exhibit the various disadvantages of decentralisation that we enumerated, as well as finding it difficult to live up to its claimed values. As instruments of pluralism, platforms for increased participation, champions of their communities, their deficiencies are manifest and have been argued and documented in the literature (e.g. King and Stoker, 1996). Nor are we challenging the ideas we dealt with in Chapter 2 about a unitary state, parliamentary sovereignty and the constitutional subordination of local government in such a state. We are, however, suggesting that a significant dispersal of power away from the centre, by extending choice, encouraging initiative and innovation, and enhancing active participation, is likely to do more for the quality of government and the health of democracy than will its centralisation and concentration. The problems associated with democratic decentralisation are minor compared with the problems associated with the excessive centralisation of power. The historical development of democratic decentralisation (i.e. elected local government) is the focus of Chapter 4.

Guide to further reading

We have already quoted from what is still one of the best introductions to the values of local government: the article by L. J. Sharpe (1970). Hill (1974) is a book-length treatment of the subject from about the same time, King and Stoker (1996) a more recent and wide-ranging one, with several useful chapters by, among others, Stoker, King and Beetham. Professors

George Jones (LSE) and John Stewart (INLOGOV) have, for two decades now, been the most prolific champions of elected local government, Jones (1997) being a helpful compilation of 'what we are against and what we are for'. The independent Commission for Local Democracy produced a radical report in 1995 designed to promote the cause of democratic local government – including elected mayors; its commissioned research is summarised in Pratchett and Wilson (1996).

Chapter 4

The Development of Local Government

Modern institutions, ancient origins

Why have we included an essentially historical chapter in a book on contemporary local government? Why not just concentrate on the present system and structure as we do in Chapter 5? The answer is disarmingly simple. It is just not possible properly to understand the present without at least some appreciation of how that present came about, of how it developed out of and differs from the past. That much would be true for any country. But it is especially true in Britain, where the system of local government, like most other institutions, has evolved gradually and piecemeal over the centuries, uninterrupted by an invasion or violent revolution that might have prompted a formal constitutional settlement.

In Britain there is no codified constitutional document setting out the rights and responsibilities of local authorities and their relationship with national government. Instead there is a set of institutions and practices, some centuries old, that were created and have been adapted in response to changing circumstances. Thus there are shires, and some shire county boundaries, dating back to Anglo-Saxon times – which, in the recent debates on reorganisation, many people made clear they did *not* want abolished and replaced by new unitary councils. There are historic cities – like Bristol, Oxford, Newcastle, Norwich, Aberdeen and Dundee – that were granted Royal Charters during the twelfth century and were centres of genuine municipal self-government until they were forcefully incorporated into their respective counties and regions in the local government reorganisation of the early 1970s.

There are magistrates or Justices of the Peace, first appointed as local agents of the Crown in the fourteenth century, some 500 years before the emergence of political parties. It is understandable that they cling on fiercely to their independent representation on modern-day police authorities – but also that the 'new magistracy' was the phrase chosen by Jones and Stewart to describe the recent spread of non-elected local government agencies (see p. 19 above). There used to be a local property tax – the rates – that originated with the Elizabethan Poor Law of 1601. Predictably enough, having been abolished by the Conservative Government in 1988, it was recognised to have had significant merits lacking in the new community charge and, when the latter was almost instantly abandoned, was substantially reincarnated in the form of the council tax.

Some sense of history and of historical continuity, therefore, is important. But this is primarily a contemporary account of local government and so we confine ourselves, and you, to a fairly breathless review of indisputably major trends and developments.

The nineteenth-century tangle

It is an irony in the history of British local government that the term 'local government' itself was coined only in the nineteenth century – at the very time when it was becoming larger and *less* local than ever before. Nonetheless, the early nineteenth century is our most appropriate starting point. Just across the English Channel, following its 1789 Revolution, France already had not only a clearly defined *system* of local government, but one that in its essentials still exists today:

- A municipality or *commune* in each town, borough, parish or rural community, and all 36,000 and more *communes*, from the smallest hamlet to Paris itself, with the same constitutional status;
- Each *commune* with its own assembly, elected by universal suffrage, and a mayor responsible to central government as well as to the *commune*.

In Britain, by contrast, there was no such 'system'; nor would there be for most of the nineteenth century. Rather, there was what Patricia Hollis has graphically labelled 'a tangle' (Hollis, 1987, pp. 2–3), comprising principally the three traditional units of British local government: the parish, the county, and the borough.

Parishes, of which there were over 15,000 by the 1830s, appointed various unpaid officers – constables, highway surveyors, overseers of the poor, as well as churchwardens – to take responsibility respectively for law and order, road maintenance, and the provision of either work or financial relief for the poor. *Counties*, into which most of the country had been divided in the Middle Ages, were administered by Justices of the Peace (JPs). These Crown-appointed officials had both a judicial role, exercised through the county quarter sessions, and increasing administrative responsibilities, for highways and bridges, weights and measures, and general oversight of the parishes. The 200 or so *boroughs*, or corporate towns, were exempt from this jurisdiction of JPs and effectively governed themselves through Corporations established by Royal Charter. They had the right to determine their own systems of government – sometimes elected, sometimes self-appointed – to decide how to raise the money due to the King, and to run their own courts. This same principle of local self-rule was being developed and extended in Scotland through a considerably larger number of *burghs*, with their councils of burgesses.

There were in addition all kinds of *ad hoc authorities*, established by local Acts of Parliament, each providing a specific service within a particular area whose boundaries might not coincide with those of any other authorities. Thus there were Turnpike Trustees, who could levy tolls on road users to maintain and provide new roads; and Improvement Commissioners, who provided rate-funded services such as paving, lighting, street cleansing, and later fire engines and gas and water supplies.

It was the pressures brought about by the Industrial Revolution – urban poverty and unemployment, overcrowding and poor sanitation, disease and crime – that showed up this 'tangle' for what it was and demonstrated the urgent necessity of reform. The existing patchwork of institutions simply could not cope with the demands of a developing industrial society.

The response of government took two contrasting forms, each reflected in the two major reform Acts of the 1830s. On the one hand, the *Poor Law Amendment Act 1834* heralded the creation of *more single-purpose ad hoc authorities*. The Act replaced the parishes for the administration of poor relief with some 700 unions, or groupings of parishes, under *elected* Boards of Guardians. These Boards were subject to strong central direction from the national Poor Law Commissioners, but the very fact of their election and resulting electoral accountability distinguishes them from most of the single-purpose authorities created more recently. Plenty of other *ad hoc* bodies followed – local health boards, highways boards, elementary school boards, sanitary districts – products in part of the delay in any more comprehensive reform of sub-national government.

The nearest the early nineteenth century came to such a reform was the second of the two 1830s statutes: the *Municipal Corporations Act 1835*. By creating some 78 multi-purpose elected local authorities which were not concerned with the administration of justice, this Act can be seen as the foundation of our present-day local government and it thus constitutes the first entry in our summary of structural legislation in Exhibit 4.1. The powers of these new councils were limited and their franchise even more so – restricted to male ratepayers of over three years' residence – but the principle of elected local self-government had been established.

A dual system emerges

Despite the reforms of the 1830s, there was nothing until almost the end of the nineteenth century that could even vaguely be called a *system* of local government. There still remained the 'tangle' of literally thousands of appointed and elected bodies, of both single- and multi-purpose authorities (see Wilson and Game, 1998, p. 45).

Exhibit 4.1 The evolution of modern local government: keynote legislation

1835 Municipal Corporations Act – birth of directly elected corporate boroughs in England and Wales to replace self-electing and frequently corrupt medieval corporations.

1888 Local Government Act – established 62 elected county councils and 61 all-purpose county borough councils in England and Wales. Paralleled by Local Government (Scotland) Act 1889.

1894 Local Government Act – established within county council areas a network of 535 urban district councils (UDCs), 472 rural district councils (RDCs) and 270 non-county borough councils. Equivalent Scottish structure established by Town Councils (Scotland) Act 1900.

1899 London Government Act – completion of the 'modern' structure of local government. Established in London County Council (LCC) area a network of 28 metropolitan borough councils (plus the City of London Corporation) to replace the 38 vestries and district boards.

1929 Local Government Act – abolished Boards of Poor Law Guardians and transferred their responsibilities to local authorities. More extensive restructuring and transfer of powers in Scotland under Local Government (Scotland) Act 1929.

1963 London Government Act – established, from 1965, the Greater London Council (GLC), 32 London Boroughs, and in the former LCC area the Inner London Education Authority (ILEA). City of London Corporation (33rd borough) survived unchanged.

1972 Local Government Act – abolished, from 1974, county boroughs and reduced counties in England and Wales to 47, incorporating 333 non-metropolitan district councils. In urban England established 6 metropolitan counties and 36 metropolitan districts.

1972 Local Government (Northern Ireland) Act – replaced 73 local authorities with 26 single-tier district councils in Northern Ireland elected by proportional representation.

1973 Local Government (Scotland) Act – reformed Scottish local government by establishing, from May 1975, 9 regional councils, 53 district councils and 3 island councils to replace the over 400 authorities which had existed from 1929.

1985 Local Government Act – abolished the GLC and the 6 metropolitan county councils with effect from April 1986. Inner London Education Authority abolished April 1990.

1994 Local Government (Scotland) and (Wales) Acts – replaced, from 1996, the two-tier systems in Scotland and Wales with, respectively, 32 and 22 unitary councils. In parallel, 46 new English unitary councils were created by Parliamentary/Statutory Orders, extending the English 'hybrid' system.

1999 Greater London Authority Act – created UK's first directly elected executive mayor and a 25–member Assembly, both elected in May 2000.

Rationalisation was clearly overdue, and it came in the form of a group of Acts passed in the last dozen years of the century. The *Local Government Act 1888* created 62 county councils, including one for London (the LCC), and 61 county boroughs, all directly elected. *County councils* varied enormously in size, from nearly 3½ million in Lancashire to 20,000 in Rutland. Initially they had only a limited range of powers – responsibility for highways and bridges, asylums, weights and measures, and partial control of the police – but, as we shall see, these would grow steadily as the twentieth century progressed.

County borough councils were all-purpose authorities, independent of the counties. The county borough status was originally intended only for large towns with populations of over 150,000. During the passage of the legislation, though, the figure was reduced to just 50,000, to the considerable resentment of the counties, whose financial viability could be seriously threatened by the loss of even a single county borough. Parallel legislation in Scotland established 33 elected county councils, with the four largest burghs – Glasgow, Edinburgh, Dundee and Aberdeen – becoming all-purpose *counties of cities:* in effect 'independent islands' like the English county boroughs.

The *Local Government Act 1894* completed the reform of English and Welsh local government outside London by creating elected *urban district councils* (UDCs) and *rural district councils* (RDCs) based on the former sanitary districts. An attempt was also made to revive parishes in rural areas, even though they had by this time lost many of their powers to larger authorities. Every parish within a rural district with more than 300 residents was required to have a *parish council,* and those without councils were to hold *parish meetings.*

In Scotland equivalent legislation extended the elective principle to parish and town/burgh councils in 1894 and 1900, respectively, although for a time, as in England and Wales, there continued in existence a complex network of *ad hoc* bodies: school boards, police commissions, county road boards, district and joint standing committees.

The *London Government Act 1899* established 28 *metropolitan borough councils* to provide the capital with a second tier of local government under the LCC. The unique City of London Corporation, with its then 700 years of history, its Lord Mayor, Court of Aldermen and Common Council – a legislative assembly in its own right – remained untouched, as it was to in all subsequent London government reforms.

Between them, these Acts at the close of the nineteenth century had brought about a small constitutional revolution. There was now a *dual system* of elected local government throughout the country: all-purpose county boroughs/burghs in the largest towns (outside London), and a two- or three-tier system elsewhere, with powers shared between the county, district/burgh and parish councils. With each level or tier of council protective of its own responsibilities and self-sufficiency, it was not necessarily the most harmonious of systems, but in its essentials it was to last for three-quarters of a century.

Structural tinkering, functional growth

The population of England and Wales was growing by an average of over 1 per cent per annum throughout the early years of the twentieth century. More significantly, this growth was distinctly uneven: concentrated in the towns which consequently spread or sprawled into the surrounding countryside. Nineteenth-century boundaries began to look outdated and there was an inevitable conflict of interest between urban and rural authorities, as more and more towns qualified for and sought county borough status. Between 1889 and 1925 21 new county boroughs were created and over 100 county borough boundary extensions granted: changes which, as Byrne notes (2000, p. 36), 'cost the county councils an estimated 3 million loss of population and some £14.5 million loss of rateable value (revenue)'. To their relief, the minimum qualifying population for county borough status was raised in 1926 to 75,000 and the procedure made considerably more difficult, with the result that no new county boroughs were established between 1927 and 1964.

Other structural changes were ushered in by two pieces of legislation in 1929. The *Local Government (Scotland) Act* completed the process of reform and rationalisation described above. The bewildering variety of burghs was reduced to two types – 21 *large burghs*, responsible for most services apart from education which by now was county-based, and 176 *small burghs*, responsible for housing, public health and amenities – the dividing line being a population of 20,000. Parishes, district and standing joint committees were all abolished and replaced in rural areas by nearly 200 *district councils*, thus completing the creation of a two-tier system across the whole of Scotland outside its four big cities.

In England and Wales the *Local Government Act 1929* began to tackle the problem of the balance of urban and rural authorities, and particularly the number of very small authorities. The outcome of ensuing boundary reviews was that between 1929 and 1938 urban districts were reduced by 159, rural districts by 169, and some 1,300 boundaries were altered. Nevertheless, many small authorities still survived. Structural reform across all authorities needed tackling in a much more concerted manner, but this did not happen until the post-war years.

A second major consequence of the Local Government Act 1929 was the abolition of what was by then the only remaining *ad hoc* authority, the Guardians of the Poor, whose functions – poor law, civil registration, and the hospital service – were transferred to the county and county borough councils. In a similar measure, responding to the growing number of motor vehicles on frequently inadequate roads, the highways powers of rural districts were also taken over by the county councils.

These kinds of functional change, and the steady acquisition of additional service responsibilities by the county and county borough councils, were what characterised the history of local government in the first half of the twentieth century far more than the comparatively minor structural reforms. The process can be visualised as the rising section of a symmetrical arch. If the whole arch represents a legislative and functional history of the first hundred years of 'modern' local government, its keystone or pinnacle would come in about the early 1930s, termed by some commentators its 'golden age' (e.g. Byrne, 2000, p. 21).

Almost immediately following their establishment in 1889 the new elected county councils had begun to add to their initially modest portfolios of responsibilities, and the process continued through until at least the 1930s: further and technical education, road maintenance, elementary education, vehicle and driver registration, school meals, maternity and child welfare, careers advice, mental health services, secondary education, 'home help' schemes, libraries, unemployment relief, planning and development control, civil defence. At the same time the county boroughs were spearheading the 1920s council housing drive and acquiring control of the public utilities – water, gas, electricity, public transport – as well as, in some instances, docks, airports, telephone systems, theatres, crematoria and slaughterhouses.

The turning point, and the start of the falling section of the arch, was signalled by the responsibility for the payment of unemployment relief or the 'dole': fleetingly assumed in 1931 and lost three years later to central government in the guise of the Unemployment Assistance Board. But the real downturn came after the Second World War, with the Labour Government's massive programme of health, welfare and nationalisation legislation, all of which took services away from local councils.

Serious structural reform at last

In the post-war years the structural problems already evident in the 1920s and 1930s were becoming ever more acute. Structures were becoming increasingly irrational as the residential pattern of communities changed. There were major disparities of size between local authorities of the same type – in particular, many authorities were proving too small, on their own, to provide efficient services. The sheer number of authorities caused a good deal of confusion, as did the fragmentation of responsibility for service provision and the need for cumbersome co-ordinating machinery. Pressure for change was mounting, and it came first in London.

London

Following a three-year review by a Royal Commission, the *London Government Act 1963* created a new two-tier structure: a substantially larger *Greater London Council* (GLC) to replace the old LCC, pushing out into the Home Counties, and 32 *London boroughs* (see Figure 4.1). As in the 1890s, the City of London Corporation survived the reform process unscathed and became effectively the 33rd borough. The boroughs – 12 (or 13) in Inner London to replace the metropolitan boroughs, and 20 in Outer London – were allocated the bulk of services: housing, social services, non-metropolitan roads, libraries, leaving the GLC with the more 'strategic' functions of fire, ambulances, main roads and refuse disposal. The maverick was education, there being a widespread wish to retain intact the high reputation service built up by the LCC. So, while the outer boroughs took responsibility also for education, inner London would have its separate service administered by a special committee of the GLC, known as the Inner London Education Authority (ILEA), consisting of elected councillors from the 12 boroughs.

Inevitably, reaction to the 1963 Act was mixed. Some argued that no reform was necessary; others maintained it did not go far enough, that the GLC boundaries had been too tightly drawn, and that it did nothing to alleviate the problems caused by the division of services between two separate tiers of councils. But, whatever its merits or defects, the reform of London government had at least demonstrated that wholesale change was possible without services being totally dislocated. It also established 'the principle that an entire conurbation, in this case with a population of eight million, should be governed as a single unit' (Elcock, 1991, p. 28). Almost inevitably, reform of the rest of the system followed.

England and Wales

In 1966, separate Royal Commissions were established, one for England (led by Lord Redcliffe-Maud) and one for Scotland (chaired by Lord Wheatley). Both reported in 1969. Wales, as in the later 1990s reorganisation, was treated differently from England. A Commission was not deemed necessary; a White Paper from the Secretary of State for Wales would suffice.

The English Royal Commission produced two reports; one by the majority of the Commissioners favouring a structure based predominantly on all-purpose unitary authorities embracing both town and country; the other a Memorandum of Dissent by Derek Senior advocatng a multi-tier system of provincial councils, city regions, district and local councils. In June 1970, however, before it had a chance to implement the majority report, the Labour Government was voted out of office, and its plans for unitary local government disappeared with it.

Figure 4.1 Elected local government in Great Britain, 1974–95

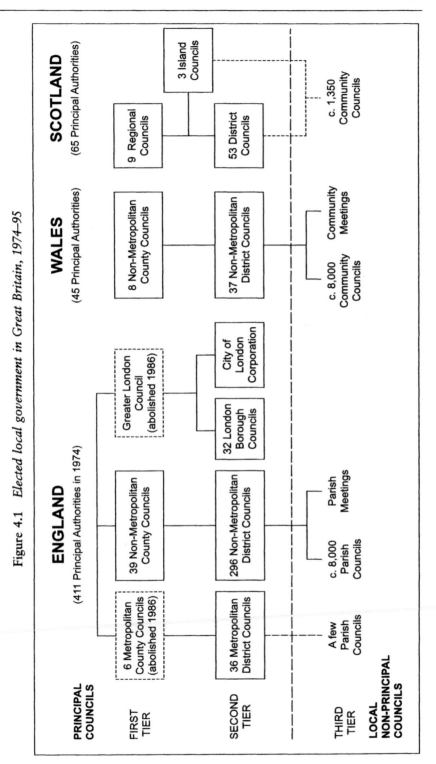

In its place came a Conservative Government committed to the retention of a two-tier system. As Alexander notes (1982, p. 36), the 'philosophical and partisan advantages of retaining the counties ensured that the Tories would, in the end, propose a county-based two-tier system'. They did, producing in early 1971 White Paper proposals for a two-tier system across the whole of England and Wales based mainly on existing counties.

The *Local Government Act 1972* abolished, from 1974, all county boroughs and reduced the 58 *county councils* in England and Wales to 47 with populations ranging at that time from 100,000 (Powys) to 1.5 million (Hampshire). Within these counties 1,250 municipal boroughs, urban and rural districts were replaced by 333 *district councils* also with hugely varying populations: from 18,760 (Radnor) to 422,000 (Bristol). In the major conurbations six *metropolitan county councils* were established – Greater Manchester, Merseyside, West Midlands, Tyne and Wear, South Yorkshire and West Yorkshire – and 36 *metropolitan districts* with populations ranging from 172,000 (South Tyneside) to almost 1.1 million (Birmingham).

Outside the metropolitan areas the old county boroughs, mostly Labour strongholds, were absorbed as district councils into the new counties. These old 'independent islands', often with several centuries of self-governing existence and a fierce civic pride, lost their positions of strength based on large-scale service provision. The loss of education and social services functions to the generally more Conservative counties was an especially bitter blow. Indeed, the maintenance of two principal tiers continued to make co-ordination of policy and administration difficult, and in those services where counties and districts had concurrent powers (e.g. planning, leisure services) the problems in some areas proved to be particularly acute.

At third tier in England outside the major cities the parish was retained. Of the more than 10,000 parishes, about 8,000 have elected councils, some of which are known as town councils. Small parishes, with under 200 electors, can instead hold parish meetings which all local electors can attend. In Wales, parishes were replaced in 1974 by *communities*, which have either elected councils or community meetings on a similar basis to English parishes. Additionally, in some urban areas neighbourhood councils have been formed which can provide a sounding board for local opinion.

Scotland

The (Wheatley) Royal Commission on Local Government in Scotland saw its proposals for a two-tier system largely adopted by the Conservative Government in the *Local Government (Scotland) Act 1973* and implemented in May 1975. As in England, the Scottish Commission identified the large numbers of small authorities as constituting a fundamental weakness of the existing system. In the final legislation those numbers were reduced proportionately by even more than had happened in England and Wales. 431 county, city, burgh and district councils were amalgamated into 9 *regions*, ranging from 100,000 (Borders) to almost 2.5 million (Strathclyde); 53 *districts*, from 9,000 (Badenoch and Strathspey) to 850,000 (Glasgow); and 3 *'most purpose' island authorities* for Orkney, Shetland and the Western Isles (see Figure 4.1). Additionally, some 1,350 communities set up their own optional *community councils* as a kind of third tier, though these have no statutory powers and a lower status than even parish councils.

The network of regional and district councils which Wheatley had proposed fitted with the Conservative Government's preference for two-tier local government. Inevitably, the size and remoteness of the regional tier were heavily criticised; as in England, shared responsibilities between districts and regions for certain services would also pose difficulties. Some small tidying up of structures occurred in the early 1980s but essentially the post-1975 system remained intact until April 1996, with the huge Strathclyde Region comprising almost half of Scotland's total population.

Northern Ireland

It will be noted in Exhibit 4.1 that Northern Ireland's local government was reformed at the same time as that in the rest of the United Kingdom. That reform, though, and the significantly different structures it produced, need to be understood in the context of the political conflicts between the province's Unionist and Catholic communities which had intensified during the 1960s.

At that time – indeed, since the Local Government (Ireland) Act 1898 – Northern Ireland had a structure of local government very similar to that on the mainland. There were two all-purpose county boroughs – Belfast and Londonderry – and a two-tier system of six counties (*not* the nine counties of the historic Ulster province) and 55 urban and rural district councils. The majority Unionist population had ensured that boundaries were drawn in such a way as to give them control of most councils and exclude the Catholic parties from any significant influence.

The resulting inequalities of service provision and particularly discriminatory housing allocations were among the principal grievances of civil rights protesters, and eventually in 1969 a Review Body was set up, chaired by Patrick Macrory. Influenced by the Wheatley Commission, the Macrory Report proposed a reformed two-tier model of elected local government. Most services – education and libraries, planning, roads, water and sewerage, fire, health and social services – would be provided by elected regional bodies, and there would be a greatly reduced number of district councils.

The *Local Government (Northern Ireland) Act 1972* implemented some of these recommendations, but, with the suspension of the Stormont government in the same year and the introduction of direct rule from Westminster, the proposed elected regional tier never materialised. In an attempt to remove sectarian bias at local level, most local authority powers in housing, personal social services, health, education and planning were placed in the hands of various non-elected boards, agencies and departments of the Northern Ireland Office.

Local democracy in Northern Ireland, therefore, was and is limited to 26 *district councils*. These are elected, by the Single Transferable Vote (STV) system of proportional representation, but, compared with their mainland counterparts, their responsibilities are very restricted – if not quite to the bins, bogs and burials that is sometimes suggested. In addition to the refuse collection and disposal, public conveniences, cemeteries and crematoria, there are leisure, recreational and cultural facilities, consumer protection, environmental health and safety, and, increasingly, tourism. Filling the democratic deficit, or the 'Macrory gap', are the area boards and other quangos providing all other services: 116 bodies in all, 'appointed by a Minister from a government which does not have a single MP anywhere in the six counties' (Vize, 1994, p. 16). District councils nominate up to 40 per cent of the members of some of these boards, but 'policy power remains with Westminster and its Stormont Castle outpost' (Vize, 1994, p. 17).

The Thatcher years: non-stop change

By the mid-1970s, then, the dual town/country structure of local government, set up at the end of the nineteenth century and fundamentally unchanged throughout most of the twentieth, had been comprehensively reformed. A two-tier system was in place across almost the whole country. It had its inevitable tensions – competing mandates, resource jealousies, the blurring of lines of responsibility and accountability for service provision – but it would, surely, see us through to the next millennium? Hardly, as you will already have gathered from Exhibit 4.1 and Figure 4.1. Parts of this new structure were to be dismantled almost before they had had a chance to establish themselves.

Despite having at the time far more councillors and controlling far more councils than any other party, the Conservative Government that took office in 1979 was not well-disposed towards local government. Ministers saw it as 'wasteful, profligate, irresponsible, unaccountable, luxurious and out of control' (Newton and Karran, 1985, p. 116). The result was a barrage of legislation aimed at remodelling the finances of local authorities, but not initially their actual structure.

Then in May 1983 the Conservative Party introduced into its General Election manifesto a pledge to abolish the six English metropolitan county councils and the GLC. As Elcock notes (1991, p. 39), the

> official reason given for this hasty proposal was that these authorities had few functions and were therefore redundant: but in 1981 all seven had fallen under Labour control and the GLC Leader, Ken Livingstone, had emerged as a colourful and effective antagonist with his headquarters just across the Thames from Mrs Thatcher's.

There was, in other words, a party political dimension to this structural reform in just the same way as there had been to the reforms of the 1970s, and as there is bound to be in any reorganisation of sub-central government in a unitary state. We should not be surprised when politicians behave politically.

In this case, the Government's arguments and the amplification of its manifesto proposals were set out in a White Paper, *Streamlining the Cities* (DoE, 1983) published in October 1983. The title was significant, emphasising the Government's concern to reduce bureaucracy, duplication and waste and generally to 'roll back the frontiers of the state'. By abolishing the top-tier authorities in the metropolitan areas and transferring the bulk of their already limited range of functions to the borough and district councils, it would be bringing government closer to the people, making it more comprehensible and accessible, and thereby enhancing local democracy. In doing so, of course, it would also be removing the irritation of the attendant policy conflicts between the top-tier metropolitan authorities and central government whenever the two were controlled by different political parties.

Despite opposition in both the Commons and the Lords, the *Local Government Act 1985* was eventually passed and from 31 March 1986 the GLC and the six metropolitan county councils ceased to exist. Their responsibilities were taken over partly by the London boroughs and metropolitan district councils, but partly also by a range of joint boards, joint committees, *ad hoc* agencies and central government departments. The result was a degree of complexity that could seem not so much a 'streamlining' of our cities as a return to the administrative 'tangle' of the nineteenth century. Hebbert and Travers (1988, p. 198) showed, for example, that almost 100 bodies with 21 different methods of revenue raising were engaged in the provision of services in Greater London. There were some two dozen *centrally appointed* bodies (e.g. Greater London Arts). Sixteen were *London-wide nominated* bodies comprising councillors from the constituent boroughs (e.g. London Fire and Civil Defence Authority). Additionally, there were numerous *localised nominated* bodies for specific parts of London with a number of participating boroughs and a lead borough (e.g. North London Waste Authority – 7 boroughs with Camden as the lead).

In the metropolitan areas outside London the picture was a little less complex: fewer functions were taken over by quasi-government agencies, but those that were so transferred were among the biggest spending and highest profile services. So in each of the six metropolitan areas there were three *joint boards* for passenger transport, police, fire and civil defence. In both Greater Manchester and Merseyside there were joint boards responsible for waste disposal. In addition, *joint committees* were established dealing with matters such as recreation, arts and economic development. None of these joint boards is *directly elected*. Most are controlled by councillors *nominated* from the constituent metropolitan districts. Directly elected local government is now weaker and more fragmented than before 1986; indirectly elected and appointed bodies have become increasingly numerous and important.

Part of the 1986 reforms, however, did not even make it through to the 1992 election. The abolition of the GLC had the effect, as we have seen, of increasing the number of part-London local bodies. The *Inner London Education Authority* had been a sub-committee of the GLC, so when the latter was abolished a new arrangement was needed. What was created, very unusually for this country in the twentieth century, was a *directly elected unifunctional* council, somewhat similar to the elected school boards in particularly the West and Midwestern United States. It could have provided an interesting study of an alternative form of local democracy. In the event, though, its almost inevitable Labour domination, allied to its high expenditure levels and perceived enthusiasm for 'progressive' education, led to its early abolition in the *Education Reform Act 1988*. Responsibility for education services passed to the individual Inner London boroughs with effect from 1 April 1990.

Summary – into the 1990s

Later that year, in November 1990, Mrs Thatcher was replaced as Conservative Party Leader and Prime Minister by John Major. Mr Major's biggest inherited local government headache by far was the hugely unpopular poll tax or community charge and how to get rid of it. By comparison, the structure of the system might have seemed reasonably straightforward and unproblematic.

A similar structure of elected local government existed throughout the *non-metropolitan areas* of England and the whole of Wales and mainland Scotland (see Figure 4.1). Throughout these areas there were two principal tiers of local authorities with each tier providing a range of services, although the division of services between tiers in Scotland was slightly different from that in England and Wales. In England and Wales the upper tier authorities were known as *counties;* in Scotland they were designated *regions.* The lower tier authorities were known as *districts*, some of which are entitled, for historic reasons, to call themselves *cities* or *boroughs*. In much of non-metropolitan Britain there were also third-tier, or 'sub-principal', authorities known as parish councils in England and community councils in both Wales and Scotland.

In *metropolitan* England and London there was only one elected tier of local government – *metropolitan districts* and *London boroughs* – and these are *unitary* or *most-purpose* local authorities. Instead of sharing responsibility for service provision with other elected authorities, they operate alongside other indirectly elected or nominated bodies. The superficial simplicity of a single elected tier is far from a reality, given the mosaic of joint authorities and boards responsible for major services such as fire and civil defence and passenger transport: hence our preference for the term 'most-purpose', rather than 'all-purpose'.

In Northern Ireland there was – and still is – a single-tier structure of 26 district councils with a very much more limited range of service responsibilities than even their non-metropolitan district counterparts on the mainland. The major functions of health, social services, education and libraries are organised through *area boards* made up of approximately one-third district councillors and two-thirds ministerial appointees. Responsibility for public sector housing is with an appointed Northern Ireland Housing Executive, administered through six regions.

Guide to further reading

Keith-Lucas and Richards (1978) provide the best overall introductory history of English local government through most of the twentieth century. The post-war period is thoroughly dealt with by Young and Rao (1997), but, for perhaps a better 'feel' for the impact of history, try Stanyer (1999) and Chapter 2 of Stewart (2000). There are several accounts of the structural reforms of the 1960s and early 1970s, including Alexander (1982), Wood (1976), and, for London, Rhodes (1970). Dearlove (1979) offers a more political, and critical, commentary. The abolition of the GLC and metropolitan county councils is recounted in Flynn *et al.* (1985) and, less disinterestedly, in the entertaining autobiography of last GLC Leader and first Greater London Mayor, Ken Livingstone (1987). Outlines of the complex post-abolition governmental structures are available in Leach *et al.* (1992) and Travers *et al.* (1993). There are several interesting commemorative publications, including Young (1989) on 100 years of county government, and Game's (1991b) collective review of the centennial publications of 28 of the 39 English counties. Last, but very far from least, there is an outstanding history of the role of women in early English local government by Patricia (now Lady) Hollis (1987).

Chapter 5

External Structures

Two chapters-worth of change

The next two chapters replace just one in the book's previous edition. It is a fair measure of the extent of the change initiated by the 1997–2001 Labour Government – both in the external structure of the country's sub-central government and in the internal working of local authorities. This chapter deals with so-called *external* structures and starts by bringing up to date the history of our system of local government begun in Chapter 4. We present literally a map, or maps, of British local government at the start of the twenty-first century – an account that culminates with the election of a uniquely structured and uniquely elected authority for Greater London.

The remainder of the chapter outlines the product of part of the Labour Government's remarkable programme of constitutional reform – its devolution of powers and responsibilities variously to the Scottish Parliament, the Welsh and Northern Ireland Assemblies, and English regional development agencies. The only mention any of these institutions could possibly have received in this book's previous edition was in Labour's 1997 manifesto (Wilson and Game, 1998, p. 276). Yet within two years they were all in operation. Significant constitutional change is not supposed, at least in Britain, to happen that fast: it is a remarkable story.

England – hybridity, or a reform too far?

We made the point in Chapter 4 that structural reform, once it becomes part of the agenda of national political debate, can acquire a momentum of its own. That is perhaps as good an explanation as any of why, following the reorganisations of local government in London in the 1960s, in the rest of the country in the 1970s, and in metropolitan England in the 1980s, we saw a further country-wide structural reform during the 1990s. Critical observers have contrasted the situation confronting the Redcliffe-Maud Commission with that 30 years on:

> In the 1960s there was a good deal of tangible evidence of the need for a reorganisation, including the palpable inability of large numbers of small authorities to deal effectively with the growth-associated problems of development and movement, especially in the more urbanised parts of

the country. It is difficult to identify similar problems that underpin the present reorganisation, in which far too much has been made of the supposed 'problems' of conflict, overlap and duplication in the existing two-tier system. (Leach, 1995, p. 50)

Few people in local government felt any compelling need for further structural reorganisation, faced as they were already with the upheaval of the poll tax and other reforms of education, community care and CCT. The impetus to reform came predominantly, Leach suggests, from a single individual, Michael Heseltine, a contender for the leadership of the Conservative Party following Margaret Thatcher's resignation, who became instead, and for the second time in his career, Secretary of State for the Environment. It was he who ensured that local government reorganisation would feature as a prominent commitment in the 1992 Conservative Party manifesto. 'We will set up a commission to examine, area by area, the appropriate local government arrangements in England', the manifesto proclaimed, the main objective of the examination being to decide 'whether in any area *a single tier* of local government could provide better accountability and greater efficiency' (emphasis ours).

That manifesto phrasing, we suggested in our previous account of the ensuing reorganisation (Wilson and Game, 1998, Ch. 17), was particularly revealing. For it seemed to suggest a *structure-led* or *cartographic* approach to the alleged problems or deficiencies of local government: a keenness to draw revised boundary lines on maps before properly deciding on the future role or purpose of local government. The commission – or, in the case of Scotland and Wales, government ministers – would determine not what local government would do in the future, or how, but where it would do it.

Insofar as there was any government blueprint for reform, it was set out most clearly in the 1991 White Paper, *Competing for Quality*:

> The Government's model for local government in the 1990s and in the 21st century is that of the enabling authority. The task of local authorities lies in identifying requirements, setting priorities, determining standards of services and finding the best way to meet those standards of service and ensuring they are met. This implies a move away from the traditional model of local authorities providing virtually all services directly and a greater separation of the functions of service delivery from strategic responsibilities.

Restructuring, then, was about enabling – but what, in practice, would an 'enabling authority' do? The difficulty was – and is – that the term is almost infinitely elastic and can mean very different things to different people. At one extreme is a minimalist position, in which the key role of the enabling authority should be simply to find a range of *other* –

preferably private sector – organisations to provide services and carry out its responsibilities. A very different and more expansive model is based on the idea of *enabling communities* meeting their needs and resolving their problems in the most effective way – which might or might not involve the local authority providing services itself.

The 1991 White Paper, with its reference to 'the best way' of doing things, read as if it favoured this more expansive interpretation. But it was questionable whether such a contestable concept was a suitable base on which to attempt to build a substantially new, predominantly single-tier structure of local government across the whole country. The restructuring process, however, had been set in motion and, even though Michael Heseltine's successors as Environment Secretary, Michael Howard and John Gummer, seemed not to share his reformist enthusiasm, it lurched on, though with less far-reaching impact than had initially been envisaged.

The Government had wanted the county-by-county structural reviews by its Local Government Commission for England (LGCE) to produce a substantial increase in the number of unitary authorities. At one time, following the Commission's draft recommendations of almost 100 new unitary councils embracing more than two-thirds of the population of the English non-metropolitan counties, that looked likely to be the outcome. The Commission was then required, however, to consult the public – who were unconvinced. Though many of them liked the *idea* of unitary local government, far more, when asked, were opposed to the Commission's detailed plans for their own counties and to their likely upheaval and cost. In most counties the weight of opinion favoured the status quo.

Figure 5.1 *Cartoon – A confusing solution*

Source: Local Government Chronicle, 16 September 1994.

The almost inevitable outcome – against a background of the Major Government's national unpopularity and its minimal parliamentary majority – was a policy retreat. Instead of unitary local government becoming the norm in England, there emerged 'hybridity', to use the technical expression, or a dog's breakfast – the latter obviously being the view presented in Figure 5.1, showing Sir John Banham, the LGCE's first Chairman, hammering a final piece of the reorganisation puzzle into place.

To be fair, the true picture, presented in Figure 5.2 and Exhibit 5.1, is not as chaotic as the cartoon suggests. A total of 46 new unitary authorities

Figure 5.2 *The local authority map of England, from 1998*

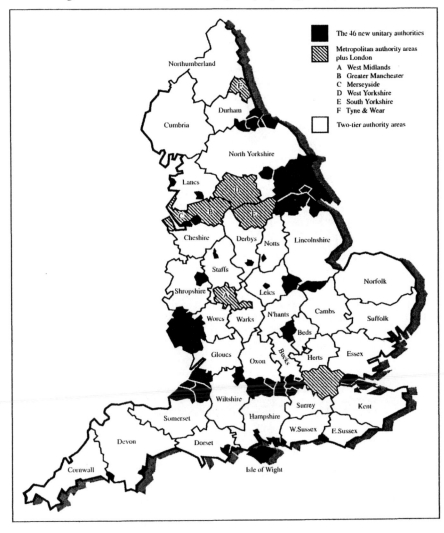

Exhibit 5.1 Was your council re-reorganised? The second-generation English unitaries and their displaced districts

	County	New Unitary	Former District Council(s)
1995	Isle of Wight	Isle of Wight	Medina BC; S. Wight BC
	Total	**1**	**2**
1996	Avon	Bristol	Bristol City C
		S Gloucestershire	Kingswood BC; Northavon DC
		North Somerset	Woodspring DC
		Bath and NE Somerset	Bath City C; Wansdyke DC
	Cleveland	Hartlepool	Hartlepool BC
		Middlesbrough	Middlesbrough BC
		Redcar and Cleveland	Langbaurgh-on-Tees BC
		Stockton-on-Tees	Stockton-on-Tees BC
	Humberside	Kingston upon Hull City	Kingston upon Hull City C
		East Riding of Yorkshire	E. Yorkshire BC; Holderness BC; Beverley BC; Boothferry BC (part)
		North Lincolnshire	Glanford BC; Scunthorpe BC; Boothferry BC (part)
		NE Lincolnshire	Great Grimsby BC; Cleethorpes BC
	North Yorkshire	York	York City C (including parts of Ryedale DC, Selby DC, Harrogate BC)
	Total	**13**	**20**
1997	Bedfordshire	Luton	Luton BC
	Buckinghamshire	Milton Keynes	Milton Keynes BC
	Derbyshire	Derby City	Derby City C
	Dorset	Bournemouth	Bournemouth BC
		Poole	Poole BC
	Durham	Darlington	Darlington BC
	East Sussex	Brighton and Hove	Brighton BC; Hove BC
	Hampshire	Portsmouth City	Portsmouth City C
		Southampton	Southampton City C
	Leicestershire	Leicester City	Leicester City C
		Rutland	Rutland DC
	Staffordshire	Stoke-on-Trent City	Stoke-on-Trent City C
	Wiltshire	Swindon	Thamesdown BC
	Total	**13**	**14**

Exhibit 5.1 continued

	County	New Unitary	Former District Council(s)
1998	Berkshire	Bracknell Forest	Bracknell Forest BC
		West Berkshire	Newbury DC
		Reading	Reading DC
		Slough	Slough BC
		Royal Windsor and Maidenhead	Windsor and Maidenhead RBC
		Wokingham	Wokingham DC
	Cambridgeshire	Peterborough City	Peterborough City C
	Cheshire	Halton	Halton BC
		Warrington	Warrington BC
	Devon	Plymouth City	Plymouth DC
		Torbay	Torbay BC
	Essex	Southend-on-Sea	Southend-on-Sea BC
		Thurrock	Thurrock BC
	Hereford and Worcester	Herefordshire	Hereford City C; S Herefordshire DC; Leominster DC (most); Malvern Hills DC (part)
	Kent	Medway	Rochester City C; Gillingham BC
	Lancashire	Blackburn with Darwen	Blackburn BC
		Blackpool	Blackpool BC
	Nottinghamshire	Nottingham City	Nottingham City C
	Shropshire	Telford and Wrekin	The Wrekin DC
	Total	**19**	**22**
GRAND TOTALS		**46**	**58**

came into existence between 1995 and 1998, covering just over a quarter of the population of non-metropolitan England. Only four of the 39 former county councils disappeared entirely from the map: the three 'newcomers', created only in the previous reorganisation in the early 1970s – Avon, Cleveland and Humberside – plus Berkshire. Hereford and Worcester, joined in 1974, was re-divided, and the Isle of Wight became a unitary county in its own right. 14 counties remained unchanged, and the remaining 19 assumed hybrid or mixed structures: one or two mainly large town unitary authorities in otherwise unchanged two-tier counties. There was thus a second generation of largely urban unitaries to add to the 36 metropolitan districts and 32 London boroughs that became unitary in

1986, following the abolition of the GLC and the six metropolitan county councils. And if that arrangement sounds a little familiar, it is: an at least partial return to the pre-1974 structure described in Chapter 4, when county boroughs were the 'independent islands' within two-tier counties.

As for the Local Government Commission, it remained in existence to undertake not structural, but periodic *electoral*, reviews – examining the total number of councillors, the number in each electoral division or ward, the ward boundaries, their names, and the timing of elections. These functions and the Commission itself have since been absorbed into the new Electoral Commission – an independent body, established in November 2000, with a remit to keep under review all UK electoral law and practice.

Scotland and Wales – Ministers halve numbers of councils, increase democratic deficit

In Scotland and Wales there were no 'rolling commissions' to examine options and make recommendations area by area. Instead the respective Secretaries of State were deputed to conduct the reviews. Preliminary consultation papers were published by the Scottish and Welsh Offices in 1991, proposing single-tier structures of authorities which it was claimed would have greater local identity, would be more efficient and more accountable. Certain amendments were made following negotiations with local authority associations and during the passage of the two Bills through Parliament. But what resulted – thanks, significantly, to the votes of overwhelmingly English Conservative MPs – were the nation-wide unitary systems that the Government sought: 32 in Scotland and 22 in Wales. Following elections in 1995, these councils came into full operation in April 1996 – see Figures 5.3 and 5.4.

In both Scotland and Wales the ministerially driven reorganisations halved the numbers of councils. These fewer elected councils inevitably cover larger areas than the former districts and also – though this was *not* inevitable – have far fewer councillors. England's reorganisation produced the same effect, though on a lesser scale: a reduction of less than 6 per cent in the number of elected councils, though one of more than a quarter in the number of councillors (see Exhibits 5.2 and 5.3). The outcome of the two bouts of reorganisation – in the 1970s and 1990s – is that Great Britain has, on average, the largest local authorities and the highest ratios of citizens to elected councillors of any country in Western Europe. The term 'democratic deficit', often applied to the alleged deficiencies of the European Parliament itself, seems more than justified here.

Figure 5.3 *Scotland's 32 unitary authorities, operational from April 1996*

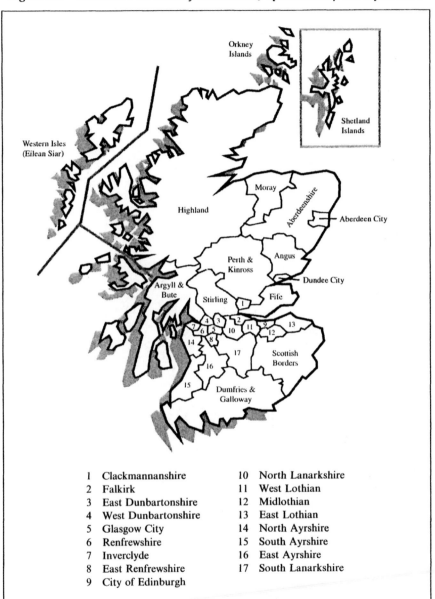

1	Clackmannanshire	10	North Lanarkshire
2	Falkirk	11	West Lothian
3	East Dunbartonshire	12	Midlothian
4	West Dunbartonshire	13	East Lothian
5	Glasgow City	14	North Ayrshire
6	Renfrewshire	15	South Ayrshire
7	Inverclyde	16	East Ayrshire
8	East Renfrewshire	17	South Lanarkshire
9	City of Edinburgh		

Figure 5.4   *The 22 unitary authorities in Wales, operational from April 1996*

1   Swansea
2   Neath Port Talbot
3   Bridgend
4   Rhondda, Cynon, Taff
5   Merthyr Tydfil
6   Caerphilly
7   Blaenau Gwent
8   Torfaen
9   Newport
10   Cardiff
11   Vale of Glamorgan

Exhibit 5.2 The growing scale of British local government

	Before 1974/75	1974/75–1996/98	New structure	Increase in scale since 1974/75
England				
No. of councils	1,246	c. 410	387	
Av. population per council	37,000	113,000	121,000	3.3×
Scotland				
No. of councils	430	65	32	
Av. population per council	12,000	78,000	153,000	12.8×
Wales				
No. of councils	181	45	22	
Av. population per council	15,000	62,000	128,000	8.5×
Great Britain				
No. of councils	1,857	520	441	
Av. population per council	29,000	106,000	128,000	4.4×

Exhibit 5.3 Unitary councillors – the missing third

	Number of councillors			
	New unitary authorities	In previous two-tier system	The democratic deficit	
			No.	%
Non-Metropolitan England	2,391	3,476	1,085	31
Scotland	1,245	1,695	450	27
Wales	1,273	1,977	704	36
Total	4,909	7,148	2,239	31

The Greater London Authority – strategic local government

The creation during the 1990s of what we have called the second generation of English unitary authorities did not quite complete the sequence of local government restructurings during the last decades of the twentieth century. There was still London – the only Western capital without a democratic voice of its own. The Labour Party, in majority control of the GLC at the time of its abolition, had consistently pledged to restore some form of directly elected government to Greater London, and in 1997 it got its chance. The party's manifesto promised (p. 34) that:

> following a referendum to confirm popular demand, there will be a new deal for London, with a strategic authority and a mayor, each directly elected. Both will speak up for the needs of the city and plan its future. They will not duplicate the work of the boroughs, but take responsibility for London-wide issues – economic regeneration, planning, policing, transport and environmental protection.

These proposals, consciously aimed at producing a novel and unique set of institutions, are best seen as a further example of hybridity – strategic local government, or a mixture of local government reform and embryonic regional government. The Greater London Authority (GLA) would be quite different from the 'modernised' mayoral town and city councils that the government was planning to legislate for the rest of England. But neither would it be permitted the self-governing powers enabling it to parallel the devolved administrations that were being simultaneously legislated for Scotland, Northern Ireland and, though to a lesser extent, Wales.

Every local government structural reform, we emphasised in Chapter 4, has its party political dimension. The GLC had been abolished because of the Thatcher Government's detestation of the way the Council was being run by 'Red Ken' Livingstone's 'municipal socialist' administration. The creation of the new GLA, and particularly the form it took, owed just as much to party and personality politics – only this time it was the *internal* politics of the New Labour Party and, extraordinarily, the personality of the same man, Ken Livingstone. Following the disappearance of the GLC, Livingstone had become a broadly left-wing, iconoclastic Labour MP, ever ready to snipe at the direction in which his party was being led and at those doing the leading. They in turn still held him, his GLC, and other like-minded Labour councils prominent in the 1980s, heavily responsible for the party's unpopularity and its series of general election defeats.

Justified or not, Tony Blair and his ministers were determined that, under no circumstances, would they permit the creation of a GLC Mark II

– a democratically legitimate body with the power and tax base to enable it seriously to challenge the policies of their own national government. Mayors in other cities and towns would be taking over existing, often unitary, councils with wide-ranging services and correspondingly large budgets. In London most of these services – education, social services, housing, environmental health and consumer protection, leisure, recreation and the arts – would continue to be provided by the 32 London boroughs, many in future probably with mayors of their own. The Greater London Mayor would be a significant figurehead and spokesperson for the nation's capital and would have considerable powers of patronage and influence in making appointments to the new executive agencies through which the Authority would exercise its responsibilities. But the Mayor's direct powers and tax-raising opportunities would be modest. Besides which, the party leadership's control of its own party machine, especially when in government, would prevent the reviled Livingstone from even winning the Labour candidacy for Mayor, let alone getting elected.

There is an observation in *Mother Courage*, the powerful play by the German playwright, Bertolt Brecht, about the finest plans always being ruined by the littleness or pettiness (*Kleinlichheit*) of those who ought to carry them out, 'for the Emperors themselves can actually do nothing'. They certainly cannot get us to vote against our inclinations, as was vividly demonstrated with the GLA. The Emperors – in this case government ministers – produced first a consultation paper, *New Leadership for London* (1997), then a White Paper, *A Mayor and Assembly for London* (1998). A London-wide referendum was held in May 1998, in which 72 per cent – albeit on a turnout of only 34 per cent – approved the Government's proposals. Legislation followed – in fact, the longest piece of legislation in post-war parliamentary history – and in November 1999, after numerous Opposition attempts to block it, the Government's massive House of Commons majority ensured that the Greater London Authority Act was passed.

With nearly 50 per cent of Londoners' general election votes and 57 out of 74 MPs, Labour was confident of winning the Mayoralty, whether against the Conservatives' initial candidate, Lord (Jeffrey) Archer or his successor, Steven Norris. The next task for the ministerial 'Emperors', therefore, was to secure the selection of a 'politically acceptable' party candidate. A bitter and much manipulated selection process ensued, riddled with *Kleinlichheit*, the Labour leadership's sole and unconcealed objective being to 'Stop Livingstone' at all costs. He was stopped, being very narrowly defeated by former Cabinet Minister, Frank Dobson, but the costs were the party's integrity and Dobson's own electability.

Opinion polls suggested that the ministerially victimised Livingstone would be almost unbeatable, prompting him to reverse previous pledges not to run against his own party's candidate and proceed to do precisely that, as an Independent. The opinion polls proved right. In a two-stage (Supplementary Vote) election, Dobson was eliminated in third place after the first stage, and, after the counting of second preferences, Livingstone was elected as Greater London's first Mayor, with over 776,000 votes against Norris' 564,000. The turnout, notwithstanding the exceptional media coverage of the campaign, was fractionally lower even than in the referendum; Livingstone's vote, however, was still the highest total ever won by a British politician – a significant mandate for an office with deliberately limited direct powers. The powers that the Mayor does have – in relation both to the Assembly and the 'functional bodies' through which most of the GLA's work is done – are outlined in Exhibit 5.4.

The arrival of the GLA completed – at least for the time being – the structural reorganisation of local government in Great Britain. The 521 principal councils created in the 1970s (Figure 4.1) have been reduced by nearly a sixth to 442, and their average population increased to nearly 130,000.

Joint arrangements

In the case of London, the re-establishment of an additional tier of elected government should clarify service responsibilities that were previously divided among several fragmented bodies and generally sharpen demo-cratic accountability. For, as we noted in relation to the earlier abolition of the GLC and the English metropolitan county councils, 'single tier' does not necessarily mean simplification. Not all the services and responsi-bilities of abolished local authorities can be easily divided up or combined together and handed over to new or different elected councils. Alongside the directly elected structures, therefore, there are frequently nowadays networks of *nominated or indirectly elected joint bodies* and other joint arrangements between councils. As described in Chapter 4, following the 1986 disappearance of the GLC and the metropolitan county councils, services such as police, fire and public transport were administered by such bodies in metropolitan England – and, of course, outside London they still are. The abolition of the two-tier structure in Scotland, Wales and parts of non-metropolitan England had a similar effect, as illustrated by the case of the Strathclyde region in Exhibit 5.5.

There are three main forms of joint arrangements through which councils work together to provide services:

- *Joint boards*. These are legally constituted bodies set up by two or more councils to provide statutorily required services. They are created by order of a minister and their membership and management are subject to ministerial approval. They do, however, have independent financial

Exhibit 5.4 The Greater London Authority (GLA)

What is it?

A unique form of strategic city-wide government for London. It comprises:

- A directly elected executive Mayor – the first in the UK. The first Mayor, elected in May 2000, is Ken Livingstone (Independent).
- A separately elected 25–member Assembly. Membership following the 2000 elections was: 9 Conservatives, 9 Labour, 4 Liberal Democrats, 3 Green Party.

The Mayor and Assembly are advised and assisted by a permanent staff of up to 500, headed by the slightly confusingly named Chief Executive, Anthony Mayer.

What does it do and how?

Its main responsibilities are *strategic* – principally transport, policing, fire and emergency planning, economic development, planning; secondarily culture, the environment, health. The London boroughs retain responsibility for education, housing, social services, local roads, libraries and museums, refuse collection, environmental health, etc.

The GLA's main responsibilities are exercised through *4 functional bodies*, members of which are mainly appointed by and accountable to the Mayor:

- Transport for London (TfL) – responsible for most public transport in London, including fare structures and future investment
- Metropolitan Police Authority – previously accountable to the Home Secretary
- London Fire and Emergency Planning Authority
- London Development Agency – a new body to promote employment, investment, economic development and regeneration in London. Similar to the other 8 English Regional Development Agencies.

Who's in charge – the Mayor or Assembly?

The Mayor decides policy – prepares plans on transport, land use, the environment, culture, etc., appoints and sets the budgets for the functional bodies.

The Assembly scrutinises and questions the Mayor's activities, and the budget, which it can overturn with a two-thirds majority. It also investigates other issues of relevance to Londoners, and makes policy recommendations to the Mayor.

How much does it spend?

The main services it took over from other bodies – transport (£780 million), police (£2,250 million), fire (£780 million), economic development (£300 million) – cost £3.7 billion in 2001/02. The cost of the GLA itself is about £36 million, most of which comes in the form of central government grant, and about 11 per cent from Londoners themselves (6p per week per council taxpayer).

Where is it?

From 2002, 'City Hall' will occupy one of London's most spectacular new buildings: Lord Foster's award-winning, glass foglamp-resembling construction alongside Tower Bridge – which seems likely to become universally known as the Mayor's glass testicle.

Exhibit 5.5 Single-tier but hardly streamlined – the case of Strathclyde

- *Until April 1996:*
  Strathclyde Regional Council
  + 19 district councils

- *After April 1996:*
  12 new single-tier or unitary councils, ranging from Glasgow (627,000) to E. Renfrewshire (88,000)
  7 joint boards for police, fire, passenger transport and valuation – made up of councillors nominated from the 12 councils
  3 strategic planning joint committees
  2 new quangos: the West of Scotland Water Authority, appointed to take over the water and sewerage services that, uniquely in Scotland, were previously the responsibility of the regional councils; also an appointed Water Customers Council
  1 new quango to run the Children's Panel Reporter service
  No responsibility for trunk roads, taken over initially by the Scottish Office.

---

powers, which include the power to raise money by 'precept' from their constituent authorities. In the English metropolitan areas there are joint boards for, principally, fire and public transport. The Local Government, etc. (Scotland) Act 1994 recognised that some of the new unitary authorities would not be able to provide police and fire services on their own and, as shown in Exhibit 5.5, created joint boards for these and certain other services.

- *Joint committees.* Two or more local authorities can determine to establish joint committees of councillors to carry out specific council functions. Such committees, unlike joint boards, are not separate legal entities and cannot employ staff. Some of the new unitary authorities are too small to provide on their own the full range of specialist services previously delivered by county or regional councils; joint committees provide one possible form of alternative arrangement. For example, facilities such as specialist schools or residential homes might be situated in one council but used by a number of others.

- *Contracts.* Local authorities can make contracts with each other for the provision of services. These have been in existence for some time (e.g. highways agency agreements between county councils and district councils), but they are likely to increase as more councils develop and explore the possibilities of their role as 'enablers'.

As noted at the end of Chapter 4, it is the proliferation of these different kinds of joint arrangements that leads critics to question the labelling of this country's unitary councils as 'all-purpose' authorities. They may constitute the only *directly* elected local authorities in their area, but they are more accurately designated 'most-purpose' councils. Joint boards and joint committees may often offer efficient and effective services and some manage to involve their constituent authorities in their decision-making. But they do inevitably add to the *fragmentation* of local government, to the potential confusion and uncertainty of the public, and to the dilution of electoral accountability. Those concerned about such developments are quick to point out that in this, as in many other respects, Britain is unusual: Luxembourg and Finland are the only other Western European countries to have unitary local government systems!

Sub-principal authorities

While this book focuses chiefly on the activities of the 'principal' local authorities in the United Kingdom, there is in non-metropolitan Britain a multitude of sub-principal authorities that should not be ignored. These sub-principal authorities – parish councils in England, community councils in Scotland and Wales – have survived the traumas of recent structural reorganisations and, indeed, have seen their role and powers enhanced.

In England, there are approximately 10,200 parishes of which almost 9,000 – predominantly in more rural areas – have parish or town councils, on which serve some 75,000 elected councillors. These 'civil' parishes – to distinguish them from the Anglican parochial church councils of 'ecclesiastical' parishes, with often non-coinciding boundaries – are a vital part (frequently in both senses of the adjective) of our system of local government: independent democratic bodies elected by and accountable to their villages, smaller towns and suburbs. 'Town council', incidentally and confusingly, is synonymous with 'parish council', and any parish council can style itself a town council, often entirely appropriately. For some of these parishes are larger than our smaller district councils, with the largest having a population of over 40,000. Most, however, are much more localised, nearly two-thirds comprising populations of under 1,000 and 40 per cent under 500 (Ellwood *et al.*, 1992). In Wales there are some 900 'communities', about 750 of which have established community councils, comparable to English parishes. Scotland is also divided into communities, but Scottish community councils are not local authorities in the same sense, as they have no statutory basis, and neither the power to tax nor any access as of right to public funds.

The principal functions of Scottish community councils, therefore, are not the provision of services, but consultation and representation: ascertaining and articulating the views of their local residents. These are obviously equally important roles for any parish, town or Welsh community council. These latter councils, however, have certain rights – to be consulted, for instance, by their district and county councils about local planning applications and footpath surveys. They also have potentially wide service-providing powers, acting either on their own initiative or as agents of their county and district councils. The services that tend most frequently to be listed are the provision and maintenance of village halls and community centres, allotments, playing fields, gymnasia and baths, footpaths, parks and open spaces, shelters and war memorials, street lighting, car parks, churchyards and burial grounds.

This permitted list was extended in one of the final enactments of the last Conservative Government, to include a range of transport and crime prevention powers (Wilson and Game, 1998, pp. 69–70). Nowadays, therefore, parishes are as likely to be involved in helping with the provision of Meals on Wheels, providing recycling facilities, organising community buses, setting up car-sharing schemes, installing CCTV cameras to prevent crime, enabling local post offices and stores to remain open, or arranging local GP clinics.

All these services, however, are *discretionary*: there is no requirement that they be provided. Where they are provided, they are financed partly by fees and charges and partly by means of a 'precept' added to the council tax collected by their district council from the area's taxpayers. These precepts vary greatly across the country, from under £10 to £100 per council tax-band D property, reflecting the equally great variation in the councils' activities. It is this wholly discretionary nature of parish and town councils' work, not primarily their size, which accounts for the limited attention they receive in this book. They are *not universal* – encompassing less than a third of the population of England and Wales – and they have *no specific duties* to provide services or facilities. These councils, though, are about far more than delivering services:

> they are about a form of democracy close to the people. They derive their legitimacy from elections, and their power comes through reflecting, mobilising and using public opinion as well as from what they can deliver directly, either on their own or in partnership with larger local authorities. (Coulson, 1998, p. 248)

There were signs towards the end of the 1997–2001 Labour Government that, albeit belatedly and cautiously, the potential of this position of parish and town councils – as arguably *the most* democratic of all local authorities – was being recognised. Ministers produced two parallel White

Papers in November 2000, addressing the futures of urban and rural England. The 'Rural White Paper' – *A Fair Deal for Rural England* – did more than repeat earlier ministerial assurances about parish councils being 'an essential part of the structure of local democracy in our country', working 'in partnership to bring government closer to their people' (DETR, 1998a, para 2.14). It set out for a re-elected Labour Government various tasks, including the creation of a new 'Quality Council' status within the framework of local government, attainable by any parish or town council seeking for itself an enhanced service-providing role.

A Quality Council would have to prove itself both capable and efficient – through, for example, having contested elections, regular meetings, training programmes for key personnel, effective public consultation procedures. Having passed this 'quality test', it would be able, both on its own and particularly working in partnership with its principal authorities, to extend the range of services it provides for its community. With an unusually large number of Labour MPs representing parished constituencies, there will be some pressure on ministers to enact this commitment.

Devolution to Scotland and Wales – the road to quasi-federalism

For an administration more frequently criticised for its undue caution than for its radicalism, and for a party with no pronounced former interest in the subject, the 1997 Labour Government's record of constitutional reform was extraordinary. Within four years it had reformed the House of Lords, introduced Human Rights and Freedom of Information Acts, codified the financing of political parties and election campaigns, introduced an avalanche of new electoral systems, and, as we have seen, continued the structural reform of local government. Arguably more far-reaching than any of these, however, was its programme of devolution to Scotland, Wales and Northern Ireland, which has changed not just the content of the British constitution but its very nature: Britain is now effectively a quasi-federal state. The Westminster Parliament remains constitutionally supreme, but in practice that supremacy now means different things in the four nations of the United Kingdom. In Scotland, Wales and Northern Ireland – though in differing ways – 'large powers have been removed from the purview of ministers and Members of Parliament' (Bogdanor, 2001, p. 149).

As with the Greater London Authority, the Government's intentions for devolution to Scotland and Wales were outlined in its 1997 manifesto (pp. 33–4):

Exhibit 5.6 Devolved government in Scotland

What is it? A form of legislative devolution: the UK Parliament's constitutional sovereignty remains unchanged, but it will not, by convention, legislate on devolved matters in Scotland: for example, health, education, local government, economic development, transport, law and home affairs, the environment, agriculture, fisheries and forestry, sports and the arts.

The Scottish Parliament – 129 members (MSPs) elected by Additional Member System form of proportional representation (see p. 219). 73 (56.5 per cent) represent individual constituencies; 56 represent 8 electoral regions. First elections in 1999 returned a 'hung' parliament: 56 Labour, 36 Scottish Nationalists, 18 Conservatives, 17 Liberal Democrats, and 3 'Others'. 48 MSPs (37 per cent) were women, third highest in the world after Sweden and Denmark.

The Scottish Executive – the government of Scotland for all devolved matters. It comprises:

- The First Minister – elected by the whole parliament; effectively Scotland's Prime Minister. Initially Donald Dewar; in 2002 Jack McConnell (Labour).
- A Cabinet/Executive of 11 Ministers, appointed by the First Minister and approved by Parliament. Reflecting the hung parliament, early Cabinets included both Labour and Liberal Democrat MSPs in a coalition administration.
- An advisory civil service, organised into 6 main departments – including Finance and Central Services, responsible for relations with local government.

Westminster's reserved responsibilities, exercised through **Secretary of State for Scotland,** include: the UK constitution, foreign policy, Europe, defence, fiscal and economic policy, employment, benefits and pensions, transport safety, broadcasting policy, the national lottery.

Financial arrangements – Westminster allocates grant to Scottish Parliament for all devolved services (approx. £20 billion). The Parliament can also choose to vary the basic rate of income tax for Scottish residents (the 'tartan tax') by up to 3p – equivalent to approx. £700 million. Council tax and non-domestic rates yield approx. £1.6 billion each. In total, therefore, the Scottish Executive can potentially raise £4 billion, or up to one-sixth of its total spending.

Parliamentary committees – much of the Parliament's work is done through its committees, which are both more powerful – combining both legislative and scrutiny/investigative functions – and more pro-active than Westminster's. Significantly, they can also initiate legislation. Committee chairs/convenerships are distributed according to the parties' shares of MSPs.

How is local government handled? There is a Minister for Finance and Public Affairs (Andy Kerr in 2002), and a parliamentary committee for local government that can question the Minister and scrutinise legislation.

Where is it? From 2002/03 in a purpose-built building at Holyrood, adjacent to the Palace of Holyrood House. Though wildly over budget and less futuristic than Ken's testicle (see Exhibit 5.4), it is a modern, innovative showcase for many indigenous materials – Kemnay granite, Caithness flagstone, Scottish oak – and companies.

Exhibit 5.7 Devolved government in Wales

What is it? A form of executive and administrative devolution: UK Parliament retains control over all primary legislation, but devolves to the Assembly the power to make secondary legislation on certain matters – similar to Scottish list – in which, by convention, UK ministers will not involve themselves.

The National Assembly for Wales – 60 Assembly Members (AMs) elected, like Scottish MSPs, by the Additional Member System. 40 (67 per cent) represent individual constituencies; 20 represent 5 electoral regions. In the first elections in 1999 no party had an overall majority: 28 Labour, 17 Plaid Cymru (Welsh Nationalist), 9 Conservatives, 6 Liberal Democrats.

The Assembly Executive – the government of Wales for all devolved matters; but, unlike the UK Government and Parliament, this executive is *part of* the Assembly, not separate from it. It comprises:

- The First Minister – elected by the whole Assembly and therefore usually the leader of the largest party. Rhodri Morgan (Labour), following resignation of Alun Michael (February 2000).
- A Cabinet/Executive of 9 Assembly Ministers, appointed by the First Minister. Alun Michael's first cabinet was an all-Labour minority administration, but in October 2000 Rhodri Morgan concluded a 3-year power-sharing partnership with the Lib Dems, following which the cabinet included 2 Lib Dems. With 5 women, it may be the only Western European executive with a female majority. Also exceptionally open, with publication of Cabinet minutes and advice papers to subject committees.
- An advisory civil service of approx. 3,000.

Financial arrangements – Westminster allocates formula-based grant to the Assembly for all devolved services (approx. £12 billion). The Assembly has no income tax-varying power.

Assembly committees – unusually inclusive: the minister is a member (but *not* chair) of the relevant subject committee, and non-executive AMs have more involvement with policy than Westminster MPs. Main responsibilities of committees are policy development – jointly with the Cabinet – scrutiny of the work of the minister, and the monitoring of public bodies. Committee chairs are shared between Labour and the Lib Dems. All Assembly business is conducted bilingually, with most broadcast on dedicated Assembly digital channel, S4C2.

How is local government handled? A Minister for Finance, Local Government and Communities (Edwina Hart in 2002), is a member of and is scrutinised by Local Government and Housing Committee. Local government remit includes: control of council tax and non-domestic rating systems, funding of local authorities, best value, councillors' allowances, regulation of housing. Assembly works collectively with local government through a 26-member Partnership Council, comprising AMs and local government representatives.

Where is it? Good question! A state-of-the-art Assembly building on Cardiff Bay waterfront was designed by Richard Rogers – of Pompidou Centre and Millennium Dome fame. But Welsh AMs, less tolerant than Scottish MSPs of the massive budget over-run, sacked Rogers. Watch the Cardiff Bay space!

As soon as possible after the election, we will enact legislation to allow the people of Scotland and Wales to vote in separate referendums on our proposals, which will be set out in white papers. For Scotland we propose the creation of a parliament with law-making powers, including defined and limited financial powers to vary revenue, and elected by an additional member system. The Scottish parliament will extend democratic control over responsibilities currently exercised administratively by the Scottish Office. The Welsh assembly will provide democratic control of existing Welsh Office functions. It will have secondary legislative powers, and will be elected by an additional member system. Following majorities in the referendums, we will introduce in the first year of the Parliament legislation on the substantive devolution proposals.

For a party that had been out of power nationally for 18 years, devolution was an unexpected priority. But the manifesto agenda was implemented almost precisely as scheduled. White papers were published within two months of the Government taking office, and referendums held in September 1997. The Scottish referendum included two questions and, on a 60 per cent turnout, 74 per cent of Scots voted for a parliament and 64 per cent for one with limited tax-varying powers. The Welsh Assembly, by contrast, was approved by only the very narrowest of majorities: just 50.3 per cent on a 50 per cent turnout.

Legislation duly followed, as did the first elections to the new bodies in May 1999. The similarities and differences between the *primary* legislative Scottish Parliament and the *executive* or *secondary* legislative Welsh Assembly can be seen from a comparison of Exhibits 5.6 and 5.7. Both institutions in their first two years received at least as much criticism as praise, which is hardly surprising. Nationalists and radical devolutionists are almost bound to be dissatisfied, while unionists see even comparatively modest devolution as an inevitable first step towards an eventual break-up of the United Kingdom. What cannot be disputed is that they have made their presence felt; they have made a difference.

Inevitably, the Scottish Parliament has had the greater impact – as many readers will need little reminding. For one of the earliest acts of the Executive was to abolish 'up-front' tuition fees for Scottish students studying in Scotland in favour of a graduate endowment. This was a direct reversal of the Blair Government's policy, prompting the Prime Minister's revealing outburst that 'you can't have Scotland doing something different from the rest of Britain ... I am beginning to see the defects in all this devolution stuff' (Ashdown, 2001). It was a prophetic remark, though hardly as intended, for by 2001 it was England that was having to come into line with Scotland. There have, though, been plenty of other policy initiatives leading to divergences between Edinburgh and Westminster, such as the introduction of free personal care services for the elderly, regardless of their financial means; a 21 per cent pay award for teachers; banning the smacking of children under the age of three.

Local government is no exception. Scottish councils are not being required to change their political management arrangements, and there are likely to be even fewer directly elected mayors/provosts north of the border than south of it. Scotland has gone its own way too in reforming local government finance, having abolished ministerially imposed spending guidelines for councils and stabilised grant distribution. In all, the Scottish Parliament passed 20 Bills in its first two years, probably 10 times as many as would have been passed by Westminster.

The Welsh Assembly, as noted in Exhibit 2.1 (Item 6), has scrapped school exam league tables, and has made clear its opposition to specialist schools and extended private sector involvement in the delivery of education. But its most publicised policy has probably been the creation, following a harrowing inquiry into abuse in children's homes, of a Children's Commissioner, to represent children's interests in relation to the social services and ensure that future complaints of abuse are investigated thoroughly. Scotland and Northern Ireland are likely to make similar appointments. On health service reform as well Wales and Scotland have gone their own way, both choosing to retain community health councils, among other structural innovations.

Northern Ireland – unplanned devolution

There was no restructuring of local government in Northern Ireland during the 1990s corresponding to the spread of unitary councils in Scotland, Wales and parts of England. The position remained – indeed, remains in 2002 – as outlined in Chapter 4, with elected local government confined to 26 district councils, relatively small in British terms, and responsible for far fewer services than their counterparts elsewhere in the United Kingdom – see Figure 5.5. Most services affecting people's daily lives continue to be administered by appointed Area Boards – 9 for health and personal social services, 5 for education and public libraries – and other public bodies, such as the Housing Executive.

It is true that the more pro-active councils and the councillors themselves have often managed to make a lot of their limited powers. In the years when there was no provincial elected assembly, they acted as an important debating forum for any key issue affecting Northern Ireland. They developed an important advocacy role, both for their own local areas and for helping individual residents, who turn out to vote in local elections

Figure 5.5   Northern Ireland's 26 district councils

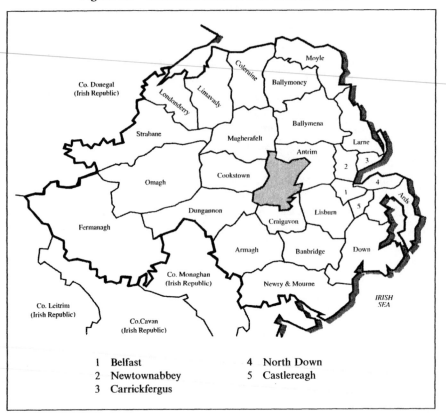

1 Belfast   4 North Down
2 Newtownabbey   5 Castlereagh
3 Carrickfergus

in far greater numbers than on the mainland. In 1994 they were given the important power to spend money on economic development in return for Unionist support of the Major Government in the parliamentary vote on the Maastricht Treaty. Some of them also worked closely with councils on the other side of the Irish border, and were highly effective in negotiating European development funding. It has long been clear, though, that devolution of further significant powers was totally dependent on there being substantial and consolidated progress in the so-called peace process.

Accordingly, Labour's 1997 manifesto pledge in respect of Northern Ireland was much vaguer than for Scotland and Wales, referring only to the 'new devolved legislative body' that was part of the package of proposals already agreed by the British and Irish governments. Yet remarkably, following the intensive negotiations that culminated in the famous Belfast 'Good Friday' Agreement in April 1998, it was actually the Northern Ireland Assembly that was the first of the three devolved regional bodies to be elected.

There were three institutional strands to the Good Friday Agreement: a Northern Ireland Assembly, an all-Ireland North-South Ministerial Council, and a British–Irish Council (see, e.g., O'Leary, 2001). Within weeks the Agreement had been endorsed in simultaneous referendums in both parts of Ireland, and barely one month later, in June 1998, the Assembly was elected. The Assembly, notwithstanding its title, is an example of full executive and legislative devolution – very similar to the Scottish Parliament. It has authority for those matters previously within the remit of the six departments of the Northern Ireland Office – agriculture, economic development, education, environment, finance and personnel, health and social services. The most obvious omissions, compared to the Scottish Parliament, are security functions, policing and the courts.

The Assembly's 108 members are elected from Northern Ireland's 18 parliamentary constituencies by the Single Transferable Vote (STV) form of proportional representation (see p. 220). STV has been used in all non-Westminster elections in Northern Ireland since 1973, specifically because it facilitates representation of the full range of opinions across the Catholic/Nationalist and Protestant/Loyalist communities. Predictably, therefore, no single party or faction emerged with an overall Assembly majority. The highest numbers of seats went, on the pro-Agreement side, to the Ulster Unionists (28), the Social Democratic and Labour Party (SDLP) (24) and Sinn Fein (18), and on the anti-Agreement side to Ian Paisley's Democratic Unionists (20).

Their respective vote shares earned these four parties representation on the 10-member power-sharing Executive Committee of Ministers that now serves as the devolved government of Northern Ireland – three posts each for the Ulster Unionists and the SDLP, two each for Sinn Fein and the Democratic Unionists. The Executive is presided over by a novel, complex, and not entirely successful 'dual premiership', comprising initially Ulster Unionist leader, David Trimble, as First Minister and the SDLP's Seamus Mallon as Deputy First Minister.

Local government is one of the responsibilities of the Minister for the Environment (Sam Foster in 2002), and it is the Department of the Environment that is formally responsible for policy in relation to local government. As in the other devolved bodies, though, Assembly members themselves, through departmental committees, play a greater role in the development of policy – e.g. the shaping of Northern Ireland's own Best Value system – as well as its scrutiny, than do Westminster MPs.

As noted in Exhibit 2.1, structural reform of local government continues to be debated, and the Executive's *Programme for Government* emphasises that 'different structures will be required under devolution, including greater accountability for all services at local level'. Such reform, though, will have to wait until the Assembly and Executive themselves have become more entrenched and accepted institutions.

English regional government

If the 1997 Labour Government delivered promptly on most of its devolution commitments – and over-delivered in the case of Northern Ireland – the one part of its programme on which it might be argued to have under-delivered was English regional government. The 1997 manifesto contained two separate policy strands. The section on promoting local economic growth promised to:

> establish one-stop Regional Development Agencies (RDAs) to co-ordinate regional economic development, help small business and encourage inward investment' (p. 16).

The section on devolution described how Labour would build on the Conservative Government's establishment of government regional offices:

> through the establishment of regional chambers to co-ordinate transport, planning, economic development, bids for European funding and land use planning.
>
> Demand for directly elected regional government so varies across England that it would be wrong to impose a uniform system. In time we will introduce legislation to allow the people, region by region, to decide in a referendum whether they want directly elected regional government. Only where clear popular consent is established will arrangements be made for elected regional assemblies. (pp. 34–5)

In its first term of office Labour fulfilled the economic pledge, but made little serious progress on the political one. The Regional Development Agencies Act 1998 produced eight new RDAs – ministerially-appointed bodies charged with improving the economic performance and competitiveness of their regions – see Exhibit 5.8. At the same time a matching set of regional chambers – often referred to now as 'assemblies' – was set up to oversee the RDAs and supposedly secure some form of local political accountability, despite the fact that they too are nominated and appointed, rather than elected.

There were no further moves in the 1997–2001 Parliament towards directly elected regional government. The Cabinet was presumed to be both divided and generally sceptical, while many in local government too were unenthusiastic, especially if a prerequisite was another bout of boundary restructuring and the establishment of predominantly unitary local government in any regions opting for elected assemblies. The 2001 Labour Manifesto suggested, in essentially an exhumation of existing policy, that this would indeed be a prerequisite:

Exhibit 5.8 English regional 'government'

9 **Regional Development Agencies (RDAs)** – regional quangos with accountability problems. Established in 1999 (2000 in London), charged with improving the economic competitiveness and success of their regions. Some known just as Development Agencies; others have gone for more macho names, reflecting their predominantly male, business-led board memberships – Yorkshire Forward, Advantage West Midlands.

Statutory purposes:
- to further economic development and regeneration
- to promote business efficiency, investment and competitiveness
- to promote employment
- to enhance development and application of skills relevant to employment
- to contribute to sustainable development.

Specific functions include:
- formulating a regional strategy
- developing a Skills Action Plan, to ensure that skills training matches the needs of the labour market
- playing a leading role in seeking European funding.

Board membership: 8–15, including 4 from local government; appointed by the Secretary of State. Worth having, at about £300 a day for two days a month – no formal qualifications required, though business experience in the region and/or voluntary community service useful; being a woman, disabled, or from ethnic minority even more so.

Regional Chambers/Assemblies
Created at the same time as RDAs – voluntary groupings of (indirectly elected) local councillors and representatives of other relevant sectors: e.g. business, trade unions, education and training, the voluntary, cultural and environmental protection sectors. Only formal role is the right to be consulted on the regional strategy, though some (e.g. East Midlands, North West, Yorkshire and Humberside) have attempted wider, more pro-active roles.

Accountabilities of RDAs
They account to ministers – Secretary of State for Trade and Industry since June 2001, previously the Environment Secretary – and consult with their chambers: a key distinction. They should *have regard for* the chamber's view in preparing their economic strategy; *consult with* the chamber on its corporate plan; be *open to scrutiny* by the chamber, but not actually accountable to it.

Exhibit 5.9 The pros and cons of elected regional government in England

PRO	CON
Democratic	
Enhanced accountability, through devolving powers from central government and unelected bodies	Reduced accountability through transferring powers from local government
More direct forum for expression of diverse regional identifications and needs	There is no deep-rooted regional consciousness in England
Economic	
Would be key driver of economic performance through development of regional economic strategies and co-ordination of development needs	Political devolution will exacerbate inter-regional competition
Could deal co-ordinatedly with cross-cutting issues like economic development, transport strategy, sustainable development	
European	
Regions are increasingly important within Europe and give access to funding and decision-making	The nation state remains pre-eminent, and countries without a regional tier of government are not obviously disadvantaged
	The uncertain benefits are not worth the domestic governmental upheaval
Technocratic	
Certain functions require a strategically co-ordinated regional approach	Local government in England is already on a very large scale. There is no need for a regional tier
Regional government would be 'better' government, in the sense of being more effective and efficient	There is no evidence of a clear relationship between authority size and effective management

Main source: DETR (2000), Ch. 2

We are committed, as RDAs take on more power, to enhance the scrutiny functions of regional chambers. For some regions this degree of political representation will be sufficient. However, in other parts of the country there may be a stronger sense of regional identity and a desire for a regional political voice.

In 1997 we said that provision should be made for directly elected regional government to go ahead where people decided in a referendum to support it and where predominantly unitary local government is established. This remains our commitment. (pp. 34–5)

It also remained, at least at the time of the election, a shambles. In January 2001 Beverley Hughes, an Environment Department Minister, had suggested that local government restructuring might *not* need to precede elected regional government (Hazell, 2001, p. 20). The September 2000 Labour Party conference had approved a policy statement talking not of referendums, but merely 'clear popular consent' (Hazell, 2001, p. 19). Deputy Prime Minister John Prescott promised a White Paper that would propose 'a similar process to that outlined for assemblies in Scotland and Wales'.

The White Paper will spell out the powers of elected regional assemblies – presumed to be broadly similar to those of the strategic GLA – their memberships, and how that may come into existence. It will also revivify the debate about the merits and demerits of elected regional government. It is one dominated by assertion and counter-assertion, in which facts and research-based evidence are at a premium. The principal arguments that tend to be deployed are set out in Exhibit 5.9 – we leave you to come to your own conclusions.

Guide to further reading

Best starting point for the various restructurings of the 1990s are two special editions of journals: *Public Administration* (Spring 1997) and *Local Government Studies* (Vol. 23.3, 1997), edited by Steve Leach. For information on the Scottish Parliament, Scottish Executive, and the Welsh and Northern Ireland Assemblies, go to their respective web sites. Taylor and Thomson (1999) is probably the most definitive of several accounts of the Scottish and Welsh devolution, and Game (2001) contains details of the elections to all these bodies, as well as to the Greater London Authority. A far racier account of the almost unbelievable 'race to become London's mayor' is D'Arcy and MacLean's aptly titled *Nightmare!* (2000).

Chapter 6

Internal Structures

A political management 'revolution'

Radical and far-reaching as they have been, the recent external structural changes to our local governmental system have been at least matched by those taking place within it – the internal reform of councils' political management structures and the advent of 'executive government'. Indeed, 'reform' is probably too moderate a term for the changes in their day-to-day working practices that many councils will be experiencing over the coming few years. In their comprehensive – and probably largely irreversible – overthrow of almost two centuries of traditional committee-based decision-making, the new mayoral or cabinet executives we shall be describing in this chapter and evaluating in Chapter 18 constitute almost a revolution.

Outlining and evaluating such change in a book of this nature, though, inevitably presents something of a problem. For, in order for you to appreciate the scale and significance of the new systems and institutions, we need first to describe the old system, even though, in your part of the country, it may well be fast disappearing. It is, therefore, with councils' traditional institutions and operations that this chapter opens, before moving on to the changes that in 2001/2 were already underway and, month by month, spreading country-wide.

Some explanations and clarifications

It is time to address in a little more detail some of the terms we have so far referred to in passing, but without further explanation: local authorities, councils, councillors, elected members, committees, departments, officers. A *local authority* may or may not be the 'political oxymoron' suggested by US Ambassador Seitz (1998, p. 272). For our present purposes it is, as we saw in Chapter 2, a semi-independent, politically decentralised, multi-functional body, created by and exercising responsibilities conferred by Parliament. The term is often used – and has already been used by us – interchangeably with *council*. Strictly speaking, though, the council is the legal embodiment of the local authority: the body of *elected councillors* who, in the British system of local government, have collectively determined and been ultimately responsible for the policy and actions of the authority. In recognition of this legal responsibility, councillors are often referred to as the elected *members* of the authority, which distinguishes them from its paid employees, the *officers* and other staff.

As we have already seen, British local authorities are mostly very large organisations and, with the spread of unitary authorities, getting larger still: 468 for the whole of the United Kingdom, or one council for every 125,000 of us. Several have more than 100 councillors and tens of thousands of full-time and part-time employees – comprising what are sometimes termed 'the two worlds' of local government. In most authorities it would be impossible for councillors to take all necessary policy decisions in full council meetings, or for officers to manage and deliver the multitude of local government services, without some kind of internal structural divisions. The way in which local authorities in this country have traditionally organised themselves is through *committees* of councillors and professionally-based *departments*.

Councillors and committees

In a word association test 'committee' would be the very first idea that many people would associate with local government – often negatively, at least sometimes positively. The committee system is one of the key features of 'the inherited world' of multi-functional authorities (Stewart, 2000, Ch. 4) that has enabled them to work efficiently and effectively, and at the same time democratically – without elected councillors handing over all policy-making to unelected officials. Committees can be seen as a council's workshops, where councillors' local knowledge and their political assessment of local needs have been brought together with officers' professional and expert advice to produce, hopefully, democratically responsive and implementable policy.

Council committees, therefore, are composed of and chaired by elected councillors and advised by officers. In the previous editions of this book we included diagrammatic illustrations of typical committee structures (e.g. Wilson and Game, 1998, pp. 72–3). A few of the committees, such as education and social services, were *statutory* and had to be set up by councils with these responsibilities. Most, though, were *permissive,* enabling councillors themselves to decide how they are going to arrange and divide up their council's work. Different councils with exactly the same set of service responsibilities, therefore, would quite likely have very different committee and sub-committee structures. Check for yourself: compare the numbers and names of your own council's listed committees with those of other councils of the same type, either through their web sites or in Volume 2 (Authorities and Members) of any recent *Municipal Year Book* in your local library.

For a council that was not an education or social services authority there was in fact no law saying it had to delegate its work to committees at all. Indeed, before the unitary reorganisation, a couple of small district councils in Scotland and Wales did choose to work entirely through full council meetings, albeit of only about a dozen councillors. But the commoner tendency was probably the reverse: for councils to acquire over time a proliferation of committees and sub-committees with correspondingly vast numbers of meetings. The sense that such systems may duplicate discussion, complicate and slow down decision-making, and be generally too time-consuming has been one of the driving forces behind the reforms we shall describing.

As already suggested, though, council committees get a bad enough press without our adding to it. In the rush to 'modernisation' and reform it is important not to overlook – or, indeed, to lose – the many very positive features of committees and committee practices that served local government well for most of its history. As detailed in our previous edition (Wilson and Game, 1998, pp. 236–7), committees:

- enable councillors to acquire specialist knowledge in specific policy areas, thereby producing more informed decision-making;
- enable councillors to develop public speaking, chairing, and other potential leadership skills;
- allow decisions to be publicly scrutinised;
- allow opposition councillors to put alternative proposals;
- allow representations of special interests;
- provide a forum for calling officers and contractors to account for their performance.

Of course, several of these positive features have their negative sides too. Councillors can over-specialise and become blinkered, failing to appreciate the work of the council as a whole. Committee meetings can be dominated by discussion of operational detail, at the expense of major policy issues, strategy, and the monitoring of service performance. Committees can also be excessively party political, creating a 'scrutiny shortfall' (Leach, 1999, p. 82), with majority party members being reluctant publicly to criticise their own leadership, and opposition members being in too small a minority to scrutinise effectively.

Perhaps most importantly for a multi-functional authority trying to present a coherent corporate image to the world, service-based or department-based committees can be become 'compartmentalised' and difficult to co-ordinate. Which is why, in recent years, almost all councils have had some kind of *central management committee,* known as Policy and Resources, Finance and Management, or some similar variant. The purpose of this usually multi-party committee, generally chaired by the

Leader of the Council and containing some of its most experienced members, has been to co-ordinate the work of specialist committees and provide the council with overall policy leadership. Some critics argue, however, that, in the absence of any *directly elected* individual leader, even the most coherent policy leadership is not going to impress itself upon local residents, service users and voters – which is part of the case for elected executive mayors.

Officers and departments

The second of our complementary and interacting worlds of local government is that of the council employees, and particularly the officers in their town and county hall departments. Notwithstanding the development of more strategic management in recent years, many local authorities still carve up their work between *departments* with a *professional* focus. Each department is headed by a *chief officer* or *director*, a qualified specialist in the functional area concerned, and will employ relevant specialist and generalist staff at lower levels. *Service departments* – such as education, social services, leisure, public protection – provide services direct to the public, while central departments – such as the Chief Executive's, the Treasurer's, Personnel, Construction and Design – have more of a servicing role for other departments.

As with committees, local authorities have considerable discretion in the departmental structures they adopt and the officers they appoint. The Local Government Act 1972 enables them to appoint 'such officers as they think necessary for the proper discharge of their functions'. This and other legislation *requires* relevant local authorities to appoint certain chief officers – a Chief Education Officer, Chief Fire Officer, Director of Social Services – but these are very much the exceptions to the rule. Councils' departmental structures have in practice varied every bit as much as their committee systems.

Chief officers have overall responsibility for implementing council policies relating to their respective departments. Though highly trained, professionally qualified and, by most standards, extremely well paid, the chief officer is as much an employee and 'servant' of *the council* as the most recently recruited manual worker. Unlike councillors – often much less formally educated and trained and much less handsomely remunerated – officers have not been elected, and their role is to ensure that the policy laid down by the councillors is implemented and that all their reasonable and lawful instructions are carried out. Note too the emphasis in the penultimate sentence: in our traditional system, where policy is formally the responsibility of the whole council, officers' responsibility has naturally been to the whole council, *not* to any particular party, whether or not it

Exhibit 6.1 Internal management structures: the 'traditional' system

Committees	Departments
• Local authorities are **governed by councillors** or **elected members**, who meet regularly and publicly in **full council** to take authoritative policy and budgetary decisions for their local area	• Local authorities are **organised** into **departments**
	• These departments are staffed by **appointed officers and other employees** – administrative, professional, technical and clerical staff, manual workers – who legally are the **paid servants** of the elected council
• Most councils delegate much of their work to **policy committees** and sub-committees of councillors which concentrate on a particular area of the council's work and are responsible for determining the council's policy in that area	
	• These officers and staff **implement council policy** as determined by its councillors, and run the authority on a day-to-day basis
• Each committee has a **chair(man)**, who chairs its meetings, speaks and acts on its behalf, and liaises with relevant officers. Chairs do **not** take policy decisions personally	• Departments can be divided into **service departments**, providing a service directly to the public, and **central** or **co-ordinating departments**, providing a service for the authority as a whole
• Council meetings are presided over by the ceremonial **mayor** or **chair(man) of the council**, elected annually by and from all members of the council	• Each department has a **chief officer**, usually a professional specialist in the work of the department and responsible for it to a committee and its chair
• The **leader of the council**, its key political figure, is generally the elected leader of the majority or largest party group on the council	• Most authorities have a **chief executive**, the head of the council's paid service, responsible for co-ordinating the operation and policy of the council, usually through a **Chief Officers' Management Team**.
• Most authorities have a co-ordinating **policy (and resources) committee** of mainly senior councillors, usually chaired by the leader	

A council's POLICY is the outcome of the formal and informal interaction between elected councillors and their appointed officers.

Councils have considerable discretion over their internal organisation; no two councils, therefore, will have precisely the same departmental and committee structures.

happens to be in majority control of the council. As we shall see, these long-cherished principles of political neutrality and a unified officer structure are under some challenge with the arrival of executive government.

Most local authorities in recent years have had a *Chief Executive*. He or she — there were some 50 women chief executives in 2002 — is the chief officer in overall charge of the council and its departments – or 'head of the paid service', as it tends to be known. An additional requirement since the Local Government and Housing Act 1989 has been that all councils must have a 'monitoring officer', to check that the council is operating within the law. This role too has been commonly taken by the chief executive. The chief executive is a kind of officers' team leader, and will generally chair a Chief Officers' Management Team, on which will sit most or all chief officers. Again, precise patterns vary from authority to authority, but almost all have some such mechanism for ensuring effective liaison and policy co-ordination across departments that can easily become almost self-contained mini-empires, with distinctive cultures and operating styles.

The internal organisation of departments has traditionally been characterised by two features: *professionalism* and *hierarchy*. Senior positions in departments have tended to be held by the dominant profession in that department, with professional boundaries marking and reinforcing departmental territories. In parallel to this there has been a strong commitment to formal accountability and hierarchical control. In service departments staff have invariably been arranged in a hierarchy of accountability running from field-worker to chief officer and through the chief officer to the committee. In such a system the span of control of any one officer is inevitably limited, and, for junior officers and the public alike, finding a route through the numerous lower tiers to deal with top-tier officers can be extremely difficult. More progressive authorities, therefore, have moved towards 'flatter' departmental structures with fewer tiers. These topics will be taken up again in Chapter 16; meanwhile, Exhibit 6.1 summarises the internal structures of local authorities *prior* to the 'modernisation' reforms that dominate most of the remainder of this chapter.

Previous approaches to internal management reform

As suggested at the start of this chapter, internal management reform at the start of the twenty-first century is all about the development of the institutions and processes of executive government: cabinets, elected mayors, council managers, overview and scrutiny committees.

The shape of reform has been almost entirely determined by the Local Government Act 2000, which itself was the product of a series of consultation papers produced in the early years of the 1997 Labour

Government. This was by no means, though, the first attempt to restructure the internal management of local authorities. Several parts of the 'traditional' system summarised in Exhibit 6.1 – policy and resources committees, chief executives, officers' management teams – developed out of earlier governmental reports and inquiries. In previous editions of this book we have described some of these earlier approaches to reform at greater length than is necessary now (Wilson and Game, 1998, pp. 76–80). With more momentous topics to address, a briefer summary will suffice.

Maud 1967 – chief executives in, management boards out

The Committee on the Management of Local Government, chaired by Sir John Maud, later Lord Redcliffe-Maud, sat at the same time as the Royal Commission on reorganisation referred to in Chapter 4. It anticipated some of the current criticisms that are made of committees encouraging elected members to concern themselves too much with details of day-to-day administration, and not enough with broad policy and strategy. Its prescriptions were radical – too radical for many.

All but the smallest local authorities, the Committee's report argued, should have a *Management Board* of between five and nine senior councillors with wide delegated powers. There should also be a radical pruning of committees and departments, and each authority should appoint a *chief executive officer* – not necessarily a lawyer, like the traditional Town Clerk – who would be the undisputed head of the authority's paid staff.

The instinctive response of most local authorities to the report was hostile. It was felt to be elitist, and, just as in the current moves towards executive government, many councillors were fearful of becoming second-class members of their councils, excluded from the Management Board, and with little or no policy influence. Nevertheless, Maud did serve as stimulus for change: many authorities did rationalise their committee systems and some did appoint chief executives. The reform process was further encouraged by the publication in the early 1970s of the Bains Report (England and Wales) and the Paterson Report (Scotland): reports which were very similar in orientation.

Bains 1972 and Paterson 1973 – corporate icing, traditional cake

These two committees were set up in 1971 to provide advice on internal management structures for the new local authorities that were established under the Local Government Acts of 1972 in England and Wales and 1973 in Scotland. Their reports received far more favourable reaction than that previously accorded to Maud. Essentially they argued that the traditional departmental attitude which permeated much of local government needed to give way to a broader corporate, or authority-wide, outlook. Maud's then controversial idea of an elite Management Board was not revived.

Following the Bains/Paterson recommendations, the vast majority of the newly established authorities appointed *chief executives*. Likewise, most set up *policy and resources committees* and *senior officer management teams* if they did not already exist. There was, therefore, in many authorities a good deal of internal *structural* change following Bains, although the effect on day-to-day working practices is more difficult to determine. Re-drawing organisation charts is comparatively easy; implanting lasting cultural changes in the way an organisation actually works is another thing altogether. New and apparently more corporate *forms* of management emerged, but the strong, co-ordinating chief executive envisaged by Bains remained the exception rather than the rule, with a strong departmentalist culture continuing to hold sway in most authorities.

Widdicombe 1986 – overdue recognition of party politics

The Widdicombe Committee was the Thatcher Government's response to its concern about the policies and campaigning activities of a number of urban Labour authorities on what came to be labelled the Municipal or New Urban Left, or 'loony left' as such councils were known in the tabloid press. A mainly younger generation of Labour councillors in London and certain other cities came into office committed to using local councils as a testing ground for new radical, interventionist policies in economic development, housing, transport and planning, and to defending their communities against central government spending cuts.

The Maud, Bains and Paterson Committees had focused mainly on organisational structures, their managerial prescriptions largely ignoring the roles and responsibilities of elected members and the increasingly prominent party political dimension of the country's local government. Widdicombe addressed these issues head-on. The spread of party politics in local government was acknowledged, investigated, and many of its positive features welcomed: more contested elections, clearer democratic choice, greater policy consistency, more direct accountability. At the same time, the Committee was concerned to safeguard the position of minority parties and of individual and non-party members.

The Widdicombe recommendations led, in the Local Government and Housing Act 1989, to the effective banning of one-party committees and sub-committees, and to senior officers being barred from all public political activity. Overall, the Committee's impact was to introduce a number of 'checks and balances', without seriously challenging the right of a majority party to determine and see implemented its policy proposals. It injected a new air of realism into discussions about local authority management, but full-scale recognition of the validity of majority party control would have to await a new millennium.

New Labour's 'modernisation' prescription – separate executives

In fact, though, until the arrival of New Labour, there were not that many serious discussions about local authority management – not at central government level anyway. The Major Government's focus, as we saw in Chapter 5, was much more on external structural reform. But, in addition to its constitutional programme of devolution to the regions, the Labour manifesto had a whole 'modernisation agenda' of reforms for local government: 'best value' services, community planning, finance reform, and – the one that particularly concerns us here – 'democratic renewal'.

The new government's thinking was presented initially in a set of consultation papers in early 1998. The first of these, *Modernising Local Government: Local Democracy and Community Leadership* (DETR, 1998b), subsequently evolved into the Local Government Act 2000, but it is still worth reading for an appreciation of the government's approach to reform. New Labour wanted to emphasise its belief in and commitment to democratic local government – in contrast, it claimed, to its Conservative predecessors. But, at the same time, it saw the existing local government system 'falling short of its great potential'. For example:

> Turnout at local elections is on average around 40% and sometimes much less. There is a culture of apathy about local democracy. The evidence is that councillors – hard-working and dedicated as they are – are overburdened, often unproductively, by committee meetings which focus on detailed issues rather than concentrating on essentials. The opportunity for councillors to have a stronger voice on behalf of local communities is being missed. (DETR, 1998b, para. 1.3)

Chapter 5 of the consultation paper, 'Modernising the way councils work', spelled out in more detail the shortcomings of a system 'designed over a century ago for a bygone age' – its inefficiency, secrecy, opacity, and lack of accountability:

- Councillors spend too small a proportion of their time in their representational work directly with their community, which should be their most important role.
- They spend too much time inefficiently – particularly in preparing for, travelling to, and attending committee meetings, which are frequently

not where the real decisions are made anyway. Rather, in most councils, these decisions are made in party group meetings, behind closed doors, with little open democratic scrutiny possible, either from opposition parties or the electorate.

- Traditional committees are also a poor vehicle for developing and demonstrating community leadership. They confuse the executive (policy-making) and representational roles of councillors. It is not always clear who has actually taken a decision and therefore who can be held to account. Few people know who the leader of their local authority is, or, just as important, who is the chair of the education committee. Local people have no say in the selection of their local leaders.

The consultation paper acknowledged that several more progressive councils had already developed innovative ways of rethinking their committee structures and involving the public in their decision-making, but faster and far more comprehensive change was required. This change, in the government's view, had to be based on a *separation* of the executive and representative roles of councillors – a contentious and consequential departure from the prevailing culture that, formally at least, saw all councillors as equal. This role separation would produce greater clarity about where decisions have been taken, by whom, and therefore who is to be held accountable. It would also enable there to be sharper scrutiny of those decisions. Indeed, the greater the degree of separation, the greater are likely to be the benefits:

> The Government is therefore very attracted to the model of a strong executive directly elected mayor. Such a mayor would be a highly visible figure. He or she would have been elected by the people, rather than by the council or party, and would therefore focus attention outwards rather than inwards towards fellow councillors. The mayor would be a strong political and community leader with whom the electorate could identify. Mayors will have to become well known to their electorate, which could help increase interest in and understanding of local government. (para. 5.14)

The choice is yours – from our three models

There were hints in the consultation paper that the government might allow councils to pilot a wide variety of managerial arrangements: cabinet systems, lead member systems, directly and indirectly elected mayors with differing ranges of functional responsibilities. However, the July 1998 White Paper, *Modern Local Government: In Touch with the People*

(DETR, 1998a), indicated that the legislation would be both narrower and more prescriptive, and so it proved. Local authorities in England and Wales would be required to choose one of just three specified forms of executive or propose some ministerially acceptable alternative arrangements, as summarised in Exhibit 6.2.

The restricted nature of this choice, plus its obvious weighting in favour of the controversial directly elected mayor, led to the legislation being fiercely opposed during its passage through Parliament, and the Government was forced to make at least some concessions. One in particular we encountered in Exhibit 2.1. Small shire districts were allowed a fourth option of a 're-vamped' committee system, provided they could demonstrate that they had the backing of their local community. All other authorities in England and Wales were required to prepare plans for new structures based on one of the three executive models, to be submitted for ministerial approval in 2001 and scheduled to be in operation by 2002.

Scotland, of course, by this time had its own Parliament and Executive and was able to go its own way. It also had a report – from the McIntosh Commission (McIntosh, 1999) – with some pertinent recommendations. McIntosh had been set up to look at the implications that the Scottish Parliament would have for Scottish local government. Reporting to the Scottish Executive in June 1999, its most publicised recommendation was for proportional representation for local elections. But it looked also at the way in which councils organised their business and political decision-making, and proposed that each of the 32 councils should review its own management arrangements against stated criteria of openness and accountability.

Thus, while the Westminster Parliament was prescribing just three executive models for more than 400 English and Welsh councils, the Scottish Executive explicitly rejected any 'central blueprint', preferring to encourage the emergence of a 'rich diversity of different models'. The individual council reviews were received by a special Leadership Advisory Panel, which reported to the Executive in April 2001. Several common themes emerged from the reviews, including strong support for separate scrutiny structures and, in more remote rural areas, for more powerful area committees. But only a few councils were in favour of 'English-style' executives, mayoral or otherwise, the majority preferring streamlined committee systems.

Where are the mayors?

It must be remembered that much of the content of the Local Government Act 2000 had been anticipated for some two years. So, although authorities still had to consult, or re-consult, their local residents, there were plenty of

Exhibit 6.2 The new 'separate executive' models of political management

The traditional committee-based structure

Council decisions could be delegated to officers, but *not* to individual councillors – not even to council leaders or committee chairs. Decisions not delegated had to be taken either in full council or by committees or sub-committees of councillors. *All* councillors, therefore, were legally part of the decision-making process.

The Local Government Act 2000 – introduced, for the first time, a clear separation between the *making and execution* of council decisions and the *scrutiny* of those decisions. The council's policy framework and budget are agreed by the full council, following proposals from the executive. The executive is then charged with implementing the agreed policy framework.

3 (or more) possible forms of executive arrangements

All councils in England and Wales – except shire districts with populations of less than 85,000 – were required, after consulting their local residents, to choose one of three specified forms of executive or propose some ministerially acceptable alternative arrangements:

(1) **Mayor and cabinet executive** – a mayor directly elected by the whole electorate, who appoints an executive of between 2 and 9 councillors
(2) **Leader and cabinet executive** – an executive leader, elected by the full council (i.e. usually the leader of the largest party), plus between 2 and 9 councillors either appointed by the leader or elected by the council
(3) **Mayor and council manager** – a mayor directly elected by the whole electorate, providing the broad policy direction, with an officer of the authority appointed by the council as a day-to-day manager
(4) **Alternative arrangements** – an alternative form of executive, approved by the Secretary of State as more suitable to the council's particular circumstances than any of the above models.

Smaller shire districts have an additional fourth option open to them:

(5) **Alternative arrangements (not involving a separate executive)** – retention of the committee system, subject to the approval of the Secretary of State that decisions will be taken in an efficient, transparent and accountable way, and that there are acceptable provisions for overview and scrutiny.

Mayoral options may only be introduced after approval in an authority-wide referendum – triggered by the council itself, by a petition signed by 5 per cent of local electors, or by direction of the Secretary of State.

Overview and Scrutiny Committees

All councils operating executive arrangements must set up overview and scrutiny committees of non-executive members (and possibly non-member co-optees), in order to hold the executive to account. These committees may make reports and recommendations, either to the executive or the authority, on any aspect of council business or other matters that affect the authority's area or its inhabitants.

Exhibit 6.3 Transitional political management structures, 1998–2000

	Political control	Executive model	Executive body Size	Executive body Party	Non-executive bodies
Breckland DC	Cons	Leader + Cabinet	9	Multi	5 Scrutiny Panels
Bournemouth BC	NOC	Leader + Cabinet	7	Multi	Service Review and Performance Panels; Policy Advisory Groups; Local Area Forums
Bury MBC	Lab	Leader + Cabinet	8	Single	5 Scrutiny & Review Panels; 6 Area Boards
Chesterfield BC	Lab	Leader + Cabinet	7	Two	4 Scrutiny Panels; 9 Community Forums
Copeland BC	Lab	Leader + Cabinet	7–9	Chosen by Leader	Policy Monitoring Board + Audit Committee; 3 standing Policy Development Groups
Dudley MBC	Lab	Leader + Cabinet	13	Single	4 Select Committees; 5 Area Committees
East Sussex CC	NOC	Leader + Cabinet	6	Two	6 Scrutiny Committees + Audit Scrutiny Committee
Enfield LBC	Lab	Leader + Cabinet	10	Single	6 Scrutiny Panels
Hammersmith and Fulham LBC	Lab	Mayor + Mayor's Board	7	Single	Committee of the Council; 5 Scrutiny Panels

Kent CC	Cons	Leader + Cabinet	7	Single	4 Scrutiny Committees; 12 Area Committees
Leeds City C	Lab	Leader + Exec. Board	9	Multi	5 'Lead Members' to support Executive; 3 Scrutiny Boards; 16 Community Involvement Panels
Mid-Suffolk DC	LD/ Lab	Leader + Executive	6	Multi	Scrutiny Committee; 4 Policy Panels + Best Value Panels
North Wiltshire DC	NOC	Leader + Cabinet	7	Single (LD)	Scrutiny Committee; 5 Area Committees
Reading BC	Lab	Leader + Exec. Board	10	Single	6 Scrutiny Panels; 5 Area Consultative Committees
Rochdale MBC	Lab	Leader + Cabinet	10	Multi	9 Policy & Review Panels; Township Committees
Slough BC	Lab	Leader + Cabinet	6	Single	Scrutiny & Overview Committee + Panels; 5 Neighbourhood/Sector Consultative Forums
Staffordshire CC	Lab	Leader + Cabinet	9	Single	Scrutiny Committees; Area Committees
Stoke-on-Trent City C	Lab	Leader + Cabinet	12	Single	5 Review Committees; Policy Committee
Wakefield MBC	Lab	Leader + Cabinet	9	Multi	6 Scrutiny panels; Community Assemblies

Note: NOC = No overall control (no single party has over 50 per cent of the seats).
Sources: IDeA (1999); Game (2000a), p. 146.

signs of their own preferences from the 'transitional arrangements' they were already operating. A fair indication of the way the wind was blowing came from a survey of some of these arrangements, summarised in Exhibit 6.3.

Government ministers clearly favoured directly elected mayors, and opinion polls suggested that the general public was at least keen on the general idea. Elected mayors had also been one of the key recommendations of the independent Commission for Local Democracy (1995). Within local government, though, there was very little support indeed. Councillors in particular were both critical and understandably concerned: critical of the concentration of power in the hands of a single individual, and concerned that, if they were not among the minority of executive councillors, they could find themselves excluded altogether from the policy-making process. Much safer, they would feel, to go for the leader/cabinet model that, although it would still involve an executive/non-executive split, would be closer to what they were familiar with.

The mayor/council manager model suffered, initially at least, from the double disadvantage of being based partly on an elected mayor and partly on another novelty in British local government, the council manager. Council manager systems are one of the most prevalent forms of urban government in the United States – in, among many other cities, Dallas, San Diego, Kansas City and Phoenix – also in New Zealand, and it is easy to understand their attraction. For they appear to combine the strong political and policy leadership of an elected mayor with the managerial expertise and experience of a professional manager, appointed by the council and responsible for day-to-day decision-making. The likelihood is that council managers may find their supporters among probably some of the smaller and less party politicised shire districts. But giving apparently a great deal of power to an appointed official is not likely to be immediately appealing to elected party politicians.

Thus, of the 19 IDeA case study authorities of all sizes and types, just one – the London Borough of Hammersmith and Fulham – opted for a mayoral structure. The remainder all preferred some version of the leader/cabinet option. It is clear, though, even from our brief summary, that there was great variation in the ways that model was being interpreted and implemented. The size of the cabinet/executive (larger in some cases than the future legislation would allow), its political composition, the scrutiny arrangements, the existence of area or neighbourhood forums – all these elements of the model varied considerably from one authority to another, just as one would expect from their very diverse locations, histories and politics.

Hammersmith and Fulham was the first major council to move from committee-based decision-making to at least a nominal mayor/cabinet system – although the 'mayor' was elected by the council, just as a leader would have been. As detailed in Exhibit 6.3, the executive was known not as a cabinet, but as the Mayor's Board, and its six members were designated Deputies, thus distinguishing them clearly from former committee chairs. The deputies' portfolios were Best Value, Regeneration, Social Inclusion, Education, Housing, Environment and Contract Services. The mayor and deputies, after appropriate advice and consultation, produced proposals, which were then available for detailed scrutiny from an all-party Committee of the Council – following either a 'call-in' by at least two councillors or a deputation of 10 or more registered voters. If not satisfied, the Committee could refer the proposal back to the Board for further consideration.

Enterprising as it was, Hammersmith and Fulham's lead attracted few followers. Indeed, there was no certainty, as the borough undertook further consultations in 2001, that it would itself move to a full-scale mayoral system. Several councils held referendums, either as part of their consultation processes or having been petitioned by 5 per cent of their electorates, but the early results – from mostly more rural councils like Cheltenham, Gloucester and Berwick-upon-Tweed – all voted down mayoral government. Watford voters, in July 2001, were the first to give referendum backing for an elected mayor – closely followed by Doncaster, Hartlepool, Lewisham, Middlesbrough and North Tyneside – but meanwhile the great majority of local councils were preparing for the formal adoption of leader/cabinet systems.

Leicestershire County Council offers us one example of such a system (see Exhibits 6.4 and 6.5). Leicestershire's new constitution – another requirement of the Local Government Act 2000 – came into operation in mid-2001, and it outlines, much more accessibly than in the past, just how the Council works. Leicestershire's is no more or less typical of leader/cabinet systems than any other, but it gives a useful insight into the kinds of new structures and terminology with which we must familiarise ourselves, and you can easily compare it with other councils' constitutions available on their web sites. You might also compare Exhibit 6.5 with Leicestershire's very different 'pre-modernisation' committee structure (Wilson and Game, 1998, p. 72), with its Policy and Resources Committee, six main service committees, plus sub-committees and working groups too numerous to list – now all swept away. In the context of British local government, a break with the past on that scale – even without directly elected mayors – does qualify as near-revolutionary.

Two-hatted officers?

As described so far, the debate about executive government has been almost entirely about the politicians' world, which, whatever structures

Exhibit 6.4 Leicestershire County Council's Leader/Cabinet system

The full County Council (54 members)

- is collectively the Council's ultimate policy making body;
- is the only body able to adopt and change the Council's *Constitution*;
- approves the Council's *Policy Framework*, comprising a series of major plans, and its budget;
- approves or rejects proposals from the Executive/Cabinet which are outside the approved Policy Framework or the budget;
- receives reports from scrutiny committees on activities of the Executive/Cabinet.

The Council's executive role

- is carried out under *delegated powers* primarily through the Executive/Cabinet acting *collectively* and chief officers;
- the *Executive* comprises the Leader of the Council – elected by the Council, and therefore usually the leader of the largest party – and a *Cabinet* (currently of 8 members) also appointed by the Council. It is responsible for the more important executive decisions needed to implement the Policy Framework and budget approved by the Council.
- Cabinet members take *lead roles* on specific services on behalf of the Cabinet, but there is (as in the traditional committee system) no delegation of powers to individual Cabinet members, including the leader;
- the Cabinet will refer to the full Council any proposal involving a significant departure from the Policy Framework or the budget;
- any meeting of the Executive at which an executive decision is taken is held in public.

The Council's overview and scrutiny role

- is directed and co-ordinated by a *Scrutiny Commission* – a politically balanced committee of *non-executive* members, chaired by the leader of the largest opposition group.
- 4 standing *Overview and Scrutiny Committees* – Education and Heritage, Health and Social Care, Planning and Environment, Finance – also comprise only non-executive members, and have roles in relation to policy development and review, as well as scrutiny.
- They can review and scrutinise decisions made by and the performance of the Executive and chief officers; they can question Cabinet members and chief officers about specific decisions, their views on issues and proposals, and their general performance; they can research and undertake in-depth analysis of policy issues and possible options; they can liaise with and scrutinise the performance of other public bodies in the area.
- The Scrutiny Commission can also appoint a number of small 5–member temporary *review panels* to carry out targeted reviews connected with Best Value or other key issues.

Exhibit 6.4 continued

The Council's regulatory role

- Regulation – of planning and conservation, health and safety, licensing, etc. – is carried out by a series of *regulatory boards* and other committees: eg the Development Control and Highways Regulatory Board, the Pension Fund Management Board.
- A *Standards Committee* – of at least two councillors + a voting member independent of the Council – will monitor standards of conduct of all elected members and officers.

Representational role of individual councillors

- to work to ensure the well-being of the community they represent;
- to bring constituents' views, concerns and grievances to the attention of the relevant bodies;
- to contribute to the overview and scrutiny of the Council's policy and performance;
- to contribute to the development of corporate policies, Best Value reviews and local initiatives.

their individual authorities adopt, is changing massively. By comparison, the officers' world is relatively stable. Again, Leicestershire serves as an illustration. While the County Council's political management structure is unrecognisable from that described in our previous edition, its departmental structure (see Exhibit 6.6) has slimmed slightly from 12 departments to 10, but is otherwise unchanged.

Yet this apparent stability may well prove deceptive, for potentially the arrival of executive government could have profound implications for officers as well as for councillors. With separate mayoral and cabinet executives, local government is becoming much more like central government, where senior civil servants' first duty is to their Minister, not to Parliament as a whole or equally to all parties. There might seem to be a case for the development of a 'local civil service', in which chief officers' responsibilities are, at least primarily, to the executive. If so, it was not a case that the government has chosen to acknowledge.

In the lengthy paper accompanying its draft legislation, *Local Leadership, Local Choice* (DETR, 1999), the roles of officers receive just six short paragraphs, the message of which is: no major change required. There is likely to be greater delegation to officers than previously, and the increased importance of direct consultation with local people and other interests is also likely to lead to new demands upon them. But they will be expected to carry out their various responsibilities wearing in effect two hats: serving both executive and non-executive members, both the policy-making

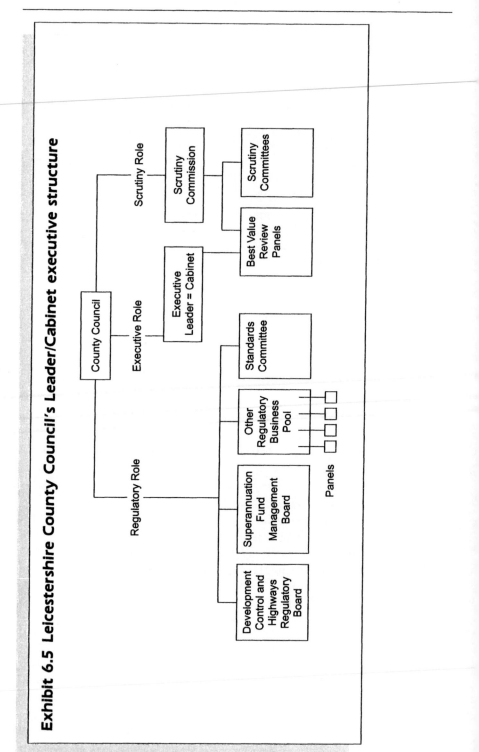

Exhibit 6.5 Leicestershire County Council's Leader/Cabinet executive structure

Exhibit 6.6 Leicestershire County Council's departmental structure, 2001

SERVICE DEPARTMENTS	CENTRAL DEPARTMENTS
Education	Chief Executive's
Libraries and Information	County Treasurer's
Museums, Arts and Records	Information Systems
Planning and Transportation	Property
Regulatory Services – including registration of births, marriages and deaths, trading standards, consumer and trader advice	
Social Services	

process and the critical scrutiny of that process, with all the potential for role conflict that entails:

> In all the new forms of local governance councils would continue to have a professional chief executive responsible for managing and securing the professional body of staff a large multi-function organisation needs to deliver modern well-focused services effectively. Council officers will be required to serve both the executive and other councillors in their several roles. They will therefore be required to maintain their political neutrality. (para. 3.82)

Fox and Leach (1999), in the most substantial early study of these issues, think that in at least some authorities – particularly any opting for mayor/cabinet systems – this balance and political neutrality may in practice prove difficult to maintain. There are likely, they suggest, to be demands for some form of dedicated staff support for both cabinet and scrutiny functions. As in almost everything to do with local government, the probability is that different solutions will be developed in different authorities. The government may have legislated for just three executive models, but it will surely find that councils' ingenuity in adapting these models to their own particular requirements is almost infinite.

Guide to further reading

The executive 'modernisation' of local government is almost entirely the Labour Government's agenda, so turn first to the key official publications: (DETR, 1998a, 1998b, 1999). The Local Government Association (LGA) web site has loads of downloadable stuff under 'Local Government Act – New Political Arrangements'. The Improvement and Development Agency (IDeA), cited in the chapter, commissions and publishes regular research aimed at making local authorities more effective – e.g. Hambleton (2000), Snape, Leach *et al.* (2000). Hambleton is also author of one of the few international comparisons of political management systems, commendably commissioned by the Scottish Office (1998). Pratchett (ed.) (2000) and Leach (2001) are both useful productions by academics at De Montfort University, and Leigh (2000), Ch. 7, gives a very good legal perspective. As ever, the 'trade' press – *Local Government Chronicle* and *Municipal Journal* – will keep you up to date with key developments – mayoral referendums and elections, 'monitoring' research studies – and individual council web sites should all have details of their constitutions and new organisational arrangements.

Chapter 7

Changing Functions

Introduction – the continuing primacy of service provision

We have already emphasised the elective, democratic history and character of the UK system of local government. The councillors and councils we elect constitute 'the government' of our city, town, county or district in the same way that ministers and the cabinet constitute the government of the country. The big difference has been that national government is not, on the whole, a large-scale provider of services. There are some major exceptions – most obviously the Department for Work and Pensions and the Home Office – but mostly ministers and their Whitehall-based departments produce *policy, not services*. They decide, through legislation, what services we citizens are to be provided with, by whom, and how they are to be financed. Others, in the main, do the actual providing, and throughout the twentieth century by far the biggest providers of local services were local councils.

That still remains the case today, although, as we have already seen in Chapter 2, things are changing fast. Councils have lost completely some of their responsibilities. Others have been and continue to be exposed to private sector competition. Sometimes out of choice, sometimes not, councils nowadays find themselves increasingly working alongside a range of other service-providing agencies in their localities. The term used to distinguish this more fragmented, multi-agency pattern of local government from the earlier 'near-monopolistic council' model is *local* or *community governance*.

Community governance implies a reduced role for local authorities as service providers. We have entered an era of alternative service delivery systems incorporating local authority, voluntary sector and private sector provision. Partnerships with the non-elected, private and voluntary sectors assume every permutation. Nevertheless, while service provision at local level is frequently more complex than it once was, it remains a major role for local authorities, albeit not necessarily through direct employment and in-house management. Midwinter was referring to Scotland (1995, p. 131), but his assertion of the continuing primacy of service provision applies to local government across Great Britain:

> Despite the welter of rhetoric, the image of radical reform, the language of the new public management, the glitz of marketing and public relations, the central role of a local authority remains – municipal provision of services.

Changing roles – from provider to commissioner?

In Chapter 1 we saw how a council could attempt to respond to the needs of its citizens 'either through the direct provision or through the sponsorship, indirect funding, regulation or monitoring' of services (p. 10). In Chapter 2 we added some more roles: licensor, registrar, certificator, facilitator, contractor (p. 31). It is time to bring some order to this lengthening list. Leach and Stewart (1992b) identify four primary roles for local government (Box 7.1).

Box 7.1 Local government – four primary roles

1. *Service Provision*: the planning, resourcing and provision, directly or indirectly, of individual local services.
2. *Regulation*: the regulation of the economic behaviour of individuals or other agencies in the public interest by insisting on their compliance with standards, rules and procedures of various kinds for exchange or provision of goods or services. This is where the licensing, inspection, monitoring, registration and certification come in.
3. *Strategic Planning*: the provision of a longer-term planning framework to influence the activities of internal departments and external organisations in relation to individual service areas or authority-wide issues.
4. *Promotion and Advocacy*: the persuasion of one or more other organisations (e.g. private industry, voluntary bodies) to carry out activities which are likely to benefit the local community (e.g. by loans to small businesses, grants to voluntary organisations).

Source: Leach and Stewart (1992b), pp. 10–19.

Unlike Leach and Stewart, who are academic analysts, David Curry, addressing the House of Commons in July 1994, was speaking as Conservative Minister for Local Government. In fact, although he did not know it at the time, he was the last, and longest serving, of no fewer than 11 local government ministers in 18 years of Conservative administration. Not surprisingly, he chose slightly differing terminology and a rather different emphasis:

> The first role is that of *regulator* ... it is clear that that role will remain. The second role is that of *service commissioner* – I use the term deliberately – because local government organises the delivery of a range of services, whether the individual services are delivered directly or through the competitive process. [The] third role is that of a *regenerator*, [something] that will be more relevant in urban areas than in some rural areas. Local government has a role to work more and more with other agencies ... so as to bring the resources of the community to tackle specific problems. (Hansard, 21 July 1994, Cols. 616–19, emphases ours)

For the Conservative minister, then, it was regulation first – which is not just remaining, but, as we saw in Chapter 6, continues even under executive government to be delivered through 'traditional' committees. Then came service provision and that only as part of a broader service-commissioning role. Regeneration, like service commissioning, involves negotiation and partnership with other agencies, and, in the minister's preferred scheme of things, a scaling down of the activity and spending of local authorities themselves. But a scaling down from what?

Still big business

It is a cliché, but true nonetheless, that local government in Britain, even after all the constraining legislation of recent years, the transfers of services, the property sales and the enforced competition, is still extremely big business. Its combined and current spending in 2001 was well over £80 billion, or more than a quarter of all government expenditure. If individual local authorities were listed in terms of their expenditure, almost a hundred would rank alongside the top 500 British companies. To take just one example, Kent County Council's 1.5 million population before the reorganisation of the mid-1990s made it larger than some 40 states of the United Nations. With an annual turnover well in excess of £1 billion, 50,000 employees and 1,400 service points, it was not only the largest employer in Kent, but larger than many national and international companies.

County councils like Kent are among the biggest of the local government 'businesses', together with the larger unitary authorities: the metropolitan districts, the London boroughs, and some of the newer big city unitaries. For, as can be seen in Exhibit 7.1, these are the authorities that are responsible for most of the council-provided services in their areas, or at least for the most labour-intensive and biggest spending ones: particularly education and social services.

The county/district division in non-metropolitan England is important to understand. It is not a hierarchical relationship. Despite the fact that in our organisation charts in Chapters 4 and 5 the counties and former Scottish regions appear above the districts, the two tiers should properly be seen as equal in status, each responsible for the range of services felt to be most appropriately provided on either a relatively larger or a more localised scale. It is, though, a severely unbalanced division, with the cost of county-provided services likely to be four or five times that of district-provided services in any district area.

Unitary authorities in principle have responsibility for all those services in the remaining two-tier parts of England that are split into counties and districts. In practice, as we saw in Chapter 5, there is also a complex network of joint boards and committees – only partially captured in our deliberately simplified Exhibit 7.1 – contributing to service provision: bodies composed of councillors not directly elected to them but nominated by their respective councils.

Then in addition there is a welter of other organisations that nowadays are likely to be involved in the governance of a community: none directly elected, many with no elective element at all. These too are very big business indeed, though even their precise numbers, let alone their financial significance, are not easy to determine. An early and authoritative study of the so-called 'quango state' (Democratic Audit, 1994, p. 36) estimated their spending on local services at well over half of the total spent by elected local government, and, with the more recent arrival of action zones and a plethora of different forms of service partnerships, the proportion has certainly not declined. These bodies have changed hugely in some cases the way in which local government services are managed and delivered, and they merit therefore separate treatment in Chapter 8, specifically on local governance. First, though, we look, in the remainder of this chapter, at the services themselves.

A classification of services – Britain's particularity

We have sought so far in this chapter to re-emphasise the importance of adopting a balanced perspective when assessing local government's present-day responsibilities – as we did when introducing our funnel of local authority discretion in Chapter 2. It is true that in Britain local government rests on a constitutionally weaker base than it does in many European countries; also that its scope and freedom of action have been significantly reduced in recent years as the result of national government policy. It is also the case, however, that local authorities are still unusually large, diverse organisations with large budgets, big workforces, and responsibility for literally hundreds of different services.

Exhibit 7.1 Who does what? Main service responsibilities of UK local authorities

	Metropolitan/London authorities				Shire/Unitary authorities		
	Metrop. districts	Joint authorities	London boroughs	GLA	County councils	District councils	Unitary authorities
Education including schools, youth service, adult education, under-5s	*		*		*		*
Housing including renovation, redevelopment, homeless persons	*		*			*	*
Social services including residential and community care	*		*		*		*
Highways including traffic regulation, road safety, on-street parking	*		*	*	*		*
Passenger transport	*	*	*	*	*		*
Strategic/structure planning	*		*	*	*		*
Local planning/development control	*		*			*	*
Fire and rescue including road accidents, safety inspection and certification	*	*		*	*		*
Libraries	*		*		*		*
Museums, galleries	*		*		*	*	*
Leisure/recreation including arts, leisure centres, playing fields, parks	*		*			*	*
Waste collection	*		*			*	*
Waste disposal	*	*	*		*		*
Consumer protection	*		*		*		*
Environmental health including food safety, pollution control, Agenda 21	*		*			*	*
Council tax collection	*		*			*	*

Cautionary note: This table is presented as a guide to usual practice. We have deliberately not complicated it with a string of detailed and technical footnotes. For details of how any particular service is provided in your area, go to the web site(s) of your own council(s)

As we shall show in more detail in Chapter 11, our local authorities are in fact much larger than those in virtually any other European country – larger in terms of their populations, but not necessarily so in the range of services they provide. In this respect, it is better to see them simply as different. British local authorities, for instance, are exceptional in *not* having direct responsibility for hospitals and preventive health services, which are of course provided through the entirely separate institutions of our National Health Service (NHS). Most social assistance benefits are administered in this country through the Department for Work and Pensions, rather than by municipalities, as is the common European practice.

But if our health and social services have been less institutionally integrated than in much of continental Europe, our education system has perhaps been more so. Education has been by far the biggest spender in British local government, because an education-providing local authority – known as a Local Education Authority (LEA) – has in fact provided almost all education services, from the building of schools, the employment of teachers, through to the books and pencils. In much of southern and central Europe local authorities provide and maintain the premises, but the national government employs the teachers. Frequently too responsibility for primary and secondary, or at least higher secondary, schools is split between different tiers of local authorities. In the United States and Canada many schools are run by elected special authorities or boards.

Exhibit 7.2 A categorisation of local services

1. Need services – eg education, personal social services, housing benefit.
    Services provided for all, regardless of means, and which therefore contribute to the redistribution of resources within the community.

2. Protective services – eg fire and rescue, and, until the creation of independent police authorities in 1995, the police.
    Services provided for the security of people, to national guidelines. Access to them cannot be restricted, and use by one person does not affect availability to others.

3. Amenity services – eg highways, street cleansing, planning, parks and open spaces, environmental health, refuse disposal, consumer protection, economic development.
    Services provided largely to locally determined standards to meet the needs of each local community.

4. Facility services – eg housing, libraries, museums and art galleries, recreational centres, refuse collection, cemeteries and crematoria.
    Services for people to draw on if they wish, sometimes in competition with private sector provision.

Another sphere in which Britain is now the exception is in provision of public utilities. In almost all other European countries municipalities retain responsibility for providing one or more of water, electricity and gas supply – all of them local government services in this country until the nationalisation legislation of the 1940s and privatisation in the 1980s. Today even the right to local authority representation is restricted to Scottish water authorities. British policing, on the other hand, has historically been and remains today more localised than in many countries. In Scandinavia, the Netherlands, Australia and New Zealand it is not a local function, whereas, even on the post-1995 independent police authorities, there is still majority local councillor representation.

These cross-national differences are worth keeping in mind as we deal briefly with the major local government services. We shall follow, partly for the sake of convenience, the fourfold classification summarised in Exhibit 7.2. This means starting with 'need services', which account in Britain for over half of total net local government spending, reflecting the role of councils as deliverers of major parts of our welfare state. In other countries, 'amenity services', for instance, might well feature more prominently.

Need services – for all of us, regardless of means

Education – the declining role of the LEA

The basis of our modern education system was the Education Act 1944, which, in a most significant clause, required the Minister/Secretary of State for Education:

> to secure the effective execution by local authorities, under his control and direction, of national policy for providing a varied and comprehensive educational system in the area.

Note the division of responsibilities. Central government legislated and set the national policy framework, the minister being answerable to Parliament for its overall implementation. But the actual provision, staffing, and running of schools were to be in the hands of local councils – Local Education Authorities. These LEAs, in the absence of any further guidance, were free to decide for themselves what pattern of schools constituted a 'varied and comprehensive system'.

For a long time there was no further guidance. Most LEAs ran 'selective' systems, using an '11-plus' examination to allocate pupils variously to grammar, secondary modern, and technical schools. Other authorities, though – most notably Leicestershire – introduced their own non-selective variations, years before Labour governments tried, first in 1965 by persuasion, then in 1976 by legislation, to establish universal 'comprehensive' secondary education. Margaret Thatcher's incoming Conservative Government in 1979 reversed the policy, and the outcome is the mixed system we have today. There are still 166 'selective' grammar schools in some 28 LEAs – most notably, Birmingham, Trafford, Kent, Ripon, and the London boroughs of Barnet and Sutton – while the rest of England, and the whole of Wales, is comprehensive.

Following that 1979 legislation there was an average of at least one Education Act each year during the 1980s and 1990s: enough to justify a funnel of diminishing discretion for education on its own. This legislative onslaught profoundly altered the role of councils – the English counties, London and metropolitan boroughs, and the unitaries – in their capacity as LEAs. They lost control altogether of polytechnics, Colleges and Institutes of Higher Education, sixth-form and further education colleges, most of which have become self-governing corporations, while their role in the management of schools was dramatically reduced.

The keynote legislation was the massive Education Reform Act 1988. It brought in the national curriculum, with its core and foundation subjects and pupil-testing against attainment targets, the results of which are now published in school performance league tables. It introduced Local Management of Schools (LMS), requiring LEAs to pass on or delegate at least 85 per cent of their education budget to the governors of schools, who thus became responsible for overseeing the running of their school and its financial operation. Even more controversially, it enabled schools, through a parental ballot, to 'opt-out' of the control of their LEA and be funded instead, as 'grant-maintained' (GM) schools, directly by central government, which then re-charged the cost to the LEA.

These parental ballots were the chosen instrument for what Conservative ministers anticipated would be an educational revolution, with the great majority of the country's 24,500 schools voting enthusiastically to sever all connections with their LEAs. But it was a revolution that never really took off. By 1998, when GM status was abolished, there had been just 1,196 'opt-outs', or less than 5 per cent of all state schools. However, although LEAs continued to maintain the other 95 per cent, their powers had been significantly reduced – partly through LMS and, so that there could be no misunderstanding about it, also in the wording of the legislation. Gone was the ministerial/LEA partnership of the 1944 Act. By the time of the 1993 Education Act, the Secretary of State had the duty of promoting the education of the people of England and Wales, while LEAs received no mention at all.

The 1997 Labour Government changed many aspects of education administration, but LEAs' increasing subordination to the Secretary of State (now for both Education and Employment) was not one of them. In fact, an education bill was drafted, containing a notorious 'clause zero' that would have swept LEAs away altogether (Smith, 1999). The eventual legislation was substantially redrafted, and education remains for the present an enormously important service for those local authorities responsible for it, but that responsibility no longer includes much involvement in day-to-day school management. The LEA provides and maintains school premises, organises certain further education and youth services, passes on funding to school governing bodies, and ensures that schools follow the national curriculum.

Among the many measures introduced in Labour's first comprehensive education legislation, the School Standards and Framework Act 1998, was a recategorisation of schools. County schools – those established by the LEA itself – became 'community schools'. Controlled or aided schools –

Exhibit 7.3 The future of secondary state education – specialist schools, selection and private sector management?

Specialist schools – first introduced in 1986, as City Technology Colleges (CTCs), by the Conservative Government. Conceived specifically for urban areas, CTCs would have an emphasis on technology, science and maths, would be independent of their LEAs, open to all pupils, and funded partly by central government and partly by private industrial and commercial sponsors. This latter funding proved much less accessible than had been hoped, and only 15 CTCs were created, instead of a projected 200.

Labour's version – extends possible specialisms to include languages, sport, the performing arts, engineering, science, business and enterprise, and introduces selection of up to 10 per cent of pupils at age of 11. The Government's green paper (2000) envisages 1,000 specialist schools by 2003 and 1,500 by 2006 – equal to 40 per cent of the maintained sector, which, say critics, would inevitably create a two-tier secondary system and, in effect, 'selection by mortgage'.

An early example of the future?

Runnymede Business and Enterprise College, Addlestone, Surrey.
Created out of a former comprehensive school by Conservative-controlled Surrey County Council, who negotiated a 7–year 'partnership' contract with a private company, Nord Anglia. Nord Anglia's early school management record was mixed: success was claimed in Doncaster and Westminster, but the company was criticised by school inspectors in Hackney. The council agrees to invest in new building and pay Nord Anglia a management fee plus bonuses for improved academic results, reduced exclusions, and an increase in parental first preference choices.

Key source: *The Guardian*, 24 May 2001.

usually established by an Anglican or Free Church, with the LEA meeting, respectively, all or some of their running costs – are now 'voluntary controlled' or 'voluntary aided'. GM schools, their maintenance now returned to their LEA, mostly became 'foundation' or 'voluntary aided'.

Much more contentiously – for a party previously committed to the principles of comprehensive education – the 1998 Act also made provision for increasing the selection of secondary school pupils. Selective 'grammar schools' would be permitted to continue, unless successfully challenged in, once again, a parental ballot. Two forms of ballot were involved, both generally acknowledged to be weighted against potential 'abolitionists': 'area ballots' of all parents resident in an area, and 'feeder school ballots' of parents of children in schools that had transferred at least five pupils to the grammar school over the previous three years.

For non-grammar schools the 1998 Act introduced the concept of 'permitted selection'. Drawing a somewhat Byzantine distinction between selection by 'ability' and by 'aptitude', the Act enabled a school claiming a specialism for a particular subject – technology, the arts, language, sports – to select up to 10 per cent of its pupil intake by their aptitude for that subject. As Exhibit 7.3 indicates, the re-elected Labour Government sees such specialist schools as representing the future of state secondary education – together with a steadily increasing role for private sector management.

Personal social services – from residential to community care

The key emphasis here is on *services*, for, as noted in Chapter 2, in the United Kingdom, most cash payments to the needy and vulnerable are made not by local government but by the Department of Work and Pensions Jobcentre Plus local offices. Local authorities, frequently working nowadays with and through voluntary and private organisations, are responsible for services to the elderly, people with learning difficulties, people with mental health problems, children, young people, and families considered to be at risk. Services provided include residential care, day care, help – such as meals, laundry, home modifications, practical aids – to enable people to remain in their own homes, one-to-one counselling, fostering and adoption, and child protection.

Like teachers, social workers live nowadays with both the continuous pressure of new legislative demands and public expectations and the seemingly inexorable squeeze on available resources. Both groups too have become used to the exceptional case that propels one or two unfortunate individuals, a single institution or department, and indirectly the whole profession, into the glare of national media headlines. For teachers it can be the allegedly 'failing school', singled out by the Secretary of State as in need of naming and shaming. For social workers it can be an even more tragic case involving the failure of child protection and the ensuing investigations into either inadequate or misguidedly zealous professional behaviour. Such cases are obviously atypical, which is why they attract the attention they do. But the very depth of their coverage, especially if they result in an official inquiry report, can reveal a great deal about the day-to-day operations of the relevant council departments.

Residential care has been and continues to be at the very heart of the work of any social services authority, but the emphasis has been gradually shifting towards domiciliary and community care, particularly since the NHS and Community Care Act 1990. This legislation represents the most striking example in recent years of local authorities having new responsibilities thrust upon them, rather than taken away. Social services departments became responsible for assessing all requests for residential and nursing home care where public funding is sought, for assessing people's overall needs, and co-ordinating the appropriate service provision. They are also required to produce, working closely with NHS authorities, annual Community Care plans evaluating how effectively the resources of various organisations and sectors are being used in meeting the diverse needs of local people.

The government's vision – naturally enough for one proclaiming a concern for 'joined-up' policy making – is of a single, integrated health and social care system, and this will be the theme of many future developments. There will be more legislation affecting both the NHS and local authority social services – like the Care Standards Act 2000, reforming the regulatory system for care services in England and Wales. There will be more joint appointments, at both local and regional level, more informal joint-working and budget-pooling arrangements – a notable example being ministers' decision in 2001 to by-pass the NHS and pay money direct to councils to avert a winter 'bed-blocking' crisis by creating additional care places in the community.

Protective services – for our security

Police service – increasing detachment

Until 1985 policing in the United Kingdom was very much a local authority service, with forces based predominantly on the counties. Except in London – where the Metropolitan Police reported directly to the Home Secretary until in 2000 they became the responsibility of the new Greater London Authority (GLA) – chief constables were accountable to the police committees of county councils: similar to other council committees, apart from their memberships which comprised two-thirds councillors and one-third local magistrates.

The Police and Magistrates Courts Act 1994 changed the role and function of police authorities by establishing them as independent authorities, with considerably enhanced powers over their own service provision, and very much more independent of and detached from their respective councils. Their composition usually now comprises nine councillors, three magistrates, and five co-opted Home Office nominees – a bare elective majority, but indirectly rather than directly elected, and the local government interest has become generally the weakest link in the 'tripartite structure' of central government, local government, and chief constable (Loveday, 1996). They are still dependent on local government for the actual collection of their revenue, and we shall see in Chapter 10 how police authorities levy what is known as a 'precept', which councils are required to include in the council tax bills they send out to their residents. When determining their local Policing Objectives, though, it is consistency with the Home Secretary's national objectives that they will observe first, rather than conformity with policies of their local councils.

Fire and rescue service

It was not until the late 1930s that fire brigades joined police forces as a statutory arm of local authorities' protective provision. Since then the police have come to prefer us to see them less as a force and more as a service, while fire authorities are concerned to emphasise that they do much more than merely fight fires. Understandably enough, for they also nowadays have to deal with road traffic accidents, chemical spillages, and personal (as well as kitty) rescue. They have important emergency planning and fire safety promotional responsibilities, and they contribute to local government's monitoring and regulatory role through their fire certification of shops, offices, factories and hotels.

Amenity services – for our community needs

Highways, transportation and traffic management

This is perhaps the most shared of all public services, covering as it does everything from motorways to bridleways and involving all levels of government from the Department for Transport, Local Government and the Regions (DTLR) to parish councils. The Secretary of State is responsible for trunk road and motorways, with decisions often being taken in the relevant regional office and most maintenance contracted out by the Highways Agency, an executive agency acting on the minister's behalf. The counties, unitaries and metropolitan districts, and in London the boroughs and the GLA, have responsibility for other primary and secondary roads. 'Responsibility' here includes the design of routes, taking into account cost, environmental impact, residential and industrial needs and safety; road building, improvement and maintenance; highway management, including parking restrictions, speed limits, street lighting, traffic signs, street cleaning and litter collection; winter maintenance and road safety. In practice, however, 'agency agreements' are common, and several of the above functions are likely in two-tier areas to be carried out by district councils.

The government's priority in its second term of office will be to progress towards its elusive integrated and sustainable transport policy, and particularly to increase the use of public transport. As in other policy areas, therefore, councils will produce plans – in this instance, Local Transport Plans – to include initiatives on road user and congestion charging, bus quality partnerships, traffic management and calming, and improving air quality.

Planning and development

This is another responsibility shared, where appropriate, between the different tiers of local government. There are in fact two principal planning roles: forward or strategic planning and development control. *Strategic planning* is the process through which local authorities decide how they would like their area as a whole to develop over, say, the next 15 years. Structure plans are drawn up, after extensive consultations, by county councils, local plans by district councils, and in unitary authorities the two are combined in a unitary plan. These plans allocate areas of land for future housing, industrial, commercial and leisure developments, taking into account national and local policies for protecting the environment. Housing allocations are likely to be especially contentious, with developers wanting more generous provision of green-field sites and the council, backed by local residential and environmental pressure groups, usually preferring more 'brown-field' redevelopment. Governments too have their own, not always consistent, views on these matters, and the Secretary of State has the power to 'call-in' a structure plan for modification or rejection.

Development control is where councils respond, usually on the basis of the relevant development plans, to applications for planning consent to make a material change in the use of existing land or buildings or to carry out physical development such as the construction, adaptation or demolition of buildings. Planning authorities are expected to respond to applications within two months, uncontentious cases being normally delegated to officers, with more controversial and complex developments determined by the council's planning committee – one of the so-called 'regulatory' committees which will continue in existence even after councils' adoption of their new executive arrangements. Various responses are available to the council – from unconditional consent, through conditional or outline consent, to refusal – a disappointed applicant having the right of appeal to a planning inspector appointed by the Secretary of State and ultimately to the High Court.

Environmental health and consumer protection

This is one of the oldest local government services, in that the modern system of borough and district councils grew out of the local boards of health and sanitary authorities set up under the Public Health Acts of the 1870s. Local government lost most of its health functions in 1948 and 1974, with the establishment and reorganisation of the NHS, leaving it 'only' with environmental health. But, as shown in Exhibit 7.4, this responsibility still gives councils far greater health promotion and disease prevention potential than any other institution, including the NHS.

Such is the comprehensiveness of councils' environmental health responsibilities that in the previous editions of this book we produced an A–Z of these services alone – from abandoned vehicles via dog fouling and tree preservation to zoo licensing (Wilson and Game, 1998, p. 26). The full list involves all those functions of inspection, regulation, registration, licensing and certification that tend to go relatively unnoticed until there is a food contamination crisis, a dangerous dogs scare, or the suspected importation of some infectious disease.

In addition, therefore, to waste collection and street cleaning – two of the few services that most of us, without prompting, can associate with local councils – there is the inspecting of premises selling and preparing food; investigating outbreaks of infectious diseases and carrying out checks at ports; control, of air, water and noise pollution, assessing over-crowding and premises unfit for human habitation; health and safety inspections of commercial and industrial premises; licensing of sex shops, riding stables, kennels, gaming machines, taxis and private hire vehicles; and pest control.

Economic development

Look at some councils' web sites and you could almost get the impression that – with their business parks and industrial estates, commercial property files, relocation grants, advisory and support services – economic development and business promotion are their principal activities. Their importance would also seem to be confirmed by councils' new well-being power – to promote the *economic*, social and environmental well-being of their area. In fact, though, explicit statutory recognition of councils' key role in economic development dates back only to the Local Government and Housing Act 1989, and it is a role that, even more than most, involves

Exhibit 7.4 If this isn't health care, what is?

Health care in Britain today is the responsibility of the NHS, not local councils?

No! Not unless you define health care only in the narrow and negative sense of treating illness. If you define it more positively as improving environmental conditions and the general quality of life, local authorities have always been centrally involved. In the 19th Century they led the public health revolution – reducing infectious diseases, improving housing and sanitation, providing public washing facilities, introducing gas lighting. They play an equivalent role today through their various environmental health responsibilities – food safety and hygiene, sanitation, waste management, housing standards, occupational health and safety.

Does central government recognise this positive health care contribution?

Yes, apparently. Local authorities' new 'power of well-being' – to promote the economic, social and environmental well-being of their area – confirms and reinforces the role of sickness prevention and health promotion.

Do local authorities recognise it?

Oh yes – and in many cases did not need the reminder of the Local Government Act 2000.

Some examples:

Adur DC's Child Home Safety project – council works with West Sussex Health Authority's Health Promotion Department to provide child safety equipment for children at risk of accidental injury in families unable to afford the purchase cost.

Brent LBC's Hospital Discharge Team – council takes pro-active approach to discharge planning by ensuring that hospitals refer directly to its Discharge Team all Brent residents who require either community-based services or permanent residential care.

Crewe & Nantwich BC's Health Development Officer – works with a range of partners – GPs, hospital dietetics and physiotherapy departments, Crewe Women's Aid, the Stroke Association – to encourage individuals from target groups to take part in leisure and exercise activities. Hospital midwives trained in ante-natal aqua-aerobics provide weekly sessions at borough's swimming pools.

Darlington BC's Before/After Group for young mothers – council's social services and education departments work with local Primary Care Trust and other agencies to meet the ante- and post-natal needs of pregnant schoolgirls who are not attending school and are not in touch with other services.

Key source: SOLACE, *Healthy Living: The Role of Modern Local Authorities in Creating Healthy Communities* (2001).

working closely in partnership with both the private sector and other bodies – chambers of commerce and trade, learning and skills councils, and, probably increasingly in the future, Regional Development Agencies. It will remain, however, a permissive or discretionary responsibility, rather than mandatory, and an interesting non-financial test of a council's seriousness is likely to continue to be the number of languages into which this particular part of its web site is translated – Hampshire having set the early pace with both Russian and Japanese.

Facility services – for all of us, if we wish

Housing – the last chapter?

If we were dealing with services not by functional categorisation but in order of their historic importance to local government, housing would have featured pages ago. In terms of its future importance, however, towards the end of the list may well be the most appropriate place, for some housing experts predict that the council home – one of the integral features of our post-war welfare state – will have virtually disappeared by about 2015. Two major government policies will have been responsible for this development: the Conservatives' 'right to buy' legislation in the 1980s, and the large-scale housing transfers initiated by the Conservatives but accelerated by New Labour.

The 1957 Housing Act made it a duty of local housing authorities to consider local housing conditions and to provide any further housing required – either by building it themselves or by buying, converting and improving existing properties. Two decades later the nation's council housing stock comprised nearly 7 million dwellings. Then in 1980 the incoming Thatcher Government's Housing Act gave council tenants the right to buy their homes at discounts of up to 70 per cent, depending on their length of tenancy. Labour councils opposed the policy and sought to resist it, concerned at the reduced housing stock that would be left available for people unable to rent privately, but they could be forced to comply. If the Secretary of State believed that a council was not allowing tenants their statutory right to buy their homes, a housing commissioner could be sent in – as happened in Clay Cross – to take over the sales process and charge the cost to the council. The 'right to buy' legislation was extended in 1988, and by the mid-1990s well over 2 million former council homes were in private ownership – the number continuing to increase by an annual rate of some 60,000 since then.

Councils also, of course, have responsibilities for repairing and maintaining their housing stock. But, as governments increasingly restricted both the revenue spending and capital borrowing of local authorities, large

Exhibit 7.5 LSVTs – the end of council housing?

LSVTs – what are they?

Large-scale voluntary transfers: they allow councils to transfer ownership and control of their homes to 'registered social landlords' (RSLs) – principally housing associations or local housing companies – provided the tenants of the homes involved vote in favour of the plan.

Why are even Labour councils willing to transfer their housing stocks?

To raise the capital investment needed to deal with a repairs and renovation backlog estimated nationally at £20 billion. Successive national governments have prohibited local authorities from borrowing money against their assets in order to undertake necessary repairs and maintenance, and RSLs are the most acceptable alternative. Instead of relaxing borrowing restrictions, the 1997 Labour Government actively encouraged wholesale transfers by agreeing to write off poor boroughs' accumulated housing debts.

So everybody's now doing it?

Yes. It started with mainly Conservative councils, but by 2001 more than 100 English councils had sold off all their homes under stock transfers – nearly 600,000 in total. Most of these transfers were to housing associations set up by the councils themselves – emphasising the 'voluntary' nature of the process – often with councillors making up a third of the new management board.

Now the biggest council landlords of all have become involved – Glasgow (94,000 homes and a repairs backlog of £1.2 billion), Birmingham (88,000 and £1 billion), Bradford, Liverpool, Sheffield (controlled by the Liberal Democrats). The government has a plan to transfer 200,000 homes p.a. – double the last Conservative government figure – and immediately after the 2001 election granted permission for 27 councils to ballot tenants on plans to transfer 328,000 homes. If the government's plans are met, RSL homes will soon outnumber those under council control, and by 2015 there will be very few indeed of the latter left.

Will this happen?

Maybe not completely. Ministers might relax their restrictions on council borrowing. And there is frequently strong opposition from both tenants and some councillors to stock transfers. The policy is seen as an irreversible, undemocratic, centrally directed piece of social engineering, that will benefit banks and building societies, consultants and surveyors, architects and builders, but will weaken tenants' rights and lead to higher rents. Several early tenants' ballots were lost, and the number could easily grow.

Key source: M. Weaver (2001).

backlogs of repairs began to build up. Rather than allowing councils to borrow the funding required to deal with these backlogs themselves, governments preferred the transfer approach. The Housing Act 1988 introduced 'tenants' choice', allowing new landlords – notably housing associations who were permitted, unlike councils, to raise private finance – to take over council housing following a ballot of tenants: a ballot whose rules were weighted heavily against the local authority. On a larger scale, the Secretary of State had powers to designate an area as a Housing Action Trust (HAT) – e.g. Castle Vale in Birmingham, Stonebridge in Brent – provided again that a majority of voted to opt-out of local authority ownership and management. Six of these HATs were set up: quangos that took over the local authority's housing and its accompanying repair and management functions.

250,000 council homes were transferred to housing associations in the decade to 1997, and they were quickly becoming the main providers of new housing for rent. The really large-scale council landlords, however, were by this time all Labour-controlled metropolitan and big city councils, whose leaders hoped that an incoming Labour government would relax borrowing controls and allow them to tackle their own repair backlogs. In fact, as we see in Exhibit 7.5, ministers encouraged instead large-scale voluntary transfers (LSVTs) which, unless reversed by the 2001 Government, are likely to result in the eventual disappearance of council housing as we have known it.

Libraries

Public libraries have been provided by local councils for over 150 years – although not until 1919 were they permitted to spend significant amounts of money actually filling them with books. In recent years, ironically, there has been no statutory limit on spending, but the limits in practice can never have been tighter. Libraries have been closed, opening hours cut, bookfunds slashed, and, not surprisingly, our usage of libraries and borrowing from them has correspondingly declined. Notwithstanding these trends, however, some 10 million of us still do visit libraries at least once a fortnight – which makes it one of several of those leisure pursuits that is more popular than attending football matches.

There are also signs that the electronic revolution, far from diminishing the role of libraries, has the capacity to enhance it. Labelled 'street corner universities' by Labour's first Culture Secretary, Chris Smith, they have a contribution to make to several of the government's key objectives: life-long learning, delivering public services online, combatting social exclusion, fostering neighbourhood renewal, and increasing our on-line access to the treasures of national and international museums. Book-lending will remain important, but alongside their expanding roles as information, reference and resource centres, as specialist service providers for schools, the blind and partially sighted, hospitals, ethnic minorities, and as community cultural and arts centres. They will also, it is worth noting, continue to receive and display details of council services, copies of agendas and reports, information on council meeting times and contact numbers and addresses for councillors.

Leisure, arts and recreation

Perhaps appropriately, these last services are the most discretionary of those we have addressed. All the others have discretionary aspects to them – different councils according them differing priorities, providing services in differing ways, with differing standards of efficiency. But most of the legislation concerning leisure and recreation is *empowering* rather than mandatory. Councils *may* provide museums and art galleries; they *may* contribute to provision by other authorities; they *may* establish orchestras, concert halls, promote tourism, and provide all manner of sports and leisure facilities. As a citizen, this discretion can prove frustrating, if you happen to live in an authority with relatively modest standards of provision, or one that imposes high charges for use of its facilities. As a student of local government, however, you can learn a great deal about a council's political, social and cultural values from its scale and patterns of leisure expenditure.

Conclusion – more sharing of the local turf

This inevitably somewhat breathless overview of local authority services rounds off appropriately, we feel, a chapter that began with our emphasising councils' continuing role as large-scale service providers. Almost all of the services we have mentioned have undergone significant transformation during the past few years. In some cases the council's former largely exclusive role is being shared with a range of other providers. Almost everywhere there is acute consciousness of financial constraint and the pressure of government-fostered competition. But in no instance – at least yet – can it really be suggested that councils as a whole are no longer playing a leading role in service determination and delivery. As Davis puts it, the balance and much of the detail have certainly changed and will equally certainly change further, but the 'traditional' picture is still recognisable:

it has never been the case that local authorities have exercised all governmental powers in any particular locality. Others have always been involved but, in the past, local authorities confidently saw themselves as the rightful and undisputed leaders of their communities. Now their position is under challenge as they find themselves sharing the local 'turf' with a whole range of bodies also exercising governmental powers at the local level. (Davis, 1996, p. 1).

Guide to further reading

Young and Rao (1997) provide a good historical overview of the major local government services, while Fenney (2000) has the most up-to-date account and one which, as an exam text for trainee journalists, is information-packed and regularly revised. Most textbooks can afford space for only brief references to individual services, whereas all major councils, and therefore quite probably your own, will have their own A–Z of services on their web sites. A surf around a few of these is now by far the best way of developing a sense of just what councils do and how they work.

Chapter 8

Governance and Partnership

Introduction – a crowded pitch, but it's not all over

Chapter 7 outlined the functions of local authorities, many of which are now carried out in partnership with private sector and not-for-profit organisations or other public bodies. This chapter further develops the themes of governance and partnership. It emphasises that elected local government is but one – albeit unique – part of a complex mosaic of organisations concerned with what is now widely known as local governance. There are also housing associations, further education colleges and foundation schools, health authorities, primary care groups, learning and skills councils, police authorities, action zones, partnerships – none of which are directly elected and thereby electorally accountable. Davis (1996) used the metaphor of local authorities getting used to 'sharing the turf'. Tony Blair's image, perhaps with the private sector more prominently in mind, is a bit more aggressive (1998, p. 10): 'There are all sorts of players on the local pitch jostling for position where previously the local council was the main game in town.' Unlike the conclusion of Kenneth Wolstenholme's immortal 1966 World Cup Final commentary, however, this pitch invasion does not signal that 'it's all over' for elected local government – simply that there have been some rather extensive changes in the rules of engagement. This chapter will map and evaluate these changing rules, and the world of policy networks, partnerships, and the ubiquitous quango.

The local quangocracy – mapping the five thousand

The Conservative years saw not only a reduction in the number of elected local authorities, but also the rapid growth of non-elected or indirectly elected bodies at the expense of directly elected councils. As summarised by Weir and Beetham in their 'democratic audit of Great Britain' (1999, pp. 251–2):

> The local quango state is now extensive and has taken over or usurped the role of local authorities in providing many services. In social housing, the Housing Corporation has taken control of most new housing investment from local authorities. It also oversees the local

133

housing associations which have become the main channel for investment in new social housing programmes locally ... A handful of housing action trusts have replaced local housing department management on some public housing estates. In education, grant-maintained schools have been removed from local authority control ...; all further education colleges, formerly run by local authorities, have been merged and transformed into quangos; polytechnics have moved from local authority control to become universities within the province of the Higher Education Funding Council; the school careers service has been taken out of local government and passed on to private companies. In planning, 12 urban development corporations were created in England to take over planning in inner-city areas ... Employment services were developed outside local authority control, through training and enterprise councils (TECs) and their Scottish equivalents, local enterprise companies (LECs) ... Local authorities lost their representatives on health authority boards; and their role on the new police authorities was further diminished.

These new associations, councils, companies, corporations, boards and trusts are all differently structured and have different working practices. But they are all bodies appointed directly or indirectly by central government, performing functions and providing services that were, until quite recently, provided mainly or exclusively by local authorities. They thus bypass local authorities and may well come into conflict with them. They add greatly to the complexity of sub-central government, and also increase the influence of their respective 'sponsoring' departments at local level – especially useful if local political control happens to differ from that at the centre. They are in a sense agents for the centre, or, as Weir and Beetham describe them, 'government's flexible friends' (1999, p. 196). Collectively, they have come to be known as 'the local quango state'.

'Quango' itself is a flexible term, definable in a multitude of ways, depending on whether the political objective is to minimise or maximise the count. Governments are minimisers, especially if they come into power like New Labour, vacuously promising 'to sweep away the quango state' (Skelcher *et al.*, 2000, p. 13). Auditors of democracy tend to be maximisers. As suggested in Exhibit 8.1, we are quite relaxed about detailed definitions, provided they embrace all those 'unelected local bodies spending public money' referred to in the previous few paragraphs.

Such definitions would at almost any time over the past decade have produced a rough total of around 5,000 local quangos in the United Kingdom. The most systematic attempt at mapping them all has been that of the House of Commons Public Administration Select Committee, whose Chairman is in the privileged position of being able to fill in any gaps by putting Parliamentary Questions to Ministers. Even the Committee

Exhibit 8.1 One thousand or five thousand – what is a quango?

We have already mentioned 'quangos' in passing, and Chapter 8 contains a lot more about them, but here seems an appropriate point for an early definition.

What is a quango?

An acronym of Quasi-Autonomous Non-Governmental Organisation.

Which means?

You can get the idea from the Cabinet Office's Quango Website:

> a body which has a role in the processes of *national* government, but is not a government department or part of one, and which accordingly operates at arm's length from Ministers (emphasis ours).

This, of course, is an official definition, used by national governments keen to minimise the scale of unelected, and electorally unaccountable, government. According to the Cabinet Office, in 2001 just over 1,000 bodies in the United Kingdom fitted this definition, and are known officially as Non-Departmental Public Bodies (NDPBs). They spend a total of just £24 million and their appointed board members total about 30,000.

An alternative, and more useful, definition

The House of Commons Public Administration Select Committee uses, in *Mapping the Quango State* (House of Commons, 2001), a much wider, and locally much more useful, definition:

> [any body] responsible for developing, managing or delivering public services or policies, or for performing public functions, under governing bodies with a plural membership of wholly or largely appointed or self-appointing persons.

This definition enabled the Committee to map a 'local quango state' of well over 5,000 'Local Public Spending Bodies' (LPSBs), spending more in £billions than NDPBs spend in £millions.

Without the pedantry

For a definition similar to the Committee's but in comprehensible English, see Charter 88's website:

> unelected bodies spending public money.

That's it!

Exhibit 8.2 The local quango state in Great Britain, April 2000

Further education institutions	511
Foundation schools (ex-GM and voluntary-aided schools)	877
City technology colleges	15
Learning and skills councils (replaced TECs in 2000)	47
Local enterprise and careers service companies (Scotland)	39
Registered social landlords	2,421
Housing action trusts	4
Police authorities	49
Health authorities/boards	114
NHS trusts	387
Primary care groups/trusts	488
TOTAL	**4,952**

Source: House of Commons Select Committee on Public Administration, *Fifth Report, 2000/01: Mapping the Quango State.*

confused in places its boards, councils and companies, but Exhibit 8.2, summarising the Committee's findings, is probably as accurate a depiction of the local quango state as was possible in April 2000.

The 5,000 or so local quangos are run by well over 60,000 mainly ministerially-appointed or self-appointed 'quangocrats', making almost three quangocrats for every councillor. Earlier Democratic Audit reports had expressed concern at the scale of this new 'local magistracy', at the arbitrary and partisan way in which quango board members were appointed, and at the serious deficiencies in the accountability and openness of many boards. The Major Government established the Nolan Committee on Standards in Public Life and set in motion a gradual reform process. But, as noted above, New Labour promised to go much further and unleash a 'quango cull'. In fact, new quangos continued to be created – not least the English Regional Development Agencies and new Welsh and Scottish bodies following devolution.

Within a year, therefore – in the foreword to the Cabinet Office paper, *Quangos: Opening the Doors* – the culling goal had been modified to one of minimising the growth of what, in office, Labour had come to see as important and appropriate instruments of government:

> Quangos perform important functions, but we will continue to scrutinise all proposals for new bodies to ensure that they are only set up where this is the most appropriate and cost-effective means of carrying out functions. We are committed to keeping the number to the minimum necessary. (Cabinet Office, 1998a)

So it all depends on how you define 'necessary' – and local government's definition tends to be more restrictive than has been that of Labour ministers. As Skelcher *et al.* show, the Quango State has continued to advance (2000, p. 5):

> Labour ministers are expanding the role of quangos, at national, regional and local levels ... at local level, a wide range of indeterminate appointed and self-appointing bodies are being added to existing 'local public spending bodies' and similar quasi-public bodies. These new quasi-public bodies include regeneration and other partnerships, the boards of education and housing zones, health and care trusts, and learning and skills councils.

They know not what they do, Skelcher and his colleagues charitably conclude. Even so, the consequences may be profound (2000, p. 5):

> We suspect that ministers do not appreciate the consequences for local democracy and elected government at local level of this expansion of quasi-governance ... But the cumulative effects are draining away the powers and functions of elected local government and vastly complicating its ability to coordinate the delivery of public services locally. For local communities and citizens, for whom the local town hall is the natural focus for inquiries, requests, complaints or demands concerning public services and duties, the uncoordinated plethora of public bodies are in effect out of reach.

No one would seriously dispute the assertion that quangos perform important functions and can do so effectively. They can bring valuable experience and expertise into government, including sections of society under-represented through the local electoral system. They may be able to bring objectivity and a non-partisan perspective to the discussion of sensitive issues. Democrats would argue, though, that taking over whole areas of policy-making and service delivery from elected and accountable local authorities runs the risk of opening up a serious democratic deficit.

In addition to their members being elected, and thereby knowable by name and readily accessible to their constituents, local authorities conduct their business relatively openly and transparently. They produce annual reports, have their accounts annually audited, advertise their meetings, publish agendas, minutes and background papers, invite complaints, and keep registers of members' interests. They are also subject to extensive central direction, inspection and regulation. Many quangos, as the Commons Public Administration Select Committee found, are required and choose to do none of these things (House of Commons, 2001, Table 11). About half of their 5,000 local quangos did publish annual reports and agendas and minutes of their committee meetings. But only a fifth, for example, admitted the public to those meetings, or conformed to the government code of practice on access to information, or consulted with their local authorities regarding their plans and policies.

None of these democratic practices in themselves – not even direct election – guarantee efficient services. They are, though, rather likelier to produce effective, responsive and improvable services than bodies some of whose members, when interviewed by Skelcher and Davis (1996), seemed uncertain who they even represented:

> [Long pause] I've never actually been asked who I'm responsible to. [Long pause] It's an interesting question. [Pause] The community probably. [Pause] The people of the area. I do feel I'm trying to do something for them. Also, of course, I represent my company.

What is local governance?

For better or worse, then, local quangos have become integral parts of the world of local governance. But what exactly is local governance? A dozen years ago the term 'governance' carried no great theoretical meaning; if used at all, it was as a synonym for government. The 1990s, however, witnessed an explosion of interest in governance as a concept. It is particularly valuable as an organising framework which enables us understand better the *processes of governing*. Local governance brings together governmental and non-governmental agencies in flexible partnerships to deal with different problems by using different strategies. Local governance is not based on a single authority, the provision of a specialised service, or a new set of structures, but on a fusion of different styles and different working relationships. Flexibility of approach is central; given that the boundaries between public and private sectors have become increasingly obscured, the traditional hierarchical and bureaucratic styles of governing are no longer appropriate. This process of change and transformation is further developing under a Labour government committed to Best Value and enhanced community leadership. The agenda for the future will be to find new ways of working which cross organisational boundaries in the interests of the whole community.

Those who hoped that the election of a Labour government critical of the Quango State would bring a swift reduction in central intervention with councils regaining some of their lost responsibilities soon realised it was not about to materialise. Indeed, Tony Blair warned in 1998 (p. 20):

> The government will not hesitate to intervene directly to secure improvements where services fall below acceptable standards. And if necessary, it will look to other authorities and agencies to take on duties where an authority is manifestly incapable of providing an effective

service and unwilling to take the action necessary to improve its performance.

There was to be no return to local authorities being near-monopolistic service providers; provision would continue to be shared with a range of partners. In fact, Labour made its own contribution to the lexicon of public administration with its introduction of *zones*. The advent of Employment Zones, Health Action Zones and Education Action Zones clearly demonstrated the new government's commitment to working through the same mixed economy of local provision that had characterised the previous decade. In a similar vein was the establishment of an £800 million New Deal for Communities programme for the regeneration of some of the country's poorest housing estates. The 'Sure Start' project, designed to support pre-school children and their families also focused on the socially disadvantaged and involved co-operation between education, health and social service agencies. These and similar initiatives reflect the Labour government's desire to embrace collaboration between agencies as a way of joining up hitherto fragmented services to meet community needs more effectively. Indeed, the development of 'joined up', more integrated government was a central theme of the 1999 White Paper, *Modernising Government* (Cabinet Office, 1999).

Rhodes (1999b, p. xvii) offers a characteristically crisp, 'stipulative' definition of governance as referring to *self-organising, interorganisational* networks: a definition that can be broken down into four key characteristics (Box 8.1).

Elected local authorities have thus become but one part of a complex network of bodies involved in local service delivery. No longer, even in a

---

Box 8.1 Governance defined

1. *Interdependence between organisations.* Governance is broader than government, covering non-state actors. Changing the boundaries of the state meant that the boundaries between public, private and voluntary sectors became shifting and opaque.
2. *Continuing interactions between network members,* caused by the need to exchange resources and negotiate shared purposes.
3. *Game-like interactions,* rooted in trust and regulated by rules of the game negotiated and agreed by network participants.
4. A significant degree of *autonomy from the state.* Networks are not accountable to the state; they are self-organising. Although the state does occupy a privileged, sovereign position, it can only indirectly and imperfectly steer networks.

Source: Rhodes (1999b), p. xvii.

city like Birmingham with a so-called unitary council, is the organisation of government relatively straightforward and comprehensible. For, in addition to the City Council, you now have to take account of, among others: the separate police authority, several joint boards, health service trusts, primary care groups, a learning and skills council, a development corporation, regeneration partnerships and task forces, boards of further education colleges and foundation schools, housing associations, a Housing Action Trust, and a City Pride Board. The city council is involved in or with all of these bodies, but it no longer has the control over, or the direct responsibility for, service delivery that it would once have done.

Councils take their partners

There is an almost inevitable resentment felt by local authorities at their loss of services and the fragmentation of their previously direct policy influence. But this has not prevented many of them working closely and productively in partnership with some of the new quasi-governmental agencies and with private sector and voluntary organisations in their localities. Birmingham's own city centre regeneration programme is a large, but not exceptional, example. If European and, more recently, Millennium Commission funding have been essential, so too has been the partnership working with many of the city's most prominent companies and business organisations, as can be seen in Exhibit 8.3.

Indeed, almost paradoxically, during this period in which local authorities have faced serious financial and other legislative constraints, many have begun to assume, much more pro-actively than in the past, a broader leadership role in the community. As Stoker (1999a, p. 15) notes, economic development, urban regeneration, environmental protection, community safety and anti-crime measures, anti-poverty initiatives, preventative health care schemes and anti-domestic violence projects are among the areas where local authorities have taken forward the vision of community governance. Central government has encouraged such developments through giving local authorities particular responsibilities in areas such as environmental protection and in part through a series of funding schemes that enable local authorities to bid for monies in partnership with other stakeholders.

Partnerships and networks

The keys – at least in principle – to overcoming some of the problems associated with the new local governance, including the fragmentation mentioned above, are partnerships and networks. They come in many

Exhibit 8.3 Birmingham's Millennium Point: a large-scale public–private partnership

What is it? Birmingham's major millennium project and the landmark building of the city's Eastside regeneration – latest phase of its long-term city centre redevelopment programme. Opened both on time and on budget (unlike some millennium ventures), it is designed as a focal point for technology-based learning, research, commerce, study and leisure.

Main features:

- **Thinktank** – a multi-media interactive science and technology museum;
- **Technology Innovation Centre** – an international centre of excellence for technological research, run in conjunction with the University of Central England (UCE);
- **University of the First Age** – a unique experiment in learning for 11–14 year olds founded by the City Council's Chief Education Officer, Prof. Tim Brighouse. The UFA is itself a partnership between schools and their local communities based on the development of 'local learning teams'.
- **The Hub** – the social centrepiece of the 5-floor building, with restaurants, bars, shops, offices and an IMAX cinema.

Funding: total cost of £114 million – £50 million from the Millennium Commission, £25.6 million from the European Regional Development Fund, £5.9 million from Advantage West Midlands (the West Midlands Regional Development Agency – see Ch.5), plus a commercial bank loan and sponsorship.

Principal partners and sponsors: Birmingham City Council, the University of Central England, Birmingham Chamber of Commerce and Industry, Specialist Computer Holdings, GPU Power, Barclays, Jaguar, Dunlop, HSBC, Birmingham Post and Mail Ltd, the Wellcome Trust, Severn Trent plc.

---

different shapes and sizes. Far from there being a single model, no two models are the same. They may be informal partnerships which take the form of networks. Alternatively they might be formalised contractual arrangements involving, for example, central government, local government, the voluntary and private sectors. In most local authority areas there is now typically a Crime and Disorder partnership, Joint Care Planning between health and social services, a partnership arrangement between the local housing authority and the housing associations in the area, a regeneration partnership, a Community Planning group, an Agenda 21 partnership, and a whole range of other joint working arrangements, like Drug Action Teams, Vehicle Crime Reduction Teams, Youth Offending Teams. The list in Exhibit 8.4 is far from exhaustive, but it does, and did to its parliamentary compilers, convey an accurate sense of the bewildering

Exhibit 8.4 The labyrinthine world of zones and partnerships

The Government's latest cliché: Like 'community', 'partnership' has become one of the great cliché concepts of our age – used so universally and unthinkingly that it has become almost meaningless. You can hardly be against these concepts in principle, but, as we try to suggest, 'partnership working' is very far from any guarantee of enhanced effectiveness. Nevertheless, for local authorities partnerships have necessarily become an even more prominent feature of day-to-day life than in the past – not least because central government departments keep creating and funding them. The following selection of 2,370 – and it is only a selection – all involve local authority officers (and sometimes councillors) from the relevant departments, representatives of other public bodies, local voluntary and, yes, community groups, and usually also of private sector and business organisations.

113   **Education Action Zones** – clusters of schools working with local organisations to raise attainment and overcome barriers to learning in areas of high deprivation.

26   **Health Action Zones** - to tackle health inequalities and key priorities – eg mental health, teenage pregnancy, drug abuse – through health and social care programmes.

15   **Employment Action Zones** – to help the long-term unemployed improve their employability through individual action plans and 'personal job accounts'.

12   **Sport Action Zones** – networks of schools, sports clubs and other bodies working to enhance the social and economic contribution of sport in deprived areas.

22   **New Commitment to Regeneration Partnerships** – to improve the quality of life and governance across a wide area and provide a framework within which other more specific local partnerships can operate.

complexity and fragmentation of today's world of local governance – particularly in the most deprived areas of the country in which there are nowadays a myriad of overlapping schemes, all attracting funding on different bases, with different monitoring and regulation regimes, and with different partners involved in each scheme.

So, while partnerships can help to overcome the fragmentation of local governance, a crucial issue remains how to manage and co-ordinate these convoluted inter-agency working arrangements. Exhibit 8.5 gives a hint of the difficulty. EYCDPs are very far from being the most all-embracing or potentially fractious of local partnerships. Yet even getting most of these 'players' together in the same place, let alone developing a shared vision and actually getting anything done, is far from easy. The difficulty, as Benyon and Edwards (1999) point out in the far more fraught context of community governance and crime control, is that resources are usually

16   **New Deal for Communities Partnerships** – to narrow gaps in housing, crime, educational attainment, health and employment prospects between deprived neighbourhoods and the rest of the country.

900   **Single Regeneration Budget Partnerships** – to address the regeneration objectives of the several government departments contributing to the SRB.

285   **Local Agenda 21 Partnerships** – to advance the principles of sustainable development, environmental conservation and preservation agreed at the 1992 Rio 'Earth Summit'.

47   **Connexions Partnerships** – to advance the goals of the Connexions Service of delivering a comprehensive support service for 13–19 year olds.

150   **Early Years Development and Child Care Partnerships** – to co-ordinate the government's commitment to good quality, affordable and accessible child care.

100   **Learning Partnerships** – to improve the planning, coherence and standards of post-16 learning and to widen participation.

139   **Sure Start Partnerships** – to improve prospects for disadvantaged pre-school children.

16   **Creative Partnerships** – to offer young people opportunities to enhance their arts and cultural education outside schools.

376   **Crime and Disorder Partnerships** – to co-ordinate action to tackle crime and crime-related issues at the local level.

153   **Community Legal Service Partnerships** – to improve access to and the delivery of legal and advice services.

Key source: House of Commons Select Committee on Public Administration, *Fifth Report, 2000/01: Mapping the Quango State.*

gained for specific projects with different time scales which frustrate co-ordination, undermining the attainment of policy goals. This may lead to failure of some projects through the lack of necessary support, e.g. attendance at meetings, overload of information and administrative systems. As Benyon and Edwards observe (1999, p. 166):

A key question for the development of community governance is whether certain social–political problems are amenable to being resolved to the satisfaction of an expanding range of different groups, and the problems of crime and community safety exemplify this challenge. They illustrate the difficulties of co-ordination, accountability and durability in a particularly stark form, given the acute inter-generational and inter-ethnic social conflicts they are capable of provoking amongst residents in the same neighbourhoods.

Exhibit 8.5 EYDCPs – the complexity of even 'simple' partnerships

What are Early Years Development and Childcare Partnerships?

They were set up in response to the Government's *National Childcare Strategy* Green Paper (1998). The paper proposed that plans for establishing and developing early years and childcare strategies should be drawn up and implemented at local level by these partnerships of governmental, voluntary and private sector representatives.

Possible bodies and interests represented on a local EYDCP

- County council officers from education, special educational needs, social services, and leisure departments
- District council(s)
- Health authorities
- Local training organisations
- School governors
- Colleges and universities
- Parents
- Voluntary sector out-of-school providers
- Private childcare providers
- Religious groups
- National Child Minders Association
- Council for Racial Equality
- Councillors
- Training and Enterprise Council
- Schools
- Voluntary special needs groups
- Employers
- Voluntary sector nursery providers
- Registered child minders
- Private out-of-school providers
- Children's Information Service
- Pre-school Learning Alliance
- Ethnic minority groups

Key source: Daycare Trust, A Survey of Early Years Development and Childcare Partnerships (DfEE, 2000)

There are, then, plenty of reasons for caution in evaluating this recent rush to partnership working. As Lowndes notes (1999b), they can be a double-edged sword for democratic practice. To critics they pose a threat to formal political accountability, as appointed bodies gaining influence at the expense of elected members. Others, though, would argue that they complement formal democratic processes by providing opportunities for a wider range of stakeholders to influence local policy-making and service delivery. Practitioners tend to differentiate between more and less effective examples. Thus former Birmingham City Council Chief Executive, Michael Lyons, has argued that 'not everything called 'partnership' is a good idea. Anyone entering into a partnership needs to ask some basic questions if it's going to work effectively.' For Lyons there are four basic rules for successful partnerships (Box 8.2).

Box 8.2 Successful partnerships

- they should be established to address a jointly recognised opportunity;
- everyone involved must feel they have something to gain;
- risks should be shared equally;
- no one participant should take all the credit.

Source: Lyons (1997), p. 10.

Lyons also stressed the importance of lateral thinking, openness and the ability to work in an innovative way if partnerships are to thrive: 'You must have an open mind about potential linkages and you must be prepared to work with different people – don't get formulaic.' (See *Local Government Management,* Vol. 1 Issue 22, Autumn 1997, p. 10.)

The Private Finance Initiative (PFI)

Virtually all the cross-sectoral bodies referred to in the past two sections of this chapter could be described as public/private partnerships (PPPs). The PFI, however, is a particularly important, and controversial, form of partnership and warrants a section of its own. It originated in the early 1990s, at a time when the Conservative government was continuing its long-term policy of reducing public spending, but was also facing the political consequences of years of under-investment in schools, hospitals, transportation and other parts of the nation's economic and social infrastructure. It was a new way of enabling the public sector to afford capital-intensive projects without inflating the government's public expenditure figures, while at the same time extending the 'privatisation' of public services.

Instead of government borrowing from the private sector to finance construction projects and then operating them itself, the private sector would be invited not only to finance the construction, but also provide some or all of the *services* associated with the project. In return, government would pay for the services over a period of time – maybe 20 or 30 years – these fees to include the costs and compensation of risk associated with the capital investment. There are several varieties of PFI schemes, some in which the entire asset and service provision is undertaken by the private sector – also known as Design Build Finance Operate (DBFO) schemes – others involving a mix of public and private funding, still others involving leasing arrangements.

PFI was slow to take off, but it gradually spread from large-scale transport projects – like the Channel Tunnel Rail Link and the Jubilee Line extension – to hospitals, prisons, roads, and new teaching and residential accommodation in further and higher educational institutions. For local government, though, the first PFI projects did not even start until 1996/97 – largely because of the tight legal and financial constraints under which British local government finance has to operate. It has been the Blair Administration, therefore, that has been very largely responsible for local authorities' now extensive use of PFI.

The White Paper, *Modern Local Government: In Touch with the People* (DETR, 1998a p. 89) made clear the new government's thinking: 'The Government regards the development of the PFI for local authorities as a high priority. The PFI is an important option within the process of seeking best value in the delivery of local authority services.' By 2001 some £4 billion of additional resources had been allocated to support about 165 council projects using the PFI approach. Exhibit 8.6 gives some examples of the kinds of projects being PFI-funded in 2001/02.

PFI has obvious attractions to central governments, even ones less predisposed towards the private sector than those during the 1990s. Most obviously, it shifts the immediate burden of government expenditure, from

Exhibit 8.6 A selection of local government PFI projects

Leeds Supertram – a new 'Supertram' will boost local transport services and help regenerate some of the run-down areas of the city.

South Hants Rapid Transit project – an environmentally friendly light rail system is to run from Fareham to Portsmouth with a cross-harbour tunnel between Gosport and Portsmouth.

Learning centre in Northamptonshire – Wootton Fields is to get a new Centre for Learning, with an emphasis on ICT and lifelong learning, and including a new primary school, secondary school and public library.

Emergency services in Dorset – an Emergency Services Partnership scheme will provide purpose-built joint fire/ambulance stations and a new divisional police headquarters.

One-stop library for Lewisham – the London borough is to have an integrated library, leisure and health facility, including two GP practices, their primary care teams, district nurses and health visitors.

Breckland's Healthy Living Leisure Centres – the Norfolk district's new centres, promoting healthy living and running after-school holiday programmes, will be linked to a community transport scheme, enabling access from the five market towns in the area.

Provision for the elderly – Hammersmith and Fulham is to increase its nursing care beds and sheltered housing and provide two new day centres for its elderly residents.

capital spending now to current spending in the future. Proponents would also point out the advantages of transferring risk to the private sector, and of having private sector management skills contributing towards the improvement of service quality. Critics, on the other hand, argue that 'such advantages may be offset ... by the concessions that may have to be made to attract private contractors' (Gray and Jenkins, 1998, p. 352), or by having to downplay environmental and other concerns, as Heald and Geaughan suggest happened with the Skye Bridge project in Scotland (1999).

The most serious criticisms, though, centre on costs. While PFI enables projects to go ahead that a resource-strapped public sector could not afford, in practice what is being achieved is an expensive accountancy trick – simply a delay in the cost to the public purse, not a saving; in fact, quite the reverse (Challis, 2000, Ch. 11) (Box 8.3).

Despite such reservations, PFI will remain an important element of the Labour government's infrastructure planning, and therefore central to many of the major partnership initiatives currently taking place at local level. The attractions to a local authority in need of capital investment are obvious. As Gray and Jenkins (1998 p. 353) remind us, its capital programme does not have to be constrained by access to government sources of capital finance; it can exploit the additional value which private sector firms can bring through design innovation and quality of service; and some of the long term operating risks (e.g. higher maintenance costs) can be transferred to the contractor, who is obliged to hand back the facility in working condition at the end of the contract. While the Labour Government has made a number of organisational adjustments to the operation of PFIs – creating a new procurement agency, Partnerships UK, and an Office of Government Commerce – it remains committed to this method of financing partnerships at local level.

Box 8.3 The costs of PFI

- PFI projects cost more, because the private sector cannot borrow at the lower interest rates available to the government;
- The private sector always needs to make a rate of return for shareholders that is not required by the public sector;
- There are additional costs arising out of PFI process itself and the need to employ consultants;
- Risk transfer produces a private sector requirement for a higher rate of return;
- There may be no 'public asset' at the end of the process;
- Negotiations at the end of the contract period may result in additional costs owing to the monopoly position of the private sector supplier.

Source: Challis (2000), Ch. 11.

Guide to further reading

An obvious starting point is Leach and Percy-Smith (2001), a good proportion of which, as its title implies, is concerned with the subject matter of this chapter. For greater depth there is Stoker (1999a), the first of two volumes presenting the findings of the ESRC's Local Governance Programme, which provides examples of partnerships and networking from a wide range of functional areas. For students wanting to look more conceptually into local governance, Rhodes (1997) is both clearer than most and comes with the bonus of a comprehensive personal bibliography. Much of the research on local quangos has been the work of Chris Skelcher and colleagues from INLOGOV – e.g. Skelcher and Davis (1995), Skelcher (1998) – the Democratic Audit at the University of Essex – e.g. Weir and Hall (1994), Weir and Beetham (1999) – or both: Skelcher *et al.* (2000). Goss (2001) provides a multitude of examples of partnerships in action as well as a helpful analytical framework. A massive quantity of information, though, including much referred to in this chapter, is now easily accessible on the internet.

Chapter 9

Central–Local Government Relations

Introduction – Britain's 'hypercentralisation'

In June 1997, just as we completed the previous edition of this book, the Council of Europe's Congress of Local and Regional Authorities of Europe (CLRAE) passed a resolution concerning the state of local democracy in its 40 or so member countries. Just six countries were defined as having 'major problems': Bulgaria, Croatia, Latvia, Moldova, Ukraine and ... the United Kingdom. Our perceived problems were not those of arbitrarily interventionist presidents or dubious electoral practices. They were arguably more serious and fundamental, for they were examples of what other Europeans tend to see as our already highly centralised – even 'hypercentralised' (Loughlin, 2001, Ch. 2) – governmental system becoming even more centralised. In particular, the Congress drew attention to the trends described in Chapter 8, of appointed quangos displacing the service-providing role of elected local authorities, and those addressed in Chapter 10, central controls on local government finance. This chapter, therefore, is positioned to be able to outline the context of central–local government relations, and perhaps to suggest how a serious observer like CLRAE can come to so critical a judgement of our local democratic health.

We begin with the formal framework and some of the instruments of central control available to Ministers individually and collectively. Formal frameworks must, however, always be studied alongside actual working relationships. The next section, therefore, looks at the dynamics of central–local relations. Next we examine the roles of the newly restructured Department for Transport, Local Government and the Regions (DTLR) and the now well established Local Government Association (LGA) and the Government Offices for the Regions (GOs). Finally a number of theoretical perspectives are considered.

The formal framework: controls and constraints

It is useful to start with an overview of the formal relations between central government departments and local authorities. We do so through a brief review of some of the main means by which local authorities are potentially able to be controlled by ministers and their departments or otherwise constrained.

Legislation

In Chapter 2 we used the term 'partial autonomy' to describe the constitutional status of British local government, and we indicated the constraints imposed by the doctrine of *ultra vires*. National governments can, through parliamentary legislation, create, abolish, restructure and amend the powers of local authorities as and when they determine. Local authorities, for their part, are authorised to provide or secure the provision of certain services, but only within a framework of national legislation. The new 'well-being power' (see p. 126) should extend local authorities' discretion, but it cannot change their constitutional position as 'creatures of statute'.

Legislation is therefore the most direct instrument of central control of local authorities and one that has in recent years been used with unprecedented frequency and impact. The Conservative governments from 1979 to 1997 produced well over 210 Acts of Parliament affecting local government, at least a third of them in major and far-reaching ways. This mountain of legislation and the associated use of the courts to enforce government intentions contrasts strikingly with what Goldsmith (1986c, p. xv) describes as 'the more informal approach generally adopted by central governments in their relations with local authorities in the years up to 1979'.

Statutory instruments

Acts of Parliament, as we noted in Chapter 5, are often referred to as 'primary legislation'. Many Acts, however, delegate law-making powers to appropriate government ministers in something like the following form of words, known in Whitehall as 'Henry VIII clauses':

> The Secretary of State shall make supplementary, incidental, consequential or transitional provisions as appear to him/her to be necessary or expedient for the general purposes or any other particular purpose of the Act.

All such secondary legislation is published and laid before Parliament. But, with some 3,500 statutory instruments currently issued each year, the detailed scrutiny most of them receives is inevitably limited. They thus constitute a significant means by which ministers can 'flesh out' their own primary legislation and thereby strengthen, if they choose, their control

Exhibit 9.1 Statutory Instruments: secondary but still significant

A small selection of the more than 3,500 Statutory Instruments that passed through Parliament in 2001

SI 2750   **Education Maintenance Allowance (Pilot Areas) Regulations.** Revises conditions relating to residence and income calculation under which certain LEAs pay allowances to students over compulsory school leaving age.

SI 2786   **Children's Commissioner for Wales Act 2001 (Commencement) Order.** Specifies that main provisions of the Act come into force on 26 August 2001.

SI 2793   **Road User Charging and Workplace Parking Levy (Classes of Motor Vehicles) (England) Regulations.** Detail procedures to be followed by local authorities wishing, under the Transport Act 2000, to introduce road user charging or workplace parking levy schemes.

SI 2944   **Education (School Performance Targets) (England) (Amendment) (No.2) Regulations.** Require that targets be set for pupils aged 15 to achieve five or more GCSE grades, including English and Maths – instead of one or more GCSE grades.

SI 2992   **Foster Placement (Children) and Adoption Agencies Amendment (England) Regulations.** Amend regulations under which persons convicted of certain offences are considered unsuitable to foster and adopt children.

SI 3384   **Local Authorities (Standing Orders) (England) Regulations.** Detail the form of the standing orders that councils must draw up for the operation of their new executive arrangements under the Local Government Act 2000.

over local authorities' actions and activities. Just because statutory instruments tend to have laborious titles and do not make media or even parliamentary headlines does not mean they are unimportant, certainly not for the councils and classes of persons affected by them (see Exhibit 9.1).

Circulars and guidance

In addition to statutory instruments, government departments will also issue circulars to local authorities containing 'advice' and 'guidance' on how they should exercise their various responsibilities. Such circulars are often perceived as further vehicles for central direction, and indeed they can be, as shown in Exhibit 9.2. But not all circulars are directive, and some are the product of genuine negotiation with local authority interests

---

Exhibit 9.2 Ugly housing – the power of a circular

Heard of 'gob-ons'? No, not local government jargon, but builders' slang for the 'adornments' they are asked by private developers to attach to the new and otherwise near-identical houses they build on estates across the country, in order to 'individualise' them – 'Georgian' porticos, 'Tudorbethan' timbering, gabled dormers, and the like.

How has this standardisation of our housing happened? At least partly because of a notorious circular (22/80) issued by the then Department of the Environment (DoE) decreeing that councillors and local authorities had the power to refuse planning permission *only* on planning grounds, not on the grounds of ugliness, unsuitability, or sheer bad taste. Private developers' tastes would prevail and, if they were initially refused planning permission, they could appeal to the DoE's own Planning Inspectorate.

Why didn't ministers intervene? They did, eventually, although there was a long disinclination of Conservative ministers to challenge the right of 'market forces' to dictate design. Planning policy guidance notes during the 1990s did give local planning authorities power to reject 'obviously poor designs . . . clearly out of scale or incompatible with their surroundings'. But non-intervention had, for many councillors and planning committees, become a habit, and the 'surroundings' had by this time lost much of their local distinctiveness anyway.

Key source: Richard Girling, 'Concrete Cancer', *Sunday Times*, 5 April 1998

---

and contain useful practical advice. Even when benign, though, their sheer volume makes them a powerful and continuous reminder of central government's presence. Planners alone, for example, will be reminded, when they check out the DTLR's web site, that, in addition to conventional departmental circulars, they should be acquainted with 25 planning policy and 15 mineral policy guidance notes, 27 good practice guidance notes, regional policy guidance, plus, of course, ministers' latest pronouncements in the form of parliamentary answers and statements.

Judicial review

British local government, then, operates within a complex and often subtle legal framework. Central government, through parliament, has ultimate authority as well as extensive powers of direction and supervision. But local authorities too, over the years, have acquired substantial powers of discretion, promotion and experimentation in relation to their service-providing responsibilities. When the priorities and policies of a local council clash with those of central government, or of any other organisation, the disputes may have to be settled in court by a process known as judicial review – something that happened with increasingly frequency in the period from 1979 onwards. In 1974 leave for judicial review was sought 160 times. By 1995 this figure had increased to 4,400.

Loughlin in particular (1996b, p. 61) emphasises the significance of this massive expansion of the formal legal dimension of central–local relations, arguing that the contemporary period has 'been one in which both Parliament and the courts have been brought back into the central–local relationship'. Indeed, following an analysis of some of the most important and contentious cases of the period – including the first three in Exhibit 9.3 – Loughlin identifies 'a remarkable pattern ... so marked that it may even be expressed in the form of a law: the further up the court hierarchy the dispute progresses, the greater the likelihood of a principle restrictive of local authority action being enunciated' (1996a, p. 408).

By no means all of even these high-profile cases, however, have gone against local authorities. Ministers lose too, and, though they can try to persuade Parliament quickly to make legal what has just been pronounced illegal, in at least the short term an adverse judgement can prove both embarrassing and a policy setback for a government. There have been plenty of these in the past three decades, the last two cases in Exhibit 9.3 being simply unusually prominent examples.

The local ombudsman

The cases in Exhibit 9.3 are obviously exceptional, in having implications extending beyond the cases themselves, and involving, on both sides, organisations, rather than individuals. Many local government judicial review cases, however, involve individuals challenging decisions of a local authority and *choosing* to pursue their grievances through the courts – 'choosing', because they are likely also to have had open to them an alternative means of seeking redress. That alternative would be through a complaint to their local ombudsman or, to give the office its proper title, the Commissioner for Local Administration (CLA).

The CLA and the separate commissions in Wales and Scotland were first appointed in 1974/75, following the creation of a national ombudsman, the Parliamentary Commissioner for Administration, in 1967. It is probably fair to say that neither nationally nor locally have these institutions had as significant an impact on the country's government as their early advocates hoped or as several of their European and especially Scandinavian counterparts have. Even so, the three English local ombudsmen alone deal nowadays with nearly 20,000 cases a year, which, in their absence, would constitute a great deal of unhealthily pent-up suspicion of council maladministration.

That is what Britain's local ombudsmen do, and that is the limit of their jurisdiction: they investigate written complaints from the public about

Exhibit 9.3 Judicial review: councils lose, but so can ministers

A. Two judgements restricting local authority action

Nottinghamshire CC v Secretary of State for the Environment (1986) The Labour County Council challenged the Conservative minister for having set targets for expenditure and thus grant distribution that discriminated particularly against a small number of authorities, including Nottinghamshire. The challenge was upheld by the Court of Appeal in a decision that would have overturned the government's whole target-based local finance policy, but was overturned when the minister appealed to the House of Lords (the UK's highest court) (see Loughlin, 1996a, pp. 282–9).

Wheeler v Leicester City Council (1985) The City Council banned Leicester Rugby Club from using a council-owned pitch, claiming the club had not fully supported the council's anti-apartheid policy and its opposition to any sporting contacts with South Africa. Peter Wheeler (then club captain, later its chief executive) challenged the council's decision, was unsuccessful in the Divisional and Appeal Courts, but had it upheld in the House of Lords, who declared the council's action 'unreasonable' (see Loughlin, 1996a, pp. 173–4).

B. An inter-authority dispute restricting local authority action

Bromley LBC v Greater London Council (1983) The Labour-controlled GLC, led by Ken Livingstone, introduced a 'Fares Fair' scheme of subsidised fares on London Transport, financed partly through additional rates (local taxes) raised from the London boroughs, including Bromley, Conservative-controlled and without any underground stations. Bromley's challenge, on behalf of its ratepayers, was dismissed in the lower Divisional Court, but upheld in the Court of Appeal and finally in the House of Lords – thus limiting the power of councils to provide grants 'as an object of social or transport policy' (see Loughlin, 1996a, pp. 231–7).

C. Two judgements restricting ministerial action

Secretary of State for Education v Tameside MBC (1977) The newly elected Conservative-controlled Tameside Council (Greater Manchester) abandoned the former Labour council's planned comprehensive reorganisation of the borough's secondary schools shortly before its scheduled introduction. When the Labour minister ordered that the reorganisation should proceed, the borough's challenge was eventually upheld in the House of Lords, who ruled that the LEA's action had not been 'unreasonable'.

Derbyshire and Lancashire CCs v Secretary of State for the Environment (1994) The two county councils won judicial reviews claiming the minister had acted illegally in trying to steer the Local Government (Reorganisation) Commission towards making recommendations for unitary, rather than two-tier, solutions for future local government in England.

injustice caused by *maladministration* on the part of their local councils, and also police and fire authorities, joint boards, education appeals panels, and (concerning admissions practices) school governing bodies. They do not initiate their own investigations. Nor do they deal with any complaints about the actual policy of a council: if you dislike that, you can complain to the councillors themselves and perhaps try to vote them out of office. The ombudsman is concerned solely with the way in which policy is administered – for example, the speed, efficiency, fairness and propriety with which it was implemented in your particular case.

The ombudsmen will accept such complaints either directly from aggrieved citizens themselves or via their local councillor. If a complaint falls within their jurisdiction, they will normally then get the local authority concerned to respond in detail and, if there seems to have been maladministration, do everything possible to bring about some local settlement – successfully in around a third of the cases they take on. In only a small minority of cases will a much more exhaustive investigation be required, resulting in a final report and published judgement of whether or not maladministration and injustice have been found. If so, the ombudsman will look to the local authority for some form of satisfactory action: an apology, financial compensation, a change of procedure in dealing with future cases. Usually acceptable action will be forthcoming, but on occasion a council will continue to dispute and resist the ombudsman's judgement, whereupon the latter is left with little sanction beyond the production of a second critical public report.

There are, then, grounds for suggesting that ultimately we are dealing here with 'Ombudsmice', the fairness of the label depending on whether you attach more weight to the exceptional case than to the generality. It can hardly be disputed that the CLA does much valuable work – notably in relation to housing benefit (21 per cent of complaints received in 2000/01), other housing matters (24 per cent), planning (18 per cent), education (8 per cent) and council tax (6 per cent). It deals with more cases each year; its costs per complaint decided (£467) have dropped by nearly a quarter since 1993/94; and waiting times for decisions have also dropped significantly from the figures quoted in our previous edition. Not least of its virtues is its contribution to sustainable development that could serve as a model for many of the authorities it investigates: bicycle allowances for staff, chlorine-free paper for stationery, replaced computers donated to developing countries.

It is also, however, an institution employing 200 staff at a cost of nearly £9 million, which finds maladministration with injustice in under 1 per cent of all the cases it decides, and even then cannot enforce any redress. Alternative and more streamlined procedures have been proposed, particularly by those arguing that since 1974 councils' own internal complaints systems and their general customer orientation have improved immeasurably and that an ombudsman-quality sledgehammer is no longer needed to crack these proverbial nuts of alleged maladministration. Better, such critics assert, to set up a more localised procedure of investigation, based on councils' own complaint systems and overseen by council-funded but genuinely independent local adjudicators, with a very much smaller-scale Commission acting as a central monitoring body. What is actually going to happen, though, as the Government announced in 2001, is that there will be created a unified public sector ombudsman, dealing with central government, local government and the NHS. Whether bigger will prove more beautiful and effective remains to be seen.

Default and intervention

Legislation sometimes confers default powers on ministers, so that a minister dissatisfied with the way an authority is providing a particular service can, as a final resort, step in and take it over or transfer responsibility to another local authority or special body. Until recently the invariably cited example of default powers being exercised has been that of Clay Cross, Derbyshire, when the Labour-controlled Urban District Council refused to increase its council house rents to the 'fair rent' level defined in the Housing Finance Act 1972. The Conservative Government sent in a housing commissioner to take over all the Council's housing responsibilities, and 11 Clay Cross councillors were disqualified from holding public office and surcharged £63,000 for the money which would have been obtained had the Act been implemented.

The sheer practical difficulties involved in government-appointed officials taking over the running of a whole council service, quite apart from the political and personal animosity they are likely to provoke, means that such default powers have been used only very rarely. Even ministers who have sensed they were being deliberately frustrated have tended to hold back and seek other solutions. Taking over or even closing an individual school, however, is a less daunting proposition, and under Labour's Education Secretary, David Blunkett, nationally prompted intervention became a key policy instrument. Adopting a more graduated and less provocative approach than at first seemed likely, the Education Department's Standards and Effectiveness Unit claimed by 2001 to have closed some 130 'failing' schools and 'turned round' nearly 800.

The Blair Government's readiness to intervene, though, far outstrips that of its predecessors and extends far beyond schools. In October 2001 Health Secretary, Alan Milburn, extended his 'naming and shaming' of poorly performing hospitals to councils' social services departments, warning that new management could be brought in if they failed to make 'significant improvements'. The previous month DTLR Secretary of State,

Stephen Byers, had used for the first time new powers under the Local Government Act 1999 to intervene in Hackney in order to 'protect and improve the key services and ensure the council tackles its budget deficit'. No fewer than five central government departments issued 'Directions' to the London borough requiring service improvements in education, social services, waste management and housing benefits, plus action to establish a new system of financial management. Other councils were rumoured to be on the minister's 'hit list' for intervention, with poorly performing services possibly being taken over by nearby high-performing councils as an additional alternative to the private sector.

Inspection

If the Thatcher Governments brought a mushrooming of judicial reviews, the Blair Governments' equivalent contribution has been inspections. There have long been government-appointed inspectorates for particular services: education, the fire and police services. By 2001, though, those already in existence had expanded, and they had been joined by a whole new army – and to some in local government that is exactly the right term – of best value inspectors. The schools inspectorate, OFSTED – the Office for Standards in Education – is an example of an inspectorate whose work has expanded in both scale and significance. Its several thousand visits to schools each year now form the basis of those ministerial judgements of whether a school has 'serious weaknesses', requires 'special measures', or is failing so fundamentally that it needs a completely 'fresh start'. In addition, OFSTED now undertakes inspections – and publishes judgements – of whole LEAs, LEA-funded youth services, early years childcare and education, education action zones, and much else besides.

The views that many teachers have held towards OFSTED and its regime have, with the arrival of the Audit Commission's Best Value Inspection Service, tended to spread right across local government. Almost all council services come within its remit, and all inspected services receive a 'star ranking' of their quality, cost effectiveness and the likelihood of their improving in the future. For outside observers, the reports and rankings – readily available on www.bestvalueinspections.gov.uk – can make fascinating reading and provide a useful insight into one's own authority. For the inspectees the experience can, at least in some instances, prove deeply dispiriting: excessively bureaucratic, confrontational, and ultimately counter-productive. 'Red book reviews' was the image left in the mind of one chief executive, who saw a more than passing resemblance to the young Red Guards from China's 1960s Cultural Revolution, 'denouncing their erstwhile comrades as they clutched Mao's *Red Book*. This time they were holding the Audit Commission's *Seeing is Believing*' (Duffield,

2000, p. 12). Hyperbole, of course, but the spread of inspection is real enough. It is also threatening, reflecting as it does the assumption that it is to central government that councils are primarily answerable, rather than to their own electorates and elected politicians.

Statutory appeals

Inspectors act at arm's length from their respective departments. In some circumstances, though, ministers may be keen to be seen acting more personally as arbitrators or defenders of the rights of local citizens. Since many local authority powers can adversely affect the interests of individual citizens – e.g. the closure of a school, the issue of a compulsory purchase or clearance order, the granting of licences, the refusal of planning permission – they may require ministerial confirmation or approval before they can be implemented, and also offer aggrieved citizens a statutory right of appeal to the minister and ultimately to the courts.

Finance

Chapter 10 is devoted entirely to finance. Here, therefore, we simply note in passing that additional means available to a central government wishing to control local authorities are through, first, regulating the amount of money which they can spend locally and, secondly, scrutinising the way in which that money is spent. The government – by, for example, effectively capping local budgets and tightly controlling capital investment – can and does tightly restrict local spending.

Scrutiny is exercised nowadays principally through the *Audit Commission* in England and Wales and the *Accounts Commission* for Scotland. These bodies are statutorily responsible for appointing external auditors for all local authorities and NHS bodies, either from their own staff (district auditors) or from private firms of accountants such as PricewaterhouseCoopers, Deloitte and Touche, and KPMG. The Audit Commission, set up in 1982, is itself appointed by the Secretary of State after consultation with local authority associations and professional accountancy bodies, and the minister is empowered to issue directives that the Commission must observe. The external auditors check an authority's accounts for:

- *Legality* – did it have the statutory authority to spend the money in the way it did?
- *Reasonableness* – did it act in the way a reasonable body would?
- *Wilful misconduct* – was anyone recklessly indifferent about whether a course of action was illegal?

They must also nowadays audit for value-for-money (VFM) and satisfy themselves that the council is securing the '3Es' – economy, efficiency and effectiveness – in its use of resources. District auditors' reports can be very wide-ranging and very hard-hitting, such as that on Westminster City Council's 'home for votes' affair in 1996 (see p. 289).

The Audit Commission, established by a government anxious to increase effective scrutiny of local authority finances, has nevertheless been far from subservient in practice. It has regularly been outspokenly critical of central government policy when it has deemed it appropriate, and also on occasion strongly supportive of individual councils' spending priorities, when it has judged them to reflect the preferences of the local population. It inevitably remains, however, a creature of central government and is the body responsible for producing the 'league tables' of Performance Indicators (PIs) which enable local authorities, and of course the government, to compare their expenditure and efficiency records with those of all other councils. More recently, as we have seen, it has also assumed responsibility for best value inspections.

Working relationships – the full complexity of sub-central government

It is important to move beyond formal legal statements about the respective powers of central and local government and look at actual working relationships. The centre, as we have seen, has plenty of capacity to legislate, regulate, direct and exhort,

> but it does so in the context of a system of sub-central government in which day-to-day control and the scope for innovation and initiative are in the hands of a range of other elected representatives, appointees and full-time officials and managers. The centre may seek to control the system but its influence is limited by the scale and fragmented character of the governmental system it oversees. (Stoker, 1990, p. 127)

Working relationships, then, are far from simple; they vary over time, from authority to authority, and from one service area to another. You should by now have come to expect local authorities to differ from one another: to have their own political outlooks and policy agendas, their own service or spending priorities, histories and traditions, and their differing sets of neighbouring councils with whom they compare themselves. The constant danger of seeking to say anything universally generalisable about 'local government' is that there is bound, somewhere, to be an exception.

It is equally important to recognise that, despite the United Kingdom's centralist political culture, central government itself is not a single uniform entity either. There are not of course as many central government departments as there are local authorities, but, just like councils, they have their own traditions, cultures, and ways of working, as well as fundamentally different – and sometimes directly conflicting – approaches to local government. The kinds of variations noted by Griffith in the 1960s among central government departments in their interactions with local authorities are just as prevalent today. Some departments tended to be conventionally *laissez-faire* in their approach, intervening as little as possible; some (e.g. the Home Office, Department of Transport) were more regulatory; and some (e.g. the then Department of Education and Science) promotional.

Today such departmental inclinations are rather more likely than in the 1960s to be overlaid by party political considerations. Thus, Goldsmith and Newton (1986a, p. 103) showed that, while the early Thatcher Government was very directive towards local authorities on council house sales, by contrast it hardly involved itself in environmental health: a reflection of the much lower priority initially given to this policy area. 'Consequently, local authorities have somewhat greater discretion in the environmental health area than they do in relation to council house sales.' By 1990, however, the Government's conversion to 'green' politics as a priority area – expressed, for example, in its Environmental Protection Act and promotion of a Litter Code – was beginning to impose more regulatory functions on local authorities. Hence another warning: observations about specific policy areas are time-bound; new policy priorities can soon introduce new sets of relationships. There is in reality something of an ebb and flow in relationships; a high political profile in a policy area (e.g. local government finance) invariably results in more intensive and interventionist central government activity.

The reality, in truth, is very complex indeed: far more so than is first suggested by the phrase 'central–local government relations'. Not only is there a multiplicity of local authorities, a diversity of central government departments and policy areas, and a constantly changing party political dimension to consider. Account must be taken too of the many other appointed and representative intermediate agencies that go to make up anything approaching a full picture of what is sometimes usefully labelled *'sub-central government'*. It was the term used by Stoker in the quote with which we began this section, but it is particularly associated with Rhodes, who adopted it as the sub-title of his comprehensive analysis of government *Beyond Westminster and Whitehall*, if only, as he put it, to draw attention to the fact that links between the centre and sub-central units of government are *not* restricted to the relationship between central departments and local authorities (1988, p. 13).

Our own 'sketch map' in Figure 9.1 is inevitably a simplification of the territory covered by Rhodes. It does incorporate some of the many other public, private and voluntary sector organisations that now make up the world of local *governance*, and it should serve as a reminder of just how

Figure 9.1 *Central–local government networks: a sketch map*

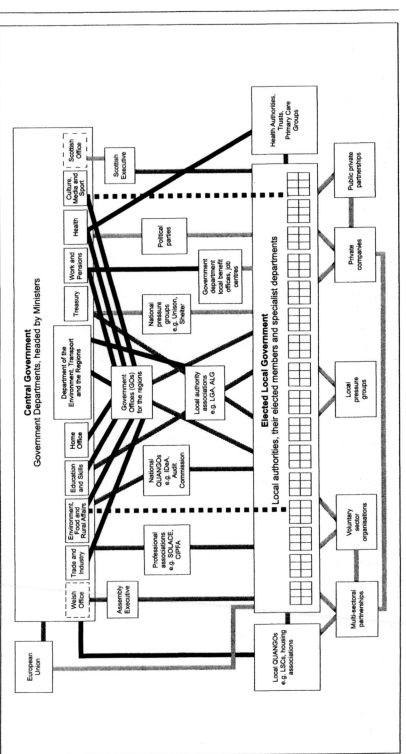

fragmented both 'central' and 'local government' really are. We have resisted, however, the temptation to relabel it a map of 'inter-governmental relations' for the same reason as we have retained 'local government' for the book's title. It is *primarily* a map of the links between central government departments and local authorities. The broken lines of communication symbolise the myriad relationships that can theoretically exist between each local authority and a range of central government departments. The unbroken lines signify that in practice much of this contact and attempted influence is necessarily channelled through 'umbrella' organisations and other agencies.

Increasing central intervention

In principle, the scale of central intervention in local authorities' affairs could be relatively easily measured. We could add up all the Acts of Parliament relating either directly or indirectly to local government, and the plethora of regulations, circulars, guidance notes, codes of practice and statutory instruments emerging from Whitehall, and doubtless conclude that the scale of central oversight and intervention is obviously massive. What is far more difficult to assess, however, is the *nature* of the relationship. In Exhibit 9.4 we identify five key phases of intergovernmental relations over the past quarter-century, progressing – or, some would say, regressing – from consultation, through corporatism, confrontation, an extended period of control, to the current state of what we have termed 'conciliation'.

The schema, designed originally to characterise changing *financial* relations, can also be applied more generally, though with the qualification that the centre's 'control' over local finance has throughout the past two decades been more direct and comprehensive than over some other policy areas. Centralisation increased greatly during this period and the formal consultative machinery between the centre and local authorities – through such bodies as the local authority associations and the Consultative Council on Local Government Finance (CCLGF) – was taken far less seriously by ministers and their Whitehall civil servants. There are as a result plenty of observers who would now question Goldsmith's sanguine conclusion in the mid-1980s (1986c, p. xiv) that 'Britain has not become a totally centralised state ... British local authorities still retain considerable discretion over the way in which they run their services and the level of service they provide.'

John Major's government made some efforts to re-establish the fractured lines of communication and consultation, and in November 1994 a set of 'guidelines' was produced, aimed at improving central–local relations. By this time, though, with the government's unpopularity leading to

Exhibit 9.4 Five key phases of intergovernmental relations, 1960s–2000s

	CHARACTER OF THE PERIOD	INTERGOVERNMENTAL RELATIONS
CONSULTATION 1960s and early 1970s	Increasing local service spending and employment, much of it encouraged and financed by central government.	*Live and let live* Considerable local discretion permitted by general (i.e. non-specific) grant funding; central direction and intervention more the exception than the rule.
CORPORATISM late 1970s	Accelerating economic decline; inflation – partly through oil price rises – necessitating loan from International Monetary Fund and tough public expenditure cuts.	*Influence through incorporation* Labour Government incorporation of local authority representative associations into policy-making to try to secure councils' voluntary expenditure restraint, reinforced by successive cuts in grant funding.
CONFRONTATION early 1980s	Conservative Government search for means to control local, and thereby overall public, expenditure – mainly through manipulation of grant system. Evolution of policy of pushing back frontiers of the local state by combination of intervention and privatisation.	*Central direction, local defiance* Consultation replaced by unilateral Ministerial decision-making; government announcements of further block grant reductions, accompanied by new detailed spending 'guidelines' for every council and grant penalties for 'overspenders', even if using their own tax revenues; increasing use of specific grants and directive legislation.
CONTROL mid-1980s to mid-1990s	Government recognition that local current spending fully controllable only through statutory limitation of rates and their eventual abolition. Radical restructuring of local government services through 'consumerist' legislation and CCT.	*If you can't persuade, abolish* Abolition of 'high-spending' GLC and MCCs; introduction of rate/ tax- and expenditure-capping; replacement of domestic rates with first community charge, then council tax; further use of specific grants, and additional legislation to reduce responsibilities and discretion of local authorities.
CONCILIATION mid-1990s onwards	With financial control effectively established, post-Thatcher and post-poll tax governments adopt less aggressive stance towards councils in era of local governance.	*It won't hurt us at least to be pleasant* Retention of tight spending and tax limits over councils increasingly stripped of direct service-providing responsibilities. Relations still distrustful, but, particularly post-1997, considerably greater consultative contact.

Sources: Dunleavy and Rhodes (1983, 1985); Rhodes (1992).

losses of dozens of councils and thousands of councillors, Conservative ministers faced a local government world dominated overwhelmingly by Labour and the Liberal Democrats. Little changed in practice, therefore, as everyone waited for the general election, New Labour's anticipated take-over, and, in the hopes of many of its supporters, the establishment of a genuine working partnership between a likeminded central and local government. It will be evident from the increasing length of the narrow neck of our funnel of discretion in Figure 2.1 that, in our judgement, such hopes were not widely realised.

Labour ministers' approach to local government, throughout its first term of office, was accurately captured in the early cartoon in Figure 9.2. It was that of the carrot and stick – or, as it sometimes seemed, carrot and semtex. The incoming government wanted to emphasise that it was far more supportive of the principles of devolution and local self-government than the outgoing Conservatives had been. However, the present state of local government was unsatisfactory in various ways and in urgent need of reform – along the lines laid down by the government in its 'modernisation agenda'. Those councils who accepted the government's diagnosis and enthusiastically adopted its prescriptions could expect to be rewarded with carrots: perhaps a relaxation of financial controls, some additional funding, or other discretionary privileges. Any that resisted, though – in the way that some had tried to thwart Conservative policies – could expect to be sharply reminded by the stick-wielding Environment Secretary and Deputy Prime Minister, John Prescott, that the national government had

Figure 9.2   *Cartoon – Carrots and Semtex: New Labour's agenda for British local government*

Source: *Local Government Chronicle*, 15 August 1997.

both the superior mandate and the greater power. If necessary, ministers could and would intervene, impose their policies, and ultimately hand over the management of the recalcitrant department or authority to another agency.

Central–local relations, therefore, continued to be characterised, on the government's part, by distrust and the insistence on retaining control. With its massive parliamentary majority, it was able to enact most of its manifesto commitments, several of which had been keenly anticipated by local government: the abolition of CCT, the 'well-being power', a mayor and assembly for London, some loosening of capital investment limits. But, as summarised in Exhibit 9.5, for each of these localist

Exhibit 9.5 Labour's central–local relations balance sheet, 1997–2001

Localist	Centralist/Non-localist
Increased funding for local services, particularly from 2000	Treasury figures show percentage of GDP spent on local government still less than under Conservatives
'Capping' of spending and council tax levels effectively abolished	Grant funding increasingly 'ring-fenced' – directed specifically towards ministers' priorities – eg schools
Some relaxation of capital funding controls	'Capping' still not actually abolished, unlike in Scotland
Compulsory Competitive Tendering (CCT) abolished	No re-localisation of business rates, or increase in percentage of revenue raised locally; no reform of council tax
Introduction of power to promote 'well-being'	Continued restrictions on capital funding force councils to transfer homes
Restoration of democratic government in Greater London	CCT replaced by Best Value regime – more bureaucratic, more interventionist
Introduction of mayoral referendums and overview/scrutiny procedures	Continued undermining of LEAs' role
	Imposition of three restrictive models of executive management, and insistence on mayoral referendums
Introduction of local public service agreements	Little done to make local quangos more accountable
Establishment of Central Local Partnership – regular meetings of senior ministers and LGA leaders.	Increased discretion is only discretion to do what central government wants and approves
	Increased contact with ministers only rarely brings policy response.

initiatives, there were usually at least one or two counterbalancing moves. Our conclusion, therefore, is that, after four years, the central–local relationship was not in a significantly healthier state than it had been in May 1997.

The DTLR – a classic quangoid department

Local authority working relationships focus in England on the Department for Transport, Local Government and the Regions (DTLR), as it suddenly became in June 2001 when the Department of the Environment, Transport and the Regions (DETR) was restructured. Its centrality for local government explains its prominence in Figure 9.1, which also, however, details some of the other central departments that deal directly with local authorities in specific policy areas. Most of these departments, together with the DTLR itself, have an additional channel of communication, through nine regional Government Offices (GOs). Local authorities in Scotland, Wales and Northern Ireland now relate largely to their own Executives.

The new department was the product of a hasty, post-foot-and-mouth reshuffling of departmental responsibilities, prompted by the political need to reincarnate the former Ministry of Agriculture, Fisheries and Food. The DETR was split into two new departments: Environment, Food and Rural Affairs (DEFRA), and DTLR. Like several other 'Whitehall departments', neither DTLR nor its recent predecessors have been located in Whitehall at all. The Department of the Environment was, until 1997, about a mile away in Marsham Street, occupying three ugly towers designed, in one of those nice quirks of history, by the disgraced architect, John Poulson (see p. 36 above). It then moved to its current address, Eland House in Bressenden Place, around the corner from Victoria Station. Labour's 2001 ministerial team can be seen in Figure 9.3, together with the department's senior civil servants and their amusingly exotic 'championship' responsibilities – reflecting, or not, the thrusting managerialism expected of our latterday Sir Humphrey Applebys, the Permanent Secretary in BBC TV's *Yes, Minister* series.

Though still obviously a conglomerate department, warranting an eight-member ministerial team, the DTLR's core staff of 3,400 means that it is only a fraction of the size of the big service-providing departments like the Home Office and the new Department for Work and Pensions. For, unlike these departments, the DTLR is not a direct service-provider; rather, as Hennessy described the old DoE, 'a bit like a Whitehall holding company in the range of activities it supervises to a greater or lesser extent at arm's length' (1990, pp. 439–40). 'It is the classic quangoid department', he goes on, with its service provision undertaken either through its executive

Figure 9.3 *The Department of Transport, Local Government and the Regions (DTLR), 2001*

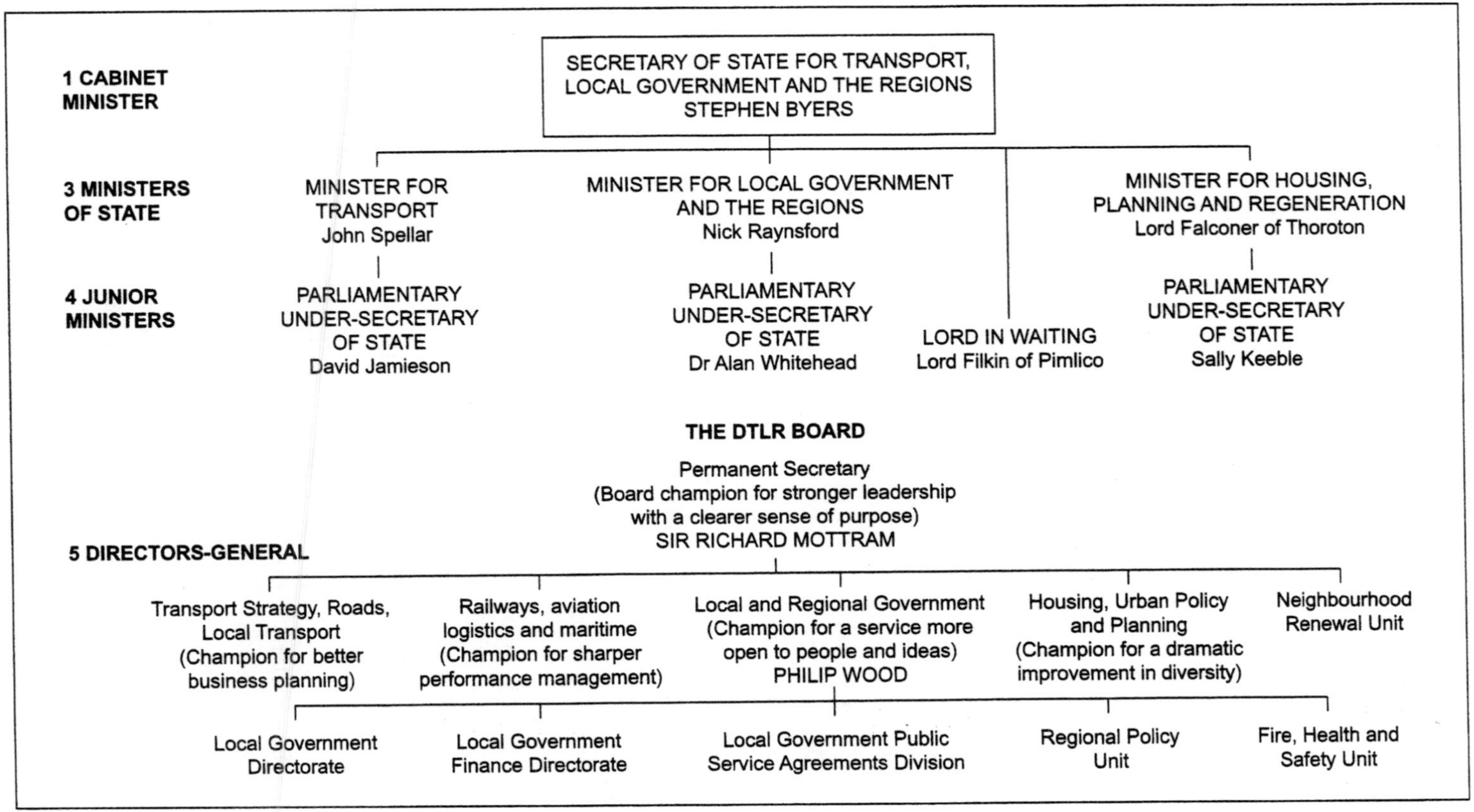

1 CABINET MINISTER

SECRETARY OF STATE FOR TRANSPORT, LOCAL GOVERNMENT AND THE REGIONS
STEPHEN BYERS

3 MINISTERS OF STATE

MINISTER FOR TRANSPORT
John Spellar

MINISTER FOR LOCAL GOVERNMENT AND THE REGIONS
Nick Raynsford

MINISTER FOR HOUSING, PLANNING AND REGENERATION
Lord Falconer of Thoroton

4 JUNIOR MINISTERS

PARLIAMENTARY UNDER-SECRETARY OF STATE
David Jamieson

PARLIAMENTARY UNDER-SECRETARY OF STATE
Dr Alan Whitehead

LORD IN WAITING
Lord Filkin of Pimlico

PARLIAMENTARY UNDER-SECRETARY OF STATE
Sally Keeble

THE DTLR BOARD

Permanent Secretary
(Board champion for stronger leadership with a clearer sense of purpose)
SIR RICHARD MOTTRAM

5 DIRECTORS-GENERAL

Transport Strategy, Roads, Local Transport
(Champion for better business planning)

Railways, aviation logistics and maritime
(Champion for sharper performance management)

Local and Regional Government
(Champion for a service more open to people and ideas)
PHILIP WOOD

Housing, Urban Policy and Planning
(Champion for a dramatic improvement in diversity)

Local Government Directorate

Local Government Finance Directorate

Local Government Public Service Agreements Division

Regional Policy Unit

Neighbourhood Renewal Unit

Fire, Health and Safety Unit

agencies – like the Driving and Vehicle Licensing Agency, the Vehicle and Planning Inspectorates – or through the kinds of quangos and partnerships encountered in Chapter 8: the Audit Commission, the Countryside Agency, Housing Action Trusts. This mode of operation means that the Department's annual budget of over £56 billion puts it considerably higher in the Whitehall league table, the great bulk of it passed on to and spent by these other public bodies, including £37 billion to local authorities.

The Bressenden Place headquarters office deals with all aspects of policy and legislation, from the modernisation of councils' powers and constitutions to electronic service delivery, from European relations to bye-laws for public conveniences. Staff include economists, statisticians, lawyers and researchers, as well as general administrators and thrusting managers, and they are involved in preparing and implementing legislation on matters including government financial support for local authorities, the government's modernisation agenda, best value, and local public service agreements.

The DTLR is at the centre of extensive formal and informal communications networks in Whitehall relating to local government matters. Numerous central government departments have their own interests in local government; they are handled through formal and informal civil service meetings, various *ad hoc* groups and committees. While the DTLR provides directives and guidance to individual authorities, it spends much of its time consulting with broader representative bodies, chief among which nowadays is the Local Government Association (LGA).

The LGA – local government's national voice

From the reorganisation of local government in the 1970s until 1997 there were three major English and Welsh local authority associations: the Association of County Councils (ACC), the Association of Metropolitan Authorities (AMA), and the Association of District Councils (ADC). In Scotland a *single* association was established, the Convention of Scottish Local Authorities (COSLA), which, it was hoped, could speak with a single voice for all Scottish authorities – regions, districts and island unitaries alike – and thus prove stronger and less potentially divisible than the separate associations in England and Wales. In 1997, after much agonising, it was decided that unification offered local government the best chance of making any political impression on national policymaking, and a unified LGA was created. COSLA remains in existence, now representing Scotland's exclusively unitary authorities; there is a separate Welsh LGA, and also an Association of London Government (ALG).

The LGA has not been without its critics, some of whom would have liked it to oppose more vigorously some of the government's centralist record in Exhibit 9.5. But few would deny that, speaking as it can claim to on behalf of its nearly 500 member authorities, it is a significantly more influential 'umbrella' organisation for local government than its predecessors. Like its member councils, the LGA is naturally a party political body. In 2001/02, therefore, with Labour controlling the largest number of councils across the country, Labour councillor representatives had a plurality – though not a majority – of seats on both the central executive and each of the 16 policy executives that steer the work of the association. An indication of the way it seeks to serve as a constant two-way channel of communication between local and central government can be seen in Exhibit 9.6, which lists a small sample of its activities during a single month of 2001.

Exhibit 9.6 The work of the LGA: a national voice for local government

Some of what the LGA was up to during September/October 2001

- **Meeting** representatives of the UK Youth Parliament to discuss their views on restructuring the school year into six terms.
- **Opposing** the Education Secretary's announced intention to take a reserve power to 'ring-fence' local education budgets.
- **Responding** to the Home Secretary's proposed changes in the processing of asylum applications, emphasising that local authorities should be better consulted on the location and suitability of sites to accommodate dispersed asylum seekers.
- **Criticising** the government's attempt to develop a single industry-wide body to speak on behalf of the tourist industry, claiming that Tourism Alliance is overwhelmingly dominated by large private sector companies and is thus narrow and unrepresentative.
- **Launching**, jointly with DTLR, a publication on credit unions, highlighting the important role they can play in tackling financial exclusion in low income areas, and the role local authorities can play in supporting them.
- **Receiving and disseminating** a government briefing on how local authorities should refine their emergency planning procedures to deal with possible biological or chemical terrorist attacks on the UK.
- **Campaigning** successfully for additional funding of £300 million for social services departments, to relieve winter pressures within the health care system and prevent hospital 'bed-blocking'.
- **Condemning** the Health Secretary for releasing 'questionable and limited data' on allegedly poorly performing social services departments on the very day of the launch of a national recruitment campaign for social workers.

Government Offices for the Regions

If the LGA is the national voice of local government, the nine Government Offices – co-ordinated now through the Regional Co-ordination Unit (RCU) in the Cabinet Office – are the regional voice of central government. They were created in 1994, to pull together the former regional offices of the Departments of Environment, Transport and the Regions, Education and Employment, and Trade and Industry. They have since taken over functions also from the Home Office, the Department for Culture, Media and Sport, and in 2001 the Department for Work and Pensions, and they are now responsible for over £6 billion of government expenditure. Their principal roles are to manage spending programmes on behalf of their 'sponsoring' departments and generally to work in partnership with local people, business organisations, local authorities, other public and voluntary sector agencies for the benefit of the region. With the RCU now providing a single focus in Whitehall for regional issues, the GOs are a key element in the drive towards 'joined-up government', and will also figure prominently in any moves towards elected regional government in England (see Chapter 5).

Some conceptual models

In this final section of the chapter we shall outline some of the models that have been applied to the study and interpretation of central–local relations. You should think and make use of these models in much the same way – to use Loughlin's analogy (1996b, p. 53) – as you would maps. For, like maps, they are deliberate simplifications of the real world that should enable us to understand its complexities and find our way through them a little more easily.

Agency model

The agency model sees local authorities as having a completely subordinate relationship to central government: as arms or agents of the centre, with little or no discretion in the task of implementing national policies. From the accounts we have given of the increasing marginalisation of local government and growing dominance of the centre, it might be supposed that the agency model is nowadays an accurate characterisation of reality. Bogdanor (1988), for example, claimed that the Conservative Government elected in 1979 was 'the most centralist since the Stuart monarchs of the 17th century'. With the steady erosion and transfer of its powers and responsibilities, and tight central control over both its taxing and spending policies, it may seem that local councils nowadays are indeed little more than central government's agents.

Such an interpretation, though, ignores the substantial policy diversity that manifestly still exists amongst our local authorities. Central government obviously does exercise tight financial control, but that control does not produce anything approaching uniform expenditure patterns or policy priorities. This can be demonstrated in many ways, but one of the most insightful is to compare – and then try to explain – the financial and other statistics compiled each year by CIPFA, the Chartered Institute of Public Finance and Accountancy. All councils are required to produce such statistics, enabling their service figures to be compared with those of other councils of the same type and size – as in Exhibit 9.7.

If you are able to find similar service indicators to those in Exhibit 9.4 for a council you know personally, you should find this kind of comparative exercise especially informative, and may feel you can begin to explain some of the variations you will almost certainly observe. All sorts of factors may occur to you: political control, pressure group activity, differences in the geography, economy, and social character of the area, but not population size, since all these statistics are *per capita* or the equivalent. You should also remember that expenditure statistics are not performance measures; they tell us simply what is being put into the provision of a service, which may or may not relate to the quality of that service or to the value for money being received by local users and taxpayers.

Trying to explain even these input variations can be a hazardous exercise and one that we do not intend to attempt here. The principal purpose of Exhibit 9.7 is to highlight the extent of expenditure and apparently policy variation that exists among councils with exactly the same statutory responsibilities. Even in the case of a largely statutory service like school education, the percentage variations may strike you as significant. But at the mainly or entirely discretionary end of the service spectrum the arts and economic development expenditure variations become massive.

You can try a similar exercise with the sets of Performance Indicators (PIs) that the Audit Commission now produces each year. All councils have to submit their PI statistics to the Audit Commission and they are also required to publicise them locally – in, for example, a double-page spread in the local paper or a pull-out supplement in the council's own free newspaper. If they make the most of this opportunity, councils can tell their residents what they are shown to be doing well, what services they are prioritising, and even why on some performance measures they appear to be lagging behind other councils of the same type.

Some councils in areas of severe economic and social deprivation clearly face heavier demands on their services and greater pressures on their tight

Exhibit 9.7 Local authority service statistics, 1999/2000: some comparisons

	SECONDARY EDUCATION		SOCIAL SERVICES	LIBRARIES	THE ARTS – CULTURE AND HERITAGE	ECONOMIC DEVELOPMENT AND PROMOTION
	Spending per pupil (£)	Pupils per qualified teacher	Net spending per capita (£)	Net spending per capita (£)	Net spending per capita (£)	Net spending per capita (£)
A. METROPOLITAN DISTRICTS						
Barnsley	2,803	18.2	275	8.1	2.7	14.3
Birmingham	2,989	22.5	338	15.1	11.0	14.6
Bradford	2,624	20.0	293	9.3	4.0	7.9
Bury	2,877	17.7	1037	11.3	1.0	0.7
Coventry	2,952	17.1	217	10.5	11.4	31.5
Dudley	2,822	15.9	310	11.2	4.0	0.24
Knowsley	3,048	16.9	153	17.4	3.5	20.0
Leeds	2,926	18.4	207	10.8	11.8	3.7
Manchester	3,208	13.7	327	22.5	11.9	N/a
Walsall	2,699	26.2	N/a	14.8	4.7	1.4
All metropolitan districts	2,868	18.1	303	13.0	6.1	7.3

Percentage variation between highest and lowest	22	91	578	178	1189	13,000
B. ENGLISH COUNTIES						
Devon	2,861	17.5	275	8.8	(0.15)	1.4
Durham	2,856	17.1	270	11.6	N/a	[7.1]
East Sussex	2,929	16.4	(229)	10.4	1.0	1.3
Essex	2,945	16.2	399	[12.9]	2.3	2.1
Lincolnshire	2,805	[33.1]	272	10.2	3.4	2.3
Norfolk	2,959	21.7	314	10.3	[4.8]	1.2
Oxfordshire	2,786	17.4	397	9.6	2.7	(0.07)
Somerset	[3,022]	19.4	[434]	(8.7)	2.3	1.0
Wiltshire	(2,485)	24.2	N/a	10.3	1.2	1.3
Worcestershire	2,524	(15.8)	N/a	8.9	1.3	0.8
All English counties	2,799	18.4	313	10.7	2.0	1.5
Percentage variation between highest and lowest	22	109	90	48	3,100	10,000

Notes: [ ] signifies highest figure; ( ) signifies lowest figure

N/a = not available

Source: CIPFA, *Local Government Comparative Statistics, 2000* (CIPFA, 2001), pp. 56–71.

budgets than do those in less stressed areas. It is difficult, however, to explain away entirely in such fashion the huge differences in, say, household waste collection and recycling rates that are shown in Exhibit 9.8 – let alone that some councils apparently expect their residents to embrace private enterprise even in the search for somewhere to relieve themselves. Councils clearly do vary in efficiency and in the priority they give to different aspects of their service provision. They have, in other words, *discretion*, which is why we suggest that, on its own, the agency model is a less than fully satisfactory representation of the central–local relationship.

Power-dependence model

This is an elaboration of the *partnership model*, which sees central government and local authorities as more or less co-equal partners. The partnership model itself is unsatisfactory in at least two respects. The concept of partnership tends to be left vague and imprecisely defined. It also appears to disregard the constitutional reality of Britain as a unitary state, and local government being necessarily, therefore, a subordinate creation of the national Parliament. To circumvent these criticisms academics developed an alternative power-dependence model. This model postulates that both central departments and local authorities have *resources* – legal, financial, political, informational, and so on – which each can use against the other and against other organisations as well (see Exhibit 9.9).

It is a model that pays particular attention to *bargaining*; it also argues that, while there are likely to be inequalities in the distribution of resources, they are not necessarily cumulative. Rhodes (1979, pp. 29–31) observes:

> The fact that a local authority or a central department lacks one resource does not mean that it lacks others. One resource could be substituted for another. For example, a central department lacking the constitutional/legal resources to prevent (or encourage) a specific local initiative can attempt to get its way by withholding (or supplying) financial resources. Conversely, a local authority which has been refused financial resources can attempt to reverse this state of affairs by embarrassing the central department. Press and television reports on the adverse consequences of the centre's decision may lead to the decision being reconsidered.

The model thus sees power in relative terms, hingeing upon a process of bargaining and exchange. Councils have significant assets of their own that they can exploit: local knowledge and professional expertise, their networking and negotiating skills, and above all their position as the elected and concerned representatives of their communities. Its obvious

Exhibit 9.8 Some Environmental Services Performance Indicators, 1999/2000

	Highest		Lowest		% variation
Public conveniences per 100,000 residents (National average = 15.4) Unitary/metropolitan authorities only	Isle of Wight Bournemouth Bath/NE Somerset	40 32 23	Liverpool Sandwell St. Helens	0 0 0	∞
% householder planning applications decided in 8 weeks (Nat. average = 75%) Unitary/metropolitan authorities only	Wirral Gateshead Thurrock	95 93 90	West Berkshire Wokingham Southampton	46 47 51	107
% pedestrian crossings with facilities for disabled (National average = 72%) Unitary/metropolitan authorities only	Bolton Stoke-on-Trent Telford & Wrekin	100 100 100	Doncaster Liverpool Stockport	22 36 43	350
% household waste recycled (National average = 12.3%) Unitary/metropolitan authorities only	Bournemouth Bath/NE Somerset	30 27	Manchester Wolverhampton Nottingham	0.6 3.2 3.7	5,000
Household waste collections missed per 100,000 collections (Nat. average = 194) Metropolitan authorities only	Wakefield Leeds Coventry	2,091 1,916 898	Gateshead Walsall N. Tyneside	3 7 7	70,000

Note: ∞ = infinity.

Source: Audit Commission, Local Authority Performance Indicators: Environmental Services in England, 1999/2000 (Abingdon: Audit Commission, 2001)

Exhibit 9.9 The resources of central and local government

CENTRAL GOVERNMENT	LOCAL GOVERNMENT
• Controls legislation and delegated powers	• Employs all personnel in local services, far outnumbering civil servants
• Provides and controls the largest proportion of local authorities' current expenditure through the Revenue Support Grant (RSG)	• Has, through both councillors and officers, detailed local knowledge and expertise
• Controls individual authorities' total expenditure and taxation levels by 'capping'	• Controls the implementation of policy
• Controls the largest proportion of local capital expenditure	• Has limited powers to raise own taxes and set own service charges
• Sets standards for and inspects some services	• Can decide own political priorities and most service standards, and how money should be distributed among services
• Has national electoral mandate.	• Has local electoral mandate.

Source: Adapted from Rhodes (1988), p. 42.

appeal is that neither central nor local government are depicted as monolithic blocs. It is also, though, one of its alleged weaknesses. For it has been regularly criticised (see, e.g., Houlihan, 1988, p. 70; Cochrane, 1993a, p. 25) for understating the superior power of central government. It is said to give insufficient attention to the internal politics of organisations, and insufficient consideration to the broader (capitalist) economic and political system within which these inter-governmental and inter-organisational relations take place. Such points should not be disregarded; nor are they by Rhodes himself (1986b), who sees the model and the conceptual debate it generated of sufficient 'continuing relevance' to justify a recent 'revisit' (Rhodes, 1999, esp. Chs 5, 6).

Policy communities and networks

The single most obvious deficiency of the power-dependence model is precisely the same as that of our own sketch map in Figure 9.1. They both focus on *institutional* or organisational relationships – at the inevitable expense of policy systems, policy communities and policy networks. The main point of studying political and governmental institutions is to understand better how they inter-relate to make and implement policies.

Box 9.1 Policy communities

- a limited number of participants with some groups consciously excluded;
- a dominant economic or professional interest;
- frequent interaction between all members of the community on all matters related to the policy issues;
- consistency in values, membership and policy outcomes over time;
- consensus, with the ideology, values and broad policy preferences shared by all participants;
- exchange relationships, with all members of the policy community having some resources;
- bargaining between members with resources;
- the hierarchical distribution of resources within the participating organisations, so that the leaders can guarantee the compliance of their members.

Source: Rhodes (1999b), p. 142.

Our local authorities are by definition multi-functional organisations and 'local authority policy-making' therefore takes place for the most part within function-specific 'policy communities' based on local authority services – education, social services, fire, and so on. The power-dependence model could thus be said to concentrate on the 'national community for local government', while substantially ignoring the multiplicity of other functional policy communities and policy networks.

Policy communities, as defined by Rhodes and Marsh, two of the most prolific contributors to these ideas, have the characteristics in Box 9.1 (Rhodes, 1999b, p. 142).

It is easy to see from this listing the thematic continuity with the power-dependence model, and also, with its emphasis on professional interests and values, its direct applicability to the profession-based world of British local government. It is also, of course, enormously research-suggestive and has generated a massive literature of its own, some of the key summaries of which are included in the suggestions of further reading below.

Guide to further reading

For many years the most insightful book-length treatment of central–local relations was Griffith (1966). It still repays study. More recently the biggest single contributor has been Rhodes. In his 'magnum opus' (1988) he reviews the various theories of inter-governmental relations and unravels the maze that was then 'sub-central government'. Parts were updated by Gray (1994), and, on a smaller scale, Stoker and John have contributed chapters on 'Government beyond Whitehall' to successive editions of *Developments in British Politics*, most recently John (1997). As noted in the chapter, in a recycling enterprise that would surely earn a high Audit Commission PI rating, Rhodes has revised his 1981 'reinterpretation of central–local relations' and, in a partly new Part II, brings the story up to date (Rhodes, 1999b). A major part of this story is policy networks, useful summaries of which are Marsh and Rhodes (1992), Rhodes (1997) and Marsh (1998). Finally, having mentioned the Audit Commission, it does of course have its own extensive web site, as do the DTLR, the Local Government Association (see particularly its Central Local Partnership page), the Government Offices for the Regions, and just about every other significant player in the world of sub-central government.

Chapter 10

Local Finance

Introduction – calm after the storm

In dealing with local finance we reverse the practice we adopted with structures. The scale of recent structural change seemed to require two chapters instead of one. Finance, however, compared with the emotion and headlines it generated in the 1980s, culminating in the brief but highly eventful appearance of the poll tax, has had a relatively calm few years. We have therefore compressed two previous chapters into one.

The form of our presentation, though, is essentially unchanged. We start by introducing the basic elements of the local government finance system and the budget-making process, and from your perspective: that of an aware, service-receiving, and probably tax-paying citizen. Specifically, we seek to arm you with the information necessary to interpret your own council tax demand and to understand the main decisions that produced it. Later in the chapter we provide some recent historical and comparative context, not least to enable us to appreciate why, as noted at the start of Chapter 9, a body like the Congress of Local and Regional Authorities of Europe (CLRAE) should see the system and process we have been describing as undemocratically centralist.

Your own tax bill

We start with the council tax, introduced by the Major Government in April 1993 as a politically necessary replacement for the poll tax or community charge – of which more later. Specifically, we suggest you look at your own council tax bill and at the accompanying explanatory information sent out by your local council – particularly the details of the council's budget. If, perhaps as a student, you have no tax bill of your own, try to borrow one. Alternatively, if, as suggested in Chapter 1, you have acquired a copy of your council's *Annual Report* or can access it on the internet, it should contain a summary of the annual accounts and budget – though in this case the budget for the previous financial year, not the current one.

At the foot of your tax bill – the bottom line figure – will be the amount that you personally or your household are required to pay. In this chapter we shall explain, using Birmingham City Council's 2001/02 budget for illustration, how that bottom line figure was calculated. You will find, though, that your council has already provided its own explanation, in the various additional leaflets it sent out with the bill. These may include:

- The budget and spending plans of the council that actually sent you the bill (the 'billing authority') – your district, borough or unitary council;
- The separate budgets and spending plans of councils and other authorities entitled to have the billing authority collect tax on their behalf – 'precepting authorities', such as county and possibly parish, town and community councils, and also passenger transport, police, and metropolitan joint fire and civil defence authorities;
- Explanatory Notes from the Treasurer's or Finance Department of the billing authority, detailing possible methods of payment, appeal procedures, discounts and benefit entitlements – often translated into relevant languages.

This information is one of the many ways in which local authorities are considerably more open and accountable than central government chooses to be. The Inland Revenue provides no such literature about central government's spending plans when it sends out tax returns for tax payers to complete.

Capital and current spending

If we turn first not to the tax bill itself but to the accompanying budget leaflet, it will be clear that we need to start with one or two basic definitions.

> *BUDGET* – a statement defining a council's policies over a specified period of time in terms of finance.

The reference to a 'specified period of time' is obviously crucial. We instinctively think of budgets as annual events, but a local authority, spending perhaps several hundred million pounds each year, cannot possibly afford to think only of the short term. It must try, as best it can, to forecast the future and plan ahead. The first thing to note, therefore, about any council's budget is its division into *current* and *capital* expenditure.

> *CURRENT (also known as REVENUE) EXPENDITURE* – the day-to-day spending needed to keep services running: staff wages and salaries, books for schools, office equipment, petrol for refuse collection vehicles, heating bills in children's homes, etc.
> *CAPITAL EXPENDITURE* – spending which produces longer-term assets, often expensive, but whose benefits will last beyond the next financial year: purchase of land, construction of buildings and roads, major items of equipment.

Far more of local government's spending goes nowadays on current running costs than on capital investment, as can be seen in Exhibit 10.1. But it was not always so. The capital:current spending ratio has increased massively over the past few decades, from 1:2 in the 1960s to 1:6 in the 1980s to over 1:11 in 1998/99, largely as the result of successive central governments' relentless pressure on local authorities to limit their capital spending. It is an eloquent measure of the extent of the country's long-term under-investment in its public service infrastructure.

The total expenditure figures at the foot of Exhibit 10.1 indicate the scale and national economic significance of local government in Britain. The £81.4 billion service expenditure represented a quarter of the country's total government spending of £328 billion, about 11p in every £ of its £900 billion Gross Domestic Product, and some £1,390 for every single resident. In Scotland especially, and also in Wales, that last *per capita* figure would be even higher; in Northern Ireland much lower, as the Northern Ireland Office, a central government department, continues to be responsible for many of the functions carried out by local authorities elsewhere in Great Britain.

Exhibit 10.1 Local authority spending 1998/99 – current vs. capital

	Current %	Capital %	Total £ billion	%
Education	32	15	25.0	31
Housing	15	38	13.7	17
Personal social services	16	2	12.4	15
Police	10	4	7.4	9
Local environmental services (including refuse collection and disposal, environmental health, planning and economic development, etc.)	7	18	6.7	8
Transport and roads	5	16	4.7	6
Fire	2	1	1.6	2
Libraries and art galleries	1	1	1.2	1
Sports and recreation	1	4	1.1	1
Other services	11	1	7.7	10
TOTAL UK (£ billion)	**74.7**	**6.7**	**81.4**	

Source: DETR, *Local Government Financial Statistics England* (2000), p. 18.

The percentage figures in Exhibit 10.1 demonstrate the still dominant positions of education and housing in the authorities that have responsibility for these services, though that dominance declined under the Conservative governments as schools opted for grant maintained (GM) status and direct central government funding, and council housing was transferred to private ownership and housing association or private sector management. The contrasting character of these two major services can be seen in the first two columns of Exhibit 10.1. Education, like social services, is labour-intensive; housing, like transport, exceptionally capital intensive.

The current spending of local authorities understandably receives the bulk of both councillors' and citizens' attention. It will be our chief concern too for most of this chapter. But we should look first at councils' capital spending programmes, for they are the embodiment of any council's longer-term political and strategic objectives. They necessarily have to be financed in very different ways from current spending; and, once started, they can have major implications for subsequent years' current budgets.

Financing capital spending

We noted above how central government has sought continuously to regulate local authorities' capital spending. The form of that regulation throughout the 1990s was based on the tough but familiar principle of *credit control*, the aim being to control all local authority capital expenditure financed by credit in one form or another. To appreciate the comprehensiveness of the system we should bear in mind that there are in fact four main methods of capital financing, three of which are directly subject to central government control.

Borrowing up to a prescribed credit ceiling

Each year, every local council is given by the government a permission to borrow, or *Basic Credit Approval* (BCA). The BCA specifies the *maximum sum* the council can borrow to finance capital projects in education, housing, social services and various other services. In addition, a council may be given a *Supplementary Credit Approval* (SCA) for specific, government-approved projects and initiatives concerning, for example, magistrates' courts, roads, rural housing and homelessness.

These credit approvals (known as net capital allocations in Scotland) account nowadays for about a third of all local authority capital investment. They permit a council to borrow from any of several available sources: from a government agency like the Public Works Loan Board (PWLB), from a British or European bank, or by issuing stocks, bonds and annuities. So a local authority may have more borrowing options open to it than we do as private citizens, but it too will have to pay the going rate of interest and repay any loan by its expiry date.

It is difficult to exaggerate how resented this form of 'control by approval' is. Responding to the government's 2000 finance Green Paper, 285 of 286 councils wanted the system abolished, together with 77 per cent of businesses and 95 per cent of other organisations. The Green Paper proposed replacing control by a self-regulated 'prudential' system. Councils would be free to borrow, without explicit ministerial permission, provided they can finance it in ways consistent with a professional Prudential Code, to be developed by the government and local authority associations. Having been outlined in the Green Paper, the necessary Bill was expected to feature in the Government's 2001/02 legislative programme. It did not, which means that credit approvals are likely to continue until at least 2004/05.

Using capital receipts

Councils may supplement their BCAs and SCAs by using money they raise by selling assets such as land, buildings and housing. Again, though, there are government-prescribed limits. For most of the 1990s councils were able to use for new investment a maximum of:

- 25 per cent of receipts from housing sales, and
- 50 per cent of receipts from the disposal of other assets.

Remaining receipts, said the Conservative Government, should be used to pay off outstanding debts. An early Labour Government overture to local authorities, however, was slightly to relax this regime by allowing them to reinvest up to £5 billion of their accumulated receipts from council house sales in building new homes and renovating old ones. As a result, this source of capital funding now accounts for nearly a quarter of the total.

Through capital grants

The government, through the Single Regeneration Budget or programmes like Sure Start and New Deal for Communities (see Exhibit 8.3), makes capital grants to local authorities for specific purposes. So too does the National Lottery, and also the European Union, both through its structural funds, like the European Regional Development Fund (ERDF) and the European Social Fund (ESF), and through more focused initiatives. These grants can be substantial and crucial to the viability of major developments – such as Birmingham's £180 million International Convention Centre and Symphony Hall, some £50 million of which came from the European Union. About a quarter of local capital spending is financed nowadays by grants, but here too there are often conditions attached: receipt of certain grants may simply lead to the government reducing a council's credit approval by an equivalent amount.

Using current (revenue) income

The one source of capital finance available to a council that is not subject to direct government control is its own revenue income – from local taxes, rents, and other charges. But in a period of financial constraint that freedom may seem like the freedom we all have to dine at the Ritz: the many more immediate calls on a council's government-capped revenue budget are likely to appear more practically and politically insistent. In this case, therefore, the last is least: only about a sixth of local government investment comes from its own revenue.

The capital budget

In summary, then, a local authority's capital spending will be shaped by the following formula:

> Its Basic Credit Approved spending,
> *plus* any Supplementary Credit Approved spending,
> *plus* the usable parts of its capital receipts,
> *plus* any capital grants,
> *plus* any revenue-financed spending.

The government, therefore, now sets most of the effective *ceilings*. But councils must choose for themselves whether to spend up to the limit of their credit approval, and whether to top that limit up with other permitted sources of finance. Capital budget profiles will accordingly vary considerably from council to council, and also from one year to the next. Biggest spending heads, depending on your council's location, size and responsibilities, are likely to be housing and regeneration, followed, usually some way behind, by highways, education, leisure and social services. Details of your own council's main capital projects should be itemised in its budget; also its principal sources of capital finance. So you should be able to compare for yourself the probably rather limited funding from the council's own revenue with the figures for borrowing under credit approval and for types of capital grants.

Contrary to what is sometimes imagined, far more of Birmingham's capital investment goes towards housing improvement – both directly on its own 88,000 housing stock and through grants to private owner occupiers – than on its 'prestige' regeneration projects. These high-profile capital programmes – the Eastside development centred on Millennium

Point (see Exhibit 8.3), the £800 million shopping centre redevelopment around the city's famous Bull Ring and Rag Market, the £210 million extensions of the Midland Metro tram line – will ultimately cost more, but that cost is spread over several years and shared with other public and private sector partners. School rebuilding and refurbishment is another key investment heading, often nowadays through PFI contracts (see p. 145).

Birmingham's capital budget in 2001/02 was £160 million, which we shall see represents a capital:current ratio of nearly 1:14. For 2002/03, though, the planned budget was down to £117 million, taking the ratio towards 1:20, which helps to explain both the attraction to even ideologically sceptical councils of PFI schemes, and also why authorities like Birmingham feel they have little option but to consider large-scale voluntary transfers of their maintenance-demanding housing stock (see Exhibit 7.5).

Current or revenue spending

How much is to be spent? On what? Where is the money coming from? The three fundamental questions we have just asked of our council's capital budget are similarly applicable to its considerably larger current or revenue budget. In fact, the answers should be more easily obtainable, for the main purpose of the tax demand literature is to set out and explain the council's revenue budget: its planned expenditure on the day-to-day provision of services for the coming financial year. With luck, yours may be one of the enterprising councils that seek to present such information in as eye-catching a manner as possible, with an imaginative use of illustrative diagrams and graphics.

But, however they are presented, you should encounter some figures set out under service or committee headings that will resemble those of Birmingham City Council in Exhibit 10.2, even if the figures themselves are on a very different scale. In order to interpret them, two further definitions are immediately required.

> GROSS SPENDING – the total cost of providing the council's services, *before* taking into account rents, fees and charges for services, and income from government grants.
> NET SPENDING – gross spending minus income from rents, fees and charges and from *specific* government grants for particular projects or services – e.g. towards rent rebates and allowances, mandatory student awards.

We can see from the first column of Exhibit 10.2 that Birmingham City Council proposed to spend a total of nearly £2.2 billion on its day-to-day service provision in 2001/02. Even after the transfer of further education

Exhibit 10.2 Birmingham City Council's revenue budget, 2001/02

MAJOR SERVICES (by Cabinet portfolio)
EDUCATION and LIFELONG LEARNING 180,000 pupils; 400 + schools
SOCIAL SERVICES and HEALTH 8,000 in residential care; 11,000 home care clients
STREET SERVICES Highway maintenance, traffic management, refuse collection, markets, etc.
LEISURE, CULTURE and TOURISM 4.9 mill. library book borrowings; 775,000 museum visits
SUSTAINABILITY and PUBLIC PROTECTION Public health, trading standards, waste disposal, recycling
HOUSING 88,000 council houses; 390,000 repairs completed
REGENERATION Economic planning and development, employment creation, business support
LOCAL and NEIGHBOURHOOD DEVELOPMENT Community development and safety, crime prevention
OTHER SERVICES (including NEC, ICC, NIA, Best Value, personnel)
Plus: contingencies
TOTAL COUNCIL EXPENDITURE
Less: contribution from balances/reserves
COUNCIL'S NET BUDGET REQUIREMENT

and sixth form colleges out of local authority control and the opting-out of some of its secondary schools, a third of the council's gross spending and over half of its net spending goes on education, with roughly 60 per cent of that sum on teachers' salaries. Next biggest net spender, similarly labour intensive, is social services, with a clientele in Birmingham of over 50,000 children, elderly and disabled people. These services derive respectively about a sixth and a quarter of their income from service charges and specific grants for designated purposes, such as nursery and childcare, special education, student awards, children leaving care, asylum seekers, and the treatment of mental illness.

GROSS EXPENDITURE		INCOME from charges and specific grants (£ mill.)	NET EXPENDITURE		
2001/02 (£ million)	% of total		2001/02 (£ million)	Change from 2000/01 (£ million)	% of total
743	34	129	614	+20	54
320	15	87	233	+4	20
140	6	44	96	+4	8
105	5	25	80	+3	7
49	2	13	36	+1	3
418	19	383	35	+4	3
44	2	26	18	+2	2
15	1	1	14	+2	1
100	5	117	(17)		(1)
10			10		
2,195	100	1,043	1,152	+41	
			(8)		
			1,144		

By comparison, over 90 per cent of Birmingham's housing expenditure is met by income, much of it from rents on the council's massive housing stock of around 88,000 dwellings. Since 1990 Housing Revenue Accounts (HRAs) have been 'ring-fenced'. Not only must they be kept separately, but no transfers are permitted between HRAs and a council's general fund, to subsidise either tenants or council tax payers. There is a housing subsidy scheme, but no longer subject to the political discretion of local authorities. They now receive a formula-defined specific grant from the government – £125 million for Birmingham in 2001/02 – to administer on its behalf. The arrangement is similar to the one-time provision of LEA mandatory student grants, though here the payment takes the form of rent rebates and allowances to low-income tenants. As a result of these two major sources of income – rents and government subsidies – Birmingham's *net* revenue spending on housing is lower than might be expected of what used – before smallness became beautiful and bigness unfashionable – to proclaim itself Western Europe's largest landlord.

Levies and precepts

Identifying the council's net spending requirements is but the first step in the determination of an individual's local tax bill. To the council-provided services listed in Exhibit 10.2 must be added the services provided for Birmingham residents by bodies that cannot themselves directly demand and collect local taxes. In Birmingham – and the other six West Midlands Metropolitan districts – there are four such bodies:

1. *The West Midlands Police Authority* – formerly a joint board, but now a separate Authority, half of whose members are councillors nominated by the West Midlands district councils and the other half local magistrates and the Home Secretary's nominees. Like all police authorities, it receives a direct central government grant equivalent to half of its net revenue expenditure.
2. *The West Midlands Fire and Civil Defence Authority* – still a joint board of nominated district councillors.
3. *The West Midlands Passenger Transport Authority* – another joint board, the largest slice of whose revenue budget provides free bus and rail travel for senior citizens and concessionary fares for children and school students.
4. *The Environment Agency* – a quango that, among other things, maintains flood defences and water resources, through a Midlands Region Flood Defence Committee.

Just like the City Council, all these bodies have their own capital and revenue budgets, funded in part through a combination of loans, grants, capital receipts and revenue income. But they also finance some of their revenue expenditure by means of a *precept* or *levy* on their tax-collecting district authorities, divided amongst them according to their population size. These latter councils are thus required to collect from their local taxpayers, in addition to their own tax demands, these other monies and then hand them straight over to the various precepting and levying authorities.

Birmingham's *total* net revenue requirement consequently includes over £70 million that it has to collect but over which it has no direct control. As may be imagined, this obligation can be distinctly irritating to city councillors, who have to take the political responsibility and blame for a tax level, part of which they can hardly even indirectly influence. But their irritation is mild compared to that of some of their shire district council colleagues. For they have to collect a county council precept that may amount to almost 90 per cent of their total tax demands, plus, in some cases, an additional few pounds in parish council precepts which, just to add to their frustration, are not even capped.

One of the tensions in the two-tier parts of our local government system is that in non-metropolitan England it is not the counties – with their bigger spending education, social services and transport responsibilities – that are designated billing and tax-collecting authorities. The council tax is a property tax and therefore most obviously collected by the local housing authorities, the much smaller and inevitably lower spending district councils (see Exhibit 7.1). This position, you may be sure, will be emphasised by district councils in their explanatory budget literature. Just look, they will say, at all the housing, leisure, environmental and community services we provide to enhance your quality of life, and all for less than the cost of a weekly pint of beer.

Financing current spending

There are two final 'technical' adjustments to be made to the spending side of our council's current account. It has to be decided how much to set aside for any unforeseen items of expenditure, known as 'contingencies', and how much to keep as balances or reserves. With those adjustments made, Birmingham City Council's *total net spending requirement* for 2001/02 amounted to a formidable £1,144 million: well over £1,000 per resident. The obvious next question: how is it to be found?

There is a certain symmetry to British local government finance. Just as there are four main methods of raising capital finance, there are four main ways of financing current or revenue expenditure.

Charges

Local authorities have always set fees and charges for the use of some of their services – passenger transport, car parks, home helps, school meals, swimming baths and other leisure facilities. They also, as noted above, collect council rents. In Birmingham's case these charges, taken together, meet a fifth (20 per cent) of the council's gross current expenditure. Since the Local Government and Housing Act 1989, councils have been able, if they wish, to introduce charges for any of their services except for education, the police and fire services, elections, and library book borrowing. This extension of charging was a key element in the

Conservative Government's programme to increase local accountability by making consumers more directly aware of the cost and value of the services they receive.

Most charges are discretionary, councils deciding for themselves what they wish to charge or what they feel the market will bear. They can try to encourage the use of a service, like adult education classes or day nurseries, by setting a *social* charge, below the full cost of provision. They can just cover the provision cost; impose a *means-related* charge based on ability to pay, as for some residential homes; or a *market* charge to maximise profit. Finally, they can try to limit the use of certain services, such as city centre car parks or cemetery burials, by imposing a *deterrent* charge.

Such decisions – whether or not to subsidise a particular service, by how much and in what way, or whether to try to maximise profit – raise some of the most fundamental of all political questions. Quite properly, they offer councillors a ready-made subject for debate whenever charges and a council's charging policy come up for review. Different economic, social and political objectives will be argued, and sometimes intriguing policy decisions taken, as can be seen in Exhibit 10.3.

Exhibit 10.3 Examples of local authority discretionary charges, 2000

	Highest (£)		Lowest (£)	
Hire of leisure centre squash court per hour (E & W average = £6.23)	Bolton	15.30	Haringey LB	2.10
	Merton LB	11.03	Coventry	2.40
	Richmond-u-Thames LB	10.50	Hartlepool	3.15
Hire of floodlit all-weather pitch per hour (E & W average = £33.58)	Hertsmere (Herts)	123.38	Enfield LB	7.20
	Reading	90.00	Forest Heath (Suffolk)	7.25
	Sheffield	81.33	Fylde (Lancs)	7.25
Weekday charge for indoor pool for senior citizens (E & W average = £1.20)	Harrow LB	2.75	Sutton LB	Free
	Camden LB	2.70	Westminster LB	Free
	Chester	2.50	Salford	Free
			Trafford	Free
Cemetery grave headstone for adult non-parishioner	Bexley LB	363	Rushcliffe (Notts)	5
	Herefordshire	300	Salisbury	11
	St. Helens	253	Hertsmere (Herts)	21

Note: E & W = England and Wales
Source: CIPFA Statistical Information Service

It is always enlightening to compare your personal experience – the cost of your LEA's school meals, for example – with that of others. You might also question what it is about Bolton's squash courts that makes them seven times as expensive as Haringey's. Or why some London boroughs seem keen to encourage their senior citizens to swim, while others try to extort as much as possible from them. Or why Hertsmere, having shocked you to death with news of its all-weather pitch charges, should be so eager to furnish your grave with a cut-price headstone. The differences in these completely discretionary service charges are, as you might expect, at least as great as the substantial variations in *per capita* expenditure and performance that we noted in Exhibits 9.7 and 9.8. Whatever possible explanations you come up with, it is difficult to argue from these figures at least that local councils have been stripped of all their powers of decision and discretion.

Government grants

Grants, like charges, have long been an integral and indispensable feature of local government finance, although, as we shall see later, their nature, role and scale have all changed significantly in recent years. Focusing on the budget process, we shall be concentrating mainly on one particular grant: the Revenue Support Grant (RSG). There are, however, numerous other grants paid by central government to local authorities, and almost as many different reasons for paying them. The two most fundamental purposes of grants, though, are compensation and persuasion.

Compensation takes a variety of forms: compensation to local councils, for instance, for providing certain necessary services – e.g. for disabled children, carers, or asylum seekers – that are acknowledged to be in the public interest and for which, therefore, local taxpayers should not be required to foot the whole bill. Councils may be compensated too for their varying spending needs and taxable resources. The rationale behind the RSG is that local authorities should be able, and be given grant incentives, to provide a common standard of service at broadly the same cost to local taxpayers across the whole country.

The *persuasion* motive for grants can be seen as a straightforward wish by central government to influence or control some aspect of local council spending: she or he who pays the piper expects to call the tune. Grants can be used to promote spending on certain services, to enforce minimum standards, to encourage councils to implement central government policy initiatives, and generally to push them in directions in which they would not necessarily otherwise go.

It ought to be that the principal purpose of a grant will suggest its most efficient form, and that a grant's form will imply its purpose. We must distinguish therefore between the two basic forms of grant – specific and general – to match our two fundamental purposes.

> SPECIFIC GRANTS (sometimes known as selective or hypothecated grants) – government grants to local authorities whose proceeds must be spent on some specified project or service – e.g. Nursery Education Grant for 4-year olds, AIDS Support Grant, Rural Bus Service Grant. As can be seen in Figure 10.3 (p. 208), specific grants have steadily increased as a proportion of total central government's contribution to local government.
> GENERAL GRANTS (also known as non-selective or unhypothe-cated grants) – grants whose proceeds may be spent at the discretion of the grantees, local councils themselves. The general grant to local government – now known as the RSG – still accounts for the biggest slice of total central government support.

The distinction between the two grant forms is important, to both central government grantor and local authority grantee. If persuasion and influence are the government's objectives, it will presumably opt for a specific grant, and define its purpose as precisely as possible. If compensation is the objective, or the retention of the maximum degree of local financial discretion, then a general grant is the logical choice. The specific:general grant ratio can thus serve as a rough and ready indicator of central government financial control. The trend in recent years towards specific grants, from a 1:4 ratio in the early 1970s to the point where they now almost match the Revenue Support Grant, is not accidental.

You will recall from Exhibit 10.2 that, together with its income from fees and charges, the *specific* grants received by Birmingham City Council were taken into account in translating the city's gross spending to a net spending requirement. We come now, therefore, to the council's single largest source of current income: a general grant known since 1990 as the *Revenue Support Grant* (RSG).

The annual RSG distribution process takes the public form of a series of government announcements, concentrated nowadays in the late autumn, or less than six months before the start of the new financial year. First, the government decides how much money in total local authorities will be permitted to spend during the coming year – their *Total Standard Spending* (TSS). Secondly, it declares the proportion of that total spending – around 80 per cent in recent years – that it will finance through national taxation, or *Aggregate External Finance* (AEF). The difference between the two figures – about 20 per cent – is the proportion that local authorities collectively will have to find for themselves.

The government then moves from the aggregate to the individual authority level. It produces an assessment of what *it* feels each authority needs to spend – both in total and in each of seven principal service areas –

in order to provide what it defines as a 'standard level of service'. These figures constitute a council's *Standard Spending Assessment* (SSA) and are absolutely critical in determining the level of grant it will receive. The government bases its calculations on a limited range of indicators, such as the total residential population of the council area, the number of people aged over 65 living alone, the number of school children aged 5–10. If it over-estimates a council's spending needs, the council will receive in effect a grant subsidy; if it under-estimates, council tax bills must rise or services be cut.

From the council's total SSA two deductions are made. The first is for the total income the government estimates the authority should receive, were it to set its council tax at a specified standard level – the *Council Tax at Standard Spending* (CTSS). The second is for the income it will receive from the government-set *National Non-Domestic Rate* (NNDR). A council's Revenue Support Grant is the figure remaining after these deductions.

Expressed as a formula:

$$RSG = SSA - (CTSS + NNDR)$$

where SSA   is the government's aggregated assessment of a council's spending needs;

CTSS   is the government's assessment of a council's income from its council tax payers at a specified standard tax level; and

NNDR is a council's population-based income from its National Non-Domestic Ratepayers at a government-set rate.

Clearly, this grant distribution process incorporates both of the fundamental purposes of grants. It seeks to compensate authorities with above-average spending needs, but within a system based on the government imposing its judgement of what these authorities ought to be doing and how much of it they should be doing.

For their part, local authorities – of all political complexions – protest and plead. They protest at the presumption of ministers and their Whitehall civil servants claiming to know better than do they themselves and their local electorates what should be spent on different services. They protest at the government's methodology – its choice of indicators, its use of unreliable and outdated information – and at the consequential anomalies. Could it really have been the case, to pick one notorious example, that there was more snow on the ground at 9.00 a.m. for more days each year – and thus higher winter road maintenance costs – in Brent than in Cumbria, and in Camden than in Lancashire (LGIU, 1993, p. 37)?

Councils protest too at the distribution of grant: that the total is inadequate and fails fully to take account of the prevailing inflation rate;

that the whole process is political; and that the wrong authorities have gained and lost. And they will plead – though rarely with marked success – their exceptional local circumstances which, they claim, the government's formulae fail to recognise and which merit special treatment.

National Non-Domestic Rate/Uniform Business Rate

The third source of current income available to local authorities is one we just touched on in describing the calculation of grant: the National Non-Domestic Rate (NNDR) or, as it is almost equally commonly known, the Uni*form* (*not* Unified, Unitary or Universal!) Business Rate (UBR). It came into operation at the same time as the community charge, though without anything like the same attendant public outcry, despite being in some ways the more constitutionally significant of the two tax reforms.

For almost 400 years prior to 1989/90 the one local tax available to local authorities in this country was a property tax, known as the *rates*. Its principles were administratively simple, which is one reason why a property tax of some kind is to be found in most developed systems of local government (see Exhibit 10.6). Every property in the area – houses, flats, shops, offices, factories – was given a valuation: its *Rateable Value*. Then each year the local council would calculate how much, in addition to the grant it would receive, it needed to collect to pay for the services it wished to provide, and would set an appropriate *Rate Poundage*: so much to be paid per £ of each property's rateable value. Domestic ratepayers paid a slightly lower rate poundage than non-domestic ratepayers because the government would pay a compensating subsidy to the local council.

In 1989 in Scotland and 1990 in England and Wales this whole system changed. Domestic rates were abolished, replaced by the community charge. Northern Ireland alone retained its rating system, no doubt to many people's relief – in both senses of the word, since, as formerly in Great Britain, a large proportion of the population is entitled to rate rebates.

The non-domestic rate was not abolished, but nationalised: hence the *National* Non-Domestic Rate. In future, central government would set each year a standard or uniform rate poundage for *all* non-domestic properties in England, and similarly in Wales – though not in Scotland, where existing rate poundages were retained. Local councils continue to send out the bills and collect the rates, but these are now paid into a national fund and redistributed back to the councils in proportion to their populations. The NNDR has become in effect part of the central government grant – its more than £15 billion in 2001/02 amounting to nearly a quarter of total central government support. Former local rate-payers have become national taxpayers, and there is no longer any direct tax link between local authorities and the businesses in their area.

In 1989/90 non-domestic rates had provided over a quarter of local government current income: more than that from domestic rates. At a stroke, therefore, local councils saw the proportion of their income that they themselves controlled fall from over a half to barely a quarter: a fraction that, as we shall see, has since declined even further.

Local taxation

It will be obvious by now that the final source of local authorities' current income is their own local taxation: traditionally the rates, then the community charge, since 1993 the council tax. We shall deal towards the end of this chapter with the respective merits and deficiencies of these and other possible forms of local taxation. For the present, we need only remind ourselves that, whereas rates were a tax on property, the community charge/poll tax was a tax on the individual: a flat-rate tax payable by most adults over the age of 18. The council tax is a combination of the two (see Exhibit 10.4). It is a domestic property tax, but with the size of the bill depending in part on the number of residents as well as on the property's value, since taxpayers living alone get at least a 25 per cent reduction, regardless of their income. It is also very different from the old rating system, with each home assigned to one of eight property bands (Figure 10.1).

Figure 10.1   *Cartoon – Council Tax assessment*

Source: Local Government Information Unit, *LGIU Briefing*, No. 55, December 1991.

Exhibit 10.4 The council tax: key features

WHAT IS IT?	A *tax on domestic property,* not people, but with a personal element. There is *one bill per household,* with a 25 per cent discount for single-person households and certain other property.
HOW MUCH?	Will depend first on the *Inland Revenue's valuation of your property.* All domestic properties were placed in 1993 in one of 8 bands, A to H, which are in a fixed proportional relationship with each other – e.g. A:D:H = 2:3:6. Band A, the bottom band, is for properties valued in 1993 at under £40,000 in England, under £27,000 in Scotland, and under £30,000 in Wales. Band H, the top band, is for properties over, respectively, £320,000 (England), £212,000 (Scotland), and £240,000 (Wales).
WHO SETS IT?	*Each local authority,* though in two-tier non-metropolitan England billing and collection are the responsibility of the district alone.
EXEMPTIONS?	Can apply only to property. Most significant addition to property types previously exempt from the community charge: *halls of residence,* flats and houses occupied solely by students.
DISCOUNTS?	Relate to the numbers and types of people occupying the property, *not* to ability to pay. 25 per cent discounts for all single householders. 50 per cent discounts for under-18s, full-time students, the 'severely mentally impaired', some carers for disabled people, and, especially controversially, second-home owners.
REBATES?	*Up to 100 per cent* available for taxpayers on low incomes.
STUDENTS?	*Do not* pay, if you are a full-time student in a hall of residence, hostel, or other *exclusively* student accommodation.
WHO IS LIABLE?	The resident, over 18, with the strongest legal interest in the property.
NON-PAYMENT?	Dealt with in essentially the same way as poll tax non-payment: summons to appear in magistrates' court, liability order issued by court, attempted recovery of money by council, imprisonment for up to 3 months (except in Scotland).
REGISTERS?	No specific register for council tax. Community charge registers retained by some councils, to enable recovery of outstanding debt.
CAPPING?	Capping powers *retained* but used more selectively by Labour ministers.
NON-DOMESTIC RATES?	No change to the 'nationalised' system introduced in 1989/90. Labour's pledge to return to local council control reversed when in government.
IS IT FAIR?	No – widely recognised (except by ministers) as regressive: those in lower bands pay far higher proportion of their income than those in higher bands.
THE FUTURE?	Don't hold your breath! Most basic aspects of the tax – e.g. splitting the top band, extending ratio between top and bottom bands from 1:3 to 1:7, abolishing discounts – could be changed by Parliamentary Order, without further legislation. But Government likely to postpone reform until after planned national property revaluation in 2005–7.

To us as local taxpayers, the two radical domestic tax changes in four years may well have made a substantial difference to our personal finances. Employed single persons, for instance, are likely to pay more in council tax than they would or did in poll tax; pensioners, single parents, the unemployed, especially those with children, mostly pay less. For those local authority officials responsible for its collection, the council tax also brought major administrative upheavals – not least because the number of tax bills sent out was roughly halved. But from the point of view of those involved in a council's annual budget process, the key decisions remain essentially the same as ever.

The tax levied is still the final residual outcome of a process in which all the other elements are now known: your own council's spending plans, those of any precepting authorities, the amount you will receive in specific grants, fees and charges, the income you will get from the NNDR pool, your RSG. The sum still outstanding has to come from the council's own local council taxpayers since, unlike their counterparts in most other countries, British local authorities have access to only the one local tax.

The last point is important, especially when considering the budgetary discretion of local authorities. Common sense suggests that an authority with access to several different local taxes, paid by different groups of taxpayers, has more options at its disposal than one forced to rely on a single tax, the burden of which falls on a single group of taxpayers.

In Belgium, to pick one particularly vivid example, they do things very differently. Their relatively small municipalities choose, as well as set, their own taxes, and have a list of more than 130 types of local taxation from which to make their selection. The list ranges from the conventional – income and property taxes – to the arcane – taxes on advertising hoardings, vehicle taxes on boats, bicycles and horses. Indeed,

> some municipalities even tax pigeon keeping. Anything is permitted as long as it is fair and in the public interest. (Gasson, 1992, p. 20)

The details, though, are less important than the principle, which is that Belgian local authorities, like most of their European counterparts, have a range of tax choices they can make which are simply not available to British councils.

Capping

It could be argued that significant local tax choice has in recent years been removed from British councils altogether. Since the Rates Act 1984, local authorities' previously limited discretion has been curtailed still further through the process known as *capping*. The term tends to be used slightly misleadingly: 'rate-capping' and 'council tax-capping', instead of what would be strictly more accurate, which is *budget-capping*. Since 1984, successive Secretaries of State for the Environment – now the Secretary of State for Transport – have had the power to cap, or impose a statutory ceiling on, the planned budget of any local authority that is, in their view, excessive. The effect is essentially the same as if the cap were placed directly on the council tax. For, with only the one local tax, that tax has to be reduced on a £ for £ basis to reflect the cut in spending demanded by the Minister.

Initially, until the end of the 1980s, Conservative ministers used their newly acquired power *selectively*, devising criteria each year that would enable them to pick out usually between 12 and 20 councils – almost all Labour – whose proposed budgets and rates they would then reduce. With the advent of the poll tax, though, capping rapidly moved from selective to *universal*, applying to all councils except parishes. If the system sounds centralist and dictatorial, that is because it was designed to be so. It is also quite simple to understand. The coming financial year's capping criteria – maximum percentage budget increases – were announced in November along with the other RSG details. Each council thus knew, before it made any of its key budget decisions, exactly how much it would be permitted to spend and to raise from its own local residents in tax. Many, indeed most, then used those figures in effect as guidelines and spent and taxed at their government-determined levels.

To local authorities of all political colours, if not to the general public, this practice of universal capping was probably more offensive than was the imposition of the community charge. It amounted to the government's setting a spending ceiling for every council in the country, leaving locally elected politicians in the position of having the framework of their budgets, if not their detailed content, determined for them. As Jones and Stewart described, there was a serious weakening of local financial responsibility and accountability:

> Most authorities now cap themselves. Once the government announces the criteria, they keep within them to avoid the uncertainties of the capping process. Balancing the need for expenditure against the costs of local taxation has always been a key local choice. Now the issue is how to reduce expenditure to the capping level. (Jones and Stewart, 1993, p. 15)

In 1996/97 over three-quarters of all authorities (77 per cent) capped themselves in this sense of setting their budgets at the government's imposed cap limit, and just six attempted to challenge their caps, even marginally. Labour, in its 1997 election manifesto, promised that this 'crude and universal capping should go' – but not completely. It would be replaced by what presumably has to be described as discriminating and selective capping, for Labour ministers would 'retain reserve powers to control excessive council tax increases' – increases, that is, that they, rather than locally elected councillors or local taxpayers themselves, judged excessive.

This legislative change was introduced in the Local Government Act 1999 – the same Act that brought in best value. The terminology has changed a little, but in effect capping has reverted to its original 1980s post-budget form: under their powers of 'Regulation of Council Tax and Precepts', ministers now 'designate' for 'limitation' any council budgets they think are 'excessive'. Most seriously considered in 2000 were the budgets of those not notoriously extravagant and revolutionary councils of Epsom and Ewell, Mid Bedfordshire, and Oxfordshire. All three eventually escaped with a ministerial warning, but the fact that the capping threat remains, together with capital controls – making our local financial system the most centrally dictated in Western Europe – speaks volumes for the fundamental lack of trust that successive governments have had even in councils of their own political complexion.

Budget setting – managing the margins

Local budgeting, from the perspective of the local councillors and officers involved, has inevitably become an exercise in 'managing the margins', to quote the sub-title of an account of the subject (Elcock *et al.*, 1989). In fact, the sub-title is intended to emphasise the almost inevitable *incremental* or marginal nature of most local budgetary decisions: adding relatively small increments to, or cutting them from, a largely unchallenged and untouched budgetary base. But it could equally suggest the management of the very tightly defined and delimited margins left to local councils' discretion, once government ministers have taken and announced all the major decisions on total spending, grant distribution, the NNDR poundage, and possible capping criteria.

Either way, there may be the temptation to see the role of 'managing the margins' as insignificant, even demeaning. The temptation should be resisted, by those in local government and by us as observers. As we emphasise throughout this book, the size, employing and spending power of local authorities are such that even their marginal budgetary decisions can have an important local impact. The government may define, and tightly, the budgetary framework, but there is still scope *within* that framework – albeit less than might be democratically desirable – for councils to respond to particular local needs and for councillors to pursue their political objectives.

To illustrate, we return to Birmingham's 2001/02 revenue budget, as set out in Exhibit 10.2 and complete the story of the setting of that city's council tax. As noted before, while the scale of Birmingham's budget may be exceptional, the basic decisions underpinning it are essentially similar and comparable to those required of your own council.

The effective starting point in both cases will have been the Government's announcement at the end of November 2000 of its proposed Revenue Support Grant Settlement. The vital data for Birmingham in that announcement were the details of its Standard Spending Assessment (SSA) – what the Government felt the council should be spending in total (£1,082 million), and specifically on education (£545 million), social services (£229 million) and so on, in order to provide a standard level of service. Those SSAs determined the RSG Birmingham would receive, even if, like most councils, it spent above the figures calculated by the government.

As noted above, the common response from local authorities to the RSG settlement has been one of almost ritualised outrage. Leading councillors are interviewed by their local media, protesting at how the government has seriously under-assessed their council's spending needs and that major service cuts, tax increases, or both will be required – for which, of course, government ministers, not councillors, must take the responsibility and blame. The Labour Government, however, has substantially disarmed such protests, by announcing three-year spending plans and encouraging councils to develop their own corresponding revenue plans. Service cuts and so-called efficiency savings still have to be found, but, by recent historical standards, the overall settlement was judged reasonable and dissent in November 2000 was relatively muted. So, advised by their officers, Birmingham's councillors – and in particular the service portfolio holders in the all-Labour cabinet – set about addressing the key policy questions:

- How and where should savings be made, in order to produce a budget and council tax increase that the Secretary of State would not deem 'excessive'?
- Which services should be prioritised, protected from cuts, and allocated extra resources?

Increasingly councils endeavour to consult their own local taxpayers and service users about *their* priorities. Birmingham thus held four public meetings across the city in early December, organised sessions with focus groups representing business and various voluntary group interests, set up a special telephone hotline and web site, and organised a deliberative workshop for the council's statistically representative 'People's Panel'. The possibly unsurprising response to these consultations was that people were keen to have extra spending ... but not if it required a big increase in council tax. They did, however, provide a rough prioritisation of the services on which they would like to see more spent, if council tax were to rise by, say, between 4 and 8 per cent: community safety, schools, social services and services for older people, better roads and street cleaning.

Some councils have chosen to consult through (usually postal) budget referendums, most notably Milton Keynes in 1999, where a good turnout of voters chose the middle of three options, involving a 9.8 per cent tax rise and a package of increased spending measures (see also p. 359). It confirmed the experience of tax referendums in other countries – that the low-tax option by no means always wins. Now that we have an independent Electoral Commission that could monitor them, we may see more of these dalliances with direct democracy in the future.

Returning, though, to Birmingham, after the various consultations and many hours of debate in committee and party group meetings, the following 'headline' policy decisions were taken and formed the basis of the council's own contribution to its budget-making process (Box 10.1).

Box 10.1 'Headline' policy decisions

- All major service areas would see at least some increase in their total net expenditure – not often the case in the recent past – but some would get proportionately more than others, reflecting the council's planned priorities and the results of the consultation process.
- Specifically, the Education and Lifelong Learning budget would increase by £20 million – about 3.5 per cent, when allowance is made for the new Learning and Skills Council taking over some of the council's adult education responsibilities. The government had increased the council's education SSA by £16.8 million and all of this additional sum would be passed on to the service.
- Similarly, the general Social Services and Health budget no longer covers Post-16 Care Leavers – now funded by a specific grant – so its percentage increase too, directed particularly towards improving staffing levels for children's services, is higher than it appears. The department will raise more money through charges than in the past.
- By far the biggest percentage budget increase (17 per cent) would go to Local and Neighbourhood Development, in line with the public concern about community safety and the council's continuing commitment to decentralisation of its policy-making and service delivery.
- Street Services would get 4 per cent, to be directed partly towards refuse collection services – more recycling sites and home composters – and partly towards better upkeep of roads and footpaths, locally decided street lighting improvements, and, perhaps bearing in mind its modest PI rating of 4 per 100,000 in the top row of Exhibit 9.8, new suburban public conveniences.
- A 3.3 per cent rise in Leisure, Culture and Tourism spending should enable the city to maintain its support of major arts programmes (see Exhibit 9.7), and in particular the new Waterhall Gallery of Modern Art – in the very hall where, when Birmingham Council was also a water authority, residents once paid their water bills.

Exhibit 10.5 Birmingham's council tax, 2001/02

	£ million
City Council's 2001/02 Net Budget Requirement (set at limit to be approved by government)	1,144
Less Revenue Support Grant (determined by government)	621 = 54.3%
Less Redistributed National Non-Domestic Rate (collected at uniform poundage set by government)	275 = 24%
Leaves Budget Requirement to be financed by council tax	248 = 21.7%
Which represents for a Birmingham property in *Band A* a council tax of	652.62
Which equals $\frac{2}{3}$ of the tax for a property in *Band D*	978.94
And $\frac{1}{3}$ of the tax for a property in *Band H*	1,957.87

These decisions and dozens of similar ones were brought together in the budget that was formally approved by the full council on 27 February 2001 (see Exhibit 10.5). They amounted to a net revenue spending increase of 3.3 per cent, which produced a council tax rise of 4.4 per cent. There is a sense, perhaps, in which such policy decisions can be regarded as 'marginal'. The most prioritised major services had their budgets increased by only a few percentage points. Similarly, the most harshly affected departments would lose only a small proportion of their staffs, and those by voluntary, rather than enforced, redundancy. The great bulk of the council's budget and all its major services remain intact.

Marginal they may have been; trivial they were not. All these decisions had costs and consequences for those involved in and affected by them. They were not inevitable; they were not made by central government; they were politically, even socially, contentious, and were the subject of much political debate, both across and within the parties represented on the council.

The fact remains, however, that it was not these policy decisions by locally elected politicians that played the crucial part in determining Birmingham's *overall* level of spending and service provision, its overall level of council tax, or the amount to be paid by the city's householders. These decisions, once the responsibility of local councillors and their electorates, were in 2001/02 all effectively settled by national politicians and civil servants in London. As can be seen in Exhibit 10.5, local taxpayers in Birmingham – as across the country – now contribute little more than a fifth of their council's net expenditure. Such a situation blurs accountability, in that voters are left uncertain as to who is actually responsible for any tax change they are asked to pay or vote for. A 'gearing effect' also acts as a big disincentive for any local authority proposing to increase its net spending. For, with central government controlling all other sources of funding – grants and the NNDR – a 1 per cent budget increase will require a nearly 5 per cent rise in council tax. It was not always so; nor, as we shall see, is it how most other countries organise their local finances.

How other countries do things

In commenting on Exhibit 10.1, we noted that local government accounted for a quarter of the country's total government spending and over one-tenth of the Gross Domestic Product (GDP). It sounds – and obviously is – a lot, and it explains why, in any local authority area, the council itself will be one of the largest employers and spenders, and frequently *the* largest.

Compared with other Western systems of local government, though, the United Kingdom is, in football parlance, in the second division. The 'Sub-central Premiership' would comprise the Scandinavian 'welfare democracies' and the federal systems of Canada, Switzerland and

Figure 10.2 *Britain's Council Tax – a small slice of a modest cake*

The Cake ↑		Under 5%	5–25%	Over 25%
Total tax revenue as a percentage of Gross Domestic Product	Over 40%	Greece (43, 1) Netherlands (41, 3)	Finland (47, 22) France (45, 10) Norway (43, 18) Italy (43, 12)	Sweden (52, 30) Denmark (49, 32) Belgium (46, 28)
	30–40%	**UK (37, 3.8)** Ireland (32, 2)	New Zealand (35, 6) Spain (34, 17) Australia* (30, 22)	Canada* (37, 46) Germany* (37, 30) Switzerland* (35, 34)
	Under 30%		Japan (28, 25)	USA* (28, 31)

The Slice →
Local/state taxes as a percentage of total tax revenue

Notes: First figure for each country is tax revenue as percentage of GDP; second is local tax as a percentage of total tax revenue. For federal countries (*) the second figure = state + local taxes.
Source: Revenue Statistics of OECD Member Countries, 1965–99 (Paris: OECD, 2000).

Germany, whose regional/provincial and local governments account for at least 16 per cent, and in Canada and Denmark over 30 per cent, of their respective GDPs. In all these countries too, state and local governments account for significantly higher proportions of their countries' total tax yields than in most other Western European countries, and certainly than in Britain (see Figure 10.2). In tax terms, British local government can be seen as contributing a very small slice to a not particularly large national cake. We are, despite what national politicians would sometimes have us believe, a comparatively modestly taxed country, and less than £1 of every £25 of tax that we pay goes direct to our local councils.

It is true that some of Britain's other EU partners have markedly smaller local government sectors than we do – notably those countries in which teachers are employed by central, rather than local, government. But, following the introduction of capping and the 1989–93 tax changes noted above – particularly the 'nationalisation' of business rates – there are no longer many countries in which local government has apparently less financial discretion. The key to that situation lies, we suggest, in Exhibit 10.6.

The detailed figures in Exhibit 10.6 are in some ways less important than the evident message:

- In very few Western countries are local authorities forced to rely on only one source of local taxation.
- In most countries local authorities can levy a variety of taxes on different groups of taxpayers and service users.
- The few exceptions are those mainly Scandinavian countries that rely very heavily on a broad-based and progressive direct tax: a local income tax.
- Britain has been unique in placing such a concentrated burden on *either* a property tax *or* a flat-rate personal tax.

The burden of a single local tax

Taxes, to quote economist Maynard Keynes, are the membership fee we pay to live in a civilised society: not inherently a 'bad' thing, as many politicians would have us believe, but a force for good, funding things we value, like universal education, social services and public transport. It is when tax liabilities are inadequately or inappropriately shared that they come to seem burdensome. For British local authorities, the enforced reliance on a single source of local taxation is burdensome in two senses: on the system itself and on those liable to pay the tax. As a local authority's responsibilities increase, more money is required from the same group of taxpayers, whose readiness and eventually ability to pay are

Exhibit 10.6 Composition of state/local tax revenues, 1998

		Income and profits	Property	Goods and services	Other
Federal countries					
Canada	State	49	6	45	–
	Local	–	93	1	6
USA	State	40	4	56	–
	Local	6	73	21	–
Belgium	State	54	6	40	–
	Local	84	14	2	–
Germany	State	50	5	45	–
	Local	79	15	6	–
Unitary countries					
Denmark		94	6	–	–
Finland		96	4	–	–
France		–	51	10	39
Italy		13	17	15	55
Japan		47	31	21	1
Netherlands		–	63	37	–
Norway		90	8	2	–
Spain		26	35	35	4
Sweden		100	–	–	–
UK pre-1989		–	100	–	–
1990–1993		–	–	–	100
1993–		–	100	–	–

Source: *Revenue Statistics of OECD Member Countries, 1965–1999* (Paris: OECD, 2000), Tables 133, 135.

finite. When, in addition, the single tax is either a flat-rate one or only loosely related to a taxpayer's changing income and wealth, problems are magnified. That, in essence, has been the story of post-war British local government.

The longstanding local rates had been effective, but their limitations became increasingly apparent as councils took on more and more services. As a property tax, they were 'regressive' – that is, not related to any ability to pay either of a head of household or of the members of that household. Domestic rates were efficient, predictable, relatively cheap and easy to collect, and difficult to evade. But during the 1970s, as they increased year by year and non-householders saw other service-users apparently 'free-loading', accusations of unfairness multiplied. The Conservatives, or more precisely the Opposition Spokesperson for the Environment – one Margaret Thatcher – produced a 1974 manifesto pledge to 'abolish the rating system within the lifetime of a Parliament and replace it by taxes more broadly based and *related to people's ability to pay*' (emphasis ours).

Of that four-part pledge, half was eventually achieved and half was not. Domestic rates were abolished, but it took three Parliaments, not one. The replacement community charge – or 'poll tax' as it became almost universally known – was certainly more broadly based, being a completely flat-rate tax payable by almost everyone; but it was emphatically not related to ability to pay. The story of its introduction is a fascinating one (see Butler *et al.*, 1994; Wilson and Game, 1998, Ch. 10), not least for the sheer chutzpah of ministers – and particularly the Prime Minister – attempting to finance a large part of a large-scale local government system through a personal tax that was unique in the Western democratic world.

The reason rating reform took a Conservative government 10 years to introduce was that it had tried and finally run out of other means of controlling local spending. The Thatcher Government came to power in what we termed the 'corporatist' phase of central–local relations (see Exhibit 9.4), and inherited Labour's policy of seeking to constrain local expenditure by annual reductions in the general grant then called the Rate Support Grant. This policy was reinforced in the Local Government Planning and Land Act 1980 by the quite unprecedented introduction for *every individual council* of spending 'targets' and grant penalties. If a council's spending significantly exceeded its supposedly 'guideline' target, its grant, far from being increased, would be cut. In the mid-1970s Rate Support Grant had funded over half of English local authorities' net spending (see Figure 10.3(a)), leaving councils themselves having to find only about a third (35 per cent) through their locally set domestic and business/ non-domestic rates. But year by year as their Rate Support Grant fell, many councils, rather than cut services, made up their loss of income by raising rates by often formidable percentages – 27 per cent on average in 1980/81, 19.4 per cent in 1981/82.

The government's response was threefold. First, a Green Paper examined a wide range of possible *Alternatives to Domestic Rates* (DoE, 1981) – local sales taxes; petrol, alcohol and tobacco duties; a local payroll tax; local income tax – and then rejected most of them, including a poll tax, on the grounds of their impracticability. Secondly, and consequently, 'rate-capping' was introduced – initially in Scotland in 1982 and two years later in England and Wales. Giving, as it did, central government complete control for the first time over the spending and taxing policies of some and eventually all local authorities, the Rates Act had a fundamental constitutional significance – more fundamental, arguably, than the third strand of the government's action: the abolition in 1985 of the 'excessively' high-spending and taxing GLC and Metropolitan County Councils.

Poll tax – a short-lived policy disaster

There had been no mention of the rating abolition pledge in the Conservatives' 1983 manifesto. But, as the government continued to cut back particularly its general grant funding, the proportion of the local government spending 'pie' contributed by ratepayers inevitably increased, as in Figure 10.3(b). It was time for another – this time uncompromising – Green Paper, *Paying for Local Government*, which outlined 'proposals for the most radical reform of local government finance in Britain this century' (DoE, 1986, p. 76). It was not exaggerating.

There were two main strands to the reform, as noted earlier:

- *Domestic rates* would be abolished, and replaced with a Community Charge, payable by all adults aged 18 and over at a level to be set by individual local authorities as a flat-rate payment.
- *Non-domestic rates* would be 'nationalised' – that is, set in future by *central* government at a uniform rate across the whole country.

The protests against the inequity of the Community Charge or poll tax were widespread, passionate and aggressive. The warnings about its operational difficulties – the compilation and maintenance of a rolling register, the problems of enforcement – were legion. Even ministers acknowledged that this 'flagship' policy of Mrs. Thatcher's third term of office would hardly be universally popular, but that merely persuaded them to introduce it 'at a single stroke', rather than, as previously planned, phase it in gradually as rates were phased out. Accordingly, 'the most celebrated disaster in post-war British politics' (Butler *et al.*, 1994) was launched – on 1 April 1989 in Scotland and 1 April 1990 in England and Wales.

The average poll tax bill for 1990/91 – £363 per adult – was some 14 times higher than the figure envisaged in the 1981 Green Paper. There were at least three times as many 'losers' as 'gainers', and the heaviest losers were those, like pensioners and single-parent families, in the smallest properties on the most modest incomes. Protests and demonstrations turned into riots. Tens of thousands were criminalised for the first time in their lives through their inability or refusal to pay, and non-collection rates rocketed. The unpopular tax was proving in practice unacceptable. In November 1990 Mrs. Thatcher lost the Conservative leadership, at least partly as a result of the damage it was doing to the party. The new Prime Minister, John Major, despite his collective ministerial responsibility for the tax, was committed to its abolition, but first he had to neutralise it. This was achieved in Chancellor of the Exchequer Norman Lamont's budget in March 1991, in which he raised Value Added Tax (VAT) from 15 per cent to 17½ per cent to finance a cut of £140 in the poll tax bill of every adult in the country. Two days later Environment Secretary Michael Heseltine announced the abolition of the poll tax and its replacement from

Figure 10.3 *The changing composition of funding for English local authority net expenditure, 1975–2001*

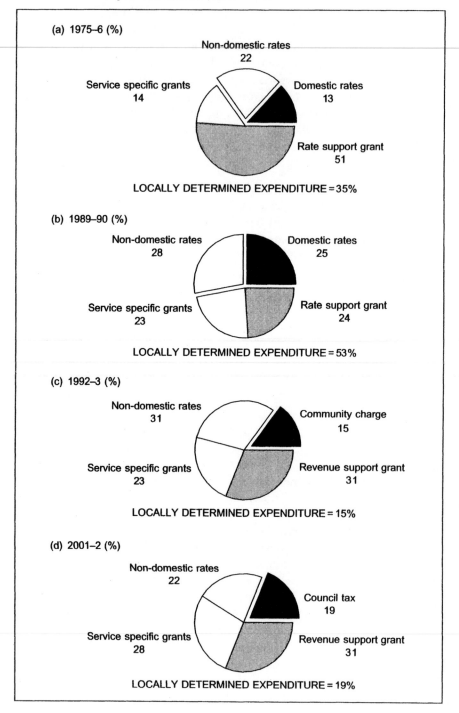

1993 by a banded property tax with some allowance for the number of adults in the household: the council tax.

The financial, fiscal, economic and employment costs of the community charge/poll tax, massive as they were, can at least be estimated (Wilson and Game, 1998, Exhibit 10.5). The longer-term social and community costs and the irreparable damage done to local government are inestimable. They are still in evidence – in people's resistance to registration and census completion, in their disengagement from local government, and in the reluctance of some to pay even the demonstrably fairer council tax. Even more damaging to local government, though, was the two-stage switch – first the uniform business rate, then the VAT increase – from local taxation funding over half of net local expenditure to its funding only one-sixth (see Figure 10.3(b) and (c)). In the ensuing decade the proportion of locally determined expenditure crept up to around a fifth. But, as we have noted, that is a much lower figure than in most other Western European countries, and too low, many observers would feel, to support a financially robust local democracy.

Marginal accountability within a command economy control system

The most obvious legacy of the post-1988 tax reforms is that British local authorities are still in the almost unique position of having access to just one source of local taxation. Not for them the 'sin taxes' on alcohol and tobacco available to many US municipalities, the French and German business taxes, the Norwegian wealth tax, or the Dutch second house tax – let alone most of these countries' substantial state or local income taxes.

As noted above, Labour reversed its opposition pledge to return business rates to local control. The likelihood, therefore, of any foreseeable government Treasury handing over to local councils a significant slice of its current 96 per cent of tax revenues – in the form, for instance, of the Scandinavian-type local income tax commended by the Layfield Committee in the 1970s – must be remote in the extreme. Partly with such *Realpolitik* considerations in mind, there are those who, like the government, argue that it is not the *overall* proportion of expenditure financed locally that really matters. Rather, local government should focus on the proportion of *marginal* or *extra* spending that is under democratic control. As evidence, they would point to Figure 10.3: was local government so much healthier in, say, 1989/90 when, after a decade of grant cuts and spending constraint, it was forced to raise over half its net revenue from the rates?

This view is perhaps most assertively expressed by the New Local Government Network (NLGN), a heavily corporately sponsored campaigning group. Unsurprisingly opposed to the return of business rates to local control, the Network argues that there are other ways in which local authorities might be given greater control over what we termed managing their budgetary margins (Stoker, 2001). Some of the remaining restrictions on charging could be lifted. Greater use could be made of 'third-party' taxes – e.g. workplace car parking and town centre congestion charges, tourist and bed taxes, that tax a third party for the costs they impose on others. Council tax capping could be finally abolished and replaced by binding tax referendums, allowing councils to increase spending following specific endorsement from their electorates.

Almost all of these measures, however, require legislation, of which in the early months of Labour's second term of office there were few signs. In the meantime, not a great deal has changed from 'the annual ritual of the RSG settlement' as described by Tony Travers in 1996:

> a spectacular example of a command economy control system in operation. The former Soviet Bloc never managed this kind of all-embracing and intricate control. A computer in London SW1 dictates the fate of a primary school roof repair in Wirral or a secondary school's music teacher in Cornwall. (*Guardian*, 3 December 1996)

In two decades local government finance has undoubtedly come a long way, but not, it would seem, along that road towards greater local accountability on which it was constantly being told it should embark back in the 1970s.

Guide to further reading

Our first recommendation will be obvious from the content of the first part of the chapter: get what information you can from your own local councils and their web sites. One of the best general introductions to the world of local government finance is that produced by the Local Government Information Unit (Challis, 2000), and the LGIU, the LGA, CIPFA, and the DTLR itself all produce masses of material on their web sites, increasingly in accessible 'plain English' form. Starkly though times have changed, the specialist reader will still find relevance in the Layfield Committee Report (1976), which is effectively the starting point of the immensely readable and self-explanatorily titled paperback by David Butler and colleagues, *Failure in British Government: The Politics of the Poll Tax* (1994). It is a kind of pathological study of modern British government, but it also incorporates some of the more specialist literature on the subject, including Bailey and Paddison (1988) and Gibson (1990). More recently, McConnell (1999) is good on local taxation generally, not just in Britain, and also contains a comprehensive bibliography.

Part 2

The Politics and People of Local Government

Chapter 11

Local Elections

Introduction

There are, as we saw in Chapter 2, several characteristics that distinguish local authorities from other institutions of public administration. One – the most fundamental of all – is the fact of their election, aspects of which provide the content of the next two chapters. Chapter 12 focuses on the products of the electoral process: the councillors. This chapter deals with the process itself: how local elections are conducted, who turns out to vote in them, and how those votes are cast.

But why are we bothering?

To hear some people talk, you might wonder why we include a separate chapter on local elections. Everyone knows that far fewer people turn out in council elections than in even the 2001 General Election. Besides, don't the few who actually vote treat them as little more than an 'annual general election', to quote Newton's portrayal of Birmingham politics in the 1960s (Newton, 1976, Ch. 2)? Are not government ministers – real, as well as fictitious ones like *Yes, Minister*'s Jim Hacker – right when they suggest that:

> Local democracy is a farce ... Most people don't even vote in local elections, and the ones who do just treat it as a popularity poll on government in Westminster? (Lynn and Jay, 1983, p. 45)

Certainly, local elections do not seem to be accorded very much importance in our national political life. Their results are analysed mainly for what they would mean *if* they had been produced in a General Election rather than for what they *actually* mean: namely, councils changing political control, policies altering, councillors winning and losing seats. One senior Cabinet Minister in the 1960s, Richard Crossman, even admitted having forgotten about them altogether when he chose the Monday of local elections week to announce a highly unpopular and electorally damaging 25 per cent increase in health service charges (Crossman, 1977, p. 47).

So why are we bothering? The answer is simple. We do not believe – even when, as in 1979, 1997 and 2001, they are held on the same day – that local elections can or should be dismissed as merely a General Election writ small. They are much more complex, and much more important, than a national popularity poll, or, as Margaret Thatcher seemed to regard them in 1983 and 1987 and Tony Blair in 2001, a handy aid for Prime Ministers seeking tactically advantageous election dates. Our view of what local elections are and are not about can be summed up in the kind of 'before and after' editorials regularly produced by our more serious national newspapers – in this instance, *The Times* in May 1990. On polling day itself, Thursday 3 May, editorial readers were instructed:

> Today's local elections are about the running of Britain's cities, towns and county districts. They are not a public opinion poll. They are not meant to be a judgement on Mrs Thatcher, on her government at Westminster, or on the vexed matter of the poll tax. They are to select the men and women who are to run local administration. Those of all political persuasions who treat local elections as surrogate general elections are merely playing the centralist game. They are enemies of local democracy.

Odd, then, and disappointing, that just two days later the same paper's editorial column should choose to play its own 'centralist game':

> Yesterday's election results showed, as predicted, that the public does not like the poll tax ... The swing to Labour on a high turnout would be enough to give Mr. Kinnock a good parliamentary majority.

Setting aside the fact that many voters demonstrably did like the poll tax, benefited from it, and voted accordingly, what happened to all those men and women running our cities, towns and county districts? The assumption is being made that national and local elections are interchangeable. A principal message of this chapter is that *they are not,* and should not be so regarded. Local elections are local political events and a great many voters, if not political commentators, clearly treat them as such. Far fewer of them actually use their votes than in parliamentary elections, but many of those doing so *consistently vote differently* in the two types of election.

They will vote on the basis of local, rather than national issues, and for or against the records or personalities of particular candidates, regardless of their party. We shall introduce some specific examples later in the chapter, but first we must outline how British local elections are actually conducted – see Exhibit 11.1.

Local elections – see how they're run

It is undeniable that some aspects of present local electoral arrangements, the product largely of historical accident, are complex and confusing. This is particularly so if you happen to live in non-metropolitan England, for you may well have to contact your local electoral registration office to find out whether yours is a 'by thirds' or 'all out' council and when you will therefore have your next chance to vote. While there are many areas of life in which variety of local practice is commendable, it is not self-evident that the organisation of elections should be one of them. The Widdicombe Committee was surely right back in the 1980s in arguing for a uniform system, even if not necessarily the 'county' system of the single-member wards and whole council elections that it favoured itself.

There are arguments for and against the 'Widdicombe' solution (Game, 1991a). *Single-member wards* are smaller, provide the strongest link between councillors and their constituents, and may encourage higher turnouts. On the other hand, they limit voters' choice of candidates, may leave them feeling inadequately represented if 'their' candidate is defeated, and they may discourage party selection committees from picking women and ethnic minority candidates.

'Whole council' elections, by giving councils a clear breathing space between elections, may encourage policy consistency, forward planning, and reduce the temptation to defer politically difficult decisions, such as school closures, tax increases, the siting of roads. They can certainly lead to sudden and dramatic changes in political control, producing large and sudden influxes of new and inexperienced councillors. But, perhaps above all, they dilute the political accountability that comes from politicians having regularly to explain and defend their policies and actions to the electorate.

The electoral system

However, the greatest controversy about current electoral practice is generated not by the mechanics of ward representation and the frequency of council elections but by the system itself: the *plurality* or *first-past-the-post* (FPTP) method of election. It is a well-tested and easily understood system, familiar to almost everyone through its longstanding use in all our governmental elections in mainland Britain. Yet there is also widespread resentment of its obvious deficiencies and biases and, as all our new devolved institutions – the Scottish Parliament, the Welsh, Northern Ireland and Greater London Assemblies – adopt more proportional methods, electoral reform for local government has inevitably become part of any constitutional reform agenda. The main arguments for and against the existing system are summarised in Exhibit 11.2.

It is easy to see what Rallings and Thrasher (1991, p. 5) mean when they suggest that 'all the evidence is that local voters are poorly served by existing methods of electing councils'. It is not our intention here to add

Exhibit 11.1 The who, when, how and why of local elections

1. **When are local elections held?**
   Every May, normally on the first Thursday of the month. *Not*, as in many countries, at weekends or on a declared public holiday, although this is one of several possibilities under consideration by the government and the Electoral Commission.

2. **Can I vote?**
   Almost certainly, yes – if you are 18 or over, a citizen of Britain, Ireland or the Commonwealth, and not a convicted prisoner.

3. **Must I register first?**
   Yes, as for Parliamentary elections. Since 2001 the United Kingdom has had a continuously maintained, or rolling, electoral register. The register, like most other aspects of electoral administration, is the responsibility of your local district or unitary council, and specifically of the Electoral Registration Officer, who should require you to complete a registration form confirming *your residence in the electoral area*. Non-registration is an offence and, as former East 17 singer and Epping Forest resident Brian Harvey discovered, can lead to prosecution and a £150 fine.

4. **Isn't there also a property qualification?**
   Not any longer. Non-residents used to be able to vote and stand as candidates if they occupied land or property in an area, but this plural voting was abolished in 1969, except in the City of London.

5. **So can I vote every year?**
   Maybe, maybe not. It depends where you live.
   Most councils are now elected *en bloc* every 4 years:

   e.g.   English Counties (1997, 2001, 2005)
   London Boroughs (1998, 2002, 2006)
   Greater London Authority (2000, 2004)
   Scottish and Welsh Unitaries (1995, 1999, 2003)
   Northern Ireland Districts (1997, 2001, 2005)

   But Metropolitan Districts are elected *'by thirds'*, one-third of councillors standing for re-election in each of the non-county years: i.e. (1998, 1999, 2000, 2002, 2003, 2004).
   Some – English unitaries and non-metropolitan districts – may *choose*. Just over a third of the mainly more urban authorities have chosen election by thirds, like the metropolitan districts; the remainder have whole-council elections every four years (1999, 2003).

6. **Whom do I elect?**
   The councillor(s) representing the particular area in which you live.
   All councils are divided into single- or multi-member electoral *divisions* (counties) or *wards* (districts, boroughs, and unitaries), each returning 1, 2 or 3 councillors for *4-year terms* of office. Until the election of the Mayor of Greater London in 2000, there were no directly elected political executives in British local government. The first mayoral elections outside London were scheduled for May 2002.

7. **When and where do I do it?**
   Traditionally, on *election day itself*, in your designated local polling station, between 7.00 a.m. and 9.00 p.m. – though, if you found it difficult or impossible to vote in person, you might have been eligible to apply for a postal or proxy vote. Belatedly, we are now seeking to boost turnout by making postal voting easier and at least piloting some of the practices of other countries: e.g. holding elections over more than one day (as in Norway, Finland, Italy, Switzerland), allowing voting in advance of polling day (as

in Sweden, Canada, New Zealand), setting up special polling stations in shopping malls and other places likely to attract large populations.

8. **Is voting easy?**
Yes – once you get your ballot paper, it could hardly be easier. In England, Wales and Scotland the same *simple plurality* or *first-past-the-post* (FPTP) system is used as in Parliamentary elections. You simply mark an X against your preferred candidate (or candidates if you are voting in a multi-member ward), and whoever gets most votes wins the seat. There is no need, or opportunity, to rank the candidates in order of preference, unless you are voting in Northern Ireland, where the *Single Transferable Vote* is used.
Counting the votes is similarly straightforward, and the complete results for many councils are often available nowadays within a couple of hours of the polls closing.

9. **Will I recognise the candidates' names?**
Not necessarily – though you may recognise your existing councillor if s/he is standing for re-election. Your ward may consist of between 1,000 and 20,000 registered electors, so even the most diligent candidate may not have been able to visit you in person. But the candidates should have delivered to your residence at least a brief 'election address', describing themselves and the policies they support. They may also describe themselves, in not more than 6 words, on the ballot paper itself, which will usually consist of their party affiliation.

10. **Could I stand as a candidate?**
Probably – provided you are over 21, a British or Irish citizen, and you have lived or worked in the local authority area for at least 12 months prior to your nomination. But there are disqualifications – for convictions, bankruptcy, etc. – the most important and controversial being that, if you are a paid employee of a local authority, you cannot also be elected to it, though you may be eligible to stand for another authority. This last disqualification was extended in 1989 to prevent senior local government officers and those in 'politically sensitive' posts standing for election at all.

11. **Would I have to be nominated?**
Yes, again as for Parliamentary elections – by 10 electors for the ward concerned.

12. **Is it expensive?**
Not terribly. It is cheaper to do badly than in Parliamentary elections, since there is no forfeitable deposit required. There is also a strictly enforced limit on each candidate's election expenditure – which in 2001 was £242 plus 4.7p for each registered elector – though very few candidates report spending up to anywhere near their permitted limit.

13. **Why is the system unnecessarily complicated?**
Good question – also raised by the Widdicombe Committee:

> a system which is as complex and inconsistent as the present one is hardly calculated to encourage electoral participation. Citizens have a reasonable expectation that, when they move from one area to another, the electoral arrangements should be the same.' (Widdicombe Report, 1986a, para. 7.15, p. 167)

The Committee's recommendation of a uniform system of single-member wards and whole council elections was rejected by the Government. For the present, therefore, it remains one of the idiosyncrasies of British local government!

Exhibit 11.2 The case for and against 'first-past-the-post' (FPTP) in local elections

For FPTP

- *Maximises chance of decisive electoral outcome* with a single party having full power to carry out its programme. Conversely, minimises the likelihood of coalition or minority government, and of protracted post-election inter-party bargaining.
- *Provides for a direct and personal councillor – constituent relationship,* unlike some systems of proportional representation in which representatives may not be directly linked to any geographical constituency.
- *Encourages parties to be broad-based, tolerant and moderate,* and discourages the creation and proliferation of new parties to represent new interests and arguments.
- *Reduces impact of extremist parties and views.*
- *Is the easiest system,* both to understand and to administer.
- *There is no alternative system* on which there is widespread agreement.

Against FPTP

- *Distorts,* often grossly and even more than in Parliamentary elections, the relationship between votes cast and seats won. Parties regularly win overwhelming control of councils on either bare majority, or even minority, votes. In other instances, a party gaining most votes may win fewer seats than rival parties with fewer votes.
- *Can effectively eliminate opposition,* producing councils on which opposition representation is either non-existent or too small perhaps even to be able to fill available committee places.
- *Wastes more votes* - in the sense of their going either to losing candidates or to build up needlessly large winning majorities – than almost any other system.
- *Reduces incentive to vote,* by reducing the proportion of potential voters who feel they can affect the result, either in their own ward or in the council as a whole.
- *Undermines perceived legitimacy of councillors,* since many, like MPs, are elected on minority votes – and usually on smaller turnouts than MPs.
- *Is electorally inefficient,* using only voters' first preferences and giving them no opportunity to express their political opinions in greater detail.
- *Is socially and geographically divisive,* benefiting the two major parties in areas in which they are already strong.
- *Is politically divisive,* encouraging adversarial politics, with more attention given to demolishing the opposition than to fostering inter-party understanding. Can make post-election negotiation and co-operation on a hung council even more difficult than it would be anyway.
- *May discriminate against women and ethnic minorities,* by making it harder for them to be selected and thus elected, though in fact female representation in British local government is higher than in at least some countries with PR systems.

greatly to the proliferating literature on electoral reform, but it may be appropriate, given the confusion that manifestly exists even among would-be reformers themselves, to make one or two fundamental points.

First, it must be emphasised forcefully that the choice of electoral systems, locally or nationally, is not simply between *either* FPTP *or* proportional representation (PR). It is probably most useful to think of there being four basic types of system, as outlined in Exhibit 11.3.

Second, by far the commonest local electoral system in Western European is the party list – but *not* the closed, blocked, depersonalised, unalterable list system UK voters were required to use in the 1999 European Parliamentary (EP) elections. Most countries use either unblocked lists, enabling voters to express personal preferences for individual candidates, or completely open lists, as in Norway, where voters can add or exclude candidates, change their list rankings, or give extra votes to their favourites.

Exhibit 11.3 Basic types of electoral system

1. *Plurality (or first-past-the-post, FPTP) systems*
   Vote for one candidate only, and the candidate with the most votes wins.

2. *Majority/majoritarian systems* – e.g. Alternative Vote (AV), Supplementary Vote (SV), double ballot
   These are *preferential* systems, usually in single-member wards/constituencies – including council-wide constituencies for mayoral elections. The main aim is not proportionality, but to eliminate, through the counting, if necessary, of voters' second and subsequent preferences, the possibility of a candidate being elected on a minority vote.

3. *Proportional systems*
   Any system, *necessarily* based on multi-member constituencies, which has as its aim the achievement of proportionality between votes cast and seats won.
   There are two main sub-types of proportional system:
   (a) *Party List systems* – which aim to represent *parties* in relation to their popular support, and in which any vote for an individual candidate is, at best, secondary to the vote for the party.
   (b) *The Single Transferable Vote (STV)* – preferential voting in multi-member constituencies, the key objective being to provide voters with a choice of candidates *within* as well as between parties.

4. *Additional Member Systems (AMS)* Hybrid systems, combining single-member constituencies and party lists, 'additional' or 'top-up' members being added to constituency members to achieve party proportionality in the elected body as a whole.

Box 11.1 The case for STV

- It is already in use in Northern Ireland – in all elections, including local elections, except those to the House of Commons – and has been found to be both readily comprehensible and widely acceptable.
- It was recommended for Scottish local elections by the McIntosh Commission on Local Government and the Scottish Parliament (1999).
- It could be comparatively easily introduced throughout Great Britain, since there are already many multi-member wards and divisions.
- It can offer voters a choice between candidates of the same party, enabling them to differentiate – as those in multi-member wards can and do already – between effective and less effective councillors, or between candidates of contrasting backgrounds or political views.
- It would probably give independent and minority party candidates a better chance of election.

Third, *if* PR were felt to be a prime objective in our own local elections – more important, for instance, than electors being represented by a single ward member, or than maximising the chances of a council being under single party majority control – there are several arguments in favour of a single transferable vote (STV), in preference to a party list system (Box 11.1).

Fourth, notwithstanding these considerations, political realism suggests that, if England is to get a more proportional system for local government elections in the foreseeable future, it is probably more likely to be an Additional Member System than STV. It is a form of election we are becoming increasingly familiar with, and, in local elections, it would create two usefully distinguishable classes of councillor: those representing their wards and those representing the council area as a whole.

An inevitable outcome of the introduction of any form of PR into local government would be a substantial increase in the already sizeable proportion of hung or 'balanced' councils: 32 per cent, or 142 out of Great Britain's 441 in 2001 (see Exhibit 14.3). Whether or not you feel this outcome to be desirable depends on your personal political views. There is, however, plenty of evidence that hung councils can work eminently satisfactorily and may 'foster a more open and democratic form of local government than that typically found in majority controlled authorities' (Leach and Game, 1992, p. 152; also Leach and Game, 1989; Leach and Stewart, 1992a).

Turnout and party competition

The one thing that everyone thinks they know about local elections is that not a lot of people vote in them. It cannot be denied. Our 59.4 per cent in the 2001 General Election put us in 24th place out of 25 in a listing of turnouts in recent Western European parliamentary elections (IDEA, 2001), ahead only of Switzerland. But that figure was roughly double the current UK average for local elections, and in that league table we are indisputably at the bottom, and have been for a long time. Even discounting the compulsory voting countries – Belgium, Luxembourg and Greece – the average turnout in most European local elections during the 1990s was between 60 and 80 per cent (European Union, 1999a). In our own local elections it was around 40 per cent and falling – fast. It is now lower than average US local turnouts during the 1990s when measured, as they conventionally are, as a proportion of total Voting Age Population (around 37 per cent) – and far lower, therefore, than the 60–65 per cent of *registered* US electors who cast local votes (Rallings and Thrasher, 2000).

A lowly 40 per cent and plummeting

Detailed turnout figures can be seen in Exhibit 11.4, which, on inspection, seems to divide roughly into two parts, the dividing point being 1992. In both periods the different authority types with their different electoral cycles produced somewhat differing patterns of results. But in the period up to 1992 a definite overall consistency is discernible. There were external events likely to have heightened voters' interest in particular years: the suspected imminence of a General Election – correctly anticipated in 1983 and 1987, incorrectly in 1991 – and certainly the controversy generated by the community charge in 1990. Even with such stimuli, though, rarely in this period did turnout rise above 45 per cent and in only two instances (both in Wales) above 50 per cent. Yet equally rarely did it drop under 40 per cent.

Since 1992 two things appear to have happened. Turnouts in all English local elections have plummeted, and in the metropolitan districts, with elections in three out of every four years, they are now consistently under 30 per cent. Similar declines have taken place in most European countries (European Union, 1999a), but mostly not so precipitous and, of course, starting from far higher baselines. The second apparent feature of the post-1992 period in Great Britain has been that turnouts in Wales and Scotland – both now with entirely unitary councils elected every four years – have held up noticeably better than those in England's mélange of authority types.

There is perhaps a clue here to a more general phenomenon: the greater readiness of people to vote in 'whole council' elections than where only a third of councillors are being returned and quite possibly, therefore, the overall control of the council is not in doubt. In 1998, for instance, even though both sets of turnouts were massively down from four years earlier, the 'all-out' London borough elections attracted significantly more voters

Exhibit 11.4 Local election turnouts, 1981–2001, as percentages

Date, type and timing of local elections	COUNTIES, REGIONS & ISLANDS + UNITARIES (U)			NON–METROPOLITAN DISTRICTS			MET DISTRICTS	LONDON BOROUGHS
	England	Wales	Scotland	England	Wales	Scotland		
1981	44	49	–	–	–	–	–	–
1982 (thirds)	–	–	43	42	–	–	39	44
1983 (all-out; anticipated Gen. Election?)	–	–	–	46	46	–	42	–
1984 (thirds)	–	–	–	40	43	44	40	–
1985	42	45	–	–	–	–	–	–
1986 (thirds)	–	–	46	42	40	–	40	45
1987 (all-out; anticipated Gen. Election?)	–	–	–	50	51	–	45	–
1988 (thirds)	–	–	–	42	41	46	40	–
1989	39	44	–	–	–	–	–	–
1990 (thirds; verdict on poll tax?)	–	–	46	48	53	–	46	48
1991 (all-out; anticipated Gen. Election?)	–	–	–	{ 49 (Eng & Wal combined) }		–	41	–
1992 (thirds; post-Gen. Election)	–	–	–	{ 38 (Eng & Wal combined) }		41	33	–
1993 (thirds)	37	39	–	–	–	–	–	–
1994 (all-out)	–	–	45	{ 43 (Eng & Wal combined) }		–	39	46
1995 (thirds)	40 (U)	49 (U)	45 (U)	42	49	45	34	–
1996 (thirds)	35 (U)	–	–	37	–	–	31	–
1997 (General Election)	73/70 (C/U)	–	–	–	–	–	–	–
1998 (thirds)	28 (U)	–	–	31	–	–	25	35
1999 (all-out)	32 (U)	50 (U)	59 (U)	36	–	–	26	–
2000 (thirds)	29 (U)	–	–	32	–	–	26	–
2001 (General Election)	58 (C/U)	–	–	–	–	–	–	–

Source: Rallings and Thrasher, *Local Elections Handbooks* (annual).

than the metropolitan districts. Similarly, in 1999 the 36 per cent turnout in English districts was made up of 37 per cent in 'all-out' councils and 32 per cent in those electing by thirds.

If voters' perception of *council marginality* is one impetus to vote, so too is perceived *ward marginality*. The smaller the majority vote of the winning candidate at the previous election, the higher the turnout is likely to be. This is hardly surprising. Voters are naturally going to be reluctant to vote if they sense they are doing so in, for them, either a politically safe or unwinnable ward, or for a member of a council that never seems to change political control. The political parties too are likely to put much more campaigning energy into a marginal ward, and this too will have a positive impact: the greater the *party competition*, the greater the likely turnout.

Ward size can also make a difference. Large wards – those with electorates of, say, significantly more than 6,000 – tend to produce lower turnouts, perhaps owing to a smaller proportion of electors actually knowing anything about the candidates. This proposition, however, has to be weighed against the fact that the wards with the smallest electorates, while producing higher average turnouts, are also precisely those that most frequently produce no turnouts at all, in that they go uncontested. Far fewer councillors nowadays are elected unopposed than used to be the case, but they are commonest in the electorally smaller – though often geographically extremely large – wards in the more rural and least partisan district councils.

More contests, more candidates

Turnout figures themselves may not have risen in the past 25 years or so, but the proportions of voters having the opportunity to turn out most definitely have. The 60 per cent or more of today's potential electors who may fail to vote in any particular set of local elections are mainly doing so *out of choice*. In the past, for millions of them, that choice would not have existed. Right up to the 1972–4 reorganisation of local government, thousands of councillors were elected, frequently term after term, without having had to fight a contested election. They were the only nominated candidates, and they were therefore returned unopposed, without necessarily having to produce an election address or ask a single voter for their support.

Harrison and Norton, in their research for the Maud Committee in the 1960s, found that:

> Of 40 859 seats for councillors above parish level which fell vacant in the three-year cycle 1962 to 1964, members were returned for 16 743 (41 per cent) without having to contest elections … It seems likely that about

one in three county councillors and about one in two of rural district councillors had never had to fight an election. (Maud, 1967b, pp. 48–9)

These figures did not change noticeably in the following decade, so that in the last major sets of elections to the pre-reorganisation authorities in the early 1970s:

- 50 per cent of the nearly 20,000 councillors 'elected' in England in 1970 were returned unopposed, including 52 per cent of all county councillors and 70 per cent of rural district councillors;
- 56 per cent of the 3,000 councillors 'elected' in Wales were unopposed, including 67 per cent of county and 65 per cent of rural district members;
- 62 per cent of the 3,100 councillors 'elected' in Scotland were unopposed, including 78 per cent of county and 87 per cent of district councillors. (Craig, 1989, p. 141)

Reorganisation brought the disappearance of almost all smaller urban and rural district councils, and many of their councillors. Previously non-partisan authorities were frequently merged with more overtly party political neighbours, and there began the long-term squeeze on Independent councils and councillors which continues through to the present day. At the same time – and with a direct causal linkage – the proportion of uncontested council seats fell immediately and dramatically from over 40 per cent to around 10 per cent. In the ensuing years it continued to decline, so that, for instance, in 2000 just 27 out of 1,947 seats in metropolitan, unitary and shire district councils (0.8 per cent) went uncontested (Rallings and Thrasher, 2000, p. xiv).

Here, though, is where the irony comes in. Almost all of those 1,947 contests were in authorities with annual elections – the very ones that produce the lowest turnouts. In 1999, by contrast, over 15 per cent of Welsh seats and around 5 per cent of Scottish and 'whole council' shire district seats had gone uncontested (Rallings and Thrasher, 1999, p. xi). But, as we saw in Exhibit 11.4, where elections did take place, turnouts were higher.

Ways of increasing turnout

Britain has not, even in the past and even in parliamentary elections, been a high voting nation. It may be regrettable; on the other hand, it may be seen as a measure of at least tolerable satisfaction with the performance of our governmental institutions. The fact is that, until quite recently, our electoral apathy has not worried most of us unduly. If it had, then there are several ways in which turnout could almost certainly have been increased.

We could make it physically easier for people to vote: by having more, and more accessible, polling stations in, for example, post offices, university campuses, shopping and DIY centres; by extending voting hours; by holding elections at weekends or declaring them public holidays. Or, if it really mattered to us, we could make voting compulsory and non-voting punishable by a fine, as in Australia, Belgium, Greece and Luxembourg. We could make much more extensive provision for postal voting, as New Zealand did over a decade ago, with an immediate doubling of many local turnouts from barely 30 per cent to over 60 per cent (Hedley, 1991, p. 18).

Now that turnouts in all types of election have fallen to internationally embarrassing levels – just 24 per cent in the 1999 European Parliamentary elections – governments have finally started to consider at least some of these administrative and procedural reforms, though *not* compulsory voting. After two years of dithering, the Home Office selected 32 volunteer local authorities to pilot a variety of alternative voting and counting arrangements at the May 2000 local elections. The projects divided roughly into three categories, dealing with when to vote, where to vote, and how to vote, the explicit emphasis of most of them being how they might increase turnout.

Most common were early voting experiments, like those in the Greater London mayoral and assembly elections, where you could vote in the preceding week as well as on election day itself. Other pilot authorities tried voting over the weekend, used mobile polling stations, and selected what they hoped might be more voter-friendly locations. Three councils piloted electronic voting systems, although set up in the same polling stations that would have been used for a conventional vote. Home-based internet voting, with accompanying network security and data encryption, may be the future, but a decidedly more distant one.

If increased turnout was the principal criterion by which these pilots were judged, the most effective by far was all-postal balloting. Disappointingly for the authorities that often went to considerable lengths and expense to raise their electors' awareness of the elections and of the new arrangements, the several versions of early voting and extended voting hours produced little, if any, improvement on turnout figures in recent elections. Nor did the electronic voting schemes. The all-postal ballots, though, certainly did increase turnouts, by an average of some 14 per cent compared with the most recent preceding elections. Further pilots – particularly of postal and electronic voting – were planned for the 2002 local elections. Meanwhile, at the 2001 General Election postal votes were available for the first time without applicants having to give a reason, about 5 per cent of voters taking advantage of this new opportunity, and most of the early mayoral referendums were also conducted entirely by post.

Conspicuously missing from this reform agenda, at least in England, is the measure that some argue – thinking back to our previous discussion – could have the most far-reaching effect of all: changing the whole electoral system. While there can be no certainty that the introduction of some form of PR in local government elections would significantly improve turnout figures, there is evidence which appears to point in that direction. A survey by Blais and Carty (1990, p. 179) looked at over 500 national elections in 20 countries and found that:

> Everything else being equal, turnout is seven percentage points lower in a plurality system, and five percentage points lower in a majority system, compared with PR.

The main impact of PR, though, would not be on turnout, but, as we noted, on the outcome of elections – namely, the greatly increased number of hung councils and the changes in political culture and the conduct of council business that would almost inevitably result. For supporters of electoral reform, these are precisely the attractions; for opponents, the threats. Credit is due, therefore, to those who – like some Labour members of the Scottish Executive and of Labour-dominated Lewisham Borough Council – are leading the local electoral reform movement, *despite* the likely short-term costs to their own party's fortunes.

Local votes

As we saw when discussing the Single Transferable Vote (STV), certain measures of electoral reform could have the effect of increasing the 'localism' of local elections. Independent, local or minority party candidacies can be encouraged, and electors given more opportunity to vote on local issues, on the merits or otherwise of the candidates, and generally to play a more involved part in influencing election outcomes. But, while an extension of these practices is always possible, they all happen *already*. Many voters require no reminders from the editor of *The Times* of the dangers of playing the 'centralist game' and of the importance of treating local elections as genuinely local events.

Local issues, local candidates

This section of the chapter returns to our starting point by introducing some actual illustrations of local voting behaviour. A comprehensive study of the subject, Miller's provocatively entitled *Irrelevant Elections?* (1988), found that, for a great many voters, local elections were far from irrelevant:

- 56 per cent of all respondents claimed to be influenced in local elections *more by local than by national issues;*
- 39 per cent of all respondents claimed to vote *more for the individual candidate* in a local election than for the party;
- 20 per cent of all respondents had *local party preferences different* from their current national party identification, a figure which rose to 34 per cent among those who 'voted for the candidate' in local elections.

In summary, up to one-fifth of electors claimed to vote for *candidates of different parties* in local and parliamentary elections. To this figure, moreover, should be added the many more who may end up supporting candidates of the same party in the two sets of elections, but on the basis of different considerations.

Split-voting evidence

A certain proportion of this differential voting behaviour will inevitably be self-cancelling; some voters preferring Party *A*'s candidate locally and Party *B*'s nationally, while others do precisely the reverse. There has, though, been a perceptible bias in recent years towards the Conservatives in parliamentary elections and to the non-Conservative parties locally, with the Liberal Democrats especially polling consistently higher locally than nationally.

The most conclusive evidence available to us of people's readiness to vote differently in parliamentary and local elections is that provided fortuitously in the so-called 'synchro-elections' in 1979, 1997 and 2001, when Prime Ministers Callaghan, Major and Blair respectively were forced or chose to call General Elections on the day already fixed for the year's local elections. Millions of voters found themselves with two votes to cast: one for their MP and one for a local – usually county – councillor.

Exhibit 11.5 shows the extent to which such people chose to split their votes in the two most recent instances, supporting candidates of different parties in the two different elections. The 33 constituencies were deliberately selected *not* for any exceptional evidence they showed of split-voting, but because their local and parliamentary boundaries precisely coincide and because each of the major parties fielded a candidate in every council contest. Interestingly, the turnouts in the two sets of elections were almost identical, but actual voting behaviour was not. Clearly, many thousands of electors did indeed split their parliamentary and local votes in both election years. Moreover, the net effect of their doing so was that the Conservative and Labour parties both fared considerably better in the General Elections, while the Liberal Democrats did very much better locally.

Exhibit 11.5 Split-voting, 1997 and 2001

33 English constituencies with 'perfect' competition

	Con %	Lab %	LD %	Other %	Turnout %
General Election	38.8	38.3	19.2	3.8	61.7
Local election	37.0	34.3	26.3	2.3	61.0
Difference: General *minus* local	+1.8	+4.0	−7.1	+1.5	+0.7
Difference in 1997	+2.0	+4.4	−8.5	+2.1	+0.6

Source: Rallings and Thrasher (2001b, p. 12).

If you happen to live in one of the areas of England that had either county or unitary council elections on 7 June 2001, you might well be able to replicate the exercise in Exhibit 11.5. Just compare the percentage vote for your MP with the total percentage for the various council candidates of the same party in the wards/divisions that make up that constituency, and you may well be able to find your own examples of split-voting.

You do not actually need synchro-elections, though. You can find plenty of evidence of the impact of local electoral influences through studying almost any set of local results. Immediately you start digging beneath the headlines and the aggregated figures, you are almost sure to be struck by the immense diversity and apparent inconsistency of the detailed ward-by-ward results. One ward is gained by the Conservative candidate, while an adjacent, previously Conservative-held ward is lost. Labour win control of one council but lose control of several others. Third and minority party candidates and Independents win seats and even whole councils against all other parties (see Exhibit 11.6).

May 2000 – Ken Livingstone was not the only 'maverick'

For our illustrations of local electoral influences at work we have chosen the millennial year elections, even more ignored than usual by the national media, whose attention was absorbed by suspended Labour MP Ken Livingstone's admittedly remarkable Independent campaign to become the first elected mayor of Greater London. Elsewhere, if there had been headlines, they would have told a story of Conservative recovery, as the party regained some of the seats and councils that it had lost four years

Exhibit 11.6 Minority parties and Independents

A few of the minority parties and independent groups contesting recent local elections

LIBERAL PARTY – NOT the Lib Dems, but the rump of the historic Liberal Party who opposed the party's 1988 merger with the Social Democratic Party. 30+ councillors, many elected against Lib Dem opposition.

GREEN PARTY – Evolved from People (1974–5) and the Ecology Party (1975–85). Peaked in 1989 with 15 per cent of vote in Euro-elections and nearly 9 per cent in locals, but has gradually extended representation from previous rural and university town base (Stroud, Oxford) into urban areas – e.g. Kirklees, Leeds, Hackney. 47 councillors in 2001, including 3 London Assembly members.

MEBYON KERNOW – 'Sons of Cornwall' or, more prosaically, 'The Party for Cornwall'. Not, as sometimes alleged, separatist, but simply for a better deal for a neglected county. Members on county council and four of the six districts.

BRITISH NATIONAL PARTY – Formed out of National Front in 1982, though NF still in existence. Created headlines and liberal consternation when Derek Beakton won by-election seat on Tower Hamlets Council in 1993 by-election. Still a presence in East End of London, but has also polled over 20 per cent in wards in Bexley, Sandwell, Burnley.

INDEPENDENT KIDDERMINSTER HOSPITAL AND HEALTH CONCERN – The ultimate single-issue party, now with its own MP, Dr. Richard Taylor. Campaign launched in 1998 to stop downgrading of local hospital and demand reopening of its accident and emergency department. Deprived Labour of overall control of Wyre Forest Council in 1999, became largest group in 2000 and part of anti-Labour coalition.

PEOPLE'S JUSTICE PARTY – also started as single-issue campaign to free two Pakistani Kashmiri separatists jailed for killing Indian diplomat. Has taken five council seats from Labour in inner city Birmingham, and changed its name to appeal to all sections of the community in these deprived areas.

RESIDENTS' ASSOCIATIONS (RAs) – A longstanding alternative to parties as a form of representative democracy. Strongholds in suburban Surrey – Epsom and Ewell, run by RAs since 1936, and Elmbridge – and East London/Essex – Epping Forest, Barking, and especially Havering, where they have been part of power-sharing administrations.

STOKE-ON-TRENT INDEPENDENTS – Self-selected group, following advert in local *Sentinel* newspaper for candidates to stand in protest against long-term near-monopolistic rule by Labour. Reduced Labour's majority to 4 and, after single election, became largest opposition group.

COVENTRY SOCIALIST PARTY – Built by and around ex-Coventry MP, Dave Nellist, and part of his national Socialist Alliance. Has taken 3 council seats from 'New' Labour.

earlier in one of the party's worst electoral performances in its history. Across the country Conservatives gained a net total of nearly 600 seats and 16 councils – albeit several that it seems almost incredible they ever lost: Eastbourne, Malvern Hills, Reigate and Banstead, Solihull, Southend-on-Sea, Torbay. Labour suffered almost matching losses, as the pendulum swung back from the party's triumphs in 1996.

Scratch around beneath those surface figures, though, and you quickly come across some apparent oddities. In among all their wins, the Conservatives somehow managed to lose nearly 50 seats they had previously held, plus their overall control of unitary Wokingham to the Liberal Democrats, who also took Oldham from Labour, but lost Herefordshire, Stockport, and Windsor and Maidenhead. Even Labour had its consolations, gaining control of Welwyn Hatfield and, as always happens, being able to attribute some of its worst results to 'exceptional local circumstances'. Its particularly poor record in the West Midlands could surely be partly blamed on government ministers appearing to do too little too late when the Rover car plant at Longbridge was threatened with closure. The 24 lost seats in Plymouth were a localised protest against housing developments and the controversial refurbishment of the sea front, and the Conservatives' winning 11 of 12 Labour seats in Tamworth was another negative vote – this time against the rise in car parking charges a few weeks before the election. The loss of Hartlepool was brought about by a dastardly pact between local Conservatives and Liberal Democrats. To all of which, the obvious response is to agree: yes, all these results, like Ken Livingstone's in London and those of the minority parties and independents in Exhibit 11.6, do stand out from any national trend, but they should not be thought of as 'deviant' or 'maverick'. They are simply the visible effects of voters' recognition that, on this occasion, it was not an MP they were being asked to elect, or a national government, but a local council to carry out local policies and provide local services.

Conclusion

This chapter has focused on the conduct of local elections, turnout patterns and differential voting. It has emphasised the 'localness' of such elections and provided a range of examples to show that local elections are not simply General Elections writ small. Local issues and local personalities are far from irrelevant in council elections, although their salience clearly varies from locality to locality. Local elections are, of course, a means to an end – namely choosing councillors to run local authorities. Chapter 12 focuses on the diverse roles of these democratically elected councillors.

Guide to further reading

No reference to local elections would be complete without a mention of the massive contributions of Colin Rallings and Michael Thrasher at Plymouth University's *Local Government Chronicle* Elections Centre and also of John and Hugh Bochel and David Denver in producing their respective compendia of detailed local results for England/Wales and Scotland – unrivalled sources of fascinating raw material and definitely worth a library investment! The product of this work is available to the general reader in Rallings and Thrasher (1997), by far the best introduction to all aspects of the subject. Keep up to date through their monthly columns in the *Chronicle* and the Elections Centre web site. The Electoral Reform Society's web site is useful on the different electoral systems, while that of the Electoral Commission should become increasingly so, now that it has taken over local election responsibilities from the Home Office.

Chapter 12

Councillors – The Voice of Choice

Introduction – beware of generalisations

This chapter explores who councillors are, what they do, why they do it, and how in future they are likely to be doing it rather differently. First, though, try to talk to one or two councillors yourself. Find out at first hand how they spend their time and how they justify their elective existences. They will not be 'typical', but part of the message of this chapter is the unhelpfulness of thinking exclusively of typical roles and behaviours. Others may generalise – like the former Conservative Welsh Office Minister, Rod Richards, whose most memorable contribution to central-local government harmony was publicly to label Labour councillors as 'fat, slimy and fundamentally corrupt' (*Local Government Chronicle*, 6 January 1995, p. 7). You should aim for a little more subtlety and sophistication in your own analysis, and you will probably find that your councillors differ one from another just as much as do our own small castlist, to which we shall now introduce you.

Five pen portraits

Maureen

Maureen has been a councillor for some 15 years: a Labour member on the Labour-controlled borough council of an East Lancashire textile town. She is in her 40s, now a single parent with three school-aged children to bring up. From a Labour-voting family, she joined the party soon after leaving school and worked her way steadily up through its local hierarchy.

She was originally selected and elected for a fairly safe Labour seat, and was quickly rewarded with the 'apprentice' post of Vice-Chair of the Allotments Sub-Committee. She later served for several years as Chair of Housing, politically responsible for the council's stock of 12,000 houses and flats. She became effectively a full-time councillor, living off income support, spending most evenings as well as daytimes at the town hall, conscious that she was seeing less of her children, and 'bribing them' with money for chips. She then started some employment training, of which politically she disapproved but it brought in an extra £10 a week. It also meant, however, that she had to fit as much of her council work as possible into her lunch hour – 'when officers are never available, unless I absolutely insist on it'.

As Housing Chair she saw through to completion a large town centre clearance programme, negotiated with a housing association the provision of good quality rented housing, and significantly reduced the council's empty properties and rent arrears. But she is prouder still of the fact that:

> with any improvement that now goes on in our council houses, people have choices. We give people budgets and they go out and choose from a range.

She explains her personal contribution to both the development and implementation of this policy:

> The single most important policy I delivered as Chair of Housing, believe it or not, was to allow our tenants the choice of colour of their front door. I could remember, as a tenant myself, the people from the council going down the street on our estate, and they used to have so many colours which they used in turn. One of the colours in my particular street was a purple and I remember counting the houses and being relieved that I just missed getting this awful purple. I didn't want the yellow I got, but I really hated that purple. So, when I was Chair, I said to officers that they had to give a choice of colour. They couldn't seem to understand at first the importance of going to someone's door and asking them what colour, of having contact with them *as tenants*, and *not* because they'd done something wrong. It's a small thing, but it gives everyone a good feeling.

Working to get the small, detailed things right is, to Maureen, much of what being a councillor is about – just as much as contributing to the large-scale policy decisions.

Richard

Richard, like Maureen, has been a senior, virtually full-time councillor, personally and politically concerned with issues of customer service. In most other respects, though, the two could scarcely offer more of a contrast.

Richard was one of 99 Kent County Councillors: a now retired but still pinstripe-suited Conservative businessman on what he hopes was seen, before it became 'hung' in the 1990s, as a businesslike Conservative council. His principal contribution was as Chairman of the County's Police Authority, in which capacity he provided the political drive behind the Constabulary's innovative Policing Charter: one of the first local government schemes to be awarded a Charter Mark by Prime Minister

John Major, 'for the raising of public service standards without increasing the cost to the taxpayer or the consumer'.

As a long-standing Conservative Party member and office-holder, it had been Richard's vague intention to 'go into local government' at the age of about 60, when his company required all directors to retire. This plan was thwarted by the Conservatives' success in the 1979 General Election. The sitting Conservative councillor for Richard's home area was elected to Parliament and resigned his council seat, and Richard was, initially with some reluctance, prevailed upon to take his place in what was about the safest Conservative seat in the county. As he himself concedes, for his first four-year term of office, while he was still working full-time, he contributed little to the Council and was very much 'learning the ropes'. After retirement he took on a series of increasingly responsible and time-consuming positions, culminating in his four years as Chairman of the Police Authority.

He did not stand for re-election in 1993. By that time he had 'spent twelve years putting something back into the community' – years which provided genuine job satisfaction but also, for a former businessman, had their definite frustrations. He resented the mainly Government-imposed constraints under which local councils must nowadays operate – 'like having not one hand, but one and a half hands, tied behind your back' – and in particular their ability to raise so little of their expenditure from their own local taxpayers.

Joan

In Lambeth, by contrast, when Labour councillors in 1985 tried to break free of the Government restraint of rate-capping, their hands were not so much tied behind their backs as metaphorically cut off. Found guilty of failing to set a legal rate, the rebel Labour councillors were ordered to pay £250,000 in surcharges and legal costs and banned from public office – to be replaced by, in many cases, totally supportive and equally radical successors, like Joan.

Joan's political career, much more than those of Maureen or Richard, has been shaped and driven by issues, rather than party. Her earliest involvement in politics was as a single parent with a young child, fighting the social security system, with the help of the local Claimants' Union, for her own and other people's benefit rights:

> I found I was much better arguing other people's cases than my own! But to get even the most simple thing out of social security usually meant occupying their offices with lots of children and forcing the issue.

Later on, as a mature student at university and with her son now at school, she again found herself drawn into campaigns and protests – for the provision of half-term playgroups, against increases in overseas students' fees – and using her personal experience to help other students with their grant and benefit claims.

Only after university, when she moved to London and obtained a council flat in Lambeth, did she actually join the Labour Party. She became constituency party secretary; then, in quick succession, as the disqualified councillors were removed from office, prospective candidate, elected councillor, and, straightaway, her party group's Chief Whip – in which responsible capacity she attended her very first council meeting.

Joyce

Joyce is another councillor who came relatively late to party politics. Her first significant contact with her council was also as a protester, and she, too, had never attended a council meeting before being elected.

Like Joan, Joyce was activated by a public issue with a personal impact: the threatened closure of her daughter's primary school by the Labour-controlled metropolitan borough council. She tried to galvanise other parents into action, but without success: the school was closed.

Shortly afterwards she was contacted by the local Liberal Democrat leader, who said how impressed he had been with her activity, and would she be interested in standing as the party's ward candidate at the following May elections? While previously a Lib Dem voter, she had never contemplated becoming a councillor. But, having given up her career as a civil servant and with her children now at school, she agreed to let her name go forward and was elected with a large majority.

From Joyce's viewpoint the Lib Dem-held ward must seem like a small yellow island in an otherwise largely red Labour sea. She feels fortunate in having been put on to the committees in which she was most interested – education, schools, and environment – but is increasingly frustrated at always being in a minority of either one or two. Almost inevitably, therefore, she finds herself spending most of her time on the representational or ward-based part of her councillor role: dealing with electors' problems.

Keith

There are thousands of councillors who could identify with both the positive and negative aspects of Joyce's position, but none better than Keith. For, several years ago, that was precisely his position; same council, same ward and same minority party.

Keith was similarly approached about standing as a Lib Dem candidate after playing a leading role in a local community protest: against the council's erection of an unwanted fence around a local housing estate. He, like Joyce a few years later, was elected at his first attempt. But disillusion swiftly set in:

> I was naive. I thought that, being a councillor, I could actually assist people in my area . . . but not as a Liberal Democrat I couldn't. My time is precious. If I was going to put 100 per cent effort in, I wanted to see results.

That, he concluded, on his perpetually Labour council, meant switching parties. So he left the Lib Dems, first becoming an Independent, and then agreeing to 'cross the floor' and join the Labour group. He was, hardly surprisingly, viewed with much suspicion, but at the same time was 'rewarded' at the next Annual Meeting with the Chair of Further Education, 'which sounds exalted, but in fact no one else wanted it'.

With his sole GCE O-level in Biology, his knowledge of further education was minimal – though, as he says, 'that's what the officers are there for'. What he knew about and was genuinely interested in was the youth and community part of his committee's responsibilities. So, for three years he threw himself into the job. He was heavily involved in the council's planned reorganisation of secondary education, and was able, at the same time, to do something for his own ward: bringing together, with the help of council officers, all the local voluntary organisations and forming a community association which now has its own Community Centre . . . in the very building that used to be Joyce's daughter's school!

Here, then, is our own small cast, to which we hope you will be able to add one or two of your own pen portraits. Three women, two men; a county councillor, a London borough councillor, one shire and two metropolitan district councillors; one Conservative, two Labour, one Liberal Democrat, and one Lib Dem-Lab switcher; two long-standing party members, three much more recent joiners; two in powerful policy-making positions, one very active ward representative, one instinctive issues campaigner, and one community politician. Plenty of labels and contrasts, but what do they have in common – among themselves and with the other 22,300 councillors across the country?

Elected local politicians – the voice of choice

To start with – and, as we shall see, it is not such an obvious statement as it may appear – they are all, all 22,300 of them, elected local politicians. Let us briefly examine the three parts of that description in turn.

There used to be a time, before the reorganisation of local government in the early 1970s, when the majority of members on many councils were unelected. Part of the reason was the existence of *aldermen*. These were usually, though not necessarily, senior and experienced councillors, who were appointed by the elected councillors to bolster their numbers by up to an additional third, and to add expertise and continuity. Their appointments were for six years – compared to councillors' then three-year term of office (now four years); they tended to take disproportionate numbers of committee chairs and vice-chairs; and they never had to seek the support of or face the prospect of defeat from a fickle electorate. They provided continuity, and most councils were able to provide examples of aldermanic members of 30, 40 or even 50 years' standing. They were undemocratic, but they unaccountably – in every sense of the word – lived on until, apart from in Northern Ireland, they and their Scottish near-equivalents, *bailies*, were finally abolished in the 1970s.

The unelected position of aldermen would have been seen as even more anachronistic than it was, had not many councillors themselves also never had to face an election. For, as we saw in Chapter 11, the sorry truth is that, throughout most of the history of UK local government, thousands of council seats at each annual set of elections were filled by unopposed returns, 40 per cent or more councillors by the 1960s winning or retaining their council memberships unchallenged.

There thus existed a kind of double democratic deficit – up to a quarter of council members who did not have to be elected and large numbers who should have been but were not. This is one local government deficit that has, since the 1972–4 reorganisation, been virtually eliminated. With over 95 per cent of seats in most parts of the country now subject to two- or three-party contests, councillors individually and councils collectively can claim with far greater legitimacy to be speaking as their community's 'voice of choice'. They are the instruments through which the residents of a particular geographical area have expressed their preferences for one set of candidates, policies, service standards and tax levels, rather than another.

Politicians all

Choice, preference, priorities … they are the currency of politics, and those who translate them into practical policies are politicians. The third attribute of all our councillors – in addition to being at least nominally elected and representing specific geographical localities – is that they are politicians. All of them – even the now small minority of self-styled 'non-partisans' and 'Independents' – perform what the late Sir Lawrence Boyle, a key member of the Widdicombe Committee, termed the 'political function':

> all governments, be they central or local, have a two-fold function to perform. They have the *service function* and the political function. The service function consists of the provision of those goods and services

which for one reason or another are supplied through the public sector. The political function, on the other hand, is the management and reduction of the conflict which arises out of the issues involved in the public provision of goods and services. It embraces such questions as *the scope, the scale and the quality of the public services and the manner in which their costs should be met.* And it should be noted that it is easier in fact to remove the service function from local government than it is to remove the political function. Because the service function, as we know, can always be privatised, but *the political function cannot and should not be delegated. If the political function is removed from local government, it ceases to be local government.* (Boyle, 1986, p. 33, emphasis ours)

That, surely, is what we expect of our elected representatives, national and local alike: that they debate and determine *themselves* – not delegate to unelected officials – the distribution of our society's resources. We, as electors, delegate the political function to them: to take on our behalf decisions about the building of houses, schools and roads, about levels of service provision and rates of taxation. That is their role and responsibility, whether or not they happen to have been elected under a party label. Most are, and that party identity shapes almost every aspect of their work, from the need to maintain a good relationship with their local ward party through to the regular meetings of their party group on the council.

Representatives, not reflections

Councillors, then, share in common the fact that they are all local elected politicians. But what *kinds* of people are they, who have the apparent arrogance or presumption to wish to exercise *their* political will on our behalf, yet who are, at the same time, prepared to plead for our votes and to risk our ridicule and rejection? How like us are they, or how different? The standard way of responding to this question tends to be by reference to councillors' personal and socioeconomic characteristics, as in Exhibit 12.1. There is nothing intrinsically wrong with such data. They are relatively easily collected and categorised – although only quite recently has there been anything that could claim to be a full-scale councillor 'census' – and they furnish us with measures of the extent to which certain social groups are over- or under-represented in the population of councillors.

It is, for instance, worth knowing – as opposed to merely suspecting – that only just over a quarter of this country's councillors are women; that the proportion of councillors over conventional retirement age is higher today than in the mid-1960s; and that only 10 per cent of councillors have current first-hand experience of the housing that they themselves are responsible for managing.

Such data, though, have their pitfalls and limitations. They can prompt unwarranted and misleading generalisations. They may obscure real and significant contrasts among councillors in different parts of the country, on different types of councils, and from different parties. They can also be seen as implying that 'representative government' is more about trying to produce, like President Clinton's first 'Mirror on America' Cabinet, a socioeconomic cross-section or statistical reflection of the electorate, rather than the representation of ideas and ideals. With these reservations in mind, we draw out a few key distinctions and implications – in the hope of *discouraging* the idea that there is a 'typical councillor'.

Gender

Most readers will surely find the gender figures in Exhibit 12.1 dispiriting, even if the proportion of women councillors has more than doubled in the past 30 years and, as ever, is substantially higher than that for the House of Commons, even after the record influx of Labour women MPs in May 1997. There are also more women *councillors* in the most senior positions in local government than there are women officers: more women leaders than chief executives, more women committee chairs than directors of departments. Perhaps more surprisingly, though lagging way behind Sweden (42 per cent), Norway (37 per cent), Finland (32 per cent), and the PR-elected Scottish Parliament and Welsh and Greater London Assemblies (all around 38 per cent), we have more women councillors than many European countries (CEMR, 2000). France, however, leads the way with 48 per cent, following its controversial Parity Act 2000, requiring political parties to nominate equal numbers of men and women as prospective commune candidates: an example for those who favour quota systems as the only effective way of changing biases in electoral representation .

Does such gender distortion matter, or make a difference? Inevitably, yes. It is difficult to claim that councils on which 75 per cent of members are men pursue the same priorities and arrive in the same way at the same decisions as would councils on which even 40 per cent, let alone 75 per cent, of members were female. The illustration usually given is that more women members would mean better child care facilities and fewer municipal golf courses. But there is much more to it than that. Women are the main users of council services. They make an estimated three-quarters of all calls to council departments. They are the majority of tenants, the family members who make most use of swimming pools and libraries, who are most likely to put the bins out for collection, and who are most conscious of and affected by the quality of the local environment – inadequate street cleansing, poor lighting, dog fouling, pot-holed roads

Exhibit 12.1 Personal characteristics of councillors, England and Wales 1997/98

	Adult pop. Eng. & Wales %	All c'llors %	Cons %	Lab %	LD %	Indep %
GENDER						
Male	49	73	74	74	66	78
Female	51	27	26	26	34	22
ETHNIC MINORITY	6	3.1	0.9	5.5	1.1	0.5
Black (gross estimated numbers)	1.8	(133)	(3)	(115)	(14)	(1)
Indian	1.6	(156)	(8)	(142)	(6)	(0)
Pakistani	0.8	(118)	(2)	(110)	(6)	(0)
Other	1.7	(246)	(26)	(178)	(29)	(8)
TOTAL		(653)	(39)	(545)	(55)	(9)
AGE						
Under 25	8	*	*	*	*	*
25–34	21	4	3	5	4	*
35–44	19	14	8	18	14	5
45–54	18	28	21	30	33	18
55–64	13	30	33	27	29	35
65–74	14	21	31	17	18	34
75 and over	7	4	5	3	2	7
AVERAGE AGE	45	56	59	54	54	61

EDUCATION – HIGHEST QUALIFICATION						
Degree or equivalent	14	32	27	33	41	19
Professional qualification	3	21	29	15	24	24
GCE A-level/HNC	13	9	12	9	9	9
GCE O-level/ONC/GCSE/CSE	30	15	16	15	13	18
Other	22	6	6	7	4	7
No formal qualifications	18	17	11	22	9	23
EMPLOYMENT STATUS						
Full-time paid employment	39	30	20	37	31	14
Part-time paid employment	12	8	6	9	10	7
Self-employed	8	15	25	8	16	29
Unemployed	4	3	1	5	2	1
Retired	22	35	41	32	32	45
Looking after home and family	6	4	5	3	5	4
Other (incl. disabled, full-time education)	9	5	2	6	4	1
CURRENT OCCUPATION (excluding council work)						
Managerial/executive	17	33	53	23	30	48
Professional/technical	17	28	26	28	32	23
Teacher/lecturer/researcher	4	12	4	16	15	4
Admin/clerical/secretarial/sales	22	13	11	14	14	13
Manual/craft	30	14	7	19	9	13
Full-time councillor	25		20	29	23	15
'Dual member' – ie of more than one council	12		15	9	15	13

Note: * = less than 1 per cent   ☐ = significantly high figure.

Source: Local Government Management Board (1998), esp. pp. 59–60.

and pavements, inadequate public transport and street crime. They are likely to have distinctive priorities and agendas. If you still have doubts, try this simple question: why is it that most public buildings have far fewer female than male toilets, instead of recognising, like the rebuilt Royal Opera House – a noteworthy exception to the rule – that roughly three times as much space should properly be allowed for women as for men?

Ethnic minorities

An equivalent argument can be directed at the under-representation on our local councils of ethnic minorities. These groups also fare a little better locally than nationally and – though, as in Exhibit 12.1, their presence is still more meaningfully recorded in absolute numbers than percentages – the election of black and Asian councillors in particular has increased significantly in recent years.

But any national figures in this instance are particularly misleading. What we want to know are both levels and details of representation in those areas with sizeable ethnic minority populations, and interpretation can be difficult. In Birmingham, for example, there are more than 20 ethnic minority members on the 117-seat City Council. Nearly 20 per cent might seem like a not unreasonable representation of the city's approximately 25 per cent ethnic minority population – until you consider the sheer diversity of that population: the African-Caribbeans; the Kashmiri restaurant owners, taxi drivers and textile industry outworkers; the Punjabi Sikhs, with their prominent role in the local economy; the small business-owning Gujuratis from both India and East Africa; the smaller Chinese and Vietnamese communities. Several of these groups are bound to regard themselves as unrepresented – not merely under-represented – on the City Council in any direct racial, religious or cultural sense, and if this is true in Birmingham, it is even more so in most other towns and cities.

Age

The world of councillors is a predominantly middle-aged and elderly one – and becoming significantly more so. In the 1985 Widdicombe Committee survey reported in this book's previous editions, over a quarter of all councillors were under 45, including a third of Labour members and nearly a half of the then Liberals. Today the proportion of under-45s (18 per cent) is lower than it was even in 1964 (21 per cent) (Wilson and Game, 1998, p. 221). At the other end of the scale, nearly 40 per cent of all today's councillors are over 60, including 53 per cent of Conservatives and over 60 per cent of Independents. Labour and the Lib Dems are the 'youthful' parties in modern-day local government, with median ages of 54 – about five years higher than that of MPs. In Scotland the average age is slightly lower, but on English county and particularly Welsh councils higher still, balanced out by the greater numbers of relatively younger members in the metropolitan districts and London boroughs. But even these councils still have some way to go, as Joyce recalls thinking at her first council meeting:

> I was really surprised by the number of elderly gentlemen. There were only about five councillors in my age group (mid-30s), and I'm the only lady councillor with young children. I'm probably the only one who has to organise arrangements for looking after their children while they're at council meetings.

Regrettable, it might be felt, for a council whose responsibilities include childminding, children's centres, crèches, day nurseries, play centres, parent and toddler groups, pre-school playgroups, toy libraries and nursery schools.

Education

The older the age group, the less likely its members are to have formal educational qualifications. Partly as a result of their elderly age profile, councillors as a whole are both better and no better educated than their constituents, who have been catching up fast. Returning again to the 1985 Widdicombe survey, the proportion of councillors with no formal qualifications (23 per cent) was half that among the adult population as a whole. Today there is virtually no difference. There are still differences, though, in lengths of formal education, with nearly a third of councillors possessing degrees or the equivalent, compared to just 14 per cent of the adult population. Such qualifications are not in themselves, of course, any measure of fitness or aptitude for government, but education is presumably one characteristic on which most of us would be happy to see our elected representatives not perfectly reflective of the population at large.

Employment

Given the long-standing tradition of council membership being a voluntary and part-time activity, it is striking that well under half of today's councillors (45 per cent) are in full-time paid employment – a figure that in total varies little across the parties, although the employed/self-employed balance predictably does. Part of the explanation of the decline from 54 per cent in 1985 is obviously the fact that over a third are now retired, compared to a quarter in 1985. The other factor, as we shall see, is that councillors' allowances have begun to increase significantly and are just reaching the levels that can support, albeit modestly, a life-style as a full-time councillor. In the past relatively few councillors would have openly admitted to being 'full-time', no matter how many hours a week they put into the job; in the LGMB's census a quarter did so, and the number will surely grow almost year by year.

With their higher educational qualifications, it is not surprising to find councillors coming disproportionately from non-manual backgrounds in general and from the professional and managerial groups in particular. There is a correspondingly low proportion of manual workers: 14 per cent of employed councillors or 7 per cent of the total. The proportion among Labour councillors has fallen from around a third in 1985 to under a fifth today, but, even so, on this particular indicator Labour can claim to be the party most reflective of its electorate.

The councillor's job description

We now know something about who councillors are. They can and do come from all kinds of backgrounds and walks of life. It is neither very easy nor helpful to talk of there being a 'typical' councillor. So does it follow that there is no such thing as a typical councillor's job? Yes, it does. Different councillors will have their differing interests, motivations, skills, aptitudes and opportunities, and they will at least endeavour to spend their inevitably limited time in differing ways. Even today, there is no neatly defined 'job spec.' to which a newly elected member can turn, and in the past it was largely left up to individual councils to produce some kind of composite job description, like the one we adopted in the previous editions of this book. Thus, the aims and purposes of the job of councillor might be said to be those in Box 12.1.

Box 12.1 The councillor's job

- To represent and be accountable to the electorate ...
- in formulating policies and practices for the Authority ...
- monitoring their effectiveness ...
- and providing leadership for the community.

This definition is not offered as something uniquely authoritative or unimprovable, and, as we shall see, in our new era of executive and non-executive councillors, any such 'blanket' listing requires careful qualification. However, it has three considerable virtues. First, it is a neat distillation of what might otherwise be a lengthy catalogue of more specific councillor duties and responsibilities.

Second, it takes us way beyond the traditional and apparently almost unthinking textbook distinctions that used to be made between 'policy' and 'administration': that councillors made policy and officers implemented and administered it, and ne'er the twain should meet. The sheer lack of realism underpinning this 'formal model', as we term it in Chapter 15, grated most with local government practitioners. Was it seriously imagined, on the one hand, that a small group of part-time, amateur councillors had the capacity – or even the inclination – to produce a 'policy' for every aspect of every council service *without* there being a necessarily substantial contribution from the numerous highly trained, experienced, and generally well-paid officers whom they themselves employed? Similarly, were councillors really supposed, having delivered their policy pronouncements like proverbial tablets of stone, to stand aside and pay no attention to how the policy was delivered and to its impact on their own local residents and electors? As Maureen might say, that is a recipe for dreadful purple doors!

This thought brings us to the third virtue of our starting definition, which is that it is expressed in language that makes sense to councillors themselves. Councillor roles and 'role orientations' have been a favourite topic of academic investigation over the years, and some insightful studies have resulted (Lee, 1963; Heclo, 1969; Hampton, 1970; Budge *et al.*, 1972; Dearlove, 1973; Jones, 1973; Corina, 1974; Jennings, 1982; Newton, 1976; Gyford, 1984). But so too has a positive lexicon of role labels: politico, delegate, trustee, representative, broad policy-maker, tribune, statesman, ministerialist, parochial, people's agent, policy advocate, policy spokesman, policy broker, party politician, ideologist, partyist, facilitator, resister, politico-administrator, communicator, populist, conventional politician, community politician.

For the reader, such a proliferation of labels can produce confusion as well as enlightenment, From most councillors, though, the response was more likely to be cynicism. Even if they recognised the actual words, they would not naturally think of using most of them to describe the behaviour of either themselves or their councillor colleagues. They would, on the other hand, recognise and identify with the language of representation and accountability, policy formulation, performance monitoring and community leadership.

Indeed, councillors tend to use these terms and ideas themselves. Maureen was conscious that, as Chair of Housing, she was both responsible and accountable for the formulation of policy across the whole of her borough, and, as she emphasised, for monitoring the effectiveness of that policy and of the overall performance of the housing department. She no longer lived in the ward she represents, and so would reluctantly acknowledge that she could not be the almost full-time resident representative that someone like Joyce is. Keith, you will recall, went to the lengths of changing parties to give himself more of a policy-making role and thereby play a more effective leadership role in his local community.

The councillor's 'traditional' job description thus embraces a wide variety of potential roles and responsibilities – as representative, policy-maker, scrutineer, and community leader. With councillors now becoming either part of their council's executive or not, some of these roles and responsibilities continue to be shared by all councillors, and all are exercised by some. But, for the first time, not all councillors are able even to claim that they have all roles. To explain, we shall examine each in turn.

Representative – on the grand scale

We start with the most fundamental role of all, yet in some ways one of the most overlooked. Under our system of local government every councillor is elected by, and is accountable to, the residents of a defined geographical area, known as an electoral *ward* or *division* – 'constituency' being primarily a parliamentary term. With the exceptional scale of UK local government, these local electorates can, from the viewpoint of councillors trying to represent them, be dauntingly large.

As shown in Exhibit 12.2, we have proportionately fewer and much larger 'local' authorities than almost any other Western country, and they are even fewer and larger following the unitary reorganisation of the 1990s. Corollaries of this scale of 'local' government are that we citizens have fewer councillors to represent us, and inevitably we are less likely to know or be known by them. If anything, the figures in the final column of Exhibit 12.2 under-state the scale of the councillor's task. When our two-tier system and many districts' multi-member wards are taken into account, an average English district councillor has an *electorate* of between 3,000 and 5,000, a county councillor one of up to 10,000, and a metropolitan district, unitary, or London borough councillor one larger still. Multiply these figures by, say, 1.5 for total residential populations, and the reality is that in large city and unitary authorities councillors may represent wards of up to 25,000 people.

As with other aspects of the job, councillors themselves decide how much energy they put into the representation of their electorate. They do not *have* to hold surgeries or advice bureaux, or publicise – preferably nowadays through the council's internet – their availability to deal with constituents' problems, complaints, queries and opinions. Most councillors, though, do choose to do these things, and much more besides. In which case, they are likely to find themselves acting in several distinct representational 'sub-roles', in addition to case-worker and individual problem-solver: as listener, advocate, ring-holder, facilitator and empowerer (Goss and Corrigan, 1999, pp. 13 ff.).

Exhibit 12.2 Britain's large-scale local government

	Population (million)	No. of principal local councils	Average pop. per council	Av. size of council	Population per elected member
France	59.6	36,700 communes	1,600	14	118
Austria	8.2	2,350 Gemeinden	3,500	17	209
Sweden	8.8	310 kommuner, etc	28,400	111*	256
Germany	83.0	15,300 Gemeinden etc	5,400	15	350
Norway	4.5	435 kommuner	10,300	28	367
Finland	5.2	452 kommuner	11,500	28	410
Italy	57.7	8,100 communi	7,100	12	608
Spain	40.0	8,100 municipios	4,900	8	610
Belgium	10.3	589 communes	17,500	22	811
Greece	10.6	1,033 dimi, koinotites	10,300	10	1,075
Denmark	5.4	275 kommuner	19,600	17	1,115
Portugal	10.1	308 municipios	32,800	29	1,131
Netherlands	16.0	548 gemeenten	29,000	19	1,555
Ireland	3.8	114 counties, etc.	33,000	14	2,336
UK	59.6	468 counties, districts, etc.	127,350	49	2,603

Notes: * Includes deputies, elected at the same time

To enable realistic comparison with other countries' local and commune councillors, these figures include only councillors of principal authorities – i.e. in the case of the United Kingdom they *exclude* the approximately 80,000 members of parish, town and community councils, which are not universal and mostly have very limited service responsibilities.

Main sources: CEMR (2000), EU Committee of the Regions (1999) – updated and corrected, where appropriate.

They *listen*, and talk of course, when they meet all the various groups, organisations and individuals within their wards: tenants' and residents' associations, community groups, housing associations, youth clubs, local fêtes, health and police authorities, local business people and journalists. They act as *advocates* in ensuring that the views, needs and problems of local people, particularly those likely to experience access difficulties, reach the appropriate sections of the council. Sooner or later they will be required to act as *ring-holder* in some dispute between individuals or groups, each convinced of the validity and justice of their case. They will go further and *facilitate*, by working with excluded, aggrieved or factionalised groups, bringing people together to discuss problems and jointly agree solutions. And on occasions they may *empower*, assisting local groups to organise, prepare and resource themselves in order to manage some council project or take over responsibility for a service.

All these activities are capable of bringing relatively swift and positive outcomes and, at least very occasionally, an expression of gratitude from those benefiting. The rewards of committee work are, at best, more diffuse, and it is not hard to understand why many councillors find that the representational part of the job is the one that brings them their greatest satisfaction (Barron *et al.*, 1987, pp. 73 ff.). But why not check for yourself? Several authorities, like Nottinghamshire and Tameside, have developed the good practice of having their councillors produce regular reports for their web sites detailing what they have been doing and what they feel they have achieved. See which councillors give more prominence to the work they have done in their ward than to the meetings they have attended in the town hall.

Policy-maker

That reference to meetings brings us to the policy role of councillors – traditionally their work in committees, sub-committees and panels in developing policy, both for the authority as a whole and for particular services. They are assisted, informed, advised, and maybe even steered by their officers, but they constitutionally have the responsibility for giving strategic direction to the authority and for determining its policy priorities.

In the past, this policy or executive role, like that of representative, was shared by all councillors, though again the nature and impact of their contribution varied enormously. A committee might be chaired by a long-serving member, seemingly as conversant with the technical details of departmental policy as most of the professional officers, but include also a neophyte and perhaps minority party backbencher, still struggling to follow the procedure of the committee, let alone its agenda. All councils, though, organised their work through committees, and all councillors would find themselves appointed to at least one or two. All councillors could thus quite properly regard themselves as contributing to policy-making in at least certain of their council's service areas and all were collectively responsible for its policy as a whole. All too, therefore, were potentially liable to be individually surcharged for supporting unlawful local expenditure, even when they themselves had received no personal benefit from the decision – quite unlike the position of, say, a government minister demonstrably responsible for a major and horrendously costly policy failure. The personal surcharge was finally abolished in the Local Government Act 2000, but even in recent years, as Joan's career demonstrates, a number of Labour councillors in Lambeth and also in Liverpool were surcharged and consequently bankrupted.

The far more comprehensive change ushered in by the 2000 Act, though, was the executive/non-executive split in councillors' roles described in Chapter 6. From 2001/02 councillors on most authorities became *either* executive *or* non-executive members. With most authorities adopting either mayor/cabinet or leader/cabinet models (see Exhibit 6.2), the small minority of executive members are usually known as cabinet, executive, or executive board members and in most cases have responsibility for a specific service portfolio. But even if that service portfolio closely resembles the title of a committee they formerly chaired, being a cabinet member is very different from being a committee chair. The key point of the executive/non-executive split is to clarify publicly who is responsible for making any particular policy decisions, and that is what executive members do: they make decisions and take public responsibility for them through the process of scrutiny by non-executive members. Some of these decisions will be taken collectively, by the cabinet as a whole, but others will be taken *individually* – in a way that previously was not legally permitted for even the most powerful committee chair or council leader.

Executive members, then, are now the key policy-*makers*, but that does not mean that non-executive members no longer have a policy role. They do, in several distinct ways. First, as ward representatives, they see and hear how the policies of the council and other bodies impact upon their own electors. If a policy is not working in the way intended or if service delivery is unsatisfactory, they are likely to be the first to receive complaints, and repeated complaints should feed in to the process of policy evaluation and review.

Secondly, they are members of the full council, which, like councillors themselves, has a much changed and enhanced role under executive government. The executive leads the preparation of the local authority's policies and budget, but the policy and budget frameworks have to be formally agreed by the full council. The full council has similarly to agree the many policy plans and strategies that authorities are now required to produce: the best value and performance plan, children's services plan, community care plan, crime and disorder reduction strategy, and the like.

Executive members take 'in-year' decisions on resources and priorities to implement agreed policies, but decisions not in accordance with the policy or budget framework, or that are not constitutionally the executive's responsibility, go to full council. The council also receives and debates all overview and scrutiny reports, which brings us to councillors' third main role.

Scrutineer

The policy process is best visualised as a continuous cycle – from initiation, through formulation, enactment, implementation, with the cycle completed by evaluation, the outcome of which may lead in turn to a further policy initiative or adaptation (see Figure 12.1). The cycle does not stop with legislation or enactment, and nor does the councillors' policy responsibilities. As John Stewart emphasises (1990, p. 27):

> Councillors are concerned not merely with policy, but with how policy is carried out, for in implementation policy succeeds or fails. Policy and implementation can never be completely separated. Policy is made and re-made in implementation.

The overview and scrutiny function is *the* key non-executive role in the government's 'modernisation' of councils' political management, and its effective development and operation will arguably be the real determinant of whether the executive/non-executive split is publicly judged a success. Fortunately, therefore, it is being given a considerably broader interpretation than at first seemed likely and promises to introduce into local government something that clearly ought to have existed previously but, by almost universal admission, did not. True, there has long been something called 'performance review', but it was almost invariably reactive

Figure 12.1   *The policy cycle*

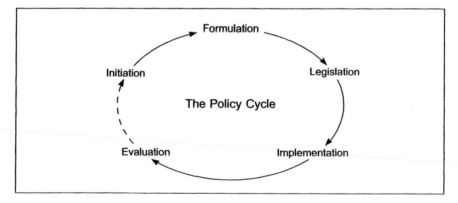

and superficial – often delegated to a single sub-committee with responsibility for monitoring the council's performance across any and all service areas. Overview and scrutiny can and should be unrecognisably different: expansive rather than delimited, pro-active rather than reactive, prospective as well as retrospective, creative and constructive as well as critical and blame-seeking (Audit Commission, 2001a, p. 9).

Quite properly, councils choose for themselves how organisationally they are going to exercise the overview and scrutiny function. There are thus differing numbers and configurations of committees and panels, of differing sizes, and with differing terms of reference. Some councils, commendably, have chairs and vice-chairs from minority parties, some not. Some invite community representatives to participate as non-voting co-opted members, others do not. All, though, *must* reflect the political balance of the council, must meet in public, and must review all matters that are the responsibility of the executive, no members of which can be members of a scrutiny committee.

Insofar as the council's constitution permits, scrutiny committees set their own agendas. They can require members of the executive and council officers to attend their meetings and be questioned about what they are planning to do (policy review), what they are doing ('call-in'), what they have done (*ex post* scrutiny), and how effective it has been (service review). If unsatisfied, they can make recommendations for further action or amendments to either the executive or the full council. They can invite evidence from other individuals and organisations. They can, if they wish, investigate the performance of other organisations and partnerships in local governance – the health service, the police authority, registered social landlords, a PFI project, or even the local university. As will be apparent, the ultimate effectiveness of scrutiny and overview involves non-executive councillors challenging not just the executive, but also their own party identities and loyalties. Majority party members have to work with colleagues from *other* parties in scrutinising and perhaps criticising in public the performance of senior executive members of their *own* party. It is neither easy nor something that is at all familiar in local government – and that is its very importance.

Community leader

It is striking that not one of the role labels listed at the start of this section included the word 'leadership', and it is a role that many councillors may not readily embrace. It is, though, one that has perhaps become relatively more important at precisely the time that councils no longer have the service-providing dominance in their areas that they once did. As service provision has become more fragmented and councils work in partnership with other organisations in a network of community governance, councillors increasingly stand out as the only democratically elected pieces in the ever more complex jigsaw. They are the ones in closest touch with the electorate and service users; they are the ones likely to have to field inquiries about non-council service providers – health authorities, housing associations, primary care groups. If their particular local community is going to have leadership, over and above mere representation, where else is it going to come from? As councils become the hub of the local authority area as a whole, so councillors can become the hub of their ward communities: the appointees to other public bodies, the human links between organisational partners, and the exercisers of what Goss and Corrigan term 'influence power', as opposed to the cruder 'control power' of former times (1999, p. 32).

The workload

It is clear that, with a ratio of well over 2,500 of us to every one of them, the job of a UK councillor in either a committee or an executive system is both multi-faceted and potentially extremely demanding. So how much time does it all take?

There is no simple answer. Like an MP, a councillor could 'get away with' doing an absolute minimum: attending the occasional council and scrutiny committee meeting and avoiding, as far as possible, all contact with constituents. All available evidence suggests there are few such councillors nowadays, and that the far more frequent behavioural pattern adopted is a maximalist and pro-active one. That was certainly the impression formed by the authors of a study of councillors and their partners that they entitled *Married to the Council?* (Barron *et al.*, 1987; also Barron *et al.*, 1991). Their findings, from an albeit limited sample of about 60 councillors from just three English county councils, were that these members were spending an average of between about 20 and 35 hours *per week* on their council duties.

Other studies, using different methods of recall and recording, have produced slightly lower figures. But there was sufficient consistency across a series of national surveys to suggest that the average time spent by members of *all types* of authority on their council work in recent years was between 75 and 80 hours per 'typical' month, or 19 to 20 hours per week (Robinson Committee, 1977; Widdicombe Committee, 1986b; Rao, 1994). Such averages, though, must be read with care. Figures for office-holding councillors and for most on urban and unitary authorities – including those in Scotland and Wales – would have been very much higher; those for 'backbench' shire district councillors much lower.

It seems likely that up to two-thirds of councillors' time in the 1980s and 1990s was in some way meeting-related: attending them, preparing for them by reading papers or meeting council officers, and travelling to and from them. By comparison, constituency and community business occupied only about a fifth of their time. It was this imbalance that was one of the considerations behind the government's political management reforms, aimed at enhancing members' representational roles and reducing the time spent relatively non-participatively in committee meetings. Whether such aspirations will be reflected in future councillors' time diaries remains to be seen.

Financial compensation

The jobs of councillor and MP may be similar in their open-endedness. In their financial rewards they are emphatically different. MPs have index-linked salaries of well over £50,000, as part of an annual pay and allowances package totalling a possible £142,000 – a sum that would cover what plenty of district councils pay out to *all* their members in the form not of salaries, index-linked or otherwise, but allowances. Yet ironically, of the two groups, it is councillors, even under the traditional committee system, that have had by far the greater and more immediate personal power – in the sense of contributing directly to decisions to spend budgets and allocate contracts of hundreds of millions of pounds. MPs can merely question, scrutinise, approve or disapprove the spending decisions of government ministers.

Times, however, are changing fast. With the arrival of executive councillors have come, on a modest scale at least, UK local government's first executive salaries – or 'pensionable remuneration' as government pronouncements seem to prefer. In the previous edition of this book we noted that most of the country's 23,000 councillors received annual allowances comparable to the then maximum undergraduate student grant – under £2,500 – although the leaders of some of the country's largest councils were for the first time able to earn at least the equivalent of an average graduate starting salary (Wilson and Game, 1998, p. 232). That statement is now at most only partially true. There are still plenty of non-executive councillors on allowances of no more than £50 per week, but the national average has risen significantly and will continue to do so, the aim being to attract a more professional type of councillor, assist family members with childcare, and set in place training budgets. Meanwhile, the payment of elected mayors and leaders of our largest councils is beginning to acknowledge the necessarily full-time nature of these posts with their greatly extended personal responsibilities.

Unlike the situation prior to 1995, local authorities are now entirely responsible for determining their own structures and rates of allowances, acting on the advice and recommendations of a local independent

Exhibit 12.3 Members' allowances deregulated

History

1972   Attendance Allowances first introduced – £10 per day maximum
1980   Special Responsibility Allowances payable to leaders, committee chairs, etc.
1991   3 allowances available to every local authority, within limits defined by Environment Secretary:
(a) Basic flat-rate Annual Allowance; (b) Special Responsibility Allowances; (c) Attendance Allowance (see Wilson and Game, 1994, p. 224)
1995   Government-imposed limits removed. Councils build *job description* for each councillor in line with their responsibilities and payable at rate of the average non-manual wage (see Wilson & Game, 1998, p. 233)

The present system – from 2001

Individual authorities continue to decide own allowances. Local Government Act 2000 requires all principal councils to establish and maintain an *Independent Remuneration Panel* of at least 3 persons to advise council on: its scheme of allowances; the amounts to be paid; the pensionability of allowances.

Allowances that must *no longer* be paid:

- *Attendance Allowance* – abolished 2001: encouraged 'attendance culture'.

Allowances that *must* be paid:

- *Basic Allowance* – flat-rate allowance paid to all council members in recognition of their time commitments in attending council and party group meetings, meeting officers and constituents, and their incidental costs – use of home, private telephone, etc.

Allowances that *may* be paid:

- *Special Responsibility Allowance* – for executive members and other councillors with significant additional responsibilities, including at least one minority party member
- *Childcare and Dependent Carers' Allowance* – new allowance payable to councillors who incur expenditure for care of dependent relatives or children while undertaking 'approved council duties'
- *Travel and Subsistence Allowance* – payable if felt not to be adequately covered in basic allowance
- *Meetings Allowance* – payable to non-elected members co-opted or appointed to certain council committees and panels (e.g. scrutiny committees, school exclusion appeals panels).

The three elements of basic allowances

1. Estimate of hours required to perform the tasks expected of a non-executive member of the council
2. Decision on the appropriate hourly/daily rate to be paid (eg median male white collar wage: £26,275 pa/£105.10 per day – often adjusted to compare with local pay rates)
3. Decision on size of Public Service Discount: in recognition of the principle of council work as voluntary service, some proportion of hours should *not* be remunerated – usually between 20% and 50%.

Average allowances – some examples, 2001/02

	Basic	Lowest	Highest	Exec member	Leader
All authorities	£4,380	£750 (Berwick-u-Tweed)	£11,957 (Birmingham)	£6,560	£12,528
London boroughs	6,532	4,200 (Kensington/Chelsea)	8,374 (Southwark)	7,475	18,995
Metropolitan districts	7,380	3,507 (Liverpool)	11,957 (Birmingham)	10,155	20,737
Shire counties	7,548	2,580 (Cornwall)	11,000 (Kent)	11,643	21,701
Shire districts	3,122	750 (Berwick-u-Tweed)	7,581 (Bolsover)	4,466	8,454
Unitaries	5,273	2,556 (Windsor/M'head)	8,000 (Brighton/Hove)	7,732	15,426

Some higher-paid leaders, 2001/02

Greater London Authority	Ken Livingstone (Mayor)	£87,000
Cardiff City C	Russell Goodway (Leader)	£58,000
Birmingham City C	Sir Albert Bore (Leader)	£55,195
Watford BC	Elected mayor, 2002	£50,000
Kent CC	Sandy Bruce-Lockhart (Leader)	£46,000
Manchester City C	Richard Leese (Leader)	£40,000

Main source: IDeA (2001)

remuneration panel. As the outcomes of these deliberations were publicised – often, most informatively, on councils' web sites – it became
evident that the ranges would be extensive, both in the basic allowances
that all councillors receive and in the special responsibility allowances
going to members of the executive. Some early examples, together with a
brief description of the new system, are shown in Exhibit 12.3.

So why do they do it?

The Government's hope, in setting up this new system of allowances, was
to address some of the existing disincentives to serving in local politics,
while recognising that 'people do not enter public service to make their
fortune' (DETR, 1998a). The latter 'recognition' hardly needed stating.
Few, if any, councillors would claim that a desire for financial reward was
their prime motivating force in becoming a councillor, and even the figures
in Exhibit 12.3 are hardly beyond the dreams of avarice. So what are
councillors' motives? What drives them to put in these large numbers of
hours for rather paltry compensation and apparently little public
recognition or gratitude?

Power, status, self-aggrandisement, ambition, compensation for personal insecurity, or even sexual inadequacy ... the drives and motives
attributed to politicians are legion, and mostly unflattering. They are
not to be ridiculed or lightly dismissed, but this is not the place in which to
speculate about councillors' essentially private motivations. Our intention
is to conclude this chapter in the way we started: with our own small
castlist of members, to see what we can conclude about *their* motivations.

Our first observation must be the apparent lack in most of their political
careers so far of any deep-rooted and single-minded wish to become
councillors. Maureen's original candidacy was a kind of natural progres-
sion from her increasingly active involvement in her local Labour Party
and her wish to further its policies and goals. Richard had had a rather
more conscious long-term plan to stand for the county council after his
retirement, but then 'events' conspired to bring the process forward. For
the other three, 'events' might almost be said to have been the key
recruiting agent: specific local issues for Keith and Joyce, and for Joan
increasingly Labour Party-related campaigns.

Far from it being carefully planned, most of our small group of members
found themselves projected almost unpreparedly into council membership.
They were not exactly 'reluctants', but neither can they be seen as very
driven 'self-starters', actively seeking and scheming for an additional
career. They were all working full-time, bringing up young children,
looking after elderly relations, or all three. As a result, the almost
insatiably time-demanding nature of council work has involved for them,

as for most councillors, potentially costly occupational choices, and at least some sacrifice of home and family life.

If they have a 'lust for power', most of our group of members manage to keep it fairly well concealed. They do seek *influence* and *involvement*: in the planning and development of their local environment, in getting a better deal for their constituents and local community, in furthering a particular cause or, more generally, the policies of their parties: activities which may bring them more direct satisfaction and sense of achievement than their day-to-day jobs. Likewise, they value being in or close to the places where decisions are taken and the quality of people's lives are determined.

They appreciate too the company of their fellow councillors, the shared interests and experience, and the gossip-laced conversations and negotiations – including those, initially unexpected, across the political divide. As Maureen recalls:

> The first meeting I went to, I didn't understand why we even sat in the same room as these Tories. But they're mostly quite helpful, and I find that most councillors are fully committed to what's good for the borough. Often you walk out of a meeting and they'll tell you privately they agree with you. These are the things nobody ever told you – that you could and do co-operate.

With executive government and the development of all-party scrutiny procedures, it was never more important for her to be right.

Guide to further reading

The significance of the change to executive government makes the recent 'practitioner' literature especially important. Many of the LGA's publications are relevant, particularly perhaps 2000a, 2000b and 2001, and the same is true of the Improvement and Development Agency (IDeA). Their *Councillor's Guide 2001* is equally useful for non-councillors, as is Taylor and Wheeler (2001), whose idea of a Hippocratic Oath for councillors is being taken up by several authorities. Less 'worthy' but perhaps a more entertaining read is *Councillors in Crisis* by Barron and her colleagues (1991). Being married to one, John Stewart has a particular insight into councillors and their 'world' (2000), and he, like we, would always optimistically recommend Winifred Holtby's wonderfully 'factional' portrayal of her mother's life as an Alderman on a rural county council in the early 1930s (1936), still probably the best English local government novel available.

Chapter 13

The Local Government Workforce

Beware (again) of generalisations – look around you

A key message in Chapter 12 was that there is no such person as a 'typical councillor', and that we should try to avoid making unthinking generalisations as if there were. There are, very roughly, one hundred times as many employees of councils as there are elected members – so it is at least as important to avoid the same trap with them. There is a potential trap, just as with councillors. Ask, say, a class of students what ideas they immediately associate with a career in local government, and their replies are likely to include things like: office work, meetings, routine, bureaucracy, nine-to-five, red tape, more meetings, job security. The reality is far more complex. This chapter will emphasise the diversity of local government employment in various ways, but we start, as we did with councillors, by suggesting that you talk to a few council workers yourself. Ask them what their day-to-day jobs entail, where they work, who with, how they actually spend their time, and so on.

As we noted in Chapter 12, the democratic scale of our so-called 'local' government system is so large that most people do not know personally their own councillors, or, in many cases, any councillors at all. Statistically this is highly unlikely to be true of employees of councils. If you know 20 employed adults, the chances are that one or more will work full-time or part-time for a council. The chances are at least equally high, though,

Figure 13.1 *Cartoon – The emotional frontline*

Source: Harry Venning (*The Guardian*).

that they will not describe themselves as council *officers*, which is one reason why this chapter is entitled as it is, rather than 'local government officers' or even 'the professionals'. When it comes to the making of policy or interacting with councillors, we shall have plenty more to add to what we have already said about the role of professional officers. For the moment, we want to look much more widely at the whole local government workforce. It covers over 500 different occupational areas and more than 3,000 job titles, which means that many employees are *not* based in offices, or even indoors, do not have their lives governed by meetings, and would not remotely conceive of themselves as bureaucrats.

Our own favourite council employee, Harry Venning's *Guardian* cartoon strip star, *Clare in the Community* (Wednesdays, the same day as all the public service job adverts), would certainly never call herself an officer, but might well hit you if you questioned her professionalism. She is a college educated, professionally trained and professionally responsible social worker, with all the compassion, care and conscience that such training imbues. She spends her days, and frequently evenings too, doing what she would describe as society's dirty work, confronting life on the 'Emotional Frontline'. She rarely, if ever, sees a councillor or goes near her council's town or county hall but works, probably from an outlying district office, as part of a five-member social work team. The team is mixed-gender and a real source of mutual support – even though managed, to the chagrin of Clare and her friend Megan, by a man. We encountered one of Clare's constant frustrations – shortage of resources – in Chapter 10, and she agonises regularly over the conflicting pressures facing those in the 'caring professions': the demands of her individual clients against those of the community, the battle between the requirements of care and control. It is perhaps hardly surprising that, as we see in Figure 13.1, she sometimes finds it difficult to 'switch off'!

Other council jobs inevitably involve completely different concerns and modes of working, as is revealed by our own small selection. Steve is a 'manager' – a Sports Marketing and Promotions Manager in the Arts and Leisure department of a large city council. His role is to ensure that the city's residents have easy access to as wide a range of sports as possible, thereby enhancing their overall physical and mental health. Steve himself does not put it quite like this, but his job is a kind of twenty-first-century extension of one of his council's earliest nineteenth-century responsibilities: public health. Much of his work entails talking with sports facility managers and others responsible for actually running sporting activities and events and then overseeing their marketing and promotion. A 'typical day', therefore, might include meeting with sports development officers to discuss 'Awards for All' promotions; checking that a Special Events Guide contains full details of disabled sports activities and minority ethnic community festival events; meeting with potential event sponsors and charity fundraisers; and providing some 'anti-racist' material for a local football club's annual report.

Ron too has a job title with distinct hints of the private sector about it. He is the sales and marketing manager of Shelforce, a company with a multi-million pound turnover that is also part of his council's Social Services Department. The company was started in 1838 as a workshop for the blind, and today is a successful business employing 81 workers, over two-thirds of them with a severe disability. Shelforce makes PVCu windows and doors, most of which it sells to the council's housing department, and beds, which are made from scratch on the premises and sold both to the hotel trade and the general public. Ron is keen to dispel the common image that 'people who are disabled aren't capable of producing a quality product. We are proud of the fact that everything we make conforms to the relevant British Standard and that we were an outright winner in 1998 in the Glassex Industry Awards.'

Marcia is a Housing Support Officer with specific responsibility for settling asylum seekers – most recently from Iraq, Albania, Iran and Somalia – into temporary accommodation while they wait for a decision on whether they can stay in the country permanently. She gets angry at the media's portrayal of her clients, pointing out not just the council's legal obligation to provide basic accommodation, but also the 'catalogue of torture' that may have driven them to leave their homes for an alien country. 'One man was forced to drink battery acid, made to eat broken glass – how can we begrudge these people a home here?' Part of her job is 'planned' – 'sorting out English classes or whatever' – and part 'unplanned', 'when I have to deal with problems as they crop up – trying to locate an interpreter or someone to fix a front door!'

Andrew is neither a manager nor an officer, but a ranger: an Urban Park Ranger. His responsibilities cover the 60 or more parks and open spaces in the south of his council's area, and his own base is an office in one of those parks. He is part of a team whose function is to develop the council's parks and open spaces to their full potential, make them safer, and to encourage families in particular to make more use of them. Most days are split between office duties and work outdoors. The former might involve answering a written complaint about the state of public toilets, designing leaflets and posters, taking bookings, and arranging for dog bins to be installed. The latter, on the day we met Andrew, had included a meeting with the gardeners in one of his larger parks, attending a consultative meeting with park users, and running a tennis session for 8- to 14-year olds.

If space permitted, we could continue indefinitely – with accounts of a job share pensions and payments assistant, a Sheltered Housing Scheme residential warden, a part-time school caretaker, a library website editor, a crèche worker, an engineering services inspector (gas), a social work assistant (Cantonese/Hakka speaking), and dozens more besides. We have now, though, to turn from the trees to the wood, and try to impose some structure on all this diversity. In the remainder of this chapter, therefore, we first identify some facts and features of local government employment; we then turn to the roles of senior managers and the importance of professional bodies. Finally we examine the advent and implications of more flexible employment structures.

Local authority employment – some quick facts and figures

Local authorities are, by any standards, major employers. They are highly labour-intensive; up to half their total expenditure goes on staff costs. The chances are that your local council is, or is close to being, the largest single employer in your area: you might try to find out. Birmingham City Council, albeit the largest in the country, employs nearly 50,000 staff or nearly 30,000 'full-time equivalents' (FTEs); Glasgow about 25,000 FTEs. The contemporary UK workforce numbers over 27 million, of whom almost 2½ million work in local government. In other words, nearly 10 per cent of all full-time and part-time jobs in the UK are provided by local authorities, with a total paybill of some £35 billion. Their division into major service areas for England and Wales in 1998/99 – when the now discontinued Joint Staffing Watch Survey last collected statistics in this form – can be seen in Exhibit 13.1. By June 2000 the total employment figure had increased to 2,167,000, to which should be added nearly 300,000 full-time and part-time staff working in Scottish local authorities.

Exhibit 13.1 Local government employment, England and Wales, 1996

Service area	Full-time ('000)	Part-time ('000)	TOTAL ('000)	% of total local government employment	% part-time	% female	% part-time female	Change since 1990
Education – teachers	356	136	492	24	28	72	22	– –
– other employees	131	507	638	30	79	88	73	– –
Social Services	156	186	342	16	54	84	50	+
Corporate functions – central admin., personnel, finance, etc.	113	31	144	7	21	59	19	n/a
Recreation, parks, baths	45	42	87	4	48	49	33	– –
Housing	61	15	76	4	19	61	17	– –
Construction	57	1	58	3	2	6	2	– –
Engineering	47	6	53	3	11	29	9	n/a
Libraries, museums	20	24	44	2	55	77	48	– –
Fire services	40	2	44	2	5	13	4	–
Planning	27	4	31	2	13	45	12	+ +
Refuse collection and disposal	25	2	27	1	8	11	6	–
Environmental health	17	2	19	1	12	41	9	–
Other services	16	23	39	2	59	60	47	n/a
TOTAL	1,113	981	2,904		47	71	42	–18%

Notes: In final column, n/a indicates not available in directly comparable form; + indicates an increase in employment since 1990; – – indicates a greater than average decrease in employment, etc.

Sources: Local Government Employment Digest (monthly).

Changing numbers

The major growth in local authority employment took place in the 1960s and the early part of the 1970s. From 1979 until the late 1980s, despite the efforts of the Conservative Government to reduce the size of the public sector, numbers remained fairly static at around 3 million – the steady reduction of manual workers during this period being largely cancelled out by the increase in non-manuals. The biggest losses during the 1980s were brought about by the abolition of the GLC and the metropolitan county councils in 1986, the change in status of bus and municipal airport staff in 1986/87, and transfer of polytechnics and higher-education institutions out of LEA control in 1989.

But at least twice the total numbers involved in these 1980s changes were lost in 1993 alone, when local government lost control of further education institutions. There was another significant drop in 1995/96, with the advent of free-standing police authorities. In total, as shown in the final column of Exhibit 13.1, local government employment in England and Wales fell during the 1990s by nearly a fifth, although this trend varied significantly from service to service – social services and planning, for example, increasing their numbers. The signs towards the end of the 1997–2001 Labour Government were that the downward trend as a whole had been arrested.

Changing composition

The composition of local government employment has changed massively in recent decades and, as can be seen in Exhibit 13.1, it is dominated nowadays, numerically at least, by part-time women. Full-time male employees, who had constituted over half of the local government workforce in 1954, were by 2000 down to 23 per cent and easily outnumbered by full-time and particularly part-time women workers (29 and 42 per cent respectively).

Over half (54 per cent) of all employee jobs are in education – a figure that, of course, includes administrators, special advisers, cleaning staff and school meal providers, as well as teachers. Social services account for around 16 per cent of employment. Again, social workers make up only part of that number; various assistants, administrators, residential carers and home helps complete the total, which, like education, is overwhelmingly female and substantially part-time. All other employment headings in Exhibit 13.1 cover rather smaller numbers of staff, including those services that tend to be most closely associated with local government in the public mind: housing, refuse collection and public libraries.

It follows from the above figures that the biggest workforces are to be found in those councils responsible for education and social services. The 34 counties thus employ nearly a third of all local government employees

(700,000), averaging around 20,000 each. They are followed by the 32 metropolitan districts with 24 per cent or around 15,000 each, and the unitaries and London boroughs that average about 7,000. Most shire districts, by comparison, employ well under 1,000.

The gender-based hierarchy – more mirror maze than glass ceiling

At the top of the local authority employment ladder is an echelon of senior managers and salaried professionals. The Chief Executive, the most senior of all managers, could receive a salary of £150,000 (e.g. Max Caller at Hackney LBC in 2000, where he was designated 'Managing Director') depending on, among other things, the size of authority and degree of difficulty associated with the job. Chief officers, senior managers and senior professionals are also well rewarded for their services. They have, though, the demanding responsibility for running the local authority or their particular department, advising councillors and cabinets, and managing budgets. With the ever-increasing amount of local partnership working, they also liaise closely with a range of other agencies, both private and public.

Senior management in local government is as narrowly a white male world as in most other sectors of UK society. While women make up 72 per cent of the total local government workforce, this numerical dominance is in no way reflected at top management levels. The numbers of women chief executives, chief and senior officers are slowly increasing – to about 12, 16 and 25 per cent respectively in 2001 – but well under 2 per cent were black, Asian or other ethnic minority (*Local Government Employment Digest*, November 2001). Blatant discrimination may be comparatively rare, but prejudice is widespread and difficult to counter. Carole Hassan, then Watford BC chief executive, argued that local authorities, for all their publicised claims to be equal opportunities employers, are guilty of complacency: 'They think we have got there but we haven't.' She called on organisations like the Local Government Association and the Society of Local Authority Chief Executives (SO-LACE) to take action on both race and gender: the few senior women in local government are busy mentoring and supporting the others and that puts huge pressure on them. It's less of a glass ceiling than a mirror maze, with new difficulties appearing at every level' (*Local Government Chronicle*, 12 November 1999).

The work of chief officers is shared with middle-ranking managers and professionals who combine an expert knowledge of a particular service or support function (e.g. finance, law, personnel, IT) with experience and involvement in overseeing the resources and employees of the authority. The number and range of both top and middle management posts are considerable, as can be seen from the very brief selection in Exhibit 13.2. The final element in this group of senior managers and salaried professionals are those with professional training operating at the service frontline, such as teachers, field social workers, environmental health officers, and development control planners.

Beneath the top managers and salaried professionals are the 'worker bees': a vast network of employees in a variety of lower-status clerical, manual and non-manual jobs. Local authorities employ nearly 750,000 administrative, technical and clerical (ATC) 'white-collar' staff – including typists, clerical assistants, clerks in schools, technicians, nursery nurses and welfare assistants. They also employ about a million full-time or part-time manual workers. These are the people who clean streets and schools, the caretakers, council gardeners, home helps and road maintenance operatives. In addition, there is a substantial number of miscellaneous workers whose jobs are neither wholly clerical or manual: cashiers in canteens, ticket sellers, pest controllers, and so on. All of these posts, as can be seen in Exhibit 13.3, are distinctly more modestly remunerated.

To summarise this section, it is clear that councils remain, by any standards, large-scale employers of extremely heterogeneous workforces. They are thus of great economic importance within their communities and in a position to serve as an example to other employers. Local authorities have at the top a range of well-paid senior managers and professionals, and beneath them a vast army of lower-status administrative, clerical, manual and non-manual employees. These people are essential to the process of service provision, yet the financial rewards they obtain are often relatively unattractive. Compare, for example, Exhibits 13.2 and 13.3 and the more than tenfold pay differentials between jobs being advertised simultaneously. Employment 'packages' incorporating negotiable benefits such as cars and private health insurance are worlds apart from the experience of manual and clerical workers.

The world of senior management

We now turn from those who actually provide the services of a local authority to those whose job is to manage them and it: the senior officers at the top of the organisation. Nowadays, certainly those at the very top are likely to be appointed at least as much for their managerial skills and experience as for their professional qualifications and expertise – as can be deduced from our very small, though colourful, selection of chief executives in Exhibit 13.4. Indeed, as departments become less tied to single services, the chief officer will be expected to play a corporate as well as a departmental role and may well not even come from the department's dominant profession (Stewart, 2000, p. 202).

Exhibit 13.2 Some officer posts and what they pay

	Advertised post (November 2001)	Approx. salary
Lancashire CC	**Chief Executive** To provide leadership and deliver successful change in organisation with £1 billion turnover, win support from our key stakeholders and communities, and speak up for Lancashire and its people.	£150,000
Newcastle City C	**Chief Executive** To work with Elected Members to lead City's response to the modernisation agenda and realise its potential as a European Regional Capital.	Package up to £140,000
Ealing LBC	**Executive Director, Diversity and Talent** New role, responsible for mainstreaming and enhancing the profile of equality and diversity across both employment and service provision in the Borough.	Package to £95,000
Blackburn w. Darwen BC	**Director of Regeneration, Housing and Neighbourhoods** To head new multi-disciplinary department and work closely with the regional government office, RDA and local strategic partnerships in delivery of innovative regeneration, housing and neighbourhood engagement policies.	Package to £80,907
Barking and Dagenham LBC	**Head of Landlord Services** To lead Council's devolution of its housing service to neighbourhoods, with 6 Community Housing Partnerships accountable for their own areas.	c. £70,000
Staffordshire CC	**Head of Cultural Services** To integrate the Council's arts, museums, library and countryside estate and benefits services and bring regional and national recognition to Staffordshire's unique culture.	To £63,500
Birmingham City C	**Head of Cabinet Office** To shape and operate the Council's new arrangements for political executive management and support the Leader in planning Cabinet business for the City.	To £51,294
Hackney LBC	**Head of Revenues** 'Fantastic career opportunity' to improve Council Tax and Business Rates collection performance in council at very bottom of relevant national league tables.	£45,816 +
Harrow LBC	**Best Value Manager** To lead radical revision of Council's programme of cross-cutting and theme-based BV reviews, following acknowledgement of early reviews as 'too functional and inward-looking'.	£36,000
Middlesbrough C	**Senior Scrutiny Support Officer** To develop and support the Overview and Scrutiny Board and scrutiny panels of councillors in one of the first authorities to have an elected executive mayor to hold to account.	£24,750 +

Exhibit 13.3 Some less well paid local government posts

Advertised post (November 2001)	Pay
Domestic Assistant, Social Services To ensure a high standard of cleanliness and hygiene throughout a residential home for the elderly and assist with the serving of meals and drinks to the residents.	£4.60 per hr
Cleaning Operative Cleaning in neighbourhood offices, libraries, and other council buildings.	£4.81 per hr
School Crossing Standby Warden Caring, reliable person to ensure the busy roads of Birmingham are safe for our children. Full uniform supplied plus first-class training.	£4.98 per hr + retainer fee
Assistant Cook, Gujarati Food To cook and prepare a full range of Asian food and assist the head cook in running the kitchen in a community day centre.	£5.14 per hr
Part-time Youth Worker, Young People's Health Project To work with young people, developing and delivering health projects that address the issues associated with teenage pregnancy.	£5.72–£6.46 per hr
Part-time Crèche Co-ordinator To co-ordinate crèche facilities for pre-school children at a council community centre and develop a 'Shoppers' Crèche'.	£11,838 pro rata
Security Officer, Housing Services To operate CCTV and electronic closed door systems, allowing *bona fide* visitors access to the council's high-rise buildings, and provide customers with a friendly, helpful and reactive service.	£11,838–£12,411
Play and/or Music Instructor To work with children who have an autistic spectrum disorder and emotional/behavioural difficulties.	£12,012+ pa
Debt Recovery Assistant, Community Care Finance To ensure that all necessary action is taken to secure early settlement of outstanding debts on charges raised by the Social Services Department.	£12,192–£14,823 pa
Development Officer (Asian Women's Textile Groups) A Museums Service post for an artistic Punjabi-speaker to run textile and other craft groups for Asian women with mental health problems.	£12,937–£14,190 pa
Technician – Bridges To assist in delivery of a large workload relating to bridge assessment, strengthening, construction, bridge inspections and maintenance.	£15,210+ pa

Exhibit 13.4 Twenty-first-century chief executives – four pen portraits

Faith Boardman (Lambeth LBC) – the civil service oddity

Brought up in Enfield – father shopkeeper, mother Methodist lay preacher. Educ: grammar school, Oxford University history degree.

Pre-Lambeth career – civil service, including HM Customs and Excise, and Chief Executive, Child Support Agency.

'I am an oddity, in that regrettably few people have stepped over the boundaries between central and local government. It's been very interesting looking at central government from a local government perspective and seeing just how un-joined up Whitehall is. On my first day in Lambeth I asked whether we had a business plan and any targets we were responsible for. They asked me which set I'd like, because they had 47 plans – all but four required by different government departments – and 470 targets, again required by central government.'

John Foster (Middlesbrough) – Barnardo's boy who returned home

Born in Middlesbrough and brought up in Barnardo's homes after parents separated. Educ: grammar school, sociology degree.

Pre-Middlesbrough career: community worker and International Socialist activist (until expelled); community development officer, Durham; secondment to Home Office anti-poverty programme; social services research department, then Director, N. Tyneside BC; Managing Director, then Chief Executive, Middlesbrough.

'I remain passionate about local government and local democracy, but we have to take scepticism on the chin. Why should we expect people always to want to participate? What's important is that every citizen has a right to know. Then they can make up their own minds afterwards.'

Carole Gilbey (North East Derbyshire DC) – from council house to council chief

Brought up in one-parent family on Sheffield council estate; Educ: girls' grammar school.

Pre-NE Derbyshire career – temp in solicitors' office; London University external law degree and solicitor's qualification; solicitor, Bassetlaw DC (Notts).

'I came from a very poor background and the only people paying the money we could live on were local authorities. I have to say that that's why I moved into local government. The councillors wanted someone who was down to earth and could empathise with a working class community, and that's what they got ... they didn't want a brilliant academic.'

Ian Stewart (Bradford MBC) – 'If you can manage a football club ...'

Pre-Bradford career – Scottish professional footballer, then 'motivational' manager of Montrose FC; civil service, including Department of Social Security – introduced incapacity benefit and developed Job Seekers Allowance; Director, Benefits Agency; Director General, Social Security Benefit Fraud Inspectorate.

'I saw the changes that had taken place in cities like Glasgow and Barcelona and wanted to be part of trying to turn a city around. Bradford's bid to be the European Capital of Culture in 2008 is the key to its rebranding. We have a range of cultures and cultural attractions here that other cities will find difficult to match'.

Key sources: Municipal Journal, 26 October 2001 (Boardman), 10–16 November 2000 (Foster), 2–8 June 2000 (Gilbey), 12 October, 2001 (Stewart).

There are today, then, at least four distinctive dimensions of the senior management role that bear examination (Box 13.1).

Box 13.1 The senior management role

- Exercising professional influence;
- supporting, advising and monitoring politicians;
- representing the authority's interests externally;
- managing staff and resources within the authority.

Exercising professional influence

Senior local government officers may now spend most of their time as managers, but still the majority are trained and qualified professionals: solicitors, treasurers, architects, planners, engineers, housing managers, education administrators, social workers and so on. Professionalism in this sense remains one of the hallmarks of British local government and one of its most powerful forces. We list in Exhibit 13.5 a small sample of the dozens of professional bodies involved in local government – some, like SOLACE, SOCPO and ACSeS, almost exclusively; others, like CIPFA and IPR, only partly. These bodies are, of course, key members of their respective policy networks and communities (see Chapter 9), but they have other roles too. They are, as Rhodes points out (1988, pp. 214–15), 'organised as "learned societies", in which capacity they recruit and train personnel, organise conferences and seminars, produce research and publications and, as with any other organised group, proselytise and lobby for their interests'. They are also 'trade unions and ... can use working to rule and strikes as a means of influencing the government. In effect, therefore, the professions can have three bites at the cherry of political influence.'

The influence of senior officers as professionals can thus be considerable, especially within those policy areas where complex technical knowledge is at a premium and of consequential value to central government. As ever, it is important not to generalise: some technical professional communities have historically been distinctly more influential than others. Both Dunleavy (1980) and Laffin (1986), for example, contrast the massive influence of local authority highways engineers and surveyors in the development of the motorway programme with the comparatively minor contribution of the housing management professions to the post-war housing boom. The latter was led much more by private sector construction interests and a combination of national politicians and civil servants. Where such professional influence does occur, though, it is more likely to

Exhibit 13.5 Some leading professional bodies – acronym clubs

1. **SOLACE – Society of Local Authority Chief Executives**
   Membership: 900 predominantly district council chief executives, plus other senior local government managers, reflecting the wish to appear democratic and increase income. But some big county, metro and unitary chief executives stick to their more exclusive Chief Executive Associations.
   Provides, for annual sub of £250+ (depending on your seniority and the size of your authority) a quarterly journal, other publications and policy papers, conference, training and professional development recruitment service.

2. **SOCPO – Society of Chief Personnel Officers**
   Membership: 400+, also recently extended to senior, as well as chief, officers.
   Provides, for the cheapest sub. of £70, practical advice and guidance, publications, conference, plus several specialist working groups.

3. **CIPFA – Chartered Institute of Public Finance and Accountancy** (pron. 'SIPFA')
   Membership: 13,400, nearly half in local government, plus 2,000 students. Open to all passing the Institute's education and training scheme.
   Provides, for £200+ sub., best staffed and slickest service among local government professional bodies: all usual perks, plus a wide range of specialist advisory services and excellent statistical information service.

4. **ACSeS – Association of Council Secretaries and Solicitors**
   Membership: 500. You do not actually have to be a CS or S, but just in charge of legal or administration work.
   Provides, for £110 sub., 'best practice' notes and guidance, close links with local ombudsman service, plus password-protected web pages, conference and cute acronym.

5. **IPR – Institute of Public Relations**
   Membership: 5000 +, but only 250 or so in local government, reflecting the profession's continuing struggle for recognition in many traditionally minded councils.
   Provides, for £175 sub., free legal and accountancy service, publications, workshops, seminars, induction training, plus discount on office equipment and the like.

Main source: Wynn Davies (1996), pp. 12–13.

constitute a force for centralisation than for localism, as Rhodes explains (1988, p. 225):

> The consequence of professional influence is the promotion of homogeneous standards, not local diversity. Their locus in policy networks places them *in*, if by origin they were not *of*, the centre. The outcome is centralization by aggregation of interests and nationalization of standards; the source is the professionals employed by sub-central organizations (emphases ours).

Working with politicians

The relationship between senior officers and councillors is explored in Chapter 15. Senior officers are likely to be involved in the process of developing strategies and policies for the authority. Much of their time is taken up meeting with councillors, writing reports for cabinet members and committees, and liaising with officer colleagues in other departments to provide policy advice and guidance. Many councils also give officers considerable *delegated powers* in, for example, the granting of certain categories of licence or planning permissions.

A more recent development has been for senior officers to exercise also a *monitoring role* in relation to the performance of the council and councillors. Part of the Conservative Government's legislative reaction to the 1986 Widdicombe Committee Report was to require local authorities to appoint a monitoring officer – most frequently the chief legal officer or council solicitor – responsible for reporting direct to the council on issues of legality, financial probity and alleged maladministration. The Local Government Act 2000 has significantly extended these responsibilities, and a monitoring officer is now charged with promoting and maintaining high standards of conduct within the local authority and for ensuring that executive decisions, together with all relevant background documentation, are made publicly available.

Senior officers stand at the heart of the decision-making processes of local authorities. Their delegated and monitoring responsibilities give them some powers, but above all it is their ability to influence the choices, thinking and approach of councillors that gives them real decision-making influence. Their proximity to the formal holders of decision-making authority – senior councillors – gives them an opportunity for influence not afforded to such a degree to employees in the lower ranks of the organisation.

External relations

As indicated even in some of the skeletal job descriptions in Exhibit 13.2, managing relations with the world outside the council has become an increasingly important part of the daily workload of senior officers in an era of local partnerships and supposedly 'joined-up' government. Links with central government regional offices, local authority colleagues in other areas, conferences and debates within professional associations all contribute to a powerful network of influence for the modern senior officer. They constitute important sources of information and ideas and provide a national forum in which senior officers can present themselves as policy entrepreneurs and learn from the knowledge and experience of others. More generally, they enable officers to make sense of the local government world and to put the work of their own department, profession and council in a broader context.

As described in Chapter 8, partnerships have become an integral part of the world of local governance. Senior officials in social service departments are thus in regular touch with voluntary groups and agencies. Land-use planners will have to represent the authority in public meetings and debates. Housing officers will attend numerous meetings with tenants' associations and community organisations. In contrast to the position 30 years ago, these senior officers have come to expect a relatively 'rough ride'. In today's consumer culture, people are less willing to accept professional explanations of what is best and far more prepared to question the policies and actions of the local authority. The need to consult with the public on a wide range of issues – a key strand of Labour's modernisation agenda – also means greater interaction than ever before with the local population.

Internal management

As we have seen, the role of senior staff within local authorities is nowadays a managerial, as well as a professional, one. Effective chief officers and senior managers in local authorities exercise a range of skills – in strategic management, decision-making, political awareness and sensitivity, leadership, business and commercial practice, negotiation – that go far beyond anything required in their professional qualifications.

The new political leadership structures established by the Local Government Act 2000 are bound, in many if not all authorities, to affect the role of senior officers – more than ministers seemed initially prepared to acknowledge. Executive members will be more involved in day-to-day decision-making and management, and officers correspondingly less so. The tensions inherent in senior officers' responsibilities to serve both the council as a whole and the current political leadership will increase. Inevitably, however, there will continue to be considerable differences in the operational styles and practices of what are, statutorily, identical authorities. It would be both naive and premature, therefore, to start discounting the influence of senior local government officers in policy-making, whatever the formal position might be. Their knowledge and expertise mean that, along with senior councillors, they are likely to remain of central importance.

From model employers to flexible employment structures

For much of the post-war period local authorities had an image as 'model' or 'good practice' employers, setting an example for other employers to follow. They were willing to recognise trade unions – 60 per cent of local government employees being union members, compared with less than half that figure for the whole economy (*Labour Force Survey*, Spring 2000). They were felt to have proper negotiating procedures, to encourage equal opportunities, pay fair wages and provide stable employment.

The period from 1979, however, ushered in changes. Local government was subjected to commercialism and competition – most notably in the form of compulsory competitive tendering (CCT). With these came private sector management ideas and personnel practices such as performance-related pay, staff appraisal procedures and decentralised negotiating and consultative arrangements. Authorities found it difficult to maintain national pay and conditions in services subject to competitive tender and there was a movement away from formal systems for the management of industrial relations towards more *ad hoc* approaches reflecting the organisational interests of management (Leach *et al.*, 1994, p. 199).

The realities of CCT meant that it became increasingly difficult for local authorities to maintain the 'model' employer tradition. If the choice were presented as one of aspiring to best employment practice, but at the possible loss of a vital contract and the associated jobs, councillors would understandably fight for the contract. In response to such dilemmas and the changing environment, many local authorities have sought to introduce greater flexibility into their employment policies. Increasing numbers of chief executives and senior officers, for example, are recruited on fixed-term contracts – considerably more than in the economy as a whole. And, as suggested in several of the salary 'packages' in Exhibit 13.2, many senior managers in local authorities now enjoy fringe benefits such as private medical care, life insurance, 'company' leased cars and pension options.

The search for flexibility involves other practices, too (Box 13.2).

Conclusion – it's not all negative

This chapter has provided an overview of the local authority workforce: an enormous variety of people involved in the process of delivering services and developing strategic local policies. Many of the human resource and

Box 13.2 Flexibility in practice

1. *More flexible establishment control* – in which an authority's personnel committee exercises detailed control over senior appointments, but below that chief officers can employ and deploy staff as required, within limits on numbers and grades set by the authority.

2. *More flexible contracts and job descriptions* – which can make it easier to transfer staff from unit to unit and adopt new working practices. Such an approach may be particularly useful for the clerical and administrative work that exists in all departments. There is also increased interest in flexible job descriptions which emphasise what the job should achieve rather than how the work is done.

3. *Performance-related pay (PRP)* – one of the more widely copied private sector practices. Used to get the personal commitment of top managers, though nothing like as extensively employed in local government as in private industry or, particularly, central government. 'PRP provides for periodic increases in pay which are incorporated into salaries resulting from assessments of individual performance and personal value to the organisation' (Farnham, 1999, p. 116). Traditionally most enthusiastically espoused in Conservative-controlled authorities, PRP is now found across the full spectrum of councils, the emphasis being on merit bonuses or awards for exceptional performance.

4. *Flexible working hours and conditions* – which can be beneficial to both the employees and the clients and service users of a local authority. Nearly a fifth of local government employees worked flexitime in 2000, compared to under 10 per cent in the economy as a whole (*Labour Force Survey*, Spring 2000). Job-sharing too is more than twice as widespread, including, for a short period, the post of Tower Hamlets LBC Chief Executive by Eleanor Kelly and Christine Gilbert. Authorities are currently experimenting with home-based working for certain categories of staff.

industrial relations issues faced in local government are similar to those found in large-scale private sector organisations. In general, the traditional bureaucratic approaches to personnel management have been replaced by managers with devolved budgets and responsibility for their own staff. The position of local authority managers, however, is complicated by their base within the public sector. Pay settlements can be controlled by national governments, as they were during the 1990s, with the effect that overall pay levels fall relatively in comparison with private industry. Policies of change and 'modernisation' are imposed from above, and issues such as redundancies, competitive tendering, and best value all become the subject of political argument and debate. The management task is further 'complexified' – intended as a less pejorative term than 'complicated' – by the involvement of councillors in the management and oversight of the authority.

It would be miraculous if local government staff were not on occasions to feel dumped on and demoralised. Yet survey evidence suggests either that such feelings are no more prevalent than in other sectors of the economy, or, if they are, there are compensations in working for public service-providing organisations. The 2001 public sector employment survey by the Chartered Institute of Personnel and Development (*Local Government Employment Digest*, November 2001) found that of the local government employees in their sample:

- 69 per cent reported that their authority had experienced some sort of major change (e.g. in working practices, the management of the authority) during the past year, compared to 47 per cent in private industry; and about half thought these changes had been badly handled;
- 84 per cent felt they were working either very hard or as hard as they could, compared to 67 per cent in industry;
- 63 per cent felt fairly rewarded for the work they do, compared to 58 per cent in the workforce as a whole; and
- 63 per cent looked forward to going to work either all or most of the time, compared to 58 per cent in private industry and just 45 per cent in central government.

These figures at least dent the unremittingly negative image sometimes painted of local government employment, while obviously confirming that there are substantial minorities who do not feel they are fairly rewarded, who do not leap joyously out of bed each working day, and so on. They also suggest clearly that there is plenty of scope within an authority, or even a section of an authority, for managers and councillors between them to provide their employees with a relatively more positive, or negative, motivation – which is something to contemplate next time you encounter one of them.

Guide to further reading

Once again, you can start by finding out some of the basic statistics about your own local authority's staffing structure and recent employment trends, which should be set out in its *Annual Report*. There is not an abundance of recent non-practitioner literature to recommend, but Farnham (1999) provides a good overview of human resource management (HRM) and employment relations across the whole public sector, while Doogan (1999) analyses the impact of contracting-out on jobs, conditions of service and labour markets. Leach *et al.* (1994) present a useful summary of modern management approaches. Pratchett (2000) provides an interesting discussion of the public sector ethos in local government.

Chapter 14

Political Parties

Introduction

Like it or not – and we conclude this chapter by examining both sides of
the case – party politics is a central feature of contemporary local
government across most of the United Kingdom. In the first part of the
chapter, therefore, we look at the current political landscape of local
government and briefly at how that landscape has come to look as it does.
We then compare the organisation and impact of the principal political
parties, inside and outside the council. We examine too the role of the
national parties and their respective policies in relation to local
government.

The survival of non-partisanship

It is important to get the balance right when dealing with party politics in
local government. Understate its significance, and you risk completely
misunderstanding how and where many of the most important council
decisions are actually made. Overstate it, and you fall into the trap of
assuming that all councils are run on tightly disciplined party lines and that
all decisions are party-based. The truth is that, as with almost everything
else to do with local government, the variety of practice is almost infinite.
Nothing is universally true of all 440 or so authorities in the country, as
can be seen in outline in Exhibit 14.1.

Exhibit 14.1 summarises the range of party, and non-party, systems in
Great Britain in 2001/02. In the metropolitan areas of the country, in most
of the English counties and unitaries, and in the larger shire districts there
are *fully developed party systems*. Nowadays over five-sixths of all
councils come into this category – those in the bottom four main rows
of Exhibit 14.1 – and, because they include nearly all county and unitary
councils, they touch the lives of almost all British voters. All or a great
majority of the councillors on these authorities are elected under the labels
of national or nationalist political parties and, having been elected, they
organise themselves into separate party groups. Independents and representatives of local or fringe parties find it hard to get elected to these
councils and are in many places non-existent (see also Exhibit 14.2).

Exhibit 14.1 Party systems in local government, Great Britain, 2001

PARTY SYSTEM AND DEFINITION		ENGLAND					WALES	SCOTLAND	GREAT BRITAIN	
		Unitaries	Counties	Non-Met Districts	Met Districts	London Boroughs	Unitaries	Unitaries	Total	%
COMPLETELY/PREDOMINANTLY NON-PARTISAN (60% or more seats held by Independents)		–	–	7	–	1	3	4	15	3
WEAK PARTISAN (20–59% of seats held by Independents)		5	1	41	–	–	8	3	58	13
MULTI-PARTY/FRAGMENTED (20% or more seats held by third party/parties)		7	8	34	3	3	–	6	61	14
TWO-PARTY (80% of seats held by two parties, neither more than 55%)		18	16	64	12	10	4	10	134	30
ONE-PARTY DOMINANT (60–75% of seats held by one party)	Cons	2	6	38	–	2	–	–	48	
	Lab	8	2	23	6	8	4	3	54	
	LD	–	–	13	1	1	–	–	15	
	(SNP)							1	1	
									118	27
ONE-PARTY MONOPOLISTIC (75% or more seats held by one party)	Cons	2	–	4	1	1	–	–	8	
	Lab	4	1	13	13	6	3	5	45	
	LD	–	–	1	–	1	–	–	2	
	(SNP)								–	
									55	12
TOTAL		46	34	238	36	33	22	32	441	100

Source: *Municipal Yearbook*, 2002.

Exhibit 14.2 Party affiliations of councillors, Great Britain, 2001/02

| PARTY AFFILIATION | ENGLAND | | | | | | | | | | WALES | | SCOTLAND | | GREAT BRITAIN | | | |
| | Unitaries | | Counties | | Non-Met Districts | | Met Districts | | London Boroughs | | Unitaries | | Unitaries | | 2001/02 | | 1979 | |
	No.	%	No.	%	No.	%	No.	%	No.	%	No.	%	No.	%	No.	%	No.	%
Conservative	734	30	1,016	46	4,052	38	413	17	542	28	76	6	108	9	6,941	31	12,143	53
Labour	1,076	44	709	32	3,057	28	1,502	61	1,045	55	556	44	542	44	8,487	38	7,351	32
Liberal Democrat	524	21	409	18	2,394	22	502	20	301	16	97	8	155	13	4,382	20	1,032	4
Nationalist Parties	–	–	–	–	–	–	–	–	–	–	208	16	210	17	418	1	278	1
Independents and Others	122	5	81	4	1,259	12	61	2	29	2	332	26	207	17	2,091	9	2,232	10
TOTAL	2,456		2,215		10,762		2,478		1,917		1,269		1,222		22,319		23,036	

Notes:
'Others' include Liberals, Social Democrats, Greens, Ratepayers' and Residents' Association members, other small local parties – the Morecambe Bay Independents (Lancaster), the Wiltshire Independents; also vacant seats.
In Northern Ireland party affiliations of the 582 district councillors following the 2001 elections were: Ulster Unionist Party 154; Democratic Unionist Party 131; Social Democratic and Labour Party 117; Sinn Fein 108; Alliance 28; Independents and others 44.
Figures for the London Boroughs exclude the 157 members of the Common Council of the City Corporation of London which claims to have no party politics.

Source: Rallings and Thrasher (2001a).

In the more rural areas of England and in Wales and Scotland the picture can be very different. Here there are many English district and Scottish and Welsh unitary councils with *weak party systems* (13 per cent as defined in Exhibit 14.1) and others that are actually or effectively *non-partisan*, almost all councillors having stood as Independents of some description.

Perhaps the best examples of near-complete non-partisanship are the three Scottish Island authorities: Orkney, Shetland and the Western Isles. But predominantly non-partisan councils are to be found in many parts of the country that are by no means parts of any Celtic fringe: Cambridgeshire, Cumbria, Devon, Dorset, Durham, Gloucestershire, Humberside, Lincolnshire, Oxfordshire, Shropshire, Somerset, Staffordshire, Surrey.

Varieties of party systems

The extent of nominal partisanship is the first clue to understanding how a council is likely to operate. At least as important, however, is its *party mix*. In Exhibit 14.1 we identify four varieties of developed party systems, shown in Box 14.1.

Box 14.1 Developed party systems

1. *Multi-party or fragmented* – relatively few Independents, but council seats divided among several party groups. Most of these councils will be 'hung' or 'balanced', in the arithmetical sense of there being no one party with an overall majority. Their actual forms of administration can vary greatly – from single-party minority rule, through different types of informal co-operation, to the rare two- or even three-party formal coalition. In countries with proportional representation systems of election multi-party hung councils are the norm, as can be seen in the footnote on Northern Ireland in Exhibit 14.3. Our first-past-the-post (FPTP) system reduces their number, but they still make up nearly a third of the total, reflecting the fact that it is far easier for third and minority party candidates to win election in the smaller wards and divisions of local councils than in our much larger parliamentary constituencies.

2. *Two-party* – relatively few third party and Independent members, council seats being split fairly evenly between the two leading parties. Depending on the actual party balance, some of these councils too will be hung. In others control will swing regularly from one party to the other.

3. *One-party dominant* – one party holds a decisive majority of seats, and will expect to run the council most of the time.

4. *One-party monopolistic* – self-explanatory; the extreme product of our electoral system, one party having unbroken, and often effectively unchallenged, control of the council.

Exhibit 14.3 Pattern of control of local authorities, Great Britain, 2001

PARTY AFFILIATION	ENGLAND										WALES		SCOTLAND		GREAT BRITAIN			
	Unitaries		Counties		Non-Met Districts		Met Districts		London Boroughs		Unitaries		Unitaries		2001		1979	
	No.	%	No.	%	No.	%	No.	%	No.	%	No.	%	No.	%	No.	%	No.	%
Conservative	5	11	16	47	75	32	2	6	4	12	–	–	–	–	102	23	256	49
Labour	22	48	7	21	52	22	26	72	19	58	8	36	14	44	148	34	113	22
Liberal Democrat	2	4	–	–	17	7	3	8	3	9	–	–	–	–	25	6	2	*
Nationalist Parties	–	–	–	–	–	–	–	–	–	–	3	14	2	6	5	1	4	1
Independent	–	–	–	–	10	4	–	–	1	3	3	14	5	16	19	4	68	13
No overall control	17	37	11	32	84	35	5	14	6	18	8	36	11	34	142	32	75	14
TOTAL	46		34		238		36		33		22		32		441		518	

Notes:

* = less than 1%.

'No overall control' is a purely arithmetic definition of councils on which no single party has more than 50 per cent of all seats. It may therefore include councils on which a single party holds exactly half the seats and, through the casting vote of the mayor or chair of the Council, may be in a position of effective overall control.

In Northern Ireland, where local elections are by the proportional Single Transferable Vote (STV) system, all 26 councils are under no overall control, as defined above.

Source: Rallings and Thrasher (2001a).

Labour's waning local dominance

The equivalent Exhibit 14.1 in the previous edition of this book (Wilson and Game, 1998, p. 260) showed that in 1996/97 – immediately before Labour came to power nationally – over three-quarters of these predominantly one-party councils were in Labour hands. To an extent this is almost invariably the case, particularly in the party's modern-day strongholds in Wales, Scotland, and much of metropolitan England. But in 1996/97 it had a less permanent element also: the by-product of the Conservatives' extended dominance of the national parliamentary stage.

A party in power nationally usually expects to lose a certain number of seats in local elections to protest votes, and by 1986 Labour, for the first time since the 1972–3 local government reorganisation, controlled more councils than the Conservatives. The trend continued, until by the early 1990s Conservative local representation had been eroded to the point where the party had fewer councillors and ran fewer councils than at any time in modern memory. The party made a small recovery in the May 1992 district elections, compounding Labour's General Election demoralisation the previous month, but then in the four-year cycle of local elections from 1993 to 1996 it suffered by far its worst sets of results on record. Across the country as a whole, therefore, Labour became for a time the overwhelmingly dominant local government party, in terms of both councillors' party affiliations (10,600 or 48 per cent of the total) and councils controlled (205 or 47 per cent). The Liberal Democrats in 1997/98 were in an unambiguous second place (4,700 councillors and 50 councils), ahead of the Conservatives, who during their 18-year period of national government lost 242 (nearly 95 per cent) of the councils they controlled in 1979 and nearly two-thirds of their 12,000 councillors (see Exhibits 14.2 and 14.3).

It is many years now since the declining number of Independent councillors was passed by the rising numbers of Liberal Democrats or their Liberal and Social Democrat predecessors. Yet it should be noted that in 1997/98 they too held sway on more councils (25) than were controlled on their own by the Conservatives (23).

It is clear in Exhibits 14.1–14.3 that in the four-year cycle of local elections following May 1997 the pendulum swung quite sharply back to the Conservatives. By 2001 they were indisputably the second party in at least English non-metropolitan local government – though still, it should be noted, with majority control of few of the country's largest and most significant councils, and none at all in either Scotland or Wales.

The history of local party politics

In the May 2000 local elections, as we noted in Chapter 11, Ken Livingstone's election as an Independent Mayor of Greater London was by no means the only remarkable result achieved by candidates challenging the major national parties. Minor party and single-issue candidates and all kinds of Independents were also getting elected, often in rather unexpected places – Barnsley, Birmingham, Bradford, Coventry, Leeds, Rotherham – in addition to their larger-scale triumphs in Wyre Forest and Stoke-on-Trent (see Exhibit 11.6). Even in combination, though, these strikingly 'localist' results were not sufficient to reverse the most consistent trend in the politics of local government in recent decades: the long-term decline of Independents.

The present-day hold of party politicians on so much of the country's local government is a comparatively recent phenomenon. At the same time, the role of parties in many towns and cities dates back at least as far as the Municipal Corporations Act 1835 (see Chapter 4). We should therefore view the emergence of a more politicised local government as 'a steady long-term trend, beginning in the nineteenth century, spreading in this century first through the major cities and then, if less evenly, to the shires' (Young, 1986a, p. 81). The trend has been well described in recent years, by Young himself and also by Gyford (Gyford *et al.*, 1989), who usefully identifies five stages to the story, which we summarise in Exhibit 14.4.

Our chief concern in this chapter is naturally with Gyford's final Reappraisal stage, incorporating as it does both a quantitative extension of the scale of party politics in local government and also some fundamental qualitative changes in its character. Much of the quantitative change occurred suddenly and immediately upon reorganisation in the early 1970s. Up to that time about half the councils in England and Wales and two-thirds of those in Scotland could be defined as 'non-partisan', in that over half their elected members resisted all conventional party labelling. There was, as ever, an urban–rural divide: between two-thirds and three-quarters of urban councils being run on party lines compared with one-third of county councils and just 10 per cent of rural district councils.

Reorganisation inevitably involved the merging of many previously non-partisan authorities with others having stronger partisan traditions. The latter invariably prevailed, and following the 1973/74 elections the proportions of predominantly partisan authorities rose immediately to nearly 80 per cent in England and Wales and to over a half in Scotland. Almost all English county councils were now party-dominated and three-quarters of all English and Welsh district councils.

In the succeeding few years this trend continued, with the Conservative Party in particular insisting that all party sympathisers stand as official party candidates and not, as often happened previously, as Independents. As we saw in Exhibits 14.2 and 14.3, Independent councils and councillors still survive in larger numbers than is often recognised, but they are being inexorably squeezed, election after election. More recently, they have been

Exhibit 14.4 The party politicisation of local government

1. *Diversity* (1835–late 1860s) – many of the new municipal councils dominated and split by party politics, but no uniform national pattern. 'Tories, Whigs, Conservatives, Liberals, Radicals, Chartists, Improvers and Economisers offered varying prescriptions in different towns' (Gyford *et al.* 1989, p. 7). Main divisive issues: role of religion in educational provision; levels of municipal spending; drink/teetotalism.

2. *Crystallisation* (1860s-1900s) – administrative rationalisation of local government accompanied by a channelling of party politics, where it existed, into a predominantly Conservative-Liberal contest. Key catalyst: Joseph Chamberlain's Birmingham Liberal Association (1860s), as both a successful electoral organisation and a radical pioneer of municipal collectivism – local government's pro-active involvement in gas and water supply, slum clearance, public health, parks and gardens.

3. *Realignment* (1900s-1940s) – Labour's displacement of the Liberals as the principal radical force in local government, offering 'a distinctive municipal programme calling for better wages and conditions for council workers, the provision of work for the unemployed, public baths and laundries, and adequate housing for working class families' (Gyford *et al.*, 1989, pp. 11–12). Anti-socialist response orchestrated by the Conservative Party through local groups labelled variously Moderates, Progressives, Municipal Alliance and Ratepayers.

4. *Nationalisation* (1940s-1970s) – of previously local government-run public utilities and hospitals and of local party politics. Increasing involvement of the national party organisations in local government; local elections fought increasingly on national issues and personalities; but most county and rural district councils still organised on non-party lines.

5. *Reappraisal* (1970s onwards) – rapid growth and change in character of local party politics following local government re-organisation. Quantitative change – increasing numbers of party-dominated councils and declining numbers of Independents – accompanied by qualitative change, through the formalisation of local party organisation and the intensification of policy debate.

Main source: Gyford *et al.* (1989, Ch. 1).

squeezed even more in Scotland and Wales by the mid-1990s' reorganisation of local government. In both countries there are now far fewer Independents on the larger unitary authorities than there were previously.

Party politicisation in practice

Counting is easy. But there is a lot more to understanding the party politicisation of local government than simply adding up the numbers of party-dominated councils. If we describe a council as 'party politicised', we should expect to find certain features of organisation and modes of operation. They are not new; they developed gradually, most notably under the direction of Labour's influential London leader, Herbert Morrison, in the 1920s and 1930s. Morrison's model party system, described by one of his biographers, George Jones (1975), comprises at least seven elements (Box 14.2).

This party political dimension is rarely included in diagrammatic representations of the organisation and working of councils. For, certainly in the past, it would inevitably complicate an otherwise fairly straightforward picture of officers and departments servicing committees of councillors who made policy decisions that were then publicly approved in full council. In our previous edition we directly addressed this complication

---

Box 14.2 Morrison's model party system

1. *The selection of candidates* by local committees of party members.
2. *The formulation of a distinctive policy programme* by a local party group, usually comprising a mix of councillors and local party representatives.
3. *The production of a party election manifesto* to which all party candidates are expected to adhere, both during the election campaign and once elected.
4. *The attempted implementation of the manifesto* in the event of the party winning a majority of seats on the council.
5. *The organisation of councillors into party groups* for the purposes of determining cabinet and committee memberships and other positions of leadership and responsibility, developing and co-ordinating party policy, determining strategy and tactics, and ensuring group discipline.
6. *The election of a group leadership,* comprising an individual leader and usually a committee of group executive officers, by members of the party group.
7. *The convening of pre-council and pre-committee party group meetings* to enable party group members to agree on policy and plan their debating and voting tactics.

and, in the interests of realism, tried to show not only where party politics fitted into the policy-making process, but how in many councils it actually drives it (Wilson and Game, 1998, Figure 14.1, p. 268).

The party groups, often omitted altogether, featured almost at the centre of our illustration. For these party groups and their respective sizes are the direct outcome of the local elections and, unless there is a directly and separately elected mayor, will determine who is to run the council and how. The elected leader of the majority or largest group would generally become Leader of the Council. The majority group's manifesto becomes the council's agenda, to be translated into practical policy proposals by the relevant departments. Councillors of the majority group would generally chair and numerically dominate all committees and sub-committees – as they now generally take all seats on the executive or cabinet. Like cabinet members, committee chairs would liaise closely with departmental chief officers in preparing their meeting agendas. Each public committee meeting would usually be preceded by private pre-committee meetings of the different party groups at which they determined their tactics: which issues to focus on, who would speak to them, how they will vote. In short, for a proper understanding of how most councils work, you need to visualise the 'unofficial' organisation of the political parties completely superimposed on the 'official' structure of committees, departments and full council.

A hung council, in which there is no overall majority party, will inevitably operate differently in practice, but not in principle. There may have to be negotiated compromises on manifesto proposals. Committees may be chaired by, and executives composed of, members of more than one party, and of course no votes in any arena can be won simply by a party exercising tight party discipline over its own members. Officers may find themselves dealing with and briefing spokespersons from two or three different parties. Those parties, though, and councillors' party affiliations remain at the heart of the policy process.

Party differences – organisation and leadership

Any political party would recognise most of the elements in Morrison's model party system, different though actuality often is from theory. For example, a dearth of willing and capable volunteers may 'informalise' candidate selection procedures, as we saw illustrated in the experience of some of our councillors in Chapter 12. Party manifestos will vary enormously in length and specificity, ranging from almost book-length productions to some that look as if they were lifted from the proverbial back of an envelope (Gyford *et al.*, 1989, pp. 167–72). Party discipline varies too, some groups treating potential or actual voting dissent with considerably greater tolerance than others (Gyford *et al.*, 1989, pp. 172–5).

Exhibit 14.5 Differences in local party organisation and operation

	LABOUR	CONSERVATIVE
1 DIRECTION FROM NATIONAL PARTY	*Model Standing Orders* and regular *NEC Action/Advice Notes* on policy and practice that local party groups are expected to follow.	*Model Constitution* for Conservative groups – completely non-binding; a guide to 'good practice'.
2 BASIC PARTY UNIT FOR LOCAL GOVERNMENT PURPOSES	Borough/District/County Labour Party, composed of delegates elected from constituency and ward parties and affiliated trade union branches.	Borough/District/County Conservative Association, less formally and less uniformly structured than in the Labour Party. Possibly also a constituency Local Government Advisory Committee.
3 KEY OPERATIONAL UNIT OF LOCAL PARTY	*Party Executive Committee*, annually elected and a potentially conflictual combination of councillors and often more radical non-councillor members.	Small group of Association officers, annually elected, plus permanent party agent, if one exists.
4 CANDIDATE SELECTION	By ward parties, but only from a *panel of approved candidates*, drawn up by the local party executive committee from ward party or union branch nominees. Process overseen by regional party. Candidates expected to have party/union experience.	More varied than in Labour Party. By ward branches, possibly but not necessarily from a panel of candidates. No long-standing party experience, or even membership, necessary.
5 PARTY GROUP ON COUNCIL	Likely to be more formally run than Conservative groups: tighter internal discipline and more frequent meetings.	Usually less tightly organised than in Labour Party, and may be more accepting of strong leadership.

6	RELATIONS BETWEEN LOCAL PARTY AND COUNCIL GROUP	'Group members are part of the local party and not separate from it.' Party representatives have right of non-voting attendance at party group meetings; group nominees should report back to local party; regular joint meetings.	Informal. Party representatives – e.g. party agent or constituency chairman – may attend group meetings, usually as observers.
7	COUNCIL POLICY	Formally the responsibility of the *local party*; in practice usually debated/ negotiated with party group, who determine implementation strategy.	Determined by council group and possibly discussed with constituency's Local Government Advisory Committee.
8	ELECTION MANIFESTO	Formally the responsibility of the local party, in consultation with the council group; sometimes drafted through a network of working groups of councillor and non-councillor members.	Usually drawn up by senior councillors, with group leader taking a leading role. Generally shorter and narrower in scope than Labour manifestos.
9	ELECTION OF GROUP LEADERS	Annually, usually by council group members only; very occasionally by 'electoral college', including outside party delegates.	By council members only. Role of leader formally more powerful than in Labour Party.
10	SELECTION OF COUNCIL COMMITTEE CHAIRS/ EXECUTIVE MEMBERS	Almost always elected by party group members.	Usually elected by party group members, but Leader or 'inner circle' of senior party members may play more significant role in nominating and even selecting.

There are also some *systematic differences* of formality and emphasis across the political parties, as exemplified in Exhibit 14.5.

The fundamental difference between the Labour and Conservative Parties derives directly from their contrasting origins and objectives. Labour is a programmatic, constitution-based, ostensibly democratic party whose local operations are governed by a set of Model Standing Orders for Labour Groups. Some local parties will adhere much more rigidly than others to these Standing Orders, but there is a greater uniformity of practice than among local Conservative parties. There is a significantly more influential role too for outside party members in the selection of candidates and, through a hierarchy of policy forums, the determination of policy. The resulting potential for internal party conflict is comparable to that at the national level between the Parliamentary Labour Party (PLP) and the Conference-elected National Executive Committee (NEC), with party activists concerned to prevent councillors becoming 'sucked into' the council and being deflected by professional officer advice from manifesto priorities.

The Conservatives, traditionally the party of the *status quo*, have evolved over a much longer period of time than Labour and are generally much less rule-bound in both their national and local organisation. There is a model constitution for Conservative groups, produced by Conservative Central Office, but it is not binding and is regarded more as a guide to good practice. Liberal Democrats too tend instinctively to favour structural flexibility and to resist externally imposed discipline, although in recent years the influential Association of Liberal Democrat Councillors based in Hebden Bridge (Yorkshire) has sought to foster the virtues of group organisation and coherence. More recently still, even Independents have had an incentive to form themselves into at least loosely knit groupings, in order to claim their entitled proportion of places on committees, as specified in the Local Government and Housing Act 1989.

A second and obviously related dimension of party difference that emerges in Exhibit 14.5 is that of the parties' attitudes towards leadership, which again are distinctive locally as they are nationally. Leach and Stewart have identified three broad types of leadership style that can be ranged, as in Figure 14.1, along an individualistic–collective continuum (Leach and Stewart, 1990, p. 6; Leach and Wilson, 2000, p. 28).

At one end of the continuum there is *leadership from the front,* where the leader is looked to by the party group – or is temperamentally inclined – to take the initiative in proposing major policy developments which the group will then generally agree and adopt. The style of the *group spokesperson* is essentially the reverse: the party group is the chief source of policy decisions, the leader's main role being to act as the group's public mouthpiece, first in the council chamber and then in dealings with the media. Somewhere in the middle of the continuum can be identified the

Figure 14.1 *Three basic political leadership styles*

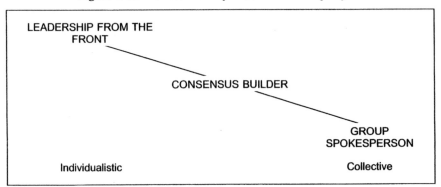

role of *consensus builder*. Here the leader actively seeks to build consensus in the party group, arguing for what s/he feels is the most desirable or attainable policy, but positively committed too to accepting and publicly advocating the eventual majority group view.

The three principal parties differ in their receptiveness to these contrasting leadership styles. Local Conservative groups, though rarely as deferential as in the past, are still the most predisposed towards leadership from the front. Leaders are expected to lead – that is what you elect them to do.

An outstanding example in recent years was Dame Shirley Porter, Conservative Leader of Westminster City Council, 1983–91. She left some very prominent and personal legacies of her leadership, including hundreds of business-sponsored white and green designer litter bins and modernistic, strategically sited 'Porterloos'. More seriously, she also left some hugely damaging accusations of wilful misconduct for having attempted to boost the Conservative vote in marginal wards through the selective sale of council houses – the 'homes for votes' scandal, as it became known. It is not the propriety of Dame Shirley's leadership that concerns us here, though, so much as its unquestionably individualistic style – visionary or authoritarian, depending on your viewpoint, and your proximity to it:

> I am synonymous with Westminster City Council. In my years as Leader I've tried to change the culture at the Council, but ... it's like taking the British Empire and turning it into Great Britain plc. You're changing a cosy establishment of both members and officers. We've had our battles ...
>
> I remember asking, 'Why don't we run this Council like a business?' One of my own side, a certain uptight gentleman with a moustache, spluttered, 'This is the Council!' That was the beginning of my wanting to change the way things were run.

Her leadership was summed up by a badge she liked to wear, saying 'YCDBSOYA':

> I'll give you the polite version. It means 'You Can't Do Business Sitting On Your Armchair'. My father, Sir Jack Cohen, who built the Tesco supermarket chain, gave one to Callaghan and one to Heath, but I haven't had the temerity to give one to Mrs Thatcher yet (Abdela, 1989, pp. 186–93).

The then Prime Minister used to figure regularly in Shirley Porter's interviews, and there were some striking similarities between the two women's pro-active leadership styles: the impatience with the traditions and conventions of public administration, the readiness to see their own colleagues as part of the problem as much as part of the solution.

In the other two parties such a highly personalised view of leadership would be much more politically risky, as evidenced by the widespread scepticism among their councillors towards the whole idea of directly elected mayors. There are still plenty of strong and highly influential Labour leaders around but, out of a combination of constitutional necessity and the politician's instinct for personal survival, they will generally take considerable care to carry their party groups with them. They will 'talk the talk' of consensus, teamwork, and even – to use a favourite expression of Birmingham's long-standing Labour Leader, Sir Richard Knowles – 'comradeship'.

David Bookbinder, Leader of Derbyshire County Council, 1981–92, was a contemporary and in some ways a Labour version of Shirley Porter: an equally high media profile and just as concerned to challenge the 'cosy' culture of local government. But, even in a personal interview, Book-binder's choice of first person pronoun was usually plural:

> For years and years it has always been the view that local government is a partnership between the councillors and those professionals employed to deliver services ... Nonsense! The officers have one role and the members have another. The members are elected and the job of any government is to govern ...
>
> We have a term – being officered. The officer will get hold of the Chair at a pre-committee meeting, explain to the Chair what they want to do, give them a report, and the Chair will instruct the committee members to deliver what is on the paper. But a member's role is not to say yes or no to the recommendation at the end of the report. We want to say what goes into the sausage machine. We are supposed to be the creators, elected on a political philosophy. We have changed people's quality of life: 80 per cent of children get school meals when it used to be 50 per cent; twice as many old folk are getting home helps; meals on wheels are the same price as when we took control in 1981; we have more nurseries. (Willis, 1990)

Party differences – policies and principles

David Bookbinder's declamation takes us neatly from organisation to policy. Our main political parties do organise themselves and operate differently from each other, but even more obvious are their policy differences.

As we have emphasised throughout this book, local government, its structure, functions and financing, have come in recent years to occupy a prime place on the UK national political agenda. Accordingly, no national party's manifesto is now complete without a selection of pledges concerning the further changes that it will impose upon local government, should it be elected to office. The three main party manifestos for the 1997 General Election were fairly typical, even if they did not differ one from another quite as markedly as those in 1992 (Wilson and Game, 1994, pp. 262–3). As can be seen in Exhibit 14.6, each party had its own proposals for the financing of local government, for the provision of some of its principal services, and even for the basic structure and organisation of sub-central government as a whole. As a result, the scale, scope and shape of our local government system were all rather different at the end of the 1997–2001 Parliament from what they would have been under either a Conservative Government or even some form of joint Labour–Liberal Democrat Administration.

The 2001 Parliament, resembling so closely that of its predecessor, will see a continuation of many of the policies and programmes of the preceding four years. In Exhibit 14.6, therefore, for the sake of comparison, we have summarised even more brutally than in previous editions the parties' key local government policies in the two relevant elections. We see, for instance, how most of the Labour's 'modernisation agenda' was anticipated in its 1997 manifesto and, as the ticks show, with only a few significant qualifications was subsequently implemented. The party has had to reiterate, though, its commitment to elected regional assemblies and emphasise local government's vital role in the provision of key public services, if only to avoid being totally outflanked by the perceptibly more radical Liberal Democrats. It was the Conservative manifesto, though, that contained some of the most eye-catching phraseology. Keen to boost at least their local electoral recovery and put recent history behind them, they promised not merely to 'revitalise' local government – without dwelling unduly on how it became devitalised – but to 'revolutionise the attitude of central government to local government'. Successful councils should get more powers and be able to become 'free'; local citizens, not central government, should decide how much their council should spend. Interesting!

The contrasts and disputes among the parties can be just as great at local elections. Councils are certainly more restricted and constrained in what they can do than they used to be. They cannot raise taxes as they might

Exhibit 14.6 The national parties' local government manifestos, 1997 and 2001

	CONSERVATIVES	LABOUR	LIBERAL DEMOCRATS
STRUCTURE	1997: No change; maintain opposition to Scottish and Welsh devolution 2001: Abolish Regional Development Agencies; oppose regional assemblies Return enterprise and development powers to county/unitary councils 'Revolutionise' attitudes of centre to local government	1997: Scottish law-making Parliament with tax-raising powers ✓ Welsh Assembly with secondary legislative powers ✓ London: strategic authority and mayor, both elected ✓ Some devolution to regional chambers of councillors ? All councils to have annual elections ✗ 2001: Maintain commitment to elected regional government, where supported in referendum and local government mainly unitary	1997: Tax-raising parliaments in Scotland and Wales Elected regional assemblies where public demand Strategic authority for London PR for all local elections Abolish quangos or increase their accountability 2001: More powers to nations and regions Referenda for elected regional assemblies Replace Lords with elected region-based Senate
FINANCE	1997: Retain capping; reduce business rates for small businesses More public-private financing. 2001: End capping, but referendums before 'inflationary' tax rises Devolve more powers to 'best' councils	1997: Retain reserve capping power ✓ Consult with businesses on business rates ✓ Fairer distribution of grant ? 2001: Extend local public service agreements; £400 mill. 'reward' fund and more financial 'flexibility' for 'successful' councils; New freedoms for capital investment	1997: Replace council tax with local income tax Allow councils to raise more funds locally Return business rates to local control 2001: Permit councils to raise bonds and parking taxes to fund improved public transport Extend rate relief to protect rural services

INTERNAL MANAGEMENT	1997: Continue CCT Restrict strikes in essential services. 2001: Abolish 'many' national targets and government-required plans.	1997: Abolish CCT ✓ Introduce best value regime with local performance plans and service targets ✓ Encourage democratic experimentation – e.g. elected mayors ? 2001: Maintain support for directly elected mayors	1997: Power of general competence for councils Increase elected membership of police authorities 2001: Define minimum standard of service for all councils
EDUCATION	1997: Encourage more grant-maintained and grammar schools; more selection and budgetary discretion to schools. 2001: Complete freedom for school heads and governors; extra £540 per pupil from saved 'council bureaucracy' More faith, charitable, company schools.	1997: Guaranteed nursery places for all 4-year olds ✓ Reduce class sizes for 5–7 year olds to 30 or less ✓ More budgetary devolution to schools ✓ OFSTED and Audit Commission inspection of LEAs ✓ 2001: £8 bill. investment in school buildings and equipment in next 3 years More faith and specialist schools More management freedom for successful schools	1997: 1p rise in income tax, to be invested in education Nursery places for all 3– and 4-year olds Double spending on books and equipment in 1 year Reduce class sizes for 5–11 year olds to 30 in 5 years More monitoring of LEAs; more powers to schools. 2001: Repeat pledge on 1p hypothecated tax increase Recruit 5,000 extra secondary teachers.
HOUSING	1997: Councils to sell empty inhabitable houses; encourage council tenants to transfer to new landlords. 2001: Abolish national housebuilding targets; streamline planning procedures Increase home ownership with better 'right-to-buy' discounts, new 'rent-to-mortgage' scheme, homesteading grants.	1997: Release of capital receipts to fund building and repairs ✓ Duty on councils to protect the unintentionally homeless ✓ 2001: £1 bill. tax cuts in next 5 years for urban capital investment Target of 60 per cent of new housing on converted 'brownfield' sites Increase home ownership with lower interest rates Cut by one-third 'sub-standard housing' by 2004 Support transfer of council housing to social landlords.	1997: Release capital receipts to fund building, repairs More public-private partnerships to build homes Powers for councils to deal with unfit private housing Rights for council tenants to manage their estates. 2001: Require landlords to bring empty homes into use Councils to specify percentage of social housing in all new developments; end council tax rebate on second homes.

Exhibit 14.7 Three local elections, 1999

SOUTH STAFFORDSHIRE DC – TAXLESS TORIES' TRIUMPHANT RETURN

Background: a whole-council election in the only West Midlands council to stay Conservative throughout the party's local government meltdown in the mid-1990s. Natural Conservative territory – the north-western, owner-occupying, suburban and green belt fringe of the W. Midlands, though, with virtually no black/minority ethnic voters, seems a world away from nearby Wolverhampton.

Conservative record: thrift-driven council has contracted out its refuse collection, earned over £50 million from council house sales, and is seeking re-election after 6 years of not charging residents any council tax: the district collects the tax, but it goes entirely to the county and parishes.

Local issues: whether the no-tax achievement is due to prudent financial management, as the Conservatives claim, or service-cutting plus the fact that the district's 27 parishes provide services – village halls, allotments, bus shelters – that elsewhere are district responsibilities. Protection of green belt from development – though cross-party agreement on this. Lib Dems argue that councillors should live in the wards they represent.

Result: Conservatives re-elected with their previous majority of 6 increased to 20.

UTTLESFORD DC – UNHOLY CON-LAB ALLIANCE SET TO CONTINUE

Background: Where is it? Surrounding Stansted Airport – a rural, historical, predominantly agricultural district in NW Essex. Unquestioningly Conservative until Lib Dems displaced them as largest party in previous whole-council elections in 1995. Brief Lib Dem minority administration ousted in 1997 by what they saw as 'unprincipled' alliance of Conservatives, Labour and Independents.

Local issues: the alliance was the issue and, for a local election, the debate was heated and personalised – to quote the Lib Dem leader: 'in this council the Labour leader, a funeral director, employs the Tory leader as a pallbearer. If that's not jobs for the boys, I don't know what is!' Nationally targeted council for Lib Dems.

Result: Conservatives and Labour swapped two seats, but no gains for Lib Dems. Alliance continued.

DONCASTER BC – LABOUR HANG ON IN DONNYGATE

Background: a mining, engineering and horse-racing district in South Yorkshire that until the 1990s was a near-monopolistic Labour stronghold. But acquired 'Donnygate' reputation as sleaziest council in England following accusations (and convictions) of expenses fraud and planning irregularities by both councillors and officers. Through party suspensions and election defeats, Labour's council majority was down by 1999 from 51 to 23.

Local issues: corruption was the big issue, certainly for the still relatively small Conservative and Lib Dem groups. Labour's third leader in 3 years and several completely new – and untainted – candidates hoped to persuade voters that it was not the most important one. They claim the council has a good record on service delivery and value for money, as evidenced in Audit Commission league tables.

Result: Labour lost a further 6 of the 22 seats contested (one-third of the council only) and had its majority cut to 11 – lowest since 1976.

wish, or even spend all the proceeds from the sales of their own capital assets. But, even though the limits of their budgets are externally defined, the *content* is still substantially theirs to determine, in accordance with the local and political priorities of the party or parties in control.

Local elections thus continue to be run by those involved in such a way as to suggest that the outcome makes a difference. Party manifestos and candidates' election addresses are likely to combine some of the national policies headlined in Exhibit 14.6 with references to local issues and circumstances, and the whole atmosphere and conduct of the election will be set by the party defending its record and those that may be seriously challenging it. We have tried to convey something of the flavour of these partisan contests in Exhibit 14.7.

The three elections summarised in Exhibit 14.7 were selected not for their typicality; if anything, the reverse. Each of these contests had strong and unique local undercurrents to them. They were almost entirely party political clashes, but by no means entirely *national* party clashes. In each case what shaped the campaign debate, and probably boosted whatever interest the media and the electorate might have in it, was the record of the *local* parties, the *local* controlling group, the *local* council leadership. As in most elections, most of the votes cast will have been party votes, but, as we saw in Chapter 11, a significant minority of them will have been for different parties than would have been supported in a parliamentary election.

The pros and cons of party politics

It is at election time that we see most clearly both the positive and negative features of the extensive role played by party politics in our modern-day local government. We have already alluded to some of the claimed positive features (Box 14.3). The logic underpinning most of these claims seems indisputable. Yet it remains the case that many of us are unpersuaded by them. When asked, as in the 1985 Widdicombe Committee survey, a majority of us (52 per cent) say we would prefer local councils to be run on non-partisan lines, with only a third of us (34 per cent) feeling that a party system is better (Widdicombe, 1986d, p. 88). We need to examine, therefore, the other side of the coin: the alleged costs and disbenefits of party politics in local government (Box 14.4).

Conclusion

Set out in this way, the arguments may seem evenly balanced. Certainly, you must form your own conclusions, preferably with reference to your

---

Box 14.3 The pros of party politics

- *More candidates, fewer uncontested seats* in local elections.
- *More active campaigning*, more information for electors, more debating of the issues.
- *Clarification of the issues*, as the parties are challenged by their opponents to defend and justify their arguments and assertions.
- *More citizen awareness and interest* in local government generally and the local council and its services in particular, resulting probably in a higher electoral turn-out.
- *Stimulation of change and initiative* – as parties with their underlying principles and collective resources develop policies to put before the electorate.
- *More opportunities for public involvement in community life.*
- *Enhanced accountability* – as the parties collectively and their candidates individually make public commitments and promises which, if elected, they must seek to implement, and for which they can subsequently and electorally be called to account.
- *Governmental coherence* – the existence, following a decisive election result, of a single-party administration, clearly identifiable by the electorate and council officers alike, able to carry out the policies on which it was elected.
- *Enhanced local democracy* – the existence of electorally endorsed party policies and programmes reducing the potential policy influence of unelected and unaccountable officers.

---

personal experience and impressions. Realists that we are, we would be inclined to point first to the historical trends we identified earlier in the chapter. The comprehensive party politicisation of most of our local government is not only here to stay, but recently received a hefty boost, with reorganisation and the spread of geographically larger, unitary authorities. And it will get another one, if the Government requires there to be predominantly unitary local government in a region before it is permitted an elected regional assembly.

Finally, we would refer back to the argument we put forward in Chapter 12: that politics, properly understood, is at the very heart of what local government is necessarily about. It is about the management and resolution of the inevitable conflict of local views concerning the provision and distribution of public goods and services. That being so, there is something to be said for these conflicting views being marshalled and articulated openly by consciously accountable party politicians, rather than by self-styled 'non-political representatives', whose motives and policy objectives may be left publicly unspecified.

Box 14.4 The cons of party politics

- *More party candidates, fewer Independents* – as the major parties, with their institutional resources, make it increasingly difficult for minority party candidates and Independents to get elected.
- *Narrower debating of the issues* – with rounded discussion displaced by the strident adversarial clash of party rhetoric.
- *Less electoral enlightenment* – as uncommitted voters become disenchanted by the polarisation of debate and by politicians' apparent convictions that their party alone possesses all the answers.
- *Electoral boredom* – with electors staying at home, invoking 'a plague on all their houses'; others not bothering to vote because the outcome seems a forgone conclusion.
- *Less public involvement* – with the many citizens not wishing to join a political party being excluded from areas of local community life.
- *Nationalisation of local elections* – as supposedly local campaigns focus much of their attention on national issues and personalities.
- *Reduced representativeness of councils* – as the winning party takes all positions of responsibility and seeks to implement its policies to the exclusion of all others.
- *Excessive party politicisation of issues* – with the parties feeling obliged to adopt usually adversarial positions on subjects that might more satisfactorily be approached consensually.
- *Reduced local democracy* – as councillors are 'disciplined' into voting with their party, regardless of their personal convictions or judgement.
- *Exclusion of professional advice* – as all effective decisions are made by party groups, usually without the benefit of professionally trained and experienced officers in attendance.

Guide to further reading

As ever, start with your own council(s) and find out what you can about their political complexions and recent electoral histories. There was a fashion in the 1970s for political studies of single towns and cities, and, although they are obviously rather dated now, the best may still repay study: Jones (1969) on Wolverhampton, Hampton (1970) on Sheffield, Dearlove (1973) on Kensington and Chelsea, Newton (1976) on Birmingham, and Green (1981) on Newcastle upon Tyne. More recently, Goss (1988) takes a longer historical perspective of the London Borough of Southwark – one of the 'municipal left' councils studied by Lansley *et al.* (1991). John Gyford has probably contributed most to our understanding of local party politics in recent years, starting with his introductory text (1984) and contributions to the sections on party politics in the

Widdicombe Committee research (Widdicombe, 1986b) and in Gyford *et al.* (1989). The nearest equivalent to the Widdicombe Committee in the 1990s was the independent Commission for Local Democracy. Among the Commission's key concerns were the extent and impact of the party domination of much of local government, which were addressed in one of its commissioned research papers (Game and Leach, 1995, 1996). Leach, with this book's other co-author, has also contributed the most recent study of local political leadership (Leach and Wilson, 2000).

Chapter 15

Who Makes Policy?

The internal and informal politics of policy-making

Chapters 12–14 have looked at three of the key elements in a local council's policy-making process: elected councillors, the professional officers who advise them, and the political parties and party groups of which most of them are members. We turn now to the end-product of the process, the actual formulation and determination of policy. We know from several of the chapters in Part 1 that much of the framework, and especially the financial framework, of local government policy is nowadays laid down by central government. But we have also seen how local authorities can still determine their own spending priorities – and non-priorities – respond to specific local circumstances, and launch their own policy initiatives. Our concern here, therefore, is mainly with the *internal*, rather than external, influences on policy-making, with the internal politics of the town or county hall.

As outlined in Chapter 6, the formal *structures* of policy-making have been undergoing near-revolutionary changes, as most councils transform themselves from committee-based to executive-based government. We described the three executive models that all councils with populations of over 85,000 have been required to choose from and adopt, and we indicated some of the other structural consequences of the executive/non-executive split in councillors' roles. We also noted, however, that by no means all the familiar features of council policy making have disappeared or become unrecognisable. The full council, for example, remains a council's ultimate policy-making body. Officers still contractually serve and advise *all* councillors, both executive and non-executive. And all the *informal* influences on policy development are still to be found, and are just as important to understand – the party groups and networks, the relationships within and between departments, the alliances between leading officers and councillors, the deals between parties when councils are hung or balanced, or where an elected mayor is not from the council's majority party. It is these largely unchanging informal relationships – the levers and channels of informal influence – that this chapter is mainly about.

Analytical models

There are three main models – not the above executive ones; these are conceptual or analytical models – which have been widely used to describe the distribution of power and influence inside local authorities. Each is considered briefly before the chapter goes on to emphasise the need to broaden out the discussion beyond the limitations of these three models.

The formal model

This model derives from the 'legal–institutional' approach that once dominated the study of local government. Its proponents saw power relationships primarily in formal terms and focussed on the formal structures of decision-making – the council, its committees and departments. The model could hardly be simpler: councillors make policy, while officers advise them and carry it out. No overlaps or qualifications are countenanced.

Advocates of this formal model would argue that, if you understand the formal, legal position, you understand reality. Critics would retort that reality, and certainly political reality, is considerably more complex, as already suggested in our discussion of councillor roles in Chapter 12. A model that saw councillors making policy through the council and its committee system, while officers merely advised and implemented, told us more about what perhaps *should* happen than about what *actually* happened. It simply fails to recognise the complexity within and the organisational variety among local authorities.

Yet one must beware of dismissing even an overly simplistic model as worthless. The confrontational Thatcher years saw real assertiveness by councillors of both the New Urban Left and the Radical Right. They set out to run authorities themselves in the way that the formal model delineates. Remember the quote in Chapter 14 from David Bookbinder that could easily have been echoed by Dame Shirley Porter: 'the officers have one role and members have another. The members are elected and the job of any government is to govern.' For a time at least, this model, often dismissed as naive, had its forthright advocates.

The technocratic model

A rival to the formal model has been the technocratic model, which views *officers* as the dominant force in local politics. Their power resides, it is asserted, in their control of specialised technical and professional knowledge unpossessed by and possibly incomprehensible to part-time, amateur, generalist councillors.

This model too, however, is something of a stereotype and should not be accepted uncritically. Highly paid, professionally trained officers, heading large departments, with all the staff and other resources of these departments at their disposal, can appear formidable to the inexperienced newly elected councillor entering the council offices for maybe the first time. But the relationship is by no means all one-sided.

Plenty of leading and long-serving councillors, particularly those in effectively full-time executive positions, will have the experience, knowledge and political skill to assert themselves effectively in any negotiation with officers. Moreover, even the neophyte councillor comes with that vital source of democratic legitimacy that no officer, however senior, can ever have: the authority of having been *elected*, on what is now an endorsed political platform, to represent all the citizens of their locality.

In Exhibit 15.1 we construct a kind of balance sheet of the respective resources of officers and councillors – a little like that in Exhibit 9.5 in which we compared the resources of central and local government. We argued then that local government has access to more resources than is sometimes suggested, and so it is with councillors in their relations with officers.

It will be apparent from Exhibit 15.1 that it has been the politicisation, and particularly the intensified *party* politicisation of local government during the past two or three decades, that has done more than probably anything else to shift the balance of power between officers and elected councillors. We come back again to the rise during the 1980s of ideologically committed and politically skilful councillors of both the new left and the new right, which inevitably served to check any independent policy aspirations of officers. In the 1990s, for example, ruling Conservative Party groups in Westminster LB, Wandsworth LB, Wansdyke DC in Avon and Rochford DC in Essex were notably assertive in the introduction of competitive tendering and the enabling/purchasing philosophy – just as a decade earlier the 'municipal left' had introduced their public transport and council housing subsidies, and their job creation and anti-discrimination policies.

Notwithstanding such examples, the professional and technical knowledge possessed by officers remains a tremendous resource, equipping them to act as powerful policy-makers *in the absence* of any positive policy lead from members. Their influence can be especially strong in smaller rural authorities dominated by Independent councillors. As professionals, they are always there to fill any policy vacuum. It is up to councillors to set their own clear and – recalling Rhodes' observations in Chapter 13 on the centralist inclination of professional influence – localist policy agendas and thus to ensure that there is no vacuum.

Exhibit 15.1 The resources of officers and councillors

OFFICERS	COUNCILLORS
• Professional knowledge, training, qualifications	• Political skills. experience; possibly training, expertise, qualifications in own field of work
• Professional networks, journals, conferences	• Party political networks, journals, conferences
• Full-time, well-paid employee of council	• Member of employing council, spending an average of 20 hours per week on council work
• Resources of whole department	• Resources of whole council
• Knowledge and working experience of other councils	• In-depth (possibly lifetime) knowledge of own council, ward, its residents and service users
• Commitment to professional values and standards	• Commitment to personal and political values, to locality and community
• UNELECTED 'servant of the council' – appointed to advise councillors and implement their policy	• ELECTED on political manifesto to make policy and represent hundreds/thousands of residents and service users

The joint elite model

Deficiencies in the formal and technocratic models prompted the development of another perspective – the joint elite model. Proposed as being more truly reflective of actual practice, it argued that policy-making is dominated by a small group of leading majority party councillors and senior officers, with minority party and what we now call non-executive members and junior officers at most only marginally involved.

It was an interpretation that found support in several empirical studies. Saunders' research in Croydon (1980, pp. 216–30) revealed a picture of town hall politics where chief officers and political leaders worked as 'close allies' maintaining a powerful control over policy-making. Cockburn in her study of Lambeth saw the backbencher 'excluded by the high-level partnership between the leadership and senior officers' and as a consequence taking 'little part in the policy planning process'. Council decision-making was, Cockburn maintained, dominated by 'a tightly-knit hierarchy under the control of a board of directors [the chief officers] in close partnership with a top-level caucus of majority party members' (Cockburn, 1977, p. 169).

But the joint elite model too had its critics, who questioned the virtual monopoly of influence apparently attributed to this elite. Young and Mills (1983) argued, for example, that the very exercise of routinised power by those at the top of a hierarchy makes them less likely *sources of policy change* than those lower down. These 'junior actors' learn from direct operational experience and often have the creative energy that is necessary for the development of new initiatives. Important though the leading councillors and officers in any authority obviously are, a thorough under-standing of the policy process requires a recognition that they will rarely constitute a united cohesive group. In the real world relationships are both more complex and also frequently characterised by tension and conflict.

Broadening the debate – additional influences

There is far more, therefore – especially with the arrival of executive government – to an understanding of the distribution of policy influence in a local authority than simply an analysis of the activities of the most senior players. As Stoker and Wilson (1986) show, other factors need to be incorporated into any genuinely realistic model. The unadorned joint elite model requires supplementing if anything like the full complexity of internal power relationships is to emerge. That is the purpose of the remainder of the chapter: to add to, qualify, and generally complicate the joint elite model, and in doing so identify some of the additional influences on real-life policy-making. Figure 15.1 provides a diagrammatic presenta-tion of the model outlined in the remainder of this chapter, the elements of which, in a clockwise order, are as follows:

- *Intra-party influences* – relations *within* especially ruling party groups, and between groups and the wider party;
- *Inter-departmental influences* – relations between and across depart-ments and professions;
- *Intra-departmental influences* – relations within departments;
- *Inter-party influences* – relations *between* party groups, especially in hung authorities, where they have to take account of one another.

The ruling party group and party networks

The ruling party group as a whole, not just its leading and executive councillors, can have a significant influence on policy-making. Very few party groups are homogeneous. Often there are factions with their own

Figure 15.1   *Power inside local authorities: a diagrammatic representation*

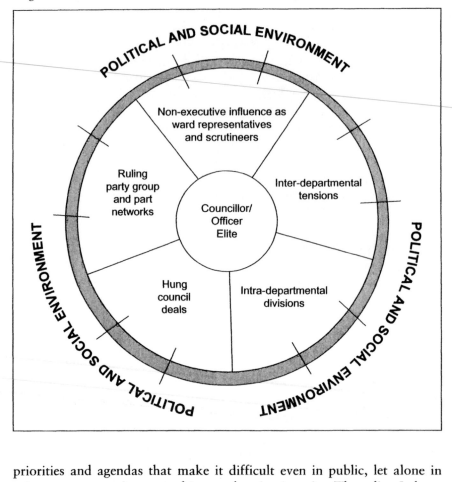

priorities and agendas that make it difficult even in public, let alone in private group meetings, to achieve and maintain unity. The ruling Labour group on Leicester City Council at the end of the 1980s was unusual in the formalisation of its factionalism, and in the fact that the party leader, Peter Soulsby, was one of the few members belonging to none of them, but it was by no means unique. There were in effect four caucuses within the group (Leach and Wilson, 2000, pp. 128–9):

- the 'left', numbering about 13, who met in a local pub, with formal agendas, in advance of Labour group meetings;
- the 'black' caucus of about 8, including one white Muslim councillor, which also held formal pre-meetings;
- the 'right' – about 8 members, largely from Leicester West parliamentary constituency, less formally organised than the left and black groups;
- the 'non-aligned' group (NAG), again of between 6 and 8 members.

Most party groups operate more informally – even haphazardly – but that does not stop them being a source of policy influence. Policy initiatives can emerge from the backbench/non-executive members of a group, who can also veto or refer back leadership proposals with which they disagree. Stoker (1991, p. 98) notes that, while over many issues and for most of the time a group may

> simply endorse decisions taken elsewhere, at the very least senior councillors and officers must be careful not to offend the core political values and commitments of backbenchers. The role of party groups in local policy-making is, with the increased intensity of party ideology and organisation, a potentially crucial area for decision-making.

Party groups nowadays expect to be consulted and listened to; leaders have continuously to cultivate their support. Upset just one or two members and they may decide to go; alienate a majority and you may have to. Defections and instances of 'crossing the floor' of the council chamber are numerically far commoner, if less publicised, than in parliamentary politics, as evidenced in almost any local election listings. Even discounting all the plain, unvarnished 'Independents', there will be plenty of candidates describing themselves as 'Independent Conservative', 'Socialist Labour', 'Independent Liberal Democrat', even 'Independent Green', and suggesting that their favoured parties cannot accommodate the ideological purity of their views – or perhaps just them personally.

On occasions party groups will flex their muscles and remove the group leader. In November 1995, for example, two majority group leaders – Stewart Foster in Leicester and Valerie Wise in Preston – were overthrown on the same day, following votes of no confidence by their respective Labour groups. It can be a heartless process, especially when the relevant group meeting comes, as it often does, in the immediate wake of an election. The best known, and fascinatingly recounted, case was the then 'Red Ken' Livingstone's displacement of the more right-wing Andrew McIntosh as leader of the Greater London Council in May 1981, within 24 hours of McIntosh having led the Labour Party to electoral victory (Livingstone, 1987, pp. 3–4). A similar fate befell Theresa Stewart, Labour leader of Birmingham City Council for nearly six years, but overthrown by supporters of Albert Bore within days of the May 1999 elections. Leaders or executive members who owe their elected positions to their group can expect to be regularly reminded of the fact – which is one powerful reason, of course, why so many councillors oppose the very principle of directly elected mayors, whose first accountability is to the electorate as a whole, rather than to them.

The *local party network* also requires consideration. Links with the wider party organisation can be a valuable resource for individual group members, especially in the Labour Party where such networks have a greater policy significance, with local election manifestos, for example, being drawn up in consultation with non-councillor party members (see Exhibit 14.5). It was thus the district parties in Walsall and Rochdale, rather than the party groups on council, who were the real originators of the decentralisation policies in those boroughs. Local councillors and council leaders must respect the role of the wider movement; disregard can easily lead to conflict.

Non-executive/backbench councillors

It would arguably have been better if the essentially parliamentary term 'backbencher' had never been applied to the very different world of local government, where, in the traditional committee system, no councillor constitutionally had more decision-making authority than any other. 'Backbencher' misleadingly and demeaningly suggests a hierarchical role division where none legally existed. We shall therefore continue, wherever possible, to talk of 'non-executive' councillors, who now have at least three quite distinct roles – as members of the full council, representatives of their wards and constituents, and overviewers and scrutineers – through which they can play a part in shaping policy, if not in actually taking policy decisions.

In promoting or defending local ward interests, councillors can sometimes enter the policy arena in a very influential way. In Leicester in 1983 two Asian Labour councillors initiated a campaign which overthrew the majority Labour group's housing policy by blocking a demolition plan in their ward (Stoker and Brindley, 1985). Local ward interests can easily cut across party interests, and in authorities with relatively weak party systems (see Exhibit 14.1) these local interests are likely to be compensatingly stronger. In such circumstances councillors can, by developing alliances and lobbying, contribute regularly and effectively to the shaping of council policy.

One of the government's intended by-products of executive government is the enhancement of councillors' ward and community roles and of their unique position as conduits of their constituents' views to the council. Freed from at least some of their former committee work, non-executive members are expected to consult with their communities on the development of policy, on the regular reviews of best value and the development of the Best Value Performance Plan, and on any other community-relevant initiatives. Councils are specifically charged with ensuring that appropriate procedures are available for members to 'feed-in' the views of their constituents to the policy development process.

These procedures include the council's overview and scrutiny arrangements, which, if properly exercised, are about far more than evaluating existing policy and holding the executive to account *after* the event – knowing whom to blame – important and satisfying though that is. The opportunities are there for the 80 per cent or more non-executive members to contribute *prospectively* to the development of policy *before* it is finalised. Scrutiny and overview is rightly presented as an integral part of effective executive government, and its potential impact is almost limitless. For it offers the non-executive members who exclusively run the process the possibility of reviewing, scrutinising, reporting on and making recommendations concerning any past, present or future policy or action of the council, or any matter affecting the council's area or its inhabitants.

If the full potential of scrutiny in this wide-ranging sense is to be realised, however, at least three conditions have to be present. First, councillors themselves must approach the process positively and in the understanding that not being part of the executive can be *empowering* at least as much as disempowering. They must realise too that new skills are likely to be required of them, which for most will mean serious training. Instead of, as often sufficed in the past, passively processing officer reports, they should now be assessing and probing, working collaboratively to draw out evidence and views from witnesses, understanding performance indicators, comparative data and financial processes in a way that few will have done previously (Audit Commission, 2001a, p. 24).

Secondly, scrutiny members need to learn not just new skills, but new ways of working – constructively across the party divide. Their role as scrutineers, even if they happen to be members of the same party as the executive, is not to defend the party line, but to explore, critically if necessary, ways in which the council can better serve its community. It is vital, therefore, that party 'whipping' and tight disciplinary regimes be relaxed – something that does not come easily to members who may have spent their entire adult lives opposing just about everything their political opponents stand for.

Thirdly, effective scrutiny requires, in addition to committed and trained members, *dedicated* officer and resource support – in both senses of the adjective. The executive's demands must not be allowed totally to hold sway. Sufficient and sufficiently senior officers need to be allocated specifically to the scrutiny process, and, like the members, they need to view the assignment positively, and not as some kind of second-class, career-blocking posting, inferior to working for the executive. Adequate financial support too is needed, so that, for instance, independent advice can be sought from outside consultants.

Inter-departmental tensions

Most councils have more than one overview and scrutiny committee, but not one for every major department. In this way, as in several others, local government practice differs from that of the largely departmentally-based select committees in the House of Commons. Councils have generally been readier to recognise that many of the most urgent and intractable problems they face – the so-called 'wicked issues' of social exclusion, environmental sustainability, community safety and the like – cannot be neatly pigeonholed into service-specific departments and committees. They have therefore set up more open-ended and flexible scrutiny arrangements, often with some formidably all-embracing titles. Birmingham's main scrutiny committees, for instance, mirror the council's performance themes and include: A Learning City; A Healthy, Caring and Inclusive City; A Safer, Cleaner, Greener City.

Such developments, though, should not be taken to imply that departmental identities and boundaries are no longer of much significance. Departments remain the main units of a council's administrative organisation, and, as ever, they represent different interests and inevitably have different, and potentially conflicting, sets of priorities. Particularly at times of zero growth or service and staffing cutbacks, these differences surface and can lead to arguments across departments in the fight for scarce resources, and conceivably for departmental survival.

There are also instinctive *professional rivalries* – between, for example, the technical departments involved in land development. 'Planners, architects, housing managers, valuation officers and engineers all claim an involvement and there is a long history of rivalry between these professions' (Stoker, 1991, p. 102). Dominance of specific departments and professions will inevitably change over time; unacceptable policies will be delayed and favoured policies will be accelerated. Increased professionalisation within the local government service has meant that inter-departmental tensions are never far from the surface. They will spill over into the policy sphere with some regularity.

According to Pratchett and Wingfield (1996), the dual impact of market competition and of the internal reforms associated with the advent of the 'New Public Management' has led to some erosion of the public service ethos in local government. The divisions of functions between client and contractor that are engendered by market competition have led to increasingly antagonistic and adversarial relations between different parts of the same organisation, encouraging more reticent and secretive behaviour within local authorities. Employee loyalty is frequently perceived nowadays to be to a specific 'cost centre' rather than to the broader authority.

Intra-departmental divisions

Intra-departmental divisions are a further factor in the policy-making equation. Individual departments are frequently no more homogeneous than are party groups. The size and diversity of many departments mean that, in effect, the span of control a chief officer can exercise must be limited, thereby providing junior officers, often with greater technical expertise by virtue of their more recent training, with scope for influence.

Most departments in larger local authorities consist of hundreds, even thousands, of employees in a range of relatively separate hierarchies and organisational divisions. Indeed, given the recent trend of merging departments into a much smaller number of strategic directorates, there is increasing scope for competing priorities and internal friction *within* a single management unit. Leicestershire County Council's Planning and Transportation Department, for example, had in 2000 no fewer than eight major areas of responsibility: public transport services; traffic; road safety; highways; street lighting; environment; planning; waste regulation. Many authorities have followed the example of Kirklees and others in streamlining a dozen or more service departments into just four or five multi-functional directorates: Housing and Direct Services; Development, Environment and Leisure, and the like. In such contexts senior managers play the role of directors of larger groups of more disparate, if related, services than would have been the responsibility of their predecessors.

Divisions within departments can also arise with the introduction of decentralised management and service delivery. Area-based housing officers, for instance, may develop a dual loyalty, not only to the local authority but also to their specific operational area and its residents. Conflict is by no means uncommon between area offices and central departments or between a number of decentralised area offices. Additionally, junior officers working in decentralised offices within a local authority can develop close ties with local ward councillors – another source of potential influence for junior officers. Failure to incorporate *junior* officials in any model of decision-making inside the town hall is to ignore a group which can be extremely influential.

'Hung' or 'balanced' councils

The prevalence nowadays of hung or balanced councils – those on which no single party has an overall majority of councillors – raises further questions about the adequacy of the joint elite model, which assumes the existence of a small group of leading majority party councillors. In 1979, 14 per cent of councils were hung; in 2001/02 that figure was more than double – over 32 per cent or 142 councils (see Exhibit 14.3). If in the future any form of proportional representation were to be introduced for local elections, the number of hung councils would be likely to double again, to around two-thirds of the total (Leach and Game, 2000, Ch. 2).

Even in the absence of electoral reform, though, in about a third of councils party groups already *have* to take account of each other's policies and actions; otherwise any proposal they put forward could in principle be defeated at any time. First, however, they need to determine among themselves how council business is actually going to be conducted. With a committee form of government there are several possible forms of 'hung' council administration, of which the three commonest have been those shown in Box 15.1.

Executive government obviously imposes different demands on a hung council and requires different solutions. For a start, the 'no administration' option ceases to be a possibility: the council is required to adopt some form of government, mayoral or otherwise. But cabinet or executive composition – whether determined by mayor, leader or the council – is subject to a similar kind of inter-party negotiation as before. The principal options are a one-party cabinet – the equivalent to minority administration – even though that party could be defeated in full council at any time; a coalition cabinet of two or more parties, in which a third party is expressly excluded; or an all-party cabinet (Leach and Game, 2000, Ch. 5). A situation in which a directly elected mayor has to work with a council

---

Box 15.1 'Hung' council administrations

(a) *Minority administration* – where one party, usually the largest, was prepared and permitted by the other parties to take all committee chairs and vice-chairs and, in this sense at least, to 'govern' as if it were in overall majority. About a third of recent hung authorities have adopted this model.

(b) *Power-sharing* – where two or more parties agreed to share committee chairs, but without, usually, any more far-reaching agreement on a shared policy programme; in other words, a deal or arrangement, rather than a formal coalition. About half of all hung authorities were run in the late 1990s by such power-sharing agreements, most frequently involving Labour and the Liberal Democrats, although, as we saw in the case of Uttlesford in Exhibit 14.7, almost any ideological permutation is possible if the motives are strong enough.

(c) *No administration/rotating chairs* – where there were no permanently held chairs, the positions being rotated for procedural purposes amongst two or more parties, but without there being any associated policy understanding.

dominated by a different party or parties could prove particularly difficult, but there are no intrinsic reasons why hung councils should not be able to adapt to executive government as effectively as many of them, if not all, operated committee administration.

Any form of hung council administration is likely to involve far more extensive inter-party contact and negotiation than is seen in most majority-controlled councils. Officers too – particularly the chief executive and chief officers – have to assume different roles, working with and briefing spokespersons from possibly several parties rather than just one. They may, indeed, perform a brokerage role, actually bringing the different parties together in order to negotiate some policy or procedural agreement. And, of course, non-executive members find their position enhanced, as every council vote becomes precious. Bargaining becomes the order of the day because there is no one-party elite of members who can be sure, unaided, of delivering a policy programme.

Conclusion – constantly shifting alliances

The three conceptual models presented in the first part of this chapter – the formal, technocratic, and joint elite models – provide insights into local policy-making but have demonstrable deficiencies. Even the joint elite model is overly simplistic. While the emergence of more corporate management structures and particularly the arrival of executive government have generally strengthened the positions of leading councillors and senior officers, it is misleading to see policy-making as a process restricted to this joint elite. While their centrality is not questioned, their exclusive dominance certainly is. Local authorities are political institutions – in both the narrowly partisan and broader senses of the word. They incorporate a whole range of additional actors and influences that may impinge on policy-making, depending on an authority's traditions, culture, leadership, political balance, and so on. The policy process in the real world is a complex and changeable one. It can be regarded as a series of shifting alliances, forming and re-forming over time and from issue to issue. These networks and alliances vary enormously, but they are by no means solely the preserve of leading councillors and officers.

Guide to further reading

No observer has an acuter understanding of the internal politics of councils of all types and cultures than John Stewart, whose most recent book (2000, esp. Chs 9, 12) distils a lifetime's experience. The Widdicombe Committee Report and accompanying research volumes (1986a–d) still have relevance, as has Gyford *et al.* (1989), which summarises much of it. Young and Mills (1983) are insightful on departmental politics, and Stoker and Wilson (1986) offer both a critique of traditional analytical models and a discussion of alternative perspectives. For more recent accounts of political parties in local government and the operation of hung councils, see Game and Leach (1996), Leach and Pratchett (1996), and Leach and Game (2000). What he terms 'the leviathan' of party group politics, from both the inside and out, has been the lifetime's study of Colin Copus (1998, 1999), and he naturally has views too about its future under executive government (2001). Leach and Wilson (2000), cited in Chapter 14, and also John and Cole (2000), are again useful on the role of local political leaders in shaping policy.

Chapter 16

Local Pressure Groups – The Exercise of Influence

Introduction

Most studies of local communities point to an extensive local pressure group universe. Newton (1976) in a study of Birmingham in the early 1970s identified no fewer than 4,264 formally organised voluntary organisations in the city. Maloney *et al.* (2000) carried out a similar mapping exercise in 1998 and found the number had risen by more than a third, to 5,781. Even in relatively small district councils Bishop and Hoggett (1986) found extensive group networks. Our interest in this chapter, though, is not so much in the numbers of groups – a sizeable proportion of which will not be politically active on any regular basis – as in the different kinds of relationships groups have with their local authorities and the nature of their influence upon policy-making and service delivery.

An all-embracing definition

It is easy to get side-tracked into discussions of alternative definitions of pressure groups – or indeed of whether it might not be more strictly accurate to label them all 'interest groups', since many in practice have little effective pressure they can bring to bear on government. We confess to being a little careless about such matters and therefore propose adopting Moran's exceedingly straightforward definition (1989, p. 121):

> any group which tries to influence public policy without seeking the responsibility of government.

An all-embracing definition of this nature acknowledges that the apparently least political of groups can be drawn into the political process, if only intermittently. Thus a local gardening association resisting a proposal to build a road over its land becomes temporarily a pressure group. At local level many groups are precisely such single-purpose groups, which burst into political life only when an issue such as a council planning decision affects them directly.

The latter part of Moran's definition is important too. For it enables us to include groups who may put up 'single-issue' candidates for local elections, alongside those from other larger and mostly nationally-based parties that most definitely *are* seeking the responsibility of government. These single-issue parties and candidates – Justice for the Elderly, Rutland Choice, the Legalise Cannabis Alliance – are using the electoral process primarily as a means of publicising their cause. They may well not field enough candidates to form an administration, even if outstandingly successful, although they can occasionally, like the Independent Kidderminster Hospital campaigners, almost inadvertently find themselves in government (see Exhibit 11.6).

Looking through the other end of the telescope, as it were, councils themselves can on occasion become pressure groups in larger political arenas, in making representations to Parliament, central government, or the European Union. Indeed, some councils nowadays employ professional parliamentary lobbyists to make their case as effectively as possible. *Westminster Advisers*, to pick just one example, has worked for Lincolnshire, Humberside and Bedfordshire CCs, helping them to campaign against nuclear waste dumping; also for Hart DC in that council's dispute with Hampshire County Council over the latter's proposed housing development in Foxley Wood.

Some classifications

The inevitable consequence of adopting a deliberately catch-all definition is that it produces a vast population of groups which then require some form of classification. In the literature on national pressure groups the most common distinction drawn is between, on the one hand, sectional or interest groups and, on the other, promotional, cause or attitudinal groups. *Sectional* groups exist to defend and advance the interests of their own members involved in usually some economic activity – e.g. trade unions, business and employers' organisations, professional associations. *Promotional* groups exist to promote or campaign for some cause or principle – e.g. the environment, civil liberties, animal rights, the welfare of children, single parents, pensioners or the handicapped.

At local level Stoker (1991, pp. 315–17) has produced an elaborated version of this classification summarised in Exhibit 16.1, which emphasises the importance of *council attitudes* in determining the nature of the relationship with different types of groups. This idea – the significance to a group of there being a *congruity* between its aims and mode of operation and the political and policy objectives of the controlling party group(s) on a council – is one to which we return regularly throughout this chapter.

Exhibit 16.1 A classification of local groups

1. **Producer or economic groups** – including businesses, trade unions, professional associations. Partnerships with such groups have grown enormously in recent years, prompted by various central government initiatives: Training and Enterprise Councils (TECs), Learning and Skills Councils, City Technology Colleges (CTCs), Action Zones, etc. – see Chapter 8.

2. **Community groups** – which draw on distinct social bases for their support, e.g. amenity groups, tenants' associations, women's groups, and groups representing ethnic minorities. They vary in their policy influence and financial and administrative support depending on the congruence of their aims and activities with those of the local authority. Grants are the major vehicle of support for such groups.

3. **Cause groups** – concerned with promoting a particular set of ideas and beliefs rather than their immediate material interests. Typically not the type of organisation that receives much official support from a local authority. Again, grants are the main form of relationship, and one would expect a consistency between the local authority's political agenda and that of any groups chosen for support.

4. **Voluntary sector groups** – organisations established to meet a perceived need in the community on a non-commercial, non-statutory basis. These groups have expanded considerably in recent years, especially since the introduction of the purchaser/provider split in social services. Increasingly the form of relationship is becoming contractual.

Source: Stoker (1991).

Another classification scheme – perhaps more useful if you want to try to find out which groups in your area are being at least partially grant-funded by your own council tax payments – is the one most readily recognised by most local authorities: by *service* or *department*. We have illustrated this approach to classification in Exhibit 16.2, which shows a small selection of the local groups supported by Birmingham City Council under four of its departmental budgets.

All the groups in Exhibit 16.2 received some kind of support from the City Council. From their point of view the financial support is almost inevitably the most important element, often determining whether they can simply stay in existence for another year. Grants may vary from a few hundred pounds to, in the case of a large council like Birmingham, several tens of thousands. With the more substantial grants in particular, the Council will naturally wish to protect its own and its taxpayers' interests, ensure that the money is spent on what it was allocated for and that a properly audited set of accounts is available. In such cases it may nominate

Exhibit 16.2 Some groups supported by four Birmingham City Council departments

Economic Development	Housing
Birmingham Co-operative Development Agency	Birmingham Women's Aid
Black Business in Birmingham	Focus Housing Association
Disability Resource Centre	Homeless Alcohol Recovery Project
Midlands Industrial Association	Housing Plus One Mother and Baby Project
Motor Industry Local Authority Network	Private Rented Sector Forum
Trade Union Resource Centre	Salvation Army
West Midlands Low Pay Unit	South Aston Housing Co-operative

Education	Leisure Services
Birmingham Social Sports Federation	Birmingham Association of Youth Clubs
The Chinese and Vietnamese Cultural School	Birmingham Readers and Writers Festival
Duke of Edinburgh Award Scheme	Birmingham Repertory Theatre
Bengali Women's Association	Cycling Advisory Group
Big Brum Theatre in Education Company	Friends of the Library
Muslim Parents' Association	Muhammad Ali Centre
	Scout Association
	Tree Lovers' League

one or more councillors to sit on the management board of the organisation, and in all instances it will designate a contact officer in the relevant department to perform a mixture of an advisory and monitoring role.

Obviously, a group receiving, let alone depending upon, funding from its local council is hardly in a position to start imposing or threatening pressure on that council, and it is here that the very term 'pressure group' can appear misleading. In the local government world especially, many groups are, as Moran notes (1989, p. 122), not so much conflictual as natural *collaborators and agents* of government in policy-making and policy implementation. Many groups, particularly in the social services field, work in *partnership* with local authorities in service provision – a tendency naturally encouraged by the growing importance of the enabling role for local councils. Only if a group finds itself excluded by its council, and apparently without realistic hope of future inclusion, will it feel it necessary or advantageous to resort to pressure as opposed to attempted persuasion.

Exhibit 16.3 SHARP: Shelter Housing Aid and Research Project

Aims	To secure a decent home for every household in Leicestershire and Northamptonshire at a price they can afford
How?	Free, confidential, impartial information and advice on housing rights and opportunities: • help and practical assistance to those unable fully to exercise their housing rights • encouragement and support for initiatives to house those currently homeless or badly housed • education and training, to develop knowledge and expertise of individuals and housing agencies
Staff	10 full-time, 4 part-time staff.
Funding	Income of £150,000: half from Leicester City Council; a quarter from Shelter HQ; remainder from donations
Caseload	About 1000 p.a., plus hundreds of enquiries
Major concern	Leicester City Council's introduction of 'Grant Aid Contracts', setting grant recipients numerical performance targets for the services it funds. 'Can those targets be met, while still enhancing the range and quality of our work?'

This brings us to a further classification, perhaps the simplest of all. Dearlove (1973, p. 168) argued that local pressure groups can be divided into two basic types: *helpful* or *unhelpful*. Helpful groups are ones whose interests reinforce those of the ruling party group and council. Unhelpful groups, by contrast, 'either do not make claims on the council, or else make claims that conflict with the councillors' own views as to the proper course of council activity'. Is the local pressure group universe quite as easily divisible as that? In Exhibits 16.3 and 16.4 we summarise the operations of two local groups active in Leicestershire. How would you classify them: helpful, unhelpful, or a possibly mixture of both?

Who benefits? The pluralist/elitist debate

We have so far mentioned almost three dozen groups by name in this chapter. Some – like the Salvation Army and Scout Association – are obviously very long-standing. Most, however, are of much more recent

---

Exhibit 16.4 ENVIRON

Aims   To provide advice on environmental management to businesses and local authorities in Leicestershire. As co-ordinators of Leicester-Environment City, to challenge the local community to care for the environment and create a better, greener future.

How?   Much of ENVIRON's work has been based on partnerships with:

- Leicester City Council – development of city centre shop-front to make people more environmentally aware; large-scale public consultation exercise to create a 'Blueprint for Leicester';
- County Council – environmental education in every school; work with community on numerous nature conservation projects;
- Leicestershire TEC and Business Link – launched advisory Business Line.

Management   Board of Directors (unpaid) from local government, local businesses, universities.

Staff   40-strong multi-disciplinary team of landscape architects, teachers, ecologists, business managers, etc.

Funding   £60,000 from central government's Urban Programme, to fund 20 community projects; £10,000 from Leicester City Council; other grants from Leicestershire County Council, Leicestershire TEC and European Commission. Quarter of income self-generated.

Other projects   'Grass Roots' – supports residents of two Leicester neighbourhoods in improving their environment by collecting residents' views; petitioning City Council on traffic speed reduction measures, improved street lighting and dog fouling prevention. Research publication of articles in local and national media.

---

origin, and local single-issue groups in particular are springing up all the time. Given this growth and, as already noted, the increasing involvement of groups in the delivery of local services, it is important to ask questions about which particular sections of society benefit from pressure groups. Is democracy enhanced by their activity, or do local groups simply reinforce the existing distribution of power in the community? Pluralists would naturally see them as an enhancement of democracy. As Dearlove puts it (1979, p. 46):

the interest group world is one of reasonably perfect competition, where the rules of the game ensure fair play and equal access for all to the favourable decisions of those in government.

Dearlove, however, concluded that in practice the world – and certainly the slice of it in Kensington and Chelsea that he studied – was not like this. He found that only a relatively small selection of groups was actually drawn into the local council's policy deliberations – in an elitist process that reinforced the dominance of producer interests, rather than opened up decision-making to a broader range of groups.

Dearlove's study (1973, Ch. 8) showed that the council's response to groups revolved around councillor assessment of group demands and communication styles. Groups were seen as either helpful or unhelpful, their demands as being either acceptable or unacceptable. Their methods of communication with the council were seen as either proper or improper. Groups judged by the ruling Conservative councillors as most helpful were those whose demands most mirrored those of the majority group. Thus, the Kensington Housing Trust was most widely regarded as very *helpful*, since it contributed towards solving local housing problems, thereby lessening the need of the local authority to build more council houses. In fact, the Council made money out of the enterprise since it charged interest on money it loaned to the Trust. Such a pressure group reinforced the policy priorities and ideological orientations of the ruling group – hence its favourable treatment.

By contrast, the *unhelpful* groups (e.g. Kensington and Chelsea Council Tenants' Association or the Kensington and Chelsea Inter-Racial Council) canvassed demands which only a minority of councillors supported and which ran counter to the policy priorities of the ruling Conservative administration. Such 'unacceptable' demands had necessarily to be channelled through what the ruling group perceived as 'improper' routes, e.g. petitions and demonstrations. 'Unhelpful' groups were thus faced with a dilemma: either continue to pursue demands which run counter to the majority group's dispositions and remain relatively powerless, or moderate their demands with a view to gaining access, acceptability and policy influence. This interpretation would see radical left groups being marginalised in Conservative-controlled authorities, and radical right groups being left equally impotent in Labour-controlled authorities.

Newton's study of Birmingham (1976) came to similar elitist conclusions. He found that 'established' groups enjoyed 'easy access to decision-makers' and were able to 'press for the maintenance of the status quo' in a 'relatively quick and unnoticed way'. On the other hand, the 'poorly established' groups frequently found it difficult to contact decision-makers and so had to resort to 'pressure group campaigns', which served only to underline how powerless they were in the local political system.

'Propositions from pluralist theory', Newton suggested (1976, p. 62), fare 'poorly against the empirical evidence'.

Writing more recently, though, Stoker (1991, p. 128) argues that times and attitudes have changed significantly and such elitist interpretations of local pressure group influence are nowadays much less valid. From the mid-1970s onwards, he maintains, 'many local authorities have opened out, providing access not only to producer groups but to a wider range of groups including community, cause and voluntary organisations'. Many groups too have changed, becoming more assertive, more skilled at acquiring funding, and more willing to become involved in service delivery. What are we to make of these conflicting views? Is the elitist model now redundant? Or do councils vary as much in their approach to and relations with local groups as they do in so many other respects?

The notion that radical groups have either to modify their policies or else remain relatively powerless certainly needs some qualification. Many Labour authorities, for example, have encouraged groups that challenge the status quo, providing some of them with generous grants. Best known was probably the Greater London Council (GLC), where the Labour administration in the early 1980s increased grants to voluntary bodies to a massive £82 million by the time of its abolition in 1985–6. While many of the groups receiving grant aid were well established, a significant number – and certainly those highlighted in Conservative Central Office publicity – were 'anti-establishment' (Livingstone, 1987, p. 292):

- Abyssinian Society
- Babies Against the Bomb
- Black Female Prisoners Scheme
- English Collective of Prostitutes
- Gay Bereavement Project
- Gay London Police Monitoring Group
- Marx Memorial Library
- Rastafarian Advisory Centre
- Women's Peace Bus

Some of these groups received only a few hundred pounds, but the better-funded ones were often drawn into the delivery of services, thereby contributing to the radical policies supported by the GLC. The increased involvement of not-for-profit organisations in local service provision, though, is not confined to Labour or urban councils. The precise mix of groups involved in service delivery or consulted on policy by a particular council will obviously depend on that council's political make-up, as well as on local needs and the assertiveness and effectiveness of groups themselves. Councils will differ one from another in their own receptivity to groups, and they will also change over time.

Service delivery through grants and contracts

As already emphasised, the significance of local pressure groups has grown partly because of the way in which many groups now collaborate with local authorities in the provision of services. It is not easy to calculate exactly what proportion of their funding groups receive from local authorities, but a Charities Aid Foundation (CAF) survey produced a total figure of some £1.3 billion in 1996/97. As always, though, it is important to recognise that different councils, even of the same type, will have different policy agendas and different approaches to service delivery. Looking at district councils within Leicestershire, for example, while Leicester City Council in 1994/95 allocated over £8 million (14 per cent of its revenue budget) on grants to voluntary bodies, Oadby and Wigston DC's allocation was a mere £34,500 (0.8 per cent). Among West Midlands metropolitan districts, Birmingham awarded £22 million (2.4 per cent of its budget) while Dudley allocated £2.5 million (1.2 per cent). There are wide variations in practice, with county councils and big cities almost inevitably spending proportionately more than smaller district authorities; and also Scottish authorities tending to spend proportionately more and Welsh authorities less than their English counterparts (see Leach and Wilson, 1998).

As the scale of local authority funding has increased, its form has also changed — away from 'no strings attached' grants and towards negotiated *service level agreements*. This enables local group agendas to be increasingly shaped by local authorities, which was one of SHARP's concerns in Exhibit 16.3. ENVIRON too (see Exhibit 16.4) faced a comparable dilemma in seeking to pressurise the city council on traffic speed, street lighting and dog fouling.

Local authorities are thus approaching relationships with local groups in a more contractual manner (see Gaster and Deakin, 1998). This does not always sit happily with small groups or with the traditional local pressure group roles of advocacy, research and campaigning. Budgets, though, including those that go to local voluntary bodies and pressure groups, are bound to reflect the policy objectives of local authorities. Does this mean that only 'conformist' groups are likely to be considered for funding? Birmingham City Council notes on one of its grant forms: 'The purpose of giving financial assistance in the form of grants is to achieve an outcome desirable in the city.' Are groups with policies and outlooks at variance to those of the local authority effectively marginalized by such a policy?

Maloney *et al.* (2000) argue that in Birmingham a culture of patronage ensures that in some areas the city appears to be 'overloaded' with voluntary and community organisations, while others have very little coverage. 'Increasing financial restraint has seen smaller, community-level groups suffer disproportionately: survival has often been related to patronage.' They cite a senior manager in a local voluntary association:

> The City Council behaves like a big funding lord; voluntary organisations are the peasants – the Council do not want the voluntary sector to have autonomy. They want control. The voluntary sector is caged.

Tighter controls over grants and, more particularly, the advent of service level agreements are, potentially, constraining influences on local group activity.

Local policy networks

In local communities informal networks develop, linking commercial and industrial enterprises with the local council. Indeed, an apparent dearth of pressure group activity in a particular sector may be 'precisely because that interest is built into the very heart of the council itself' (Dearlove, 1979, p. 49). In even a former mining area the interests of the National Union of Mineworkers (NUM) are likely to permeate the local authority, just as in rural Norfolk agricultural interests will be prominently represented. Pressure group activity by these sectors may appear low key *because* their interests are being defended at every level of the local political system. As 'insiders' already, they have no need to 'go public'. Producer groups too – Chambers of Trade and Commerce, local branches of the Institute of Directors – may well have particularly close links with their respective local authorities, although closeness does not necessarily mean cordiality (see Stoker, 1991, p. 122). The obligation imposed by the 1984 Rates Act upon local councils to consult specifically with representatives of non-domestic ratepayers during their budget-making process led in at least some cases to acrimony rather than harmony.

In recent years local authorities have paid increasing attention to what has become known as their 'public service orientation' – recognising more pro-actively than they once did that they exist to provide services for the public. All councils nowadays thus use questionnaires and other devices to identify the needs and views of their residents about existing services and how they might be improved. This 'opening out' of debate about service delivery has to some extent gone hand in hand with the 'opening out' of the local pressure group world and the growing involvement of community and voluntary organisations in service delivery that we have described.

Conclusion – a more complex world

The world of local pressure groups and their interactive relations with local authorities were probably always more varied and complex than apparently simple classification schemes implied. Certainly that is the case today. Many councils, as we have seen, now create and maintain sizeable networks of voluntary and community groups that are likely to develop sufficient dynamism of their own to survive considerable political change on the part of their sponsoring councils.

For, in today's more fragmented world of local governance, local authorities are no longer the automatic hub of the local political system. Groups are increasingly – partly from necessity, partly from choice – finding sponsorship and support from other elected and non-elected agencies, as we saw, for instance, with ENVIRON (Exhibit 16.4) and its multi-source international, national and local funding.

At the same time, though, there have been several key legislative changes that have increased the dependence of local authorities on the voluntary sector to implement its programmes and deliver its services. Community Care is one obvious illustration. Cochrane (1993a p. 114) has highlighted the dilemma:

> Those voluntary organizations which look and operate most like businesses are likely to benefit most from these arrangements. Other smaller community-based organizations, often run by women who are the main users of the services involved, are in danger of being so dependent on financial support from councils that they find it hard to retain their autonomy.

There are no signs that such dilemmas will go away. Indeed, the increasingly specific grants and service level agreements offered to groups by local authorities promise to focus the issue even more sharply.

Guide to further reading

First, see if you can obtain from your own council details of their grant funding and formal links with outside groups and organisations. You will probably need to go, as we have, to individual departmental reports and to the council's yearbook. For pictures of other authorities see Jones (1969) on Wolverhampton; Hampton (1970) on Sheffield; Newton (1976) on 'the politics of the four thousand' in Birmingham; and Dearlove (1973) on Kensington and Chelsea – but remember our discussion of councils' changing attitudes. Gyford (1984) and Stoker (1991) discuss as well as classify local interest group activity, while Stoker and Wilson's journal article (1991) seeks to shed light on 'the lost world of local pressure groups'. A useful contribution to the literature is Baggott (1995), as, more recently, are several chapters in Stoker (ed.) (2000). Leach and Wilson (1998) focus on the advent of contracts; Maloney *et al.* (2000) provide some excellent contemporary material on pressure group activity in Birmingham.

Part 3

From Change to Modernisation

Chapter 17

Management Change

Introduction – local government's two fundamental functions

Let us take you right back to our introduction and our assumption that your previous experience of local government would probably have been as customers, consumers, clients and citizens. Our ordering of this short alliterative list was not accidental. The terms cover the two fundamental functions that local government – indeed, any government – performs: the *service* function and the *political* function (Boyle, 1986). It provides certain goods and services, and it is the setting in which the key questions concerning the public provision of those goods and services – their scale and distribution, their quality, cost and mode of financing – are argued out and resolved. Fundamental as both are, we have already suggested that it is the political function that is utterly indispensable. The service function can be – and has been – contracted out, wholly or partly privatised. Remove the political function, though, and what is left is not local government, but, at most, local administration.

The 'values or justifications' of local government itemised in Chapter 3 (Exhibit 3.1) clearly embrace both functions. But the focus of central government attention over most of the past two decades has been disproportionately on the service function – how to provide services more efficiently, more cheaply, more homogeneously, more competitively, more privately – while the political function has been relatively neglected. Put another way, the public, already inclined to think of councils more as service providers than as *their* local government, have been seen first as customers, consumers and clients for those services, and only secondarily as citizens.

This customer/citizen distinction serves as a useful backdrop to the final section of the book, which returns once more to the theme of change. We have two chapters in which to deal with some profound changes in the management of local government developed during – and substantially prompted by – national governments of two different parties. However, just as those parties' terms of office have – so far – been very unequal, so the division of our chapters is not a neat pre- and post-1997 one. Rather, we adopt the service/political distinction, which also, we suggest, makes broad sense chronologically.

The greater part of this chapter, therefore, will be about the radical managerial changes that took place during the Thatcher/Major years and that transformed hugely the way in which business is conducted and services are organised in town and county halls across the country. The most profound of these changes was CCT – Compulsory Competitive Tendering – which justified its own chapter in our previous edition (Wilson and Game, 1998, Ch. 19). Nearly five years on, though, it is more appropriately presented alongside other contemporary managerial trends and as a trail for its successor regime, Best Value services.

Best Value was one of the core planks in the New Labour Government's 'Modernisation Agenda' for local government. The Agenda as a whole is formidably comprehensive – even more so, arguably, than the three-part review of finance, structure and internal management launched in the early 1990s by John Major's Environment Secretary, Michael Heseltine (Wilson and Game, 1998, Chs 17–18). In particular, it has at its heart the programme of 'democratic renewal' that we encountered in Chapter 6, that seems to address local government's political function rather more directly and extensively than the more service-directed reforms of the Conservative era. The same concern is detectable in the split title of the Government's 2001 White Paper, *Strong Local Leadership – Quality Public Services*. There is an apparent interest in the public as voters, as members of communities, as consultees, as participants in service planning and delivery, as citizens, in addition to their role as service consumers. But, perhaps significantly, the legislation incorporating most of the democratic renewal programme – the Local Government Act 2000 – had to take second place to the 1999 Act that abolished CCT and introduced Best Value. Further delayed by the 2001 General Election, it is only being implemented as we write, which makes it a particularly appropriate topic for the book's concluding chapter.

CCT and the contract culture

Of all the changes introduced by the 1979–97 Conservative governments, the most far-reaching were surely those associated with CCT – particularly if it is seen, properly, as one dimension of the 'New Right' privatisation or contracting-out strategy of those governments. Essentially, the process required a comparison of the costs of continuing in-house provision of specified services with those of any interested private contractors and the award of the contract to the most competitive bidder. That meant the *lowest* bidder, and councils were prohibited from imposing conditions on such issues as trade union rights, employment protection, sickness benefit, pensions, training, and equal opportunities that might 'have the effect of restricting, distorting or preventing competition' (Local Government Act 1988, s.7(7)). Cost was always the ultimate criterion, rather than quality.

It must be emphasised that it was the *competitive tendering* – the cost comparison – that was made compulsory, *not* the contracting-out of the service, which might or might not eventuate, depending on the competing bids. If, after competition, no alternative bid was received or the in-house bid proved the lowest, the local authority would continue to provide the service, but in an organisationally different way. The part of the authority carrying out the service became known as a Direct Service Organisation (DSO) and these DSOs were obliged to maintain separate trading accounts which had to make a specified percentage surplus.

Three key pieces of legislation drove the CCT process, the first drafted within months of the Thatcher Government coming to power in May 1979 (Box 17.1). It sounds ideological and it was, owing much to the New Right 'think tanks' – the Adam Smith Institute, the Institute of Economic Affairs (IEA), and the Centre for Policy Studies (CPS). Their argument and that of likeminded politicians – notably Nicholas Ridley (1988) and Michael Forsyth (1982) – was that the contracting-out of services formerly provided monopolistically by central and local government or by agencies like the NHS would lead to both improved service provision and reduced costs. It would challenge the 'dependency culture' imbued by the Welfare State and would lead to less and smaller government. For local authorities it would mean them entering a brave new world of *sharing* the provision of services with a range of other bodies – private industrial and commercial concerns and voluntary organisations.

Those opposed to CCT, on the other hand, noted that it potentially reduced the role not only of elected and democratically accountable local authorities but also of trade unions. It was seen as – and obviously was –

Box 17.1 Driving the CCT process – key legislation

1. *The Local Government, Planning and Land Act 1980*, which introduced CCT for building construction and maintenance and highways construction and maintenance;
2. *The Local Government Act 1988*, which extended CCT to building cleaning; grounds maintenance; vehicle maintenance; school meals, welfare and other catering (e.g. staff canteens); refuse collection; street cleaning; plus sports and leisure management;
3. *The Local Government Act 1992*, which extended it beyond these technical services into housing management and many other mainly 'white collar' activities at the very heart of the local authority – legal, personnel, financial, IT services, etc.

part of the Government's comprehensive attack on trade union power and public sector pay bargaining and on the strong financial and institutional links between the public sector unions and the Labour Party. More tellingly, it was argued – and studies purported to show – that claimed cost savings from CCT came largely not from increased efficiency, but from cuts in employees' pay and conditions and from safety-challenging changes in working practices.

The impact of CCT – managerial and financial

As with many innovations, the immediate impact of CCT was not as dramatic as the more strident claims of either its proponents or opponents predicted. No near-universal 'takeover' by the private sector materialised, and the overall picture was very much what you should by now have come to expect – extremely varied from service to service and from one council to another. Some services were far more amenable to private sector bids than others, but only in building cleaning and construction were more than half of all contracts won by outside bidders. At the other end of the scale DSOs were successful in retaining at least three-quarters of contracts in leisure and housing management and legal services. In all services DSOs tended to win a disproportionate share of the larger contracts, so that while around 40 per cent of the total, they amounted to only around 25 per cent of the total contract value. In Scotland both those figures were significantly lower, but even in England and Wales more than one in every six authorities had no outside contracts at all. What the Labour Government inherited in 1997, therefore, was a mixed economy of in-house and external provision in a majority of authorities.

The financial savings or otherwise achieved by CCT were notoriously difficult to evaluate authoritatively. Annual cost savings were undoubtedly achieved – perhaps of around 8 per cent across the board – but neutral observers tended to suggest that these owed more to the introduction of competition than to the awarding of contracts to private firms. The major savings came from the reductions in the numbers of staff employed to do the work, often by 20–30 per cent, which happened even under DSO contracts. Then there were cases of service failure – some comic, others tragic (Wilson and Game, 1998, p. 349) – and councils' termination of contracts not being satisfactorily fulfilled. They were only ever a small proportion of the total, but, not surprisingly, termination was commoner among private sector contracts.

It might be imagined that, with the majority of larger contracts staying in-house, CCT left much of local government relatively unchanged. In fact, such an idea could hardly be further from the truth. Whether retaining or 'losing' contracts, all authorities had to adapt quite fundamentally their patterns of management and organisation in response to CCT. The major change was the need to separate the roles of client and contractor within the authority. *Clients* are those responsible for the specification and monitoring of services; *contractors* are those responsible for the direct production and delivery of the service. The separation of these roles can be made within a single department or by creating separate contractor departments.

Other managerial trends

The CCT story contains within it a certain irony. As we have seen, it certainly did not spell even the beginning of the end of local authorities as direct providers of services, and in one way it had almost the reverse effect. For, in presenting authorities with the challenge of winning contracts in-house, it encouraged them to streamline and strengthen their management systems so that they were better able to do precisely that. The client/contractor split and creation of internal markets were an important part of this managerial reform programme, but there were several other noteworthy strands too.

The customer service revolution

Without doubt, one of the most momentous developments in the public service in the past two decades has been what Skelcher has termed 'the service revolution' (1992): the proclaimed commitment to put customers first, or, at least, to label them 'customers' and then tell them they are being put first. Traditionally local authorities have had residents, tenants, clients and claimants *to* whom, rather than *for* whom, they provided services in the way and to the standards they felt most appropriate. Then, prompted to an extent by the private sector, came what was variously termed the *public service orientation* (PSO) or *customer care*. Councils gradually came to realise that these previously passive recipients of their services should be treated more as customers, with at least a voice, if not totally free choice, and an entitlement to be consulted and even actively involved in decision making.

The practical manifestations of a council's customer focus can be seen in a host of ways: user surveys and residents' questionnaires, advertised complaints procedures, service days, customer care training, neighbourhood forums, user groups, public question times at council meetings, and, perhaps most notably, *customer charters* and *service guarantees*. Charterism, and specifically the Citizen's Charter, has come to be associated with John Major, whose July 1991 White Paper, *The Citizen's Charter*, sought to empower the citizen as an individual service consumer, if not more ambitiously as a participant, in the process of local self-government. In fact, Major's initiative was predated both by the Labour Party's *Quality Street* policy review following the 1987 General Election, which included service guarantees with redress mechanisms and financial compensation, and also by a number of mainly Labour councils developing their own charters and customer contracts. Of these latter, York City Council's was one of the most interesting:

> not merely as an example of local government innovation anticipating a major central government initiative, but because of the way it attempts to weave together the concerns of citizens, customers and community. The commitment to citizenship – to people's *civic rights* as citizens of York – is explicitly stated in terms of rights to know; rights to be heard and to influence; rights to be treated honestly, fairly and courteously; rights to participate and be represented. These general civic rights are subsequently translated into practical entitlements, through, for example, the establishment of:
>
> – area committees where you can have your say about decisions affecting your neighbourhood;
> – special arrangements to involve some of the people who are not often listened to: people with disabilities and other special needs.
>
> (Prior, 1995, pp. 91–2, emphasis ours)

The Citizen's Charter movement, with its subsidiary charters for council tenants, parents and other groups, was part of local authorities' recognition that they should try to get 'closer' to those they served. At the very least, local charters clarify the nature of the relationship between an authority and its citizens by using the language of rights, entitlements and responsibilities which can be checked and monitored (Prior, 1995, p. 100). Essentially, though, they – like Labour's 1998 relaunch of the Citizen's Charter under the title *Service First* – are about a rather narrow, consumerist concept of citizenship, in which consumerist values are substituted for democratic ones.

Quality systems and quality assurance

If 'customer first' initiatives are to be more than pious rhetoric, there needs to be a genuine institutional commitment and capacity to translate them into service quality. This recognition prompted many authorities to develop quality control (QC), quality assurance (QA), and total quality management (TQM) systems, as means of improving their service quality. The three processes are clearly differentiated and discussed by Skelcher (1992, Ch. 8).

Quality control 'is an inspection and checking process which occurs *after* the service has been or is ready to be provided' (emphasis ours). Its purpose is to measure performance against pre-set standards and thereby identify any failure rate in the service provision. An example would be a post-repair tenant satisfaction survey. Knowledge of tenants' dissatisfaction will hopefully help improve the service next time.

Quality assurance is the attempt to stop the sub-standard service being provided in the first place. It involves designing delivery systems and procedures so that a certain standard of service can be guaranteed every time. Originally developed in the manufacturing sector, where product standards can be precisely measured and specified, QA does not translate easily into the local government world of personal service delivery. Nevertheless, the British Standards Institute (BSI) developed a recognised benchmark (BS 5750), against which local and NHS authorities could assess their QA systems and a number received accreditation. Developing an accreditable QA system can be a protracted and resource-intensive exercise, necessitating as it does the detailed codification of policies, procedures, performance standards and monitoring systems. On the other hand, confronted, say, with a case of alleged child abuse in a council residential home, it is not hard to see it as a worthwhile investment.

Total quality management can be seen as making service quality the driving force of the whole organisational culture of the authority – 'a way of involving the whole organisation; every department, every activity, every single person at every level' in the commitment to quality (Oakland, 1989, p. 14). Its demands are obviously immense, which is one reason why Stewart suggests that it 'is often an aspiration imperfectly realised or perhaps understood' (1996a, p. 19). As he adds, however, 'the search for quality remains important'.

Strategic management

Self-evidently, any authority aspiring to quality management requires a *strategic approach*, ensuring that its multiplicity of activities and policies are consistent and are all contributing to the corporate objectives and values. Increasingly, though, all authorities have come to see the need systematically to take stock of their activities in a constantly changing environment, and either set new directions or at least state some vision of where the authority will be in so many years' time and what it will be doing.

That, in essence, is what strategic management and planning are about: providing information and developing decision-making processes that enable elected members and officers alike to set priorities, direct their energies to key issues, and thereby develop a means of coping assertively with change. It can be contrasted to, and is a means of getting away from,

Exhibit 17.1 Strategic vs. operational management

Strategic management can:	... where operational management:
● Be long-term	● Is short-term
● Expose choices	● Reinforces continuities
● Be guided by political priorities	● Emphasises professional concerns
● Encourage the organisation to pause for thought before deliberation	● Produces a ceaseless treadmill of activities and routinised meetings
● Take account of the changing environment	● Is grounded in the organisation
● Be concerned with the impact of its activities	● Is concerned with getting activities done
● Look outwards to the network of community organisations	● Is limited by organisational boundaries
● See interrelationships between tasks	● Is centred on specific tasks

Source: Adapted from M. Clarke and J. Stewart, *Strategies for Success* (LGMB, 1991), p. 15.

the limitations of operational or reactive management, as indicated in Exhibit 17.1. It involves standing back from the everyday pressures of operational management and taking a broader, corporate, longer-term view of the authority and its function.

As an additional way of fostering strategic thinking and breaking down traditional departmental and professional boundaries, many authorities, as we noted in Chapter 16, have appointed *strategic directors*, who may oversee a number of combined departments, but who are freed from the day-to-day responsibility of departmental management. The intended outcome is a streamlined strategic management team, comprising the chief executive and strategic directors, who are better able to focus on major policy issues and secure co-ordination between services (see Griffiths, 1992).

Devolved, cost centre management

An almost necessary concomitant of strategic management is a devolution of actual management responsibility. If an authority's overall objectives and policies are to be achieved, they need to be translated into clearly defined targets or key tasks for individual managers. Somebody, in short, has to be accountable. But, to make their accountability meaningful, that person has to be given the necessary discretion to deploy financial and other resources in such a way as to attain the specified targets. The principle behind such devolved management is that it releases initiative among middle and junior managers who would previously have been constrained within a steep management hierarchy, and thereby leads to greater efficiency and, in the case of a local authority, a better quality service to the public.

The managerial logic is the same as that behind the Next Steps Initiative within the civil service, which has involved setting up separate units or executive agencies to perform the executive functions of government which were previously the responsibility of Whitehall departments. Next Steps Agencies – ranging from the massive Jobcentre Plus to the Vehicle Inspectorate, Royal Mint, and Public Record Office – remain part of the civil service, but, under the terms of individual framework documents, they have responsibility for their own financial, pay and personnel decisions. Similarly, cost centre managers, whether within a university or local authority, remain part of the corporate body, but have the authority to use the resources they have been allocated to achieve the key tasks and standards of performance with which they have been entrusted.

Performance management

The establishment of cost centres is likely to lead in turn to performance management (PM): the specification, measurement, and evaluation of the performance both of individuals and of the organisation. Tasks are devolved to cost centres and expressed in measurable terms, enabling the performance of the cost centre and the cost centre manager to be regularly reviewed, appraised, and then rewarded or penalised accordingly. Generally, when it is the organisation that is being evaluated, the term used is performance review (PR); when an individual, performance appraisal (PA).

But what, for a service-providing local authority, is 'performance'? For the Audit Commission, it meant the '3Es': Economy, Efficiency and Effectiveness (Box 17.2). It will be immediately apparent that any attempted measurement of these '3Es' is likely to be much more difficult for a political, sometimes monopolistic, multi-service delivering local authority than for a single-product, profit-maximising manufacturing company. At the very least, account has to be taken of the council's political values and objectives, which are likely to be considerably more complex than the maximisation of profit. There are obvious problems too in even defining, let alone measuring, outcomes of, say, the educational experience or some of the social services.

Controversial and provocative though they can prove, a wide selection of measures have been used over the years to assess aspects of council

Box 17.2 The '3Es'

- *Economy* – relates to *inputs*, and is concerned with minimising the cost of resources involved in producing any given standard of service.
- *Efficiency* – is concerned with the *relationship between inputs and outputs*. It is not, as is often wrongly supposed, a measure of cost, but of the relationship of output quantity and quality to the cost of inputs. It is about getting more or better for less: either minimising inputs in relation to outputs, or maximising outputs in relation to inputs, or both.
- *Effectiveness* – is also about a *relationship, between intended and actual outputs*, or, to put it slightly differently, between outputs and outcomes.

performance. As we saw in Chapter 9 (Exhibit 9.8), all councils are now required to produce for the Audit Commission and also to publish themselves dozens, even hundreds, of these Performance Indicators (PIs). In Exhibit 17.2 we list some of the commonest *types* of (PIs) and relate them to their corresponding Es.

Exhibit 17.2 Performance Indicators and the '3Es'

Type of indicator	Corresponding 'E'	Example
Cost indicators	Economy	Annual cost per aged person in residential accommodation
Productivity indicators	Efficiency	No. of library books issued per staff member per hour
Time targets	Efficiency and Effectiveness	Response time for dealing with grant application
Quality of service indicators	Effectiveness	Percentage of users/clients satisfied with the service
Demand for service indicators	Effectiveness	Numbers using a service
Availability of services	Effectiveness and Equity	Access to library service in different areas
Outcome of policy indicators	Effectiveness	Reduction of unemployment through operation of training scheme

Sources: Jackson and Palmer (1989), pp. 5–6; Fenwick (1995), p. 116.

New Labour – Best Value and performance plans

CCT had been opposed from the outset by Labour – by its shadow spokespersons in Parliament and even more vehemently by the steadily increasing numbers of Labour councils. Customer care, quality service, strategic and performance management, however financially and commercially driven you may consider them to be, are more difficult to argue against, and the New Labour Party being primed for government by Tony Blair had no inclination to try. The Party's 1997 manifesto made clear how, having transferred the first capital 'C' from competitive tendering to something called Best Value, it would work with and build upon some of the other parts of the New Public Management edifice (p. 34):

> Councils should not be forced to put their services out to tender, but will be required to obtain best value. We reject the dogmatic view that services must be privatised to be of high quality, but equally we see no reason why a service should be delivered directly if other more efficient means are available. Cost counts but so does quality.
>
> Every council will be required to publish a local performance plan with targets for service improvement, and be expected to achieve them. The Audit Commission will be given additional powers to monitor performance and promote efficiency. On its advice, government will where necessary send in a management team with full powers to remedy failure.

Within two months of taking office, John Prescott's new Department of the Environment, Transport and the Regions had issued '12 Principles of Best Value' (Wilson and Game, 1998, p. 350), which were followed up in early 1998 by one of the Government's six 'modernisation' consultation papers. This paper outlined the parameters of what was in fact a new duty on local authorities – to deliver services to clear standards by the most economic, efficient and effective means available (DETR, 1998c, para. 7.2):

> In carrying out this duty, local authorities will be accountable to local people and have a responsibility to central government in its role as representative of the broader national interest. Local authorities will set these standards – covering both cost and quality – for all services for which they are responsible. But in those areas such as education and social services, where the Government has key responsibilities and commitments, the Government itself will set national standards.

It was already clear to local government that, while it would be rid of the deeply unpopular CCT regime, Best Value would prove every bit as centrally prescriptive and potentially even more interventionist. It applied, moreover, to every single service and function.

Best Value in practice

CCT was repealed and the Best Value framework statutorily introduced in the Local Government Act 1999. The full BV regime, outlined in Exhibits 17.3 and 17.4, came into operation for all English local authorities in April 2000 and in Wales three months later. Well before that, though, the Government had launched an extensive pilot programme, in which some 40 authorities volunteered to apply Best Value (BV) on a test basis to various selected services, enabling there to be an early evaluation of its impact and an opportunity to disseminate advice and good practice.

The evaluation was undertaken by a team of independent consultants from Warwick Business School. Their final report (DETR, 2001) was not published until well after full implementation, but its findings were still revealing. On the positive side – and of course highlighted in ministerial press releases – the consultants concluded that the BV framework does have the potential to drive service improvement and they gave several examples from the pilot authorities of both service improvements and cost savings (Box 17.3). The evaluation report also, however, highlighted some serious difficulties, not all of which can brushed aside as teething problems. The pilot authorities proved far better at comparing and consulting than at the other two Cs – challenging and competing. Few were found to have examined rigorously the underlying need for a service, as opposed to thinking up ways of improving it. Competition too was a tough requirement, particularly for those authorities strongly committed to in-house provision, who hoped that the disappearance of CCT had seen the end of having to compete constantly with the private sector.

Elected members, at least at this early pilot stage, seemed generally disengaged from the whole BV exercise and particularly from the preparation of BV Performance Plans. These tended to be seen as documents

---

Box 17.3 Some early BV service improvements

- Camden's productivity gains helped provide an extra 70,000 hours of extra social care over two years at no extra cost;
- Portsmouth Council was able to teach twice as many dyslexic children as before and to a higher standard;
- Greenwich made major improvements in its social transport services, reflected in a large fall in the number of complaints from service users;
- Newark and Sherwood DC made £150,000 savings in the cost of administering its housing repair service;
- Lewisham LBC made efficiency savings of £500,000 in its revenue and benefits service.

Exhibit 17.3 Best Value – what it is, how it works

BV's key purpose – to make a real and positive difference to the services that people receive from their local authority

How? By requiring councils to make arrangements – in the form of an annual BV Performance Plan (BVPP) and regular service-specific and cross-cutting Reviews – to secure *continuous improvement* in the way they undertake *all their service responsibilities*, having regard to their economy, efficiency and effectiveness. Councils must review all their services every 5 years to ensure they are applying continuous improvement principles.

BV Performance Plans – assess existing performance, set future targets, and outline the authority's programme of BV Reviews; the principal means by which an authority is held to account for the efficiency and effectiveness of its services and for its plans for the future.

BV Reviews – in reviewing all services on a 5-year cycle, an authority should follow the 4Cs:

- **Challenge** why, how, and by whom a service is being provided and be able to show that alternative approaches to service delivery have been considered;
- **Compare** its performance with that of similar authorities across a range of relevant national and local indicators, taking into account the views of both service users and potential suppliers;
- **Consult** local taxpayers, service users, external partners and the wider community in setting new and demanding performance targets and an action plan that will deliver continuous improvements;
- **Compete**, wherever practicable, in order to secure efficient and effective services.

Review questions would typically include:

- *What* does the service do now?
- *How well* does it do it, and for what cost?
- *What* do its customers want of it?
- *How well* does it do it in comparison with others?
- *Could* the benefits of the service be obtained in some other way?
- *Could* some other organisation provide it better and/or cheaper than the council?
- *Can* we do the job better (and by how much)?
- *Can* we make customers happier (and by how much)?
- *How* can we get the same benefits to the people while spending significantly less?
- *Should* we be providing the service at all?

Inspection – all functions of an authority are subject to inspection at least once every 5 years by either an existing special inspectorate – e.g. OFSTED, the Social Services Inspectorate, the Benefit Fraud Inspectorate – or by the Audit Commission's Best Value Inspectorate. All inspection reports are published (see Exhibit 17.4) – over 1,000 by 2001/02.

Failing services – the Secretary of State has wide-ranging powers to intervene where an authority is judged by inspectors not to be delivering a BV service, and ultimately to remove responsibility for the 'failing' service from the authority altogether.

Exhibit 17.4 An Inspector Calls – Some Best Value inspections, 2001   (www.bestvalueinspections.gov.uk)

BV Inspections – score each service/function on two 4–point scales:

- *Quality of the service*: poor = no stars; fair = 1 star; good = 2 stars; excellent = 3 stars;
- *Prospects for improvement*: no; unlikely; probably; yes.

The good, the bad and the ugly

1. *Herefordshire Council – Homelessness and Housing Advice Service*
   Excellent 3-star service that will probably improve
   Good features – accessible service to rural, dispersed community through network of offices and outreach services; maximum use of Council's own well-maintained accommodation, rather than bed and breakfasts; excellent reception facilities, all offices wheelchair-accessible, with toys for children and enthusiastic staff; positive approach to victims of domestic violence; vacant properties let in less than two weeks on average; regular inspection of hostels and other accommodation.
   Likely improvements – more direct support for clients with additional needs in temporary accommodation; collect more monitoring information on issues of disability, race, gender and ethnicity; improved equal opportunities training for staff and elected members.

2. *Bedfordshire CC – Library Service*
   A good 2-star service that will probably improve
   Good features: responsiveness to public priorities of extended opening hours (incl. Sundays) and IT access; good core book-lending and enquiry service; facilities for children – eg homework centres in especially deprived wards, with welcoming, interactive staff; positive work with disabled through Library Link service; provision of other-language newspapers and free internet access for recent refugees; libraries mostly bright and welcoming (except Bedford Central); good user satisfaction ratings.

prepared by officers for the benefit of external auditors, rather than the product of what might be expected to be an intensely political debate about values, priorities and resource allocation. Councillors and officers alike were critical of the costs and time that the new regime seemed to demand, and there was extremely widespread antipathy to the inspections – hardly surprisingly, when over 60 per cent of the first wave of inspected services were judged either poor or fair, with the poorest services also frequently reckoned the least likely to improve. It was significant, therefore, that one of the first post-election pronouncements of the new Local Government Minister, Nick Raynsford, conceded explicitly the need to

Likely improvements: increase usage and take-up by black and ethnic minority communities, by relevant welcome signs, displays and promotional material; rely less on user surveys and develop more informal user groups.

3. *Brighton and Hove City Council – Cross-cutting review of Public Access*
   A fair 1-star service with promising prospects for improvement
   Good features: adoption of drive to improve public access as one of Council's core values; piloting of one-stop shops as way of tackling social exclusion; organisation of internet website around 'life events' better than classifying information under departmental headings.
   Improvements needed: variable opening hours for council services can confuse public; over-reliance on voicemail in some areas of council; most council buildings not accessible to disabled customers; staff dealing with public not always replaced when they leave, because of council's 'difficult' financial situation.

4. *Castle Morpeth BC – Housing Maintenance and Capital Programme*
   A poor, no star service, unlikely to improve
   Poor features: no formal maintenance appointments system, too many jobs done on 'urgent' basis; no effective monitoring of contractors' performance; council's 'over-ambitious' modernisation programme will take 100 years to complete, which 'falls a long way short of tenants' aspirations'; unco-ordinated maintenance programmes lead to inefficient use of scarce resources; no regular and systematic customer feedback sought; no tenant involvement in development of services or in BV review.
   Improvements unlikely: because no effective system of performance management with tenant involvement yet in place; low staff morale; 'departmentalism' hinders corporate and co-operative working; concerns about capacity of council to drive through the level of change and continuous improvement required by BV.

streamline the 'over-bureaucratic' BV inspection process and move 'away from rather limited service-focused inspections' (*Local Government Chronicle*, 22 June, 2001).

The message from Scotland was harsher still. There, all 32 unitary authorities, rather than selected 'pilots', were obliged to operate a BV regime earlier than in England. Any beneficial influence of BV on service standards, early observers concluded (Midwinter and McGarvey, 1999, p. 99), was outweighed by the constraint on organisational performance of the level of financial resources, which 'remains unaddressed' in Scotland – as, effectively, it does in England and Wales.

Beacons of light and PSAs

Best Value was New Labour's comprehensive assault on local government service provision, applying to all functional responsibilities of all councils. It was backed up, though, by plenty of other more selective initiatives, one of which was Beacon Councils (Exhibit 17.5) – a scheme for identifying excellent performance in individual local councils and disseminating news of that performance to the rest of local government through open days, publications, conferences and the like.

Keen to be seen as vanguard 'modernisers', over half of all English and Welsh authorities nominated themselves for beacon recognition in the first round of applications, 42 of whom were eventually successful in the seven selected service areas. One of the 'winners' was Wakefield MDC, which won beacon status for a social services partnership project with the children's charity, Barnardo's, designed to give care leavers a better start in life. The Council's leader, Peter Box, was clearly taken with the new accolade: 'Being chosen as a Beacon Council is a huge boost for the whole district and means our exceptional best practice has been nationally recognised.'

By implication, not being chosen, or perhaps even shortlisted, must have come as a major disappointment, which may explain the subsequent rather sharp drop in applications. By the third round (2002/03), the initial 269 applications from 211 bidding councils had fallen to 131 applications from 94, which at least increased the chances of recognition. Beacons, however, received no specific mention in Labour's 2001 manifesto, which suggested that another initiative for rewarding high-performing councils, Local Public Service Agreements (PSAs – see Exhibit 17.6), would play a relatively more prominent role in the future:

> We want to give successful local councils more leeway to meet local needs using a £400 million reward fund. We have piloted local public service agreements to offer new investment and greater financial flexibility in return for higher performance. We will extend this reform to all upper-tier councils. We will offer further flexibility for high-performance authorities, with reformed inspections and more local discretion to encourage civic renewal (p. 34).

Labour Mark II – a change of focus?

The 2001 election was followed by an immediate reshuffle of departmental responsibilities and ministerial portfolios. Stephen Byers and Nick Raynsford replaced John Prescott and Hilary Armstrong as, respectively, Secretary of State and Minister responsible for local government. Both new

Exhibit 17.5 Beacon Councils and the IDeA

What are Beacon Councils (BCs)? Councils formally recognised by government as 'best performers' in a particular service area, who can be used, during the year in which they hold beacon status, to disseminate best practice to other authorities. In exchange, they may be allowed to test new freedoms and flexibilities that might subsequently be applied to local government more widely.

Other beacon schemes – there are also beacon schools and NHS beacons that operate on the same principle: they are supposed to set the pace of change and act as centres of excellence by spreading best practice and sharing their expertise. The aim of BCs is to raise service quality by enabling all councils to learn from the best.

The beaconising process

- Each year, Ministers from across government select *themes* in service areas that have a direct impact on the quality of life of local people. Councils apply, either singly or jointly, under the themes where they can demonstrate that an excellent service is being provided.

  The 11 themes for the 3rd Round of Beacons (2002/03) included Adoption, Better Access and Mobility, Crime Reduction in Rural Areas, and Libraries as a Community Resource.

- Councils are shortlisted, principally by an expert 10-member Advisory Panel on BCs, supported by the BC team of civil servants in the DTLR. Shortlisted councils are then visited and assessed, and final recommendations for beacon status are made to Ministers by the Advisory Panel. There are usually about 40 BCs at any one time.

- To be selected, a BC must show:
  - *Excellence* in a beacon theme;
  - *Good* general performance
  - *Plans for effective dissemination* – e.g. showcase events, open days, workshops, seminars, mentoring opportunities, etc.

Dissemination and the IDeA – throughout the dissemination process councils work closely with the *Improvement and Development Agency (IDeA)*. The IDeA was formed in 1999 by the Local Government Association (LGA) as one of the two successor organisations to the LGMB (Local Government Management Board – not 'Loser Geeks and Misery Bitches'!).

The *Employers' Organisation* took over LGMB's pay negotiating role, IDeA its management and development role – though, under its first executive director, Mel Usher, in an unrecognisably more dynamic style. In addition to supporting the BC scheme, IDeA runs a voluntary Peer Review Programme for councils, undertaking reviews of councils as a 'critical friend', rather than a regulatory inspector; runs elected member and manager development programmes; and has a useful website to compensate for its computer-unfriendly acronym.

Exhibit 17.6 Local Public Service Agreements (PSAs)

What are they? A particular form of central-local partnership between the Government and *individual* local authorities, involving specific shared local performance goals, government help in achieving them, and cash rewards for success – 'something for something' agreements, as the Government described them.

The 3-part PSA sets out:

- The authority's commitment to deliver, within about three years, a dozen or so *specific and measurable improvements in service performance, over and above* any targets in its BV Performance plan. The improvement targets, as well as being 'stretching', should be defined as precisely as possible and in terms of *outcomes*, not outputs or inputs. They should comprise both national and local priorities, but must include at least one relating to each of the national priorities of education, social services and transport.
- The Government's commitment to help the authority achieve these agreed improvements, by providing interim 'pump-priming' grants and possibly allowing scope for extra borrowing.
- The Government's commitment to pay the authority extra Performance Reward Grants if/when the performance improvements are verifiably attained.

History and significance: 20 authorities concluded pilot PSAs in 2000/01, and, having been highlighted in Labour's 2001 manifesto, they have been extended to all top-tier authorities and constitute a central element in the Government's evolving modernisation agenda.

An example – Birmingham City Council's PSA (2001–04)

The Government will pay 'pump-priming' grants of £1,050,000 in 2001/02 to cover the Council's increased expenditure involved in implementing the PSA. If all 12 targets are met in full, the Council will receive extra Performance Reward Grants of nearly £28 million by 2005/06.

The Council's performance commitments include:

- to increase the percentage of 14–year olds at level 5 in key Stage 3 tests e.g. in English from 57 per cent in 2000 to 71 per cent in 2003, instead of 68 per cent without the PSA;
- to increase the percentage of pupils obtaining 5 or more GCSEs at grades A* to C from 38 per cent in 2000 to 50 per cent in 2003, instead of 47 per cent without the PSA;
- to increase the percentage of children leaving care with 5 GCSEs at grades A* to C from 1 per cent in 2000 to 17 per cent in 2003 instead of 15 per cent without the PSA;
- to reduce incidence of accidental fires, fire-related injuries and deaths in the home e.g. accidental fires from 1,453 in 2000 to 1,207 in 2004, instead of 1,245 without the PSA;
- to increase amount of waste recycled and composted from 8.4 per cent in 2000 to 17 per cent in 2004, instead of 12 per cent without the PSA;
- to increase the percentage of council transactions available electronically and increase the numbers of online services in libraries e.g. e-transactions from 10 per cent in 2000 to 100 per cent in 2004, instead of 70 per cent without the PSA.

ministers had served previously as councillors and they at least presented their plans for reform in rather more tempered and less interventionist language than their predecessors. A key early policy document was the December 2001 White Paper, *Strong Local Leadership – Quality Public Services*. Almost echoing some of our own observations in Chapters 8–10, the White Paper (DTLR, 2001a, paras. 4.2–4.4) acknowledged just how strangulating had become the micro-management of central government controls:

> over inputs (e.g. by controlling borrowing, and ring-fencing resources), processes (by requiring the production of plans or establishment of partnerships) and decisions.

Over the years, the cumulative effect has become significant:

- the level of ring-fenced [specific] grant is in danger of rising to levels that seriously restrict councils' financial room for manoeuvre;
- councils are now required to produce some 66 separate plans and strategies, with top-tier councils alone required to produce more than 40;
- the Regional Co-ordination Unit has identified some 30 key initiatives targeted at deprived areas and neighbourhoods.

This accumulation of central requirement and initiatives can become counter-productive.

The White Paper promised that in future the Government would shift its focus from controls on inputs, processes and local decisions to assuring delivery of outcomes through a national framework of standards and accountability. Furthermore (paras 4.6–4.7):

> Over the course of this Parliament we will give councils more space to innovate, to respond in ways that are appropriate to local circumstances, and to provide more effective leadership. We will provide greater freedom for councils to borrow, invest, trade, charge and set spending priorities.

Though few of these 'freedoms' – possessed already by principal authorities in most purportedly democratic countries – came with timescales attached, several of them are potentially significant and have been touched on earlier in this book. They include (Ch. 4):

- *Abolition of credit approvals for capital investment,* and their replacement by a local 'prudential' regime under which individual authorities decide how much they can afford to borrow – subject, of course, to 'Government reserve powers';
- *Greater freedom to supply and charge for goods and services* to others in the public, private and voluntary sectors;

- *Restriction of ring-fenced grants* to 'cases which are genuine high priorities for Government';
- *Reduction in the numbers of plans required of local authorities, and of area-based initiatives (ABIs).*

More goodies – for the good children

The motivational theory is that, released from some of these long-term constraints, most, if not all, councils will become more innovative, entrepreneurial, and generally better service deliverers. That is no reason, though, to abandon performance management; quite the contrary. The 2001 White Paper (para. 3.12) conceded that, as well as too many controls, plans and initiatives, there were also too many overlapping performance measurement frameworks. As Faith Boardman discovered on her first day as Lambeth's Chief Executive (Exhibit 13.4), 'the cumulative effect of these can be an overload of confusing measures and a loss of focus on priorities'.

Again, the White Paper pledged (paras 3.13–3.15), the future would be different – though not, apparently, for backsliders. There would be 'a more coherent and integrated system of performance measures' across the whole range of local services, based on a national PSA for local government.

> In partnership with local government and other stakeholders, we will aim to put in place a framework in which there are:
>
> - defined standards focused on priority areas identified in the national PSA; and
> - clear criteria against which performance can be assessed for each defined standard.
>
> All authorities will be assessed against [these standards] through inspections and comprehensive performance assessments. Where councils fail to deliver, they will be expected to put things right. Where necessary, the Government will take decisive remedial action.

The comprehensive assessments, based obviously on BV experience and, noticeably, the judgements of collections of people *not* in any way involved in the locality – inspectors, auditors, civil servants, ministers – would be 'a cornerstone of the Government's performance framework'. They would provide Government, councils and the public 'with a *clear performance profile* for each council' (para. 3.17) – or a single, rather facile, and potentially destructive label, depending on your viewpoint. All councils would be sorted into one of four categories – high performers, strivers, coasters, and poor performers – and would, or would not, be rewarded with various 'additional freedoms' – see Exhibit 17.7.

Exhibit 17.7 High performers, low performers, strivers and coasters

Comprehensive performance assessments: In its second term of office the Labour Government intends to move towards a more coherent and integrated system of performance measurement, in which all councils will be assigned to one of four categories. Those in the higher categories will be rewarded with 'additional freedoms', over and above those deregulations promised to all councils.

- **High performers** – high performance in the Government's priority service areas (education, social care, transport), no poorly performing services, and a proven capacity to improve.
  Possible additional freedoms: less ring-fencing of non-educational grants; freedom from threat of capping; more freedom to use income from fines; further reductions in plan requirements; reduction in ring-fencing of capital investment.

- **Strivers** – not top performers, but with proven capacity to improve.
  Possible additional freedoms: a 'lighter touch' inspection regime; more discretion over BV review programmes; more freedom to trade in areas of high performance.

- **Coasters** – not top performers, and limited or no proven capacity to improve.
  Possible additional freedoms: like other councils, through their local PSAs, plus support for 'capacity building' in areas of weakness; more freedom to trade in areas of strong performance.

- **Poor performers** – consistently near bottom of performance spectrum, with limited or no proven capacity to improve.
  Possible additional freedoms: not much, and plenty of additional monitoring and intervention to tackle corporate or service weaknesses – including transfer of functions to other providers and placing the council into the hands of Government-appointed administrators.

Both their detailed content and the language in which these categorisations are presented are fascinatingly revealing of the centre's view of what the Prime Minister, in his Foreward to the 2001 White Paper, repeatedly refers to as the '*partnership* between central and local government' (emphasis ours). This partnership, evidently, is one between parents, striving belatedly to make amends for years of authoritarian child abuse which even they now recognise may have been excessive, and their wayward teenage children, who they are certain will seriously misbehave immediately their backs are turned. Quite unfit, in their parents' eyes, to be treated as adults, these children can be controlled only by playing them off against each other – offering bribes to the brown-nosers and resorting again to violent threats for the others.

The 'bribes' too are instructive – of the demeaning nature of the control regime within which local councils now operate: *not* having discretion to spend their own income from fines, or to buy and sell services from each other, or to decide at what rate to tax their own residents and voters. The financial sections of the 2001 White Paper (Part II) made it clear that there would be no significant change in:

- the central–local balance in the funding of local revenue expenditure – with the centre contributing at least three-quarters;
- ministers' retention of their council tax- and expenditure-capping powers;
- business rates remaining a national tax;
- councils' right to raise revenue from additional forms of local taxation.

The phrase used by ministers in advance of the White Paper for the 'reward' of new freedoms and flexibilities to high-performing councils was 'earned autonomy'. It features less prominently in the White Paper itself – advisedly, recalling our own discussion of 'partial autonomy' in Chapter 2. In our system of government, local authorities can never be autonomous or the equal partners of central government; this latest concession of strictly limited 'freedoms' simply emphasises the constitutional imbalance of the relationship.

Conclusion – the primacy of the consumer

Diligent readers may have noted that the word 'citizen' disappeared completely from this chapter after about the first third. The changes and initiatives described have all been about what we termed the service function of local government and about our relations with our local councils purely as service users and consumers. Because of this thematic continuity, we moved straight from the New Public Management (NPM) innovations of the Thatcher/Major Conservative Governments to those parts of New Labour's 'modernisation agenda' that adopted, adapted and, in some cases, overturned them. The overturnings are important, confirming that there are some notable *dis*continuities between the Blair Government's approach to service delivery and that of its predecessors, as Martin (1999b) identifies:

- it conspicuously addresses a cross-cutting agenda – e.g. in the areas of crime and social exclusion;
- there is a more pro-active and pragmatic style of policy-making – more experimental, more concern with 'evidence-based' policy;
- policy development is both more risk-taking, in its openness to new methods of service delivery, and less risk-taking, with its much heavier reliance on the piloting and evaluation of new schemes.

A further change, as we noted in our introduction, is that Labour's modernisation agenda has a major additional governmental element to it – its democratic renewal programme, addressed to our role as citizens, as well as consumers. That is the subject of Chapter 18.

Guide to further reading

There are several useful evaluations of CCT and the other market-driven policies of the Conservative Governments, a couple of which (Stewart and Stoker, eds, 1995 and Leach, Davis *et al.*, 1996) enable us to mention the inimitable contributions of our late INLOGOV colleague, Kieron Walsh, who is still, academically and personally, sorely missed. Horton and Farnham (1999) deal comprehensively with 'the New Public Management'. Boyne (ed.) (1999) recounts the transition from CCT to BV, and Martin (2000), who led the pilot evaluation team, has produced a good early overview of BV. Labour's modernisation agenda is probably best followed through the succession of consultation papers, Acts, and advisory guides to local authorities, all of which are on the DTLR's website. Stoker's paper (1999b) contains a useful synthesis of the agenda. As its full title implies, Atkinson and Wilks-Heeg's volume (2000) has an interesting slant on several of the topics in this chapter, and, indeed, in others.

Chapter 18

Democratic Renewal?

Introduction – the neglected political function

In Chapter 6 we suggested that the changes taking place in the day-to-day political management of our town and county halls were of such a magnitude and broke so fundamentally with long-standing previous practice that they might be claimed to constitute a minor revolution. At the heart of these changes were the new structures and processes of executive local government – directly elected mayors, cabinets, council managers, council constitutions, overview and scrutiny committees, standards committees. All these were being debated, consulted about, voted on, introduced, and adapted to in the opening years of the twenty-first century as the 'democratic renewal' part of Labour's modernisation agenda took legislative and institutional shape. In 2001/02 the revolution was still in progress, its eventual impact still unknowable – hence the question mark in the title of this chapter. The chapter, therefore, is inevitably a kind of stock-taking snapshot of the reforms – not all, by any means, to do with political management – affecting primarily local government's *political* function, rather than its service function.

This political function, we suggested, had been comparatively neglected in the welter of managerial changes of the 1980s and 1990s. There were, however, exceptions. One Conservative minister in particular, Michael Heseltine, was seriously interested in modernising what he saw as councils' antiquated and inefficient political processes, and it is with his initiatives in the early 1990s that we open. But few of the minister's colleagues shared his enthusiasm, and it was left to an assortment of others to pick up the baton of reform – the Commission for Local Democracy, the House of Lords, and, latterly, the then opposition Labour Party and its leader, Tony Blair. Ultimately, of course, it was only Labour's interest that mattered, and the bulk of this chapter outlines the evolution and stuttering progress of what has come to be known as democratic renewal.

Forerunners of democratic renewal – the mayorists and the experimentalists

The 1990s opened with the arrival of a new Prime Minister, John Major, and a new Environment Secretary, Michael Heseltine, whose challenge to

350

Mrs Thatcher's leadership had been responsible for the change of Premiers. Mr Heseltine immediately launched a wide-ranging review of the local government system, focusing on finance, structure, and internal management. Finance meant the abolition of the poll tax, as swiftly and unembarrassingly as possible (see Chapter 10). Structure meant the spread of unitary authorities, although in England nothing like as extensively as the government initially intended (see Chapter 5). Internal management meant, to Michael Heseltine, separate executives and preferably elected mayors.

He wanted to raise the fundamental questions about the political operation of UK local government that the Widdicombe Committee had left dormant. He challenged the 'British model', the committee system, in which policy was made openly and corporately by the elected council, working through committees with delegated powers but no independent authority, and on the advice of officers serving the council as a whole, not, as in the civil service, just the majority party and its leadership. Consequently, his 1991 consultation paper, *The Internal Management of Local Authorities in England* (DoE, 1991b), put forward a range of alternative models, most of which involved replacing the committee system with some form of either elected or appointed separate executive – including directly elected mayors – thus splitting the executive and representational roles of the council (Wilson and Game, 1998, pp. 332–4).

Local government's reception of the minister's consultation paper was barely lukewarm. Councillors were predictably unimpressed by any 'streamlining' of the decision-making process that would a result in a reduction in the numbers of elected members, and there was also a notable vagueness about how some of the alternative models would actually operate. The government's next move, therefore, was to set up a departmental working party, which produced in 1993 a report entitled *Community Leadership and Representation: Unlocking the Potential* (DoE, 1993), the potential in question being that of councillors (Wilson and Game, 1998, pp. 335–6). Councillors' roles should be strengthened and they should be better supported, better trained, and more adequately remunerated. Councils should review their internal management arrangements and at least consider the merits of more radical models, the piloting of a diverse range of which should be actively encouraged by the government.

In the hands of Michael Heseltine, the Department of the Environment's working party report might have produced some useful experiments from which central and local government alike could have learned. By the time it was published, however, even his successor as Environment Secretary, Michael Howard, had come and gone and ministerial interest had largely evaporated. Others, though, were more stimulated.

From academia, Stoker and Wolman (1991, 1992) drew on US experience and claimed that such mayors in the United Kingdom could provide a focal point and driving force for a more dynamic and influential local government. The mayoral system, they argued, produces a high-profile figure whom the public can identify and hold to account. Stoker was also one of the members of the independent Commission for Local Democracy (CLD), whose 1995 report advocated a separate executive headed by a directly elected mayor:

> We believe that revitalising local democracy demands that the ASSEMBLY and the EXECUTIVE be separated. They should be clearly distinguishable in the public mind, and the executive should derive its own democratic legitimacy at the ballot box (para. 4.3, emphasis in the original).
>
> This proposal is designed to attack head-on the central weaknesses of local government in Britain. These we have identified as low turnout at elections; citizen ignorance of local politics and leadership; the gap between formal and informal accountability for decisions; excessive party involvement in local elections; too much councillor time spent on management, not enough on representation and scrutiny. (para. 4.4)
>
> There are many models for a directly elected executive structure in local government. Our proposal is for one in which the Leader/Mayor heads the administration of the Authority and appoints its senior officers, but is subordinate to the Council in so far as the latter has control over the budget and the broad policy plan. The Leader/Mayor must negotiate with the Council for resources and thus for general policy approval. (para. 4.9)

Two schools of reformist argument were developing. Both favoured a separation of powers, but, while one school strongly supported a separate executive headed by a single individual – a directly elected mayor – the other, represented by the DoE working party, preferred diversity and experimentation. Lord Hunt of Tanworth was definitely an experimentalist. He had chaired an influential all-party House of Lords Select Committee on Relations between Central and Local Government (1996), which, among other things, had been severely critical of the steady erosion of powers experienced by local government during the 1980s and 1990s (Wilson and Game, 1998, pp. 114–15). In early 1997 Lord Hunt introduced a Local Government (Experimental Arrangements) Bill, which would implement one of the key recommendations of his Select Committee.

As advocated by the DoE working party, the Bill would allow local authorities to apply to the Secretary of State for permission to pilot, for up to 8 years, alternative decision-making structures and arrangements that would be likely to lead to decisions being taken more efficiently, accountably and transparently. They should also include provisions for members of the authority to scrutinise the exercise of any functions to which the new arrangements related. Legislative authority would be required, and the

Secretary of State would make an Order, temporarily modifying existing legislation to enable approved schemes to proceed.

Several possible sets of arrangements were put forward, each capable of being implemented in a variety of different ways:

- *a formal single-party advisory committee*, to make recommendations to the authority as a whole;
- a *single-party executive committee* with responsibility for certain decisions and the overall strategy of the authority;
- *a lead-member system*, with responsibilities delegated to individual councillors;
- *a cabinet system*, combining executive responsibilities for lead members with others performed jointly by the executive committee of which they are members;
- *an executive mayor – directly or indirectly elected* – with executive responsibilities that could be delegated to either lead members or a mayor-appointed cabinet.

Introduced at the same time as Labour leaders were putting the final touches to the party's 1997 manifesto, Lord Hunt's Bill seemed closely to reflect the party's own thinking about the value of learning from experimentation (p. 34):

> We will encourage democratic innovations in local government, including pilots of the idea of elected mayors with executive powers in cities.

The sting, though, was in the tail; as New Labour's modernisation agenda took shape, the experimentalists would soon turn into mayorists.

The New Labour approach – modernise our way or else!

New Labour's approach to local government became clear within weeks of the government taking office. As characterised in Chapter 9 (Figure 9.2), it was one of sticks and carrots, or, to put it as positively as possible, carrots and sticks (Game, 2000). Led by Deputy Prime Minister and Environment Secretary John Prescott, ministers were keen from the outset to emphasise their genuine belief in and commitment to a strong, democratically elected local government. Things would be very different under Labour from the constraint and marginalisation that councils had suffered under the Conservatives. After years of Vitamin A deprivation, carrots would be available again – in the form of the 'freedoms and flexibilities' we encountered in Chapter 17. But they, as ministers in the popularly elected national government, would be the ones deciding just *how* things would be different – and what would happen if councils attempted to resist change in the way that some had tried to do under the Conservatives. And change there would have to be, before any carrots were distributed at all, for, as the first of the new government's six consultative Green Papers spelled out, several aspects of local government's current operation and performance were not to be tolerated.

Turnouts in local elections were far too low, reflecting people's general apathy about local democracy; councillors worked hard, but unproductively; committees spent too much time on details, not enough on essentials; councillors were unrepresentative of their local electorates.

It was, obviously, a one-sided centralist critique. Few neutral observers, for instance, would nominate Parliament as a model of modernity, efficiency or productivity. MPs and ministers, though slightly younger on average than councillors, are in most other respects – and certainly in their gender balance – even less socio-economically representative of their constituents. And, as we saw in June 2001, those constituents are not exactly queuing in the streets to vote for them either. They, however, were the governors, and they called the shots.

Local government must modernise, they decreed, in accordance with their agenda, which involved:

> a radical programme of *democratic renewal*, enabling local authorities to *engage directly* with their communities, to whom they should be able to provide *visionary leadership*, while working *in partnership* with other agencies, companies and organisations, guaranteeing by these means, *Best Value services* for all, and a system of local government characterised by the *highest standards of conduct*. (DETR, 1998b, emphasis ours)

Councils responding positively to this agenda would earn the right to work in partnership with government, delivering on its mandate to 'modernise' Britain. There may even be more material 'carrots' in the form of a relaxation of certain financial controls and a greater freedom of action. But the 'sticks' are an equally important part of the deal, as the Prime Minister himself emphasised (Blair, 1998, pp. 20, 22):

> Where councils show that they can embrace this agenda of change and show that they can adapt to play a part in modernising their locality, then they will find their status and power enhanced. [But] if you are unwilling or unable to work to the modern agenda, then the government will have to look to other partners to take on your role.

The commitment to democratically elected local government, then, was a qualified one. Councils judged to be failing or simply recalcitrant could be stripped of key powers and see them handed over to unelected business or voluntary organisations – akin in its impact less to a stick of wood than a stick of dynamite.

Democratic renewal

As will by now be apparent, the term 'modernisation' has come to refer to the full catalogue of local government reforms proposed by New Labour in its 1998 consultation papers (DETR, 1998b–f) and in an ensuing White Paper, *Modern Local Government: In Touch with the People* (1998a). The catalogue would include the service improvement schemes outlined in Chapter 17 – Best Value, Beacon Councils, Local PSAs – partnership working (see Chapter 8), electronic government, financial reforms, as well as the discrete set of proposals under the banner of 'democratic renewal'.

Democratic renewal was the collective heading for the radical changes felt to be required if councils were to engage effectively with and provide 'visionary leadership' for their local communities. More specifically, as itemised in the first consultation paper, *Modernising Local Government: Local Democracy and Community Leadership* (DETR, 1998b, para. 2.3), there was a need to:

- *modernise local electoral arrangements*, in order to improve the accountability of councils and increase participation in local elections;
- *develop new ways in which councils listen to their communities and involve people in their decisions*, and in their policy planning and reviews;
- devise new ways of working for councils, giving them *clearer political management structures;*
- strengthen councils' role as *leaders of their local communities.*

We shall deal with each of these policy strands in turn.

Elections – PR stands only for procedural reform

The Government made it clear from the outset that the 'modernisation' of electoral arrangements did *not* mean electoral reform of the sort the Electoral Reform Society stands for, or that we discussed in Chapter 11. Notwithstanding that one of its claimed concerns about the existing state of local government was the large number of councils dominated by a single party – a problem that would largely disappear under almost any form of proportional representation (PR) – this kind of electoral reform was effectively excluded even from discussion. Attacking a claim that no one was on record as having made, the first consultation paper announced that:

> The Government believes that changes in the voting system are not a panacea for the current weaknesses in local government (para. 3.47).

It is a stance that has come to seem increasingly perverse, as elections to the three regional assemblies, the European Parliament, and the Greater London Assembly have all been held under various forms of PR. For the present, though, the only arrangements to be considered for modernisation were the more technical aspects of local elections:

- voter registration;
- the number and siting of polling stations;
- the days on which elections are held;
- the hours during which we may cast our votes;
- absentee and postal voting;
- telephone and electronic voting.

There was also a controversial proposal from Labour's 1997 manifesto for annual elections – or, to quote the precise words, that 'a proportion of the councillors in each locality will be elected annually'. The laudable intention was to increase councils' and councillors' accountability, by enabling the electorate each year to give its verdict on their performance. It seemed odd, though, to try to reduce voters' apathy about elections by increasing their frequency, quite apart from the administrative difficulties that would be created by annual elections in some of the country's more sparsely populated areas, and the pledge failed to reappear in the 2001 manifesto.

The procedural reform proposals, which many authorities were ready, willing and able to pilot just as soon as they received permission to do so, were referred to a Home Office working party, which took no less than two years to produce its final report. The principal outcomes of the working party's deliberations were three provisions in the Representation of the People Act 2000: rolling registration, automatic postal voting, and local election pilots. Rolling registration enables people moving house to register their new address on a monthly basis, rather than having to wait until a designated day the following October. Automatic postal voting means that, outside Northern Ireland, these votes are now available to anyone without their having to state a reason. Thirdly, selected local authorities were to be permitted to test new ways of voting in the May 2000 local elections.

The principal types of new arrangements piloted were:

- elections entirely by postal vote;
- early voting, with one or more polling stations open in advance of polling day;
- mobile polling stations and out-of-area polling stations – e.g. voting in supermarkets;
- electronic voting and counting, using machines sited in polling stations.

As noted in Chapter 11 (see also Game, 2000a), only the all-postal ballots produced any really significant increases in turnout and they, together with various forms of electronic voting, were prominent among the second phase of pilots in 2002. The government's preoccupation with making voting easier and lazier, though, is not to everyone's taste. None of these measures will do much to overcome your disincentive to vote if you happen to live in a politically safe or politically hopeless ward. Nor will they enthuse you if you happen to think that local government nowadays is so centrally controlled that little your local council can do, whichever party runs it, is likely to have a great impact on your life. As we have endeavoured to indicate, we do not take that latter view, but we are tempted to adapt the government's own dismissal of electoral reform: we believe that increases in electoral turnout are not a panacea for the current weaknesses in local government. Low turnout is a symptom of the problem, not the problem itself.

More listening than hearing?

The second strand of democratic renewal required councils to develop 'new ways of listening' to their communities and involving local people in their decision-making, policy planning and review. While acknowledging that 'many authorities are already pursuing initiatives to involve their communities in their decision-making on a regular basis', the government's view was that even the best authorities could go further and that their best practice should become the norm. As with the rest of the modernisation agenda, local authorities were not to be trusted to improve themselves; statutory backing was required.

Included, therefore, in the Local Government Act 1999 that implemented Best Value was a new statutory duty on local authorities to consult service users, local taxpayers and the business community. Moreover, while recognising that different forms of consultation are likely to be appropriate at different stages in the development of a policy or strategy, the government set out certain initiatives as being especially worth considering:

1. **Seeking citizens' views, through:**

   - *citizens' juries* – 'representative' groups of 12–16 citizens brought together to consider an issue in depth, scrutinise evidence, cross-examine expert witnesses, and make recommendations about it over a period of, typically, 3–5 days;
   - *focus groups/survey panels/citizen conferences* – ad hoc groups of varying sizes meeting together at length or regularly to give considered views on a particular question, service or problem;

- *deliberative opinion polls* – much larger and more statistically representative than citizens' juries, and starting and finishing with 'baseline' and 'attitude change' opinion surveys, the latter following extended discussion of written and oral evidence.

2. Involving citizens directly in decision-making, through:

   - *standing citizens' panels* – statistically representative samples of residents used by a council as a regular sounding board;
   - *community/user group forums* – to consider policies or proposals affecting their particular community or area of interest, possibly with some delegated authority and devolved budgets;
   - *local referendums* – either mandatory or advisory.

3. Developing the citizen's watchdog or scrutiny role, through:

   - *panels of inquiry/public scrutiny committees* – committees of residents having the right to ask for papers and evidence from key councillors and officers;
   - *direct service scrutiny committees.*

4. Opening up the authority, through:

   - *Public question times* at council meetings;
   - *Co-options* to council committees;
   - Experiments with *alternative meeting times and venues*;
   - *Devolution/localisation* of council decision-making.

Few, if any, of these ideas were completely new to local government. As we noted in Chapter 3 (Exhibit 3.3), most were already being used by some authorities somewhere before the Labour Government even came to power and several were almost standard practice: service user and neighbourhood forums, co-options, public question and answer sessions at council meetings. A quarter of authorities also claimed to have interactive web sites – at a time when most ministers' interest in e-government extended no further than trying to out-fox the millennium bug.

The more interesting feature of the list, therefore, is that in places it clearly did acknowledge that our relations with our local councils are not restricted to our roles as service consumers, but that we are citizens as well. We have parts to play – and not merely as voters – in their political as well as their service function, and they have responsibilities to us beyond simply providing us with services and fielding our complaints about them. The role distinction is a vital one. A customer's concern with a service is whether it is *right for them*, and when their use of the service ends, so does their interest in it, in both senses. The citizen's concern is whether the service is *right, period*. Even if they no longer use it, or never used it, citizens may still have an interest in it, views about it, and a right to have those views heard.

Box 18.1 Harlow BC's citizen's charter

The rights of Harlow citizens:

- to be heard and listened to;
- access to the authority and those who speak on behalf of the authority;
- to information;
- to be met with fairness, equity and justice;
- to be actively involved in the governing of the local community.

Indeed, Harlow's citizens have at least five sets of rights, as spelled out in the district council's citizen's charter (quoted in Stewart, 2000, pp. 260–1) (Box 18.1).

By comparison with the attention given by councils to developing new ways of consulting with their publics as consumers, innovations in citizenship or democratic engagement were relatively neglected – though there were, as ever, exceptions, documented regularly throughout the 1990s by John Stewart (1995c, 1996b, 1997, 1999). Several local and health authorities convened citizens' juries. Leicester set up citizen panels to consider budget spending priorities. Stirling established a novel 60-member Civic Assembly representing various community interests. Nottinghamshire was one of several authorities to organise community visioning exercises. Walsall, using an approach known as System Alignment, brought together stakeholders for two-day structured conferences on community safety and employee and user participation.

Local referendums too started to make an appearance, well before they were required in connection with elected mayors. They had always been permitted – on matters relating to the functions of a principal authority or where there would be likely to be direct benefit to the area. But in recent years they had tended to be limited in both number and subject: Sunday opening for Welsh pubs, transfers of local authority schools and housing stock. Then, in February 1999, Milton Keynes BC held a well-publicised referendum on its forthcoming budget and council tax levels. Residents were offered three options: a tax rise of 15 per cent, 9.8 per cent or 5 per cent, with corresponding packages of service increases or savings. On a turnout of over 44 per cent – compared to the previous local election figure of 26 per cent – a decisive plurality of 46 per cent chose the 9.8 per cent rise, which the Council pronounced itself morally bound to implement.

In February 2001 Bristol and Croydon followed Milton Keynes' lead, though with rather different results. A majority of Bristol electors voted for a complete tax freeze in preference to any of three modest increases, requiring the council to make cuts of some £4.5 million, mainly in education. In Croydon too residents chose the lowest tax rise on offer, while tenants voted themselves a rent freeze. As we noted at the end of

Chapter 10, binding council tax referendums have now found their way on to the finance reform agenda. All three of these forays into direct democracy, therefore, will have been watched with considerable interest – not least because, with their seemingly 'encouraging' postal turnouts of 35–45 per cent, they highlight some of the key issues about enhanced participation in general.

The reality is that, even when offered freepost, freephone and internet response options, sizeable majorities in all three of these council tax referendums chose *not* to join in. Many of these abstainers, undoubtedly, were precisely those most reliant on council services, which, incidentally, in Bristol would now have to be cut by a further £120,000 to pay for the referendum. Participation methods abound, none of them cost-free, but the question remains: so what? Have all the various initiatives we have described actually broadened the base of decision-making? Activity and effectiveness are not the same thing. We can be swamped with participatory initiatives – as hard-pressed voluntary organisations often feel themselves to be – but the policy impact for certain sectors of the population may be minimal. Councils' best intentions can all too easily reinforce existing patterns of social exclusion and disadvantage.

None of these reservations is intended to question the many values and benefits of participation, or to criticise policies that, belatedly at least, appear to recognise the importance of citizenship in our local governance. They do, however, lead us fairly directly to the next strand of democratic renewal – political management and political leadership. All the signs are that most of us do not really want to be much more actively 'engaged' with our local councils than we already are. Certainly we appear to be disenchanted to the point of abstention with the existing form of local representative democracy. Could it be that we would be happier with a stronger, more visible, more personalised form of local leadership?

Elected mayors – few are chosen, yet

The third, and most profound, requirement of democratic renewal involved modernising the way councils work and, in particular, getting away from the traditional committee system, which, 'designed over a century ago for a bygone age . . . is no basis for modern local government'. We outlined in Chapter 6 the government's critique of committees and their operation and also its prescribed remedy: a separation of the executive and representatives roles of councillors and an executive headed, preferably, by a strong directly elected mayor.

Within months, though, the consultation paper preference had become something to be forcefully promoted in legislation. The experimentalists, in favour of allowing councils to pilot a wide variety of executive managerial arrangements, had become fervent mayorists. By the time reform reached the White Paper stage, as we saw in Chapter 6, all local authorities in England and Wales were to be required to select one of just three proposed models, two of which were based on a directly elected mayor. They were free, of course, to choose the third option – an indirectly elected leader and cabinet. Even so, they might still be forced to hold a mayoral referendum, following a petition from 5 per cent of local electors or possibly the intervention of the Secretary of State, if councillors were felt to be ignoring or misinterpreting the electorate's own preference.

Having been outlined in the July 1998 White Paper, the three models were explained further and included in a draft Bill in early 1999, the Local Government (Organisation and Standards) Bill. So too was the requirement that every council consult its local community – about 'which new form of local governance will be best suited to give it the leadership it needs'. Councils decided for themselves which methods of consultation they would use, and naturally the range was considerable: consultative referendums, opinion polls, self-completion questionnaires, public meetings, focus groups. Whatever the method, though, they had to produce some kind of explanatory information, setting out in a balanced, supposedly unbiased way the merits and possible drawbacks of each of the three models, as in Exhibit 18.1.

Just how urgently such information was needed was borne out in the first government-commissioned survey on public attitudes to mayors in the summer of 2001. IFF Research, an independent market research company, carried out approximately 1,100 telephone interviews in each of 10 large towns and cities, chosen in part because of the differences in their proposed new council constitutions – Liverpool, Bristol, Birmingham, Plymouth, Derby, Oxford, Harrow, Westminster, Middlesbrough and Preston. By the time of the survey, political management reform and mayors had been under discussion for well over three years, yet barely a quarter of the total IFF sample (26 per cent) recalled having 'heard or seen any information on different ways that decisions could be made'. Over a third of the sample (34 per cent) admitted to understanding either not very well or not at all well the different ways councils could make decisions – an eloquent argument in itself against those inclined to claim that local government wasn't broke, so why try to fix it. It could be seen as a strong argument too for citizenship education, due to become a compulsory part of the National Curriculum from August 2002.

Notwithstanding their casual acquaintance with the issues, almost all those questioned by IFF were prepared to express preferences and, as can be seen in Exhibit 18.2, three-quarters supported something like a mayor/cabinet model. The actual question asked was inelegant, convoluted, and deliberately omitted all references to 'mayors', but there was an undeniable consistency of response across most of the survey authorities, with the

Exhibit 18.1 The three executive models – for and against

New Option 1 – Indirectly Elected Leader and Cabinet

You would go to the polls as now and elect your city councillors, who in turn would select (and later vote out if they are unhappy with their performance) a few senior councillors to form a Cabinet and elect one councillor to become Council Leader. Most of the present service committees would be abolished. The Leader and Cabinet between them would make big council decisions, and the remaining councillors would scrutinise and keep a watch on them. Each Cabinet member would take responsibility for running a council service, like education, housing, or social services, and would be accountable for that service to the people of the city and other councillors.

Those who like this system say: it speeds up decision-making and improves accountability, as Cabinet Members would become locally well known; it retains important checks and balances on the exercise of power; non-Cabinet members would have more time to represent their wards.

Those who don't like it say: it's a fudge, and not a sufficient change from the present system; people would not be any more interested or involved; decisions would not be taken as quickly as with an executive Mayor.

New Option 2 – Directly Elected Mayor and Cabinet

This new system would abolish most council committees and transfer most of their power into the hands of a Mayor elected by all voters once every 4 years. The Mayor would be supported by a small Cabinet of councillors, each one covering a major service area. The other councillors would perform the scrutiny role, vetting the decisions of the Mayor and Cabinet and representing their constituents.

Those who like this system say: a high-profile Mayor will reinvigorate public interest in the council; decisions will be made more quickly and more accountably.

Those who don't like it say: it puts too much power in the hands of the Mayor, who cannot be removed from office for 4 years; no strong decision-making role for other councillors; could lead to worse and less accountable decisions because so few people involved; no guarantee that it will increase people's interest or participation.

New Option 3 – Directly Elected Mayor and Council Manager

As in New Option 2, a Mayor would be elected by the people directly. But in this model the council would appoint a Council Manager, and possibly other chief officers too, to run services on a day-to-day basis.

Those who like this system say: it has the advantages of Option 2, but, without a Cabinet, decisions could be made even quicker; with only 2 people responsible for policy-making, it would be easier for the public to know who to hold to account.

Those who don't like it say: it gives too much power to just 2 people, one completely unelected and neither of whom is directly accountable to councillors; it is anti-democratic and has few checks and balances on power; too many decisions would be made behind closed doors, rather than in open Cabinet meetings.

Exhibit 18.2 Public attitudes to directly elected mayors, 2001

Question: Say [council name] works so that most decisions are made by a small group of councillors with a leading councillor, and their decisions are checked by the whole council. If that happened, do you think this leading councillor should be chosen at an election at which everyone in the city can vote?

	(%)
ALL 10 CITIES – AVERAGE	75
Most 'pro-mayoral' – Middlesbrough	86
Least 'pro-mayoral' – Westminster	62
Other strongly 'pro-mayoral' groups:	
18–24 year olds	79
Socio-economic groups DE (manual workers)	80
Women	79
Other less strongly 'pro-mayoral' groups	
Over 65s	70
Socio-economic groups AB (higher/middle managerial, professional)	66
Men	71

Question: A directly elected mayor would have the power to take some decisions on the council's behalf. A number of councillors would then check that council services and policies would meet the needs of local people. With this in mind, how strongly would you agree or disagree with each of these statements relating to this idea?

	Agree strongly + agree (%)
Having an elected mayor for [council name] would ...	
... mean there was someone who could speak up for the whole area	78
... mean it was always clear who was responsible when things go wrong	66
... make it easier to get things done	65
... make local politics more interesting	58
... give too much power to one person	46
... mean local councillors would have too little say	35
... mean the council tax would go up	33
... mean local services like schools and refuse collection would get worse	12

Question: Do you think you would be more or less likely to vote in an election for a mayor of [council name] than in an election for your local councillor?

More likely 31%   Less likely 13%   No difference 54%

Source: DTLR, *Public Attitudes to Directly Elected Mayors* (2001).

London borough of Westminster alone in having more than a quarter of respondents favouring a continuation of the present system of a councillor-elected leader. Support for direct election was highest by some way in Middlesbrough, a view reflected later in the year in the unitary authority's mayoral referendum, which was one of the earliest to endorse a mayor/cabinet form of government.

As in other surveys, the younger age groups were most in favour of change – those, as it happens, who are least inclined to vote in local elections and who were least likely to recall having seen any information. Socio-economically, the same pattern can be seen: those who could be presumed to have given the subject most consideration were the least enamoured of the idea of mayors, the single group most sceptical of direct election, with only 59 per cent in favour, being those in higher management and the professions.

Once it was confirmed that a leading councillor decided by the public was a directly elected mayor, respondents were asked for their strength of agreement to a series of opinion statements on the impact or effect they thought a directly elected mayor might have. In broad consistency with the support for the principle of popular election, there was most agreement on the 'positive' effects. Around two-thirds or more agreed that a directly elected mayor would be able to speak up for the whole area, be a focus of responsibility when things went wrong, and would make it easier to get things done.

For those hoping, though, that mayors would immediately and significantly boost local election turnouts, the evidence from this DTLR survey was distinctly qualified. Under half of all respondents thought it was 'very likely' that they would actually 'go and vote' in a mayoral election, and in only two of the 10 authorities – Middlesbrough and Westminster – was there even a third of respondents who said they would be 'more likely' to do so. Majorities everywhere thought it would make no difference, which, as we noted in Chapter 5, had been the case in Greater London, where, after the most publicised campaign imaginable, only a third of the electorate turned out to vote either for or against Ken Livingstone.

If the public are generally, if not knowledgeably, in favour of elected mayors, those most immediately and personally affected by the issue – existing councillors – have been overwhelmingly opposed. We noted in Chapter 6 (Exhibit 6.3) how the very great majority of councils introducing 'transitional arrangements' had opted for variants of the leader/cabinet model, and, once in place, the new structures and processes were able to be used as an additional argument against making any further change. In some cases, though, councils' consultations with their local communities persuaded them that pro-mayoral sentiment was so strong that they should hold a full-scale mayoral referendum, as required by the Local Government Act 2000.

The first of these binding, as opposed to consultative, referendums was held in England's northernmost town, Berwick-upon-Tweed, following a successful petition of 5 per cent of the modest-sized electorate. Coinciding with the June 2001 General Election, the turnout was a relatively impressive 64 per cent, but only just over a quarter supported the proposal for a directly elected mayor. The remainder of 2001 saw a further 15 referendums: two in London boroughs (Lewisham, Harrow), four in metropolitan districts (Doncaster, Kirklees, Sunderland, North Tyneside), three in unitaries (Hartlepool, Middlesbrough, Brighton and Hove), and six in non-metropolitan districts (Cheltenham, Gloucester, Watford, Sedgefield, Redditch, Durham). Most were held by postal ballot; even so, only in North Tyneside and Middlesbrough did the turnout exceed a third of the electorate. In six cases the council's mayoral proposal was supported and the following councils, therefore, were due to hold the country's first mayoral elections – after, of course, the Greater London Authority – in May 2002: Doncaster, Hartlepool, Lewisham, Middlesbrough, North Tyneside and Watford. Of these six, by far the strongest pro-mayoral vote was Middlesbrough's 84 per cent, thanks largely to a campaign centred around the possibility of Ray Mallon, a suspended senior policeman with a big local following, standing as a 'People's Candidate'.

Having weighted the legislation so strongly towards elected mayoral models, the government cannot fail to have been disappointed that, as St. Matthew nearly said, so few were chosen. Of particular concern was the absence from the mayoral list of any really major cities that might act as role models for others. Ministers, therefore, were examining very closely the consultation processes used by some big city authorities like Birmingham and Bradford, to check whether they had fairly sought and interpreted local opinion, or whether there was justification to intervene and require them to hold binding referendums. It would be an unfortunate way of having to keep alive a policy that was supposed to be about strengthening the voice and autonomy of local government.

With or without mayors, though, executive local government began to take root in England in 2001 in all but the smaller district councils. Decision-making procedures and institutions changed fundamentally, as should be confirmed by a glance at your own authority's web site. You should now be able to find listed a complete record of significant decisions by date and decision-maker – the cabinet collectively, an individual cabinet member, or a chief officer – plus supporting reports and a Forward Plan of upcoming 'key decisions' to be considered by the council. You can also go and see the cabinet in session, because, as local government minister Lord Whitty assured the House of Lords in July 2000: 'where a decision will have any significant impact on the community, the electorate involved should be able to influence that decision. That means that it must be made openly and in public.' All these decisions too are subject to the overview and scrutiny of the non-executive members of the council, as described in Chapter 12. As already emphasised, effective scrutiny is an indispensable element of effective executive government; to watch and monitor the two sets of processes developing in parallel should prove, to say the least, educative.

Community leadership and promotion of well-being

It was not particularly our intention, but the final principal section of this chapter and therefore the book brings us right back to where we started in Chapter 1. For the fourth element of the government's democratic renewal programme involved a strengthening of council's community leadership role. Its thinking was spelt out in the July 1998 White Paper, *Modern Local Government: In Touch with the People*:

> Community leadership is at the heart of the role of modern local government. Councils are the organisations best placed to take a comprehensive overview of the needs and priorities of their local areas and communities and lead the work to meet those needs and priorities in the round (para. 8.1 – original typography corrected by the authors for convenience).

The stated intention was to introduce legislation 'to place on councils *a duty to promote the economic, social and environmental well-being of their areas* and to strengthen councils' powers to enter into partnerships' (para. 8.8 – our emphasis). This new duty would have the effect of enshrining in law 'the role of the council as the elected leader of its local community with a responsibility for the well-being and sustainable development of its area' (para. 8.10 – original grammar corrected by the authors for convenience).

For a time it seemed that the government had frightened itself by the Pandora's box of possibilities it might have opened up, and the proposed new duty was omitted from the draft Bill published in March 1999. But, thanks largely to some effective lobbying by the Local Government Association, it reappeared as a power in the eventual Bill and became Part I of the Local Government Act 2000.

Taken together, the affirmation of local government's community leadership role and the new well-being power are of major importance, substantively, historically and symbolically. As we have indicated throughout this final part of the book, there has always been a tension between local authorities' service and political functions – between their role as service deliverers and a potentially much wider role as the elected governments of their particular areas and communities. The wider role has always been there, as we suggested in our discussion of 'local self-government' in Chapter 2. Clarke and Stewart provide some illustrations (2000, p. 127):

> Local authorities have campaigned against the closure of local stations or local hospitals. Faced with growing unemployment [in the 1980s], local authorities built a role in economic development before they had specific powers to do so.

Yet the reality is that the whole organisation and operation of local authorities have been driven by their service-providing responsibilities, and the statutory framework of *ultra vires* within which they had to work meant that their scope for promoting more general 'well-being' was severely constrained. The Local Government Act 2000 goes some way to providing local authorities with a new legal framework.

There are, inevitably, limitations. The new power is *not* directly equivalent to the 'power of general competence' possessed by local authorities in most other European countries. Most significantly, it cannot be used to raise money. Nevertheless, on the face of it at least, the wording of some of the Act's accompanying guidance sounds positive and expansive. The specific actions an authority may undertake include the incurring of expenditure, providing staff, goods and services, entering into partnership arrangements, and carrying out functions for other bodies, such as health authorities. These actions are expected to be directed towards innovation and joint action in policy areas where previously councils would have had to check that they had specific powers:

- tackling social exclusion;
- reducing health inequalities;
- promoting neighbourhood renewal;
- improving local environmental quality.

Conclusion – mixed messages

It would be tempting to end right here – in similar upbeat tenor to that in which we began. Unfortunately, though, all the talk of new institutions, new powers and opportunities has to be set alongside the retained and refined mechanisms of control that feature in the 2001 White Paper, the government's opening statement of intent for its second term of office. We dealt with that White Paper in Chapter 17, because that is where it fitted. Its title, *Strong Local Leadership – Quality Public Services*, turned out to be misleadingly inverted. Its focus was on how, most politically and managerially effectively, to get councils to deliver their own definitions of quality services. The democratic renewal agenda that has occupied us in this chapter received barely a passing reference.

The mixed messages abound, perhaps most vividly in the proposed new comprehensive performance assessments of authorities as high-performers, low-performers, strivers and coasters. Setting aside the serious methodological questions raised, it is hard in the extreme to see what councillors and voters are likely to make of these umbrella labels. Are voters going to rush more excitedly to the polls to elect representatives to a council they are told is a 'coaster'? Are they going to understand why they are being punished further for living in a 'low-performing' authority? Are they going to be stimulated into becoming more actively involved, or even putting themselves forward for election to a body that cannot be left unsupervised even to set its own rate of local taxation? Unlikely.

As we regularly emphasise to our students, it is important to get the balance right. There can be can be little doubt that the climate of central–local government relations has improved greatly since we wrote the first edition of this book. Moreover, many of the genuinely positive and stimulating changes currently taking place would almost certainly not have evolved without a strong national governmental lead. But we must remember the baseline from which we started, as well as the direction of travel. During the last quarter of the twentieth century UK local authorities gradually came to be about the most tightly centrally controlled of any in Europe. Five years into a self-proclaimedly devolutionist government, most objective observers would say they still are – and that the detailed content of the 2001 White Paper confirms that judgement, rather than repudiates it.

Guide to further reading

Two special issues of journals are good starting points, particularly for democratic renewal but also for other aspects of the modernisation agenda: *Local Government Studies*, 25: 4 (Winter 1999) and *Local Governance*, 26: 3 (Winter 2000). For the full story, all the consultation papers and White Papers, referenced in the text, are on the DTLR's website. Tony Blair's pamphlet (1998) is certainly worth a look: he may not have written it, but it's rare enough for a Prime Minister even to lend their name to anything to do with local government. Gerry Stoker (e.g. 1998) is the leading academic advocate of democratic renewal in general and mayors in particular; both his academic and 'popular' writings are worth following. He is also Chair of the corporately-sponsored New Local Government Network, similarly strongly pro-mayorist, whose website keeps a useful record of mayoral referendums. The chapter by Rao and Young (1999) on revitalising local democracy is a mine of fascinating attitudinal data. Several essays in Pratchett and Wilson (eds) (1996) are relevant, and a more theoretical perspective can be found in King and Stoker (eds) (1996).

Bibliography

Abdela, L. (1989) *Women With X Appeal: Women Politicians in Britain Today* (London: Optima).

Alexander, A. (1982) *The Politics of Local Government in the United Kingdom* (Harlow: Longman).

Allen, H. J. B. (1990) *Cultivating the Grass Roots: Why Local Government Matters* (The Hague: International Union of Local Authorities).

Armstrong, H. (1999) 'The Key Themes of Democratic Renewal', *Local Government Studies*, 25:4, pp 19–25.

Ashdown, P. (2001) *The Ashdown Diaries, Vol. II: 1997–1999* (Harmondsworth: Penguin).

Atkinson, H. and Wilks-Heeg, S. (2000) *Local Government from Thatcher to Blair: The Politics of Creative Autonomy* (Oxford: Blackwell).

Audit Commission (1988) *The Competitive Council* (London: HMSO).

Audit Commission (1997) *Representing the People* (Abingdon: Audit Commission).

Audit Commission (2000) *Seeing is Believing: How the Audit Commission Will Carry Out Best Value Inspections in England* (Abingdon: Audit Commission).

Audit Commission (2001a) *To Whom Much is Given: New Ways of Working for Councillors Following Political Restructuring* (Abingdon: Audit Commission).

Audit Commission (2001b) *Local Authority Performance Indicators: Environmental Services in England, 1999–2000* (Abingdon: Audit Commission).

Baggott, R. (1995) *Pressure Groups Today* (Manchester: Manchester University Press).

Bailey, S. and Paddison, R. (eds) (1988) *The Reform of Local Government Finance in Britain* (London: Routledge).

Bains, M. (Chairman) (1972) *The New Local Authorities: Management and Structure* (London: HMSO).

Barnes, M., Harrison, S., Mort, M., Shardlow, P. and Wistow, G. (1999) 'The New Management of Community Care: User Groups, Citizenship and Co-Production', in Stoker, G. (ed.) *The New Management of British Local Governance*, pp. 112–27.

Barron, J., Crawley, G. and Wood, T. (1987) *Married to the Council? The Private Costs of Public Service* (Bristol: Bristol Polytechnic).

Barron, J., Crawley, G. and Wood, T. (1991) *Councillors in Crisis* (London: Macmillan).

Benyon, J. and Edwards, A. (1999) 'Community Governance of Crime Control', in G. Stoker (ed.), *The New Management of British Local Governance*, pp. 145–67.

Bishop, J. and Hoggett, P. (1986) *Organizing Around Enthusiasms: Mutual Aid in Leisure* (London: Comedia).

Blair, T. (1998) *Leading the Way: A New Vision for Local Government* (London: Institute for Public Policy Research).

Blais, A. and Carty, R. J. (1990) 'Does Proportional Representation Foster Election Turnout?', *European Journal of Political Research*, 18, pp. 167–81.

Bogdanor, V. (1988) *Against the Overmighty State: A Future for Local Government in Britain* (London: Federal Trust for Education and Research).

Bogdanor, V. (2001) 'Constitutional Reform', in A. Seldon (ed.), *The Blair Effect: The Blair Government 1997–2001*, (London: Little, Brown), pp. 139–56.

Boyle, Sir L. (1986) 'In Recommendation of Widdicombe', *Local Government Studies*, 12:6, pp. 33–9.

Boyne, G. (1999) 'Introduction: Processes, Performance and Best Value in Local Government', *Local Government Studies*, 25:2, pp 1–5.

Boyne, G. (ed.) (1999) *Managing Local Services: From CCT to Best Value* (London: Frank Cass).

Boyne, G. (2000) 'External Regulation and Best Value in Local Government', *Public Money and Management*, 20:3, pp 7–12.

Boyne, G. et al. (1995) *Local Government Reform: A Review of the Process in Scotland and Wales* (London: LGC/Joseph Rowntree Foundation).

Brooke, R. (1989) *Managing the Enabling Authority* (Harlow: Longman).

Budge, L, Brand, J., Margolis, M. and Smith, A. L. M. (1972) *Political Stratification and Democracy* (London: Macmillan).

Burns, D., Hambleton, R. and Hoggett, P. (1994) *The Politics of Decentralisation. Revitalising Local Democracy* (London: Macmillan).

Butler, D., Adonis, A. and Travers, T. (1994) *Failure in British Government: The Politics of the Poll Tax* (Oxford: Oxford University Press).

Byrne, T. (1994) *Local Government in Britain*, 6th edn (Harmondsworth: Penguin).

Byrne, T. (2000) *Local Government in Britain: Everyone's Guide to How It All Works*, 7th edn (Harmondsworth: Penguin).

Cabinet Office (1998a) *Quangos: Opening The Doors* (London: HMSO).

Cabinet Office (1998b) *Service First: The New Charter Programme* (London: HMSO).

Cabinet Office (1999) *Modernising Government*, Cm 4310 (London: HMSO).

Challis, P. (2000) *Local Government Finance* (London: LGIU).

Chandler, J. A. (ed.) (1993) *Local Government in Liberal Democracies* (London: Routledge).

Chartered Institute of Public Finance and Accountancy (CIPFA) (2001) *Local Government Comparative Statistics, 2000* (London: CIPFA).

Clarke, M. and Stewart, J. (1988) *The Enabling Council* (Luton: LGTB).

Clarke, M. and Stewart, J. (1991) *The Choices for Local Government for the 1990s and Beyond* (Harlow: Longman).

Clarke, M. and Stewart, J. (2000) 'Community Leadership', *Local Governance*, 26:3, pp. 127–33.

Cochrane, A. (1993a) *Whatever Happened to Local Government?* (Buckingham: Open University Press).

Cochrane, A. (1993b) 'Local Government', in R. Maidment and G. Thompson (eds), *Managing the United Kingdom* (London: Sage).

Cochrane, A. (1996) 'From Theories to Practices: Looking for Local Democracy in Britain', in D. King and G. Stoker (eds), *Rethinking Local Democracy*.

Cockburn, C. (1977) *The Local State* (London: Pluto).

Commission for Local Democracy (CLD) (1995) *Taking Charge: The Rebirth of Local Democracy* (London: Municipal Journal Books).

Copus, C. (1998) 'The Councillor: Representing a Locality and the Party Group', *Local Governance*, 24:3, pp. 215–24.

Copus, C. (1999) 'The Party Group: A Barrier to Democratic Renewal', *Local Government Studies*, 25:3, pp. 76–97.

Copus, C. (2001) *It's My Party: The Role of the Group in Executive Arrangements* (London: LGA Publications).

Corina, L. (1974) 'Elected Representatives in a Party System: A Typology', *Policy and Politics*, 3:1, pp. 69–87.

Coulson, A. (1998) 'Town, Parish and Community Councils: The Potential for Democracy and Decentralisation', *Local Governance*, 24: 4, pp. 245–48.

Council of European Municipalities and Regions (CEMR) (2000) *Women in Local Politics in the European Union* (Brussels: CEMR).

Cousins, P. (1976) 'Voluntary Organisations and Local Government in Three South London Boroughs', *Public Administration*, 54: 1, pp. 63–83.

Crossman, R. (1977) *The Diaries of a Cabinet Minister, Vol. 3: Secretary of State for Social Services* (London: Hamish Hamilton and Jonathan Cape).

D'Arcy, M. and MacLean, R. (2000) *Nightmare! The Race to Become London's Mayor* (London: Politico's).

Davis, H. (1996) 'Quangos and Local Government: A Changing World', *Local Government Studies*, 22: 2, pp. 1–7, Special Issue on Quangos.

Dearlove, J. (1973) *The Politics of Policy in Local Government* (Cambridge: Cambridge University Press).

Dearlove, J. (1979) *The Reorganisation of British Local Government* (Cambridge: Cambridge University Press).

Democratic Audit (1994) *Ego Trip: Extra-Governmental Organisations in the United Kingdom and their Accountability* (London: The Charter 88 Trust).

Department for Education and Employment (DfEE) (2000) *Daycare Trust: A Survey of Early Years Development and Childcare Partnerships* (London: DfEE).

Department of the Environment (DoE) (1981) *Alternatives to Domestic Rates*, Cmnd 8449 (London: HMSO).

Department of the Environment (DoE) (1983) *Streamlining the Cities*, Cmnd 9063 (London: HMSO).

Department of the Environment (DoE) (1986) *Paying for Local Government*, Cmnd 9714 (London: HMSO).

Department of the Environment (DoE) (1991a) *The Structure of Local Government in England* (London, HMSO).

Department of the Environment (DoE) (1991b) *The Internal Management of Local Authorities in England* (London: HMSO).

Department of the Environment (DoE) (1993) *Community Leadership and Representation: Unlocking the Potential*, Report of the Working Party on the Internal Management of Local Authorities in England (London: HMSO).

Department of the Environment, Transport and the Regions (DETR) (1998a) *Modern Local Government: In Touch with the People* (London: DETR).

Department of the Environment, Transport and the Regions (DETR) (1998b) *Modernising Local Government: Local Democracy and Community Leadership* (London: DETR).

Department of the Environment, Transport and the Regions (DETR) (1998c) *Improving Local Services Through Best Value* (London: DETR).

Department of the Environment, Transport and the Regions (DETR) (1998d) *A New Ethical Framework* (London: DETR).

Department of the Environment, Transport and the Regions (DETR) (1998e) *Capital Finance* (London: DETR).

Department of the Environment, Transport and the Regions (DETR) (1998f) *Improving Financial Accountability* (London: DETR).

Department of the Environment, Transport and the Regions (DETR) (1999) *Local Leadership, Local Choice* (London: DETR).

Department of the Environment, Transport and the Regions (DETR) (2001) *Improving Local Public Services: Final Evaluation of the Best Value Pilot Programme* (London: DETR).

Department for Transport, Local Government and the Regions (DTLR) (2001a) *Strong Local Leadership – Quality Public Services* (London: DTLR).

Department for Transport, Local Government and the Regions (DTLR) (2001b) *Public Attitudes to Directly Elected Mayors* (London: DTLR).

Doig, A. (1984) *Corruption and Misconduct in Contemporary British Politics* (Harmondsworth: Penguin).

Doogan, K. (1999) 'The Contracting-Out of Local Government Services: Its Impact on Jobs, Conditions of Service and Labour Markets', in G. Stoker (ed.) *The New Management of British Local Governance*, pp. 62–78.

Duffield, C. (2000) 'Red Book Reviews', *Local Government Chronicle*, 15 December, p. 12.

Dunleavy, P. (1980) *Urban Political Analysis* (London: Macmillan).

Dunleavy, P. and Rhodes, R. A. W. (1983) 'Beyond Whitehall', in H. Drucker *et al.* (eds), *Developments in British Politics* (London: Macmillan).

Dunleavy, P. and Rhodes, R. A. W. (1985) 'Government Beyond Whitehall', in H. Drucker *et al.* (eds), *Developments in British Politics 2* (London: Macmillan).

Dynes, M. and Walker, D. (1996) *The Times Guide to the New British State* (London: Times Books).

Elcock, H. (1989) 'The Changing Management of Local Government', in I. Taylor and C. Popham (eds), *An Introduction to Public Sector Management* (London: Unwin Hyman).

Elcock, H. (1991) *Local Government* (London: Methuen).

Elcock, H. (1994) *Local Government: Policy and Management in Local Authorities*, 3rd edn (London: Routledge).

Elcock, H., Jordan, C. and Midwinter, A. (1989) *Budgeting in Local Government: Managing the Margins* (Harlow: Longman).

Ellwood, S., Nutley, S., Tricker, M. and Waterston, P. (1992) *Parish and Town Councils in England: A Survey* (London: HMSO).

Ennals, K, and O'Brien, J. (1990) *The Enabling Role of Local Authorities* (London: Public Finance Foundation).

European Union, Committee of the Regions (1999a) *Voter Turnout at Regional and Local Elections in the EU, 1990–1999* (Brussels: European Union).

European Union, Committee of the Regions (1999b) *The Proportion of Women Members in Regional and Local Parliaments and Assemblies in the EU* (Brussels: European Union).

European Union, Committee of the Regions (1999c) *Regional and Local Democracy in the European Union* (Brussels: European Union).

Evans, M. (1997) 'Political Participation' in Dunleavy, P. *et al.*, *Developments in British Politics 5* (Basingstoke: Macmillan), pp. 110–25.

Fanning, P. (2000) 'Pipeline to prosperity', *Local Government Chronicle*, 28 April 2000, pp. 22–3.

Farnham, D. (1999) 'Human Resources Management and Employment Relations', in S. Horton and D. Farnham (eds), *Public Management in Britain*, pp. 107–27.

Farnham, D. and Horton, S. (1999) 'Managing Public and Private Organisations', in S. Horton and D. Farnham (eds), *Public Management in Britain*, pp. 26–45.

Fenney, R. (2000) *Essential Local Government 2000* (London: LGC Information).

Flynn, N., Leach, S. and Vielba, C. (1985) *Abolition or Reform? The GLC and the Metropolitan County Councils* (London: Allen & Unwin).

Forsyth, M. (1982) 'Winners in the Contracting Game', *Local Government Chronicle*, 10 September.

Fox, P. and Leach, S. (1999) *Officers and Members in the New Democratic Structures: A Research Report* (London: LGIU).

Fox, P. and Leach, S. (1999) 'What about the Officers?', *Municipal Journal*, 9–15 July.

Freedland, J. (1998) *Bring Home the Revolution: The Case for a British Republic* (London: Fourth Estate).

Game, C. (1991a) 'How Local are Local Elections?', *Social Studies Review*, 6:5, pp. 202–7.

Game, C. (1991b) 'County Chronicles: A Collective Appreciation', *Local Government Policy Making*, 18: 2.

Game, C. (1997) 'Unprecedented in Local Government Terms – The Local Government Commission's Public Consultation Programme', *Public Administration*, 75:1, pp. 67–96.

Game, C. (2000a) 'Local Government Modernisation: Much More Than Just Elected Mayors', in S. Lancaster (ed.), *Developments in Politics: An Annual Review, Vol. 11* (Ormskirk: Causeway Press), pp. 125–52.

Game, C. (2000b) 'Changes in Voting Arrangements: A Distinctly Non-Radical Programme of Democratic Renewal', *Local Governance*, 26:3, pp. 135–49.

Game, C. (2001) 'Britain's Changing and Unchanging Electoral Systems' in S. Lancaster (ed.), *Developments in Politics: An Annual Review, Vol. 12* (Ormskirk: Causeway Press), pp. 49–75.

Game, C. and Leach, S. (1993) *Councillor Recruitment and Turnover: An Approaching Precipice?* (Luton: LGMB).

Game, C. and Leach, S. (1995) *The Role of Political Parties in Local Democracy, CLD Report No 11* (London: Commission for Local Democracy/Municipal Journal Books).

Game, C. and Leach, S. (1996) 'Political Parties and Local Democracy', in L. Pratchett and D. Wilson (eds), *Local Democracy and Local Government*, pp. 127–49.

Gasson, C. (1992) 'Freedom at a Cost', *Local Government Chronicle*, 4 December.

Gaster, L. and Deakin, N. (1998) 'Local Government and the Voluntary Sector: Who Needs Whom – Why and What For?', *Proceedings of the 3rd International Conference of the International Society for Third-Sector Research*, Geneva, Switzerland, pp. 1–27.

Gibson, J. (1990) *The Politics and Economics of the Poll Tax: Mrs Thatcher's Downfall* (West Midlands: EMAS Ltd).

Goldsmith, M. (1986a) *Essays on the Future of Local Government* (Wakefield: West Yorkshire Metropolitan County Council).

Goldsmith, M. (1986b) 'Managing the Periphery in a Period of Fiscal Stress', in M. Goldsmith (ed.), *New Research in Central–Local Relations* (Aldershot: Gower).

Goldsmith, M. (ed.) (1986c) *New Research in Central–Local Relations* (Aldershot: Gower).

Goldsmith, M. and Newton, K. (1986a) 'Central–Local Government Relations: A Bibliographical Study', *Public Administration*, 64:1, pp. 102–8.

Goldsmith, M. and Newton, K. (1986b) 'Local Government Abroad', in Widdicombe (1986e), pp. 132–58.

Goss, S. (1988) *Local Labour and Local Government* (Edinburgh: Edinburgh University Press).

Goss, S. (2001) *Making Local Governance Work* (Basingstoke: Palgrave).

Goss, S. and Corrigan, P. (1999) *Starting to Modernise: Developing New Roles for Council Members* (London: New Local Government Network/Joseph Rowntree Foundation).

Gray, A. and Jenkins, W. (1998), 'The Management of Central Government Services', in B. Jones *et al.*, *Politics UK* , 3rd edn (London: Prentice Hall) pp. 348–66.

Gray, A. and Jenkins, W. (1999) 'Democratic Renewal in Local Government: Continuity and Change', *Local Government Studies*, 25:4, pp. 26–45.

Gray, C. (1994) *Government Beyond the Centre* (London: Macmillan).

Green, D. (1981) *Power and Party in an English City* (London: Allen & Unwin).

Greenwood, J., Pyper, R and Wilson, D. (2002) *New Public Administration in Britain* (London: Routledge).

Griffith, J. A. C. (1966) *Central Departments and Local Authorities* (London: Allen & Unwin).

Griffiths, D. (1992) 'Strategic and Service Management – The Kirklees Experiment', *Local Government Studies*, 18: 3, pp. 240–8.

Gyford, J. (1984) *Local Politics in Britain*, 2nd edn (London: Croom Helm).

Gyford, J. (1991) *Citizens, Consumers and Councils* (London: Macmillan).

Gyford, J., Leach, S. and Game, C. (1989) *The Changing Politics of Local Government* (London: Unwin Hyman).

Hall, W. and Weir, S. (1996a) *The Untouchables: Power and Accountability in the Quango State*, Democratic Audit Paper No. 8 (University of Essex: The Scarman Trust and Human Rights Centre).

Hall, W. and Weir, S. (1996b) 'Rise of the Quangocracy', *Local Government Chronicle*, 30 August, p. 12.

Hambleton, R. (1998) *Local Government Political Management Arrangements: An International Perspective* (Edinburgh: Scottish Office Central Research Unit).

Hambleton, R. (2000) *The Council Manager Model* (London: IDeA).

Hampton, W. (1970) *Democracy and Community* (London: Oxford University Press).

Hazell, R. (2001) *Unfinished Business: Implementing Labour's Constitutional Reform Agenda for the Second Term* (London: The Constitution Unit).

Heald, D. and Geaughan, N. (1999) 'The Private Financing of Public Infrastructure', in G. Stoker (ed.) *The New Management of British Local Governance*, pp. 222–36.

Hebbert, M. and Travers, T. (eds) (1988) *The London Government Handbook* (London: Cassell).

Heclo, H. (1969) 'The Councillor's Job', *Public Administration*, 47: 2, pp. 185–202.

Hedley, R. (1991) 'First Principles – The Reorganisation of New Zealand Local Government', *Local Government Chronicle*, 11 January, p. 18.

Hennessy, P. (1990) *Whitehall*, rev. edn (London: Fontana).

Hill, D. (1974) *Democratic Theory and Local Government* (London: Allen & Unwin).

Hollis, G. *et al.* (1990) *Alternatives to the Community Charge* (York: Joseph Rowntree Trust/Coopers and Lybrand Deloitte).

Hollis, P. (1987) *Ladies Elect: Women in English Local Government, 1865–1914* (Oxford: Oxford University Press).

Holtby, W. (1936) *South Riding* (London: Collins).

Horton, S. and Farnham, D. (eds) (1999) *Public Management in Britain* (Basingstoke: Macmillan).

Houlihan, B. (1988) *Housing Policy and Central-Local Government Relations* (Aldershot: Avebury).

House of Commons (2001) *Select Committee on Public Administration Fifth Report, 2000/01: Mapping the Quango State* (London: HMSO).

House of Lords (1996) *Select Committee on Relations Between Central and Local Government, Vols I–III* (London: HMSO).

Improvement and Development Agency (IDeA) (2001) *A Councillor's Guide* (London: IDeA).

International Institute for Democracy and Electoral Assistance (IDEA) (2001) *Voter Turnout from 1945 to Date* (Sweden: Strömsberg).

Jenkins, S. (1995) *Accountable to None: The Tory Nationalisation of Britain* (London: Hamish Hamilton).

Jennings, R. E. (1982) 'The Changing Representational Roles of Local Councillors in England', *Local Government Studies*, 8: 4, pp. 67–86.

John, P. (1997) 'Local Governance', in P. Dunleavy *et al.* (eds) *Developments in British Politics 5* (Basingstoke: Macmillan), pp. 253–76.

John, P. (2001) *Local Governance in Western Europe* (London: Sage).

John, P. and Cole, A. (2000) 'Political Leadership in the New Urban Governance: Britain and France Compared', in L. Pratchett (ed.), *Renewing Local Democracy?*, pp. 98–115.

Jones, G. (1969) *Borough Politics* (London: Macmillan).

Jones, G. (1973) 'The Functions and Organisation of Councillors', *Public Administration*, 51, pp. 135–46.

Jones, G. (1975) 'Varieties of Local Politics', *Local Government Studies*, 1: 2, pp. 17–32.

Jones, G. (1997) *The New Local Government Agenda* (Hemel Hempstead: ICSA Publishing).

Jones, G. and Stewart, J. (1992) 'Selected not Elected', *Local Government Chronicle*, 13 November, p. 15.

Jones, G. and Stewart, J. (1993) 'Different Domains', *Local Government Chronicle*, 8 April, p. 15.

Jones, G. and Travers, T. (1996) 'Central Government Perceptions of Local Government', in L. Pratchett and D. Wilson (eds), *Local Democracy and Local Government*, pp. 84–105.

Keith-Lucas, B. and Richards, P. (1978) *A History of Local Government in the Twentieth Century* (London: Allen & Unwin).

Kent CC/Price Waterhouse (1992) *Facing the Challenge: Making Strategic Management Work* (Kent CC).

King, D. and Stoker, G. (eds) (1996) *Rethinking Local Democracy* (Basingstoke: Macmillan).

Labour Party (1995) *Renewing Democracy, Rebuilding Communities* (London: Labour Party Publications).

Labour Party (1997) *New Labour – Because Britain Deserves Better* (London: Labour Party Publications).

Labour Party (2001) *Ambitions for Britain – Labour's Manifesto 2001* (London: The Labour Party).

Laffin, M. (1986) *Professionalism and Policy: The Role of the Professions in the Central-Local Relationship* (Aldershot: Gower).

Lansley, S., Goss, S. and Wolmar, C. (1991) *Councils in Conflict: The Rise and Fall of the Municipal Left* (London: Macmillan).

Layfield Committee (1976) *Report of the Committee of Enquiry into Local Government Finance*, Cmnd 6543 (London: HMSO).

Leach, R. and Percy-Smith, J. (2001) *Local Governance in Britain* (Basingstoke: Palgrave).

Leach, S. (1995) 'The Strange Case of the Local Government Review', in J. Stewart and G. Stoker (eds), *Local Government in the 1990s*, pp. 49–68.

Leach, S. (1999) 'Introducing Cabinets into British Local Government', *Parliamentary Affairs*, 52: 1, pp. 77–93.

Leach, S. (2001) *Starting to Modernise: Balancing Good Government and Open Decision Making* (London: New Local Government Network).

Leach, S., Davis. H. *et al.* (1996) *Enabling or Disabling Local Government: Choices for the Future* (Buckingham: Open University Press).

Leach, S. and Game, C. (1989) *Co-operation and Conflict: Politics in the Hung Counties*, Common Voice Research Study, No. 1 (London: Common Voice).

Leach, S. and Game, C. (1992) 'Local Government: The Decline of the One-Party State', in G. Smyth (ed.), *Refreshing the Parts: Electoral Reform and British Politics* (London: Lawrence & Wishart).

Leach, S. and Game, C. (2000) *Hung Authorities, Elected Mayors and Cabinet Government: Political Behaviour Under Proportional Representation* (York: Joseph Rowntree Foundation).

Leach, S. and Pratchett, L. (1996) *The Management of Balanced Authorities* (Luton: LGMB).

Leach, S. and Stewart, J. (1990) *Political Leadership in Local Government* (Luton: LGMB).

Leach, S. and Stewart, J. (1992a) *The Politics of Hung Authorities* (London: Macmillan).

Leach, S. and Stewart, M. (1992b) *Local Government: Its Role and Function* (York: Joseph Rowntree Foundation).

Leach, S. and Wilson, D. (1998) 'Voluntary Groups and Local Authorities: Rethinking the Relationship', *Local Government Studies*, 24: 1, pp. 1–18.

Leach, S. and Wilson, D. (2000) *Local Political Leadership* (Bristol: Policy Press).

Leach, S. and Wingfield, M. (1999) 'Public Participation and the Democratic Renewal Agenda: Prioritisation or Marginalisation?', *Local Government Studies*, 25: 4, pp 46–59.

Leach, S. *et al.* (1987) *The Impact of Abolition on Metropolitan Government* (Birmingham: INLOGOV).

Leach, S. *et al.* (1992) *After Abolition: The Operation of the Post-1986 Metropolitan Government System in England* (Birmingham: INLOGOV).

Leach, S. *et al.* (1994) *The Changing Organisation and Management of Local Government* (London: Macmillan).

Lee, J. (1963) *Social Leaders and Public Persons* (London: Oxford University Press).

Leigh, I. (2000) *Law, Politics and Local Democracy* (Oxford: Oxford University Press).

Livingstone, K. (1987) *If Voting Changed Anything, They'd Abolish It* (London: Collins).

Local Government Association (LGA) (2000a) *Real Role for Members – The Role of Non-executive Members in the New Structures* (London: LGA).

Local Government Association (LGA) (2000b) *A Role for All Members – The Council Meeting* (London: LGA).

Local Government Association (LGA) (2001) *Representing the People: Democracy and Diversity* (London: LGA).

Local Government Information Unit (LGIU) (1993) *The LGIU Guide to Local Government Finance* (London: LGIU).

Local Government Management Board (LGMB) (1993) *Fitness for Purpose: Shaping New Patterns of Organisation and Management* (Luton: LGMB).

Local Government Management Board (LGMB) (1998) *First National Census: Survey of Local Authority Councillors in England and Wales in 1997* (London: LGMB).

Loughlin, J. (2001) *Subnational Democracy in the European Union: Challenges and Opportunities* (Oxford: Oxford University Press).

Loughlin, M. (1996a) *Legality and Locality: The Role of Law in Central–Local Relations* (Oxford: Clarendon Press).

Loughlin, M. (1996b) 'Understanding Central–Local Government Relations', *Public Policy and Administration*, 11: 2, pp. 48–65.

Loughlin, M., Gelfand, M. and Young, K. (eds) (1985) *Half a Century of Municipal Decline, 1935–1985* (London: Allen & Unwin).

Lowndes, V. (1996) 'Locality and Community: Choices for Local Government', in S. Leach, H. Davis *et al.*, *Enabling or Disabling Local Government*, pp. 71–85.

Lowndes, V. (1999a) 'Management Change in Local Governance', in G. Stoker (ed.) *The New Management of British Local Governance*, pp. 22–39.

Lowndes, V. (1999b) 'Rebuilding Trust in Central/local Relations: Policy or Passion?', *Local Government Studies*, 25: 4, pp. 117–37.

Lowndes, V. and Stoker, G. (1992) 'An Evaluation of Neighbourhood Decentralisation Part 2: Staff and Councillor Perspectives', *Policy and Politics*, 20: 2, pp. 143–52.

Lowndes, V. *et al.* (1998a) *Enhancing Public Participation in Local Government* (London: DETR).

Lowndes, V. *et al.* (1998b) *Modern Local Government: Guidance on Enhancing Public Participation* (London: DETR).

Lowndes, V. *et al.* (2001) 'Trends in Public Participation: Part 1 – Local Government Perspectives', *Public Administration*, 79: 1, pp. 205–22.

Lynn, J. and Jay, A. (1983) *Yes, Minister: The Diaries of a Cabinet Minister, Vol. 3 – The Challenge* (London: BBC).

McConnell, A. (1999) *The Politics and Policy of Local Taxation in Britain* (Wirral: Tudor).

McIntosh, N. (Chairman) (1999) *Commission on Local Government and the Scottish Parliament*, Report (Edinburgh: Scottish Executive).

Macrory, P. (Chairman) (1970) *Review Body on Local Government in Northern Ireland, Report*, Cmnd 540 (NI) (HMSO: Belfast).

Maloney, W., Smith, G. and Stoker, G. (2000) 'Social Capital and Urban Governance: Adding a More Contextualised 'Top-down' Perspective', *Political Studies*, 48: 4, pp. 802–20.

Marsh, D. (ed.) (1998) *Comparing Policy Networks* (Buckingham: Open University Press).

Marsh, D. and Rhodes, R.A.W. (eds) (1992) *Policy Networks in British Government* (Oxford: Oxford University Press).

Martin, S. (1999a) 'Picking Winners or Piloting Best Value? An Analysis of English Best Value Bids', *Local Government Studies*, 25: 2, pp. 53–67.

Martin, S. (1999b) 'Best Value' – paper delivered at Local and Regional Government Research Unit Seminar, DETR, 26 November.

Martin, S. (2000) 'Implementing 'Best Value': Local Public Services in Transition', *Public Administration*, 78: 1, pp. 209–27.

Maud, Sir John (Chairman) (1967a) *Committee on the Management of Local Government, Vol. 1: Report* (London: HMSO).

Maud, Sir John (Chairman) (1967b) *Committee on the Management of Local Government, Research Volume 5: Local Government Administration in England and Wales* (London: HMSO).

Midwinter, A. (1995) *Local Government in Scotland: Reform or Decline?* (London: Macmillan).

Midwinter, A. and McGarvey, N. (1999) 'Developing Best Value in Scotland: Concepts and Contradictions', *Local Government Studies*, 25: 2, pp 87–101.

Miller, W. (1988) *Irrelevant Elections? The Quality of Local Democracy in Britain* (Oxford: Clarendon Press).

Milton Keynes Liberal Democrats (1995) *Quangos in Milton Keynes* (Milton Keynes: Liberal Democrats publication).

Moran, M. (1989) *Politics and Society in Britain* (London: Macmillan).

Newton, K. (1976) *Second City Politics: Democratic Processes and Decision-Making in Birmingham* (Oxford: Oxford University Press).

Newton, K. and Karran, T. (1985) *The Politics of Local Expenditure* (London: Macmillan).

Nolan, Lord (Chairman) (1997) *Committee on Standards in Public Life: Report on Local Government* (London: HMSO).

Norton, A. (1994) *International Handbook of Local and Regional Government: A Comparative Analysis of Advanced Democracies* (Aldershot: Edward Elgar).

Oakland, J. (1989) *Total Quality Management* (London: Butterworth Heinemann).

O'Leary, B. (2001) 'The Belfast Agreement and the Labour Government', in A. Seldon (ed.), *The Blair Effect: The Blair Government 1997–2001* (London: Little, Brown), pp. 449–87.

Paddison, R. and Bailey, S. (eds) (1988) *Local Government Reform: International Perspectives* (London: Routledge).

Painter, C. and Isaac-Henry, K. (1999) 'Managing Local Public Services', in S. Horton and D. Farnham (eds), *Public Management in Britain*, pp. 162–79.

Pateman, C. (1970) *Participation and Democratic Theory* (Cambridge: Cambridge University Press).

Paterson, I. V. (Chairman) (1973) *The New Scottish Local Authorities: Organisation and Management Structures* (Edinburgh: Scottish Development Department).

Perri 6 *et al.* (1999) *Governing in the Round* (London: DEMOS).

Poole, K. P. and Keith-Lucas, B. (1994) *Parish Government 1894–1994* (London: National Association of Local Councils).

Pratchett, L. (2000) 'The Inherently Unethical Nature of Public Service Ethics', in R.A. Chapman (ed.), *Ethics in Public Service for the New Millennium* (Aldershot: Ashgate).

Pratchett, L. (ed.) (2000) *Renewing Local Democracy? The Modernisation Agenda in British Local Government* (London: Frank Cass).

Pratchett, L. and Wilson, D. (eds) (1996) *Local Democracy and Local Government* (London: Macmillan).

Pratchett, L. and Wingfield, M. (1996) 'The Demise of the Public Sector Ethos', in L. Pratchett and D. Wilson (eds), *Local Democracy and Local Government*, pp. 106–26..

Prior, D. (1995) 'Citizens' Charters', in J. Stewart and G. Stoker (eds), *Local Government in the 1990s,* pp. 86–103.

Rallings, C. and Thrasher, M. (annual) *Local Elections Handbook* (London: LGC Communications).

Rallings, C. and Thrasher, M. (1991) 'Local Elections: The Changing Scene', *Social Studies Review*, 5:4, pp. 163–6.

Rallings, C. and Thrasher, M. (1997) *Local Elections in Britain* (London: Routledge).

Rallings, C. and Thrasher, M. (1999) 'An Audit of Local Democracy in Britain: The Evidence from Local Elections' *Parliamentary Affairs*, 52: 1, pp 58–76.

Rallings, C. and Thrasher, M. (2000) *Turnout at Local Elections: Influences on Levels of Local Registration and Electoral Participation* (London: DETR).

Rallings, C. and Thrasher, M. (2001a) 'Every Which Way You Lose', *Local Government Chronicle*, 15 June, p. 17.

Rallings, C. and Thrasher, M. (2001b) 'Aspects of Voting at the Local and General Elections, 2001', paper presented at the Elections, Parties and Polls Conference, University of Sussex, September.

Ranson, S. *et al.* (1999) 'The New Management and Governance of Education', in G. Stoker (ed.), *The New Management of British Local Governance*, pp. 97–111.

Rao, N. (1994) *The Making and Unmaking of Local Self-Government* (Aldershot: Dartmouth).

Rao, N. and Young, K. (1999) 'Revitalising Local Democracy', in R. Jowell, J. Curtice, A. Park and K. Thomson (eds), *British Social Attitudes: the 16th Report – Who Shares New Labour Values?* (Aldershot: Ashgate), pp. 45–63.

Redcliffe-Maud, Lord (Chairman) (1969) *Royal Commission on Local Government in England 1966–1969, Vol. I Report*, Cmnd 4040 (London: HMSO).

Redlich, J. and Hirst, F. W. (1958) *The History of Local Government in England*, rev. edn (London: Macmillan).

Rhodes, G. (1970) *The Government of London: the Struggle for Reform* (London: Weidenfeld & Nicolson).

Rhodes, R. A. W. (1979) 'Research into Central–Local Relations in Britain: A Framework for Analysis', unpublished paper, Department of Government, Essex University.

Rhodes, R. A. W. (1986a) *The National World of Local Government* (London: Allen & Unwin).

Rhodes, R. A. W. (1986b) *Power Dependence, Policy Communities and Intergovernmental Networks*, Essex Papers in Politics and Government, No. 30 (University of Essex).

Rhodes, R. A. W. (1988) *Beyond Westminster and Whitehall* (London: Allen & Unwin).

Rhodes, R. A. W. (1991) 'Now Nobody Understands the System: The Changing Face of Local Government', in P. Norton (ed.), *New Directions in British Politics?* (Aldershot: Edward Elgar), pp. 83–112.

Rhodes, R. A. W. (1992) 'Local Government Finance', in D. Marsh and R. A. W. Rhodes (eds), *Implementing Thatcherite Policies* (Milton Keynes: Open University Press).

Rhodes, R. A. W. (1997) *Understanding Governance: Policy Networks, Governance, Reflexivity and Accountability* (Buckingham: Open University Press).

Rhodes, R. A. W. (1999a) 'Foreword: Governance and Networks' in G. Stoker (ed.), *The New Management of British Local Governance*, pp. xii–xxvi.

Rhodes, R. A. W. (1999b) *Control and Power in Central–Local Government Relations*, 2nd edn (Aldershot: Ashgate).

Ridley, N. (1988) *The Local Right* (London: Centre for Policy Studies).

Robinson, D. (Chairman) (1977) *Remuneration of Councillors: Vol I: Report; Vol II: The Surveys of Councillors and Local Authorities*, Cmnd 7010 (London: HMSO).

Robson, W. (1954) *The Development of Local Government*, 3rd edn (London: Allen & Unwin).

Saunders, P. (1980) *Urban Politics: A Sociological Interpretation* (Harmondsworth: Penguin).

Seitz, R. (1998) *Over Here* (London: Phoenix).

Sharpe, L. J. (1970) 'Theories and Values of Local Government, *Political Studies*, 18: 2, pp. 153–74.

Skelcher, C. (1992) *Managing for Service Quality* (Harlow: Longman).

Skelcher, C. (1998) *The Appointed State* (Buckingham: Open University Press).

Skelcher, C. and Davis, H. (1995) *Opening the Board-Room Door: The Membership of Local Appointed Bodies* (London: LGC Communications/ Joseph Rowntree Foundation).

Skelcher, C. and Davis, H. (1996) 'Understanding the New Magistracy: A Study of Characteristics and Attitudes', *Local Government Studies*, 22: 2, pp. 8–21.

Skelcher, C. *et al.* (2000) *Advance of the Quango State* (London: Local Government Information Unit).

Smith, B. C. (1985) *Decentralization: The Territorial Dimension of the State* (London: Allen & Unwin).

Smith, P. (1999) 'Countdown to the Relaunch of Clause Zero', *Local Government Chronicle*, 8 January, p. 8.

Snape, S. (ed.) (2000) 'Special Issue on Local Government Modernisation', *Local Governance*, 26: 3.

Snape, S., Leach, S. *et al.* (2000) *New Forms of Political Management Arrangements* (London: IDeA/DETR).

Stanyer, J. (1999) 'Something Old, Something New', in G. Stoker (ed.), *The New Management of British Local Governance*, pp. 237–48.

Stewart J. (1990) 'The Role of Councillors in the Management of the Authority', *Local Government Studies*, 16: 4, pp. 25–36.

Stewart, J. (1995a) 'The Internal Management of Local Authorities', in J. Stewart and G. Stoker (eds), *Local Government in the 1990s*, pp. 69–85.

Stewart, J. (1995b) 'A Future for Local Authorities as Community Government', in J. Stewart and G. Stoker (eds) *Local Government in the 1990s*, pp. 249–67.

Stewart, J. (1995c) *Innovation in Democratic Practice* (University of Birmingham: INLOGOV).

Stewart, J. (1996a) *Local Government Today: An Observer's View* (Luton: LGMB).

Stewart, J. (1996b) *Further Innovation in Democratic Practice* (University of Birmingham: School of Public Policy).

Stewart, J. (1997) *More Innovation in Democratic Practice* (University of Birmingham: School of Public Policy).

Stewart, J. (1999) *From Innovation in Democratic Practice Towards a Deliberative Democracy* (University of Birmingham: School of Public Policy).

Stewart, J. (2000), *The Nature of British Local Government* (Basingstoke: Macmillan).

Stewart, J. and Game, C. (1991) *Local Democracy – Representation and Elections* (Luton: LGMB).

Stewart, J. and Stoker, G. (eds) (1995) *Local Government in the 1990s* (London: Macmillan).

Stoker, G. (1990) 'Government Beyond Whitehall' in P. Dunleavy *et al.* (eds), *Developments in British Politics 3* (London: Macmillan).

Stoker, G. (1991) *The Politics of Local Government*, 2nd edn (London: Macmillan).

Stoker, G. (1996) 'Understanding Central–Local Relations: A Reply to Martin Loughlin', *Public Policy and Administration*, 11: 3, pp. 84–5.

Stoker, G. (1998) Democratic Renewal: Issues for Local Government (London: LGMB).

Stoker, G. (ed.) (1999a) *The New Management of British Local Governance* (Basingstoke: Macmillan).

Stoker, G. (1999b) *Remaking Local Democracy: Lessons from New Labour's Reform Strategy*, University of Manchester, Department of Government Golden Anniversary, September.

Stoker, G. (ed.) (2000) *The New Politics of British Local Governance* (Basingstoke: Macmillan).

Stoker, G. (2001) *Money Talks: Creating a Dialogue Between Taxpayers and Local Government* (London: New Local Government Network).

Stoker, G. and Brindley, T. (1985) 'Asian Politics and Housing Renewal', *Policy and Politics*, 13: 3, pp. 281–303.

Stoker, G. and Wilson, D. (1986) 'Intra-Organizational Politics in Local Authorities', *Public Administration*, 64: 3, pp. 285–302.

Stoker, G. and Wilson, D. (1991) 'The Lost World of British Local Pressure Groups', *Public Policy and Administration*, 6: 2, pp. 20–34.

Stoker, G. and Wolman, H. (1991) *A Different Way of Doing Business – the Example of the US Mayor* (Luton: LGMB).

Stoker, G. and Wolman, H. (1992) 'Drawing Lessons from US Experience: An Elected Mayor for British Local Government', *Public Administration*, 70: 2, pp. 241–67.

Taylor, B. and Thompson, K. (1999) *Scotland and Wales: Nations Again?* (Cardiff: University of Wales Press).

Taylor, M. and Wheeler, P. (2001) *In Defence of Councillors* (London: IDeA).

Travers, T. *et al.* (1993) *The Impact of Population Size on Local Authority Costs and Effectiveness* (York: Joseph Rowntree Foundation).

Vize, R. (1994) 'Northern Ireland: The Acceptable Face of Quangos', *Local Government Chronicle*, 25 November, pp. 16–17.

Walsh, K. (1995) 'Competition and Public Service Delivery', in J. Stewart and G. Stoker (eds), *Local Government in the 1990s*, pp. 28–48.

Walsh, K. (1996) 'The Role of the Market and the Growth of Competition', in S. Leach, H. Davis *et al.* (eds), *Enabling or Disabling Local Government*, pp. 59–70.

Weaver, M. (2001) 'Housing Transfers: The Issue Explained', www.society. guardian.co.uk/housing.

Weir, S. (1995) 'Quangos: Questions of Democratic Accountability', *Parliamentary Affairs*, 48: 2, pp. 306–22.

Weir, S. and Beetham, D. (1999) *Political Power and Democratic Control in Britain: The Democratic Audit of Great Britain* (London: Routledge).

Weir, S. and Hall, W. (eds) (1994) *EGO TRIP: Extra-governmental Organisations in the UK and their Accountability*, Democratic Audit Paper, No. 2 (University of Essex: Human Rights Centre).

Welsh Office (1993) *Local Government in Wales: A Charter for the Future* (London: HMSO).

Wheatley, Lord (Chairman) (1969) *Royal Commission on Local Government in Scotland*, Report, Cmnd 4150 (Edinburgh: HMSO).

Widdicombe, D. (Chairman) (1986a) *The Conduct of Local Authority Business: Report of the Committee of Inquiry into the Conduct of Local Authority Business*, Cmnd 9797 (London: HMSO).

Widdicombe, D. (Chairman) (1986b) *Research Volume I – The Political Organisation of Local Authorities* (by S. Leach, C. Game, J. Gyford and A. Midwinter), Cmnd 9798 (London: HMSO).

Widdicombe, D. (Chairman) (1986c) *Research Volume II – The Local Government Councillor*, Cmnd 9799 (London: HMSO).

Widdicombe, D. (Chairman) (1986d) *Research Volume III – The Local Government Elector*, Cmnd 9800 (London: HMSO).

Widdicombe, D. (Chairman) (1986e) *Research Volume IV – Aspects of Local Democracy*, Cmnd 9801 (London: HMSO).

Willis, J. (1990) 'David Bookbinder: Behind the Mythology', *Local Government Chronicle*, 12 January, pp. 24–5.

Wilson, D. (1995) 'Quangos in the Skeletal State', *Parliamentary Affairs*, 48: 2, pp. 181–91.

Wilson, D. (1996a) 'Structural Solutions for Local Government: An Exercise in Chasing Shadows?', *Parliamentary Affairs*, 49: 3, pp. 441–54.

Wilson, D. (1996b) 'The Local Government Commission: Examining the Consultative Process', *Public Administration*, 74: 2, pp. 199–220.

Wilson, D. (1998) 'From Local Government to Local Governance: Re-Casting British Local Democracy', *Democratization*, 5: 1, pp. 90–115.

Wilson, D. (1999) 'Exploring the Limits of Public Participation in Local Government', *Parliamentary Affairs*, 52: 2, pp. 246–59.

Wilson, D. and Game, C. (1994) *Local Government in the United Kingdom*, 1st edn (London: Macmillan).

Wilson, D. and Game, C. (1998) *Local Government in the United Kingdom*, 2nd edn (London: Macmillan).

Wistow, C. *et al.* (1992) 'From Providing to Enabling: Local Authorities and the Mixed Economy of Social Care', *Public Administration*, 70: 1, pp. 24–45.

Wood, B. (1976) *The Process of Local Government Reform, 1966–74* (London: Allen & Unwin).

Wynn Davies, R. (1996) 'Club-wielding Power', *Local Government Chronicle*, 13 December.

Young, K. (1986a) 'Party Politics in Local Government: An Historical Perspective', in Widdicombe (1986e) (London: HMSO).

Young, K. (1986b) 'The Justification for Local Government', in M. Goldsmith (ed.), *Essays on the Future of Local Government* (Wakefield: West Yorkshire Metropolitan County Council), pp. 8–20.

Young, K. (ed.) (1989) *New Directions for County Government* (London: ACC).

Young, K. and Mills, L. (1983) *Managing the Post-Industrial City* (London: Heinemann).

Young, K. and Rao, N. (1997) *Local Government Since 1945* (Oxford: Blackwell).

Index